DATE DUE			

GLADSTONE

WILLIAM EWART GLADSTONE

After the portrait by Sir J. E. Millais

GLADSTONE

ERICH EYCK

Translated by
BERNARD MIALL

Reprints of Economic Classics
AUGUSTUS M. KELLEY PUBLISHERS
New York 1968

Published by Frank Cass & Co. Ltd.,
10 Woburn Walk, London W.C.1
by arrangement with George Allen & Unwin Ltd.

Published in the United States by
Augustus M. Kelley, Publishers
New York, New York 10010

First edition   1938
New impression   1966

Library of Congress Catalog Card No. 68–56055

Printed in Holland by
N.V. Grafische Industrie Haarlem

CONTENTS

I

THE HOPE OF THE TORIES

1. *"A Man is Uprisen"*

It was the 17th of May, 1831, at Oxford. In the Union, that nursery
of English politicians, in which the undergraduates debate and
vote upon their motions in accordance with the procedure of the
House of Commons, there was forgathered an unusually numerous
assembly of young men in a fighting mood. Electoral reform was
the order of the day; the very question on whose account Parliament had just been dissolved after an embittered contest. These
were stirring times; for only last July, in France, a king who was
the last monarch of an ancient dynasty was tumbled off the throne,
and the propertied bourgeoisie seized the reins of government,
led by a new king, himself a bourgeois heart and soul. The incident
did not leave England unmoved, and the electors, who constituted
only a thin stratum of the nation, were sufficiently alive to the
spirit of the new age to send to Westminster, in the elections of
the previous autumn, an unprecedented majority of progressively-
minded members, all in favour of reform. And now the new
Ministers of the Whig Government, although they were pre-
dominantly members of the oldest and most aristocratic families—
like Earl Grey, the Prime Minister, and the ruthless little Lord
John Russell—had the courage to introduce a Reform Bill which
proposed to abolish, with startling thoroughness, the abuses which
had slowly come into being through the centuries, and had been so
affectionately cherished, and to transfer the political power which
had hitherto lain in the hands of the landed nobility and gentry
to the merchants, manufacturers, and bankers of the cities which
had been increasing in prosperity and importance. True, the Lords
had opposed the measure, but in order to overcome their opposition the Ministers, with the support of King William IV, had
appealed to the people.

Could Oxford quietly look on while such things were done? Oxford, the great guardian of the tradition that gave to her colleges, dating from the thirteenth and fourteenth centuries, their incomparable and indelible character; Oxford, the stronghold of the pure doctrine of the Anglican Church, which had just deprived the Conservative leader, Sir Robert Peel, of his mandate, because he had carried Catholic Emancipation; the rallying-point of the sons of the old aristocracy, the class to whom government was second nature? Among the Oxford undergraduates the battle for the new political ideals was keenly fought, and the issue uncertain. They flocked into the doors of the Union all the more eagerly when they knew that the President of the Union, young William Ewart Gladstone, was going to speak.

For Gladstone was known to be a convinced Tory. Men smiled to remember that at Eton, when he was only sixteen, he had proudly said of himself: "I am well aware that my prejudices and my predilections have *long* been enlisted on the side of Toryism." But they knew, also, that he was an unusually serious and passionately ambitious young man, who excelled all his competitors in scholarship, and exerted an irresistible influence over the more distinguished undergraduates of his time. He counted among his devoted friends many young noblemen—such as Lord Lincoln, the son of the Duke of Newcastle—although he himself was of middle-class origin. His father was a Liverpool merchant, who had amassed considerable wealth, and was the owner of coffee and sugar plantations in the West Indies. It was known that he had been counted among the friends of the great Canning, who had died so suddenly four years earlier, and who, in 1822, had been waiting in his house for the ship that was to take him to India as Governor-General, when Castlereagh's suicide had opened for him the path to the Ministry, and to a political career which, brief though it was, had revolutionized European politics. In the spirit of Canning young Gladstone, speaking in the Union, had defended Catholic Emancipation, which after many years of conflict had been passed in 1829. But in the spirit of Canning he was a declared opponent of the electoral reform advocated by the Whigs, and in the Union he had introduced a motion in which he described it, with youthful dogmatism, as not merely a complete alteration of the form of government, but as destructive of the very foundations of the social order. Naturally, all were eager to hear what he had to say.

Now the youthful politician—he was twenty-one years of age—was on his feet, facing his audience. He was tall and raven-haired, and those who had once seen him never forgot the great eyes, full of life and enthusiasm. He spoke in the keen, logical dialectic which Oxford taught her sons, in a voice whose resonance and wealth of modulation held the hearer spellbound. What the young Gladstone said in his forty-five minutes' speech no stenographer recorded for posterity. But many of his listeners described, in after years, the impression which he had made upon them. "When Gladstone sat down we all of us felt that an epoch in our lives had occurred," wrote one of them; and another, who afterwards became a bishop, declared that he felt certain, even then, that this young man "would one day rise to be Prime Minister of England." But Lord Lincoln wrote to his father, the Duke of Newcastle, that so soon as a seat in any constituency under his control was vacant, he must offer it to no one but his friend William Ewart Gladstone. "A man is uprisen in Israel."

The excitement of politics did not prevent him from distinguishing himself in the schools, and winning the highest obtainable honours. Now, thanks to his father's wealth, he was able to choose his profession without regard to the question of a livelihood. This matter of a vocation was one to which he had given serious thought during his undergraduate days. In the summer of 1830 he wrote his father a letter whose exceptional length bears witness to his thoroughness, no less than to his father's patience. In an irresistible torrent of words he explained that the state of his soul and the necessitousness of his fellow-men pointed to the clerical vocation. He felt strongly urged to bring "to fellow-creatures sitting in the darkness and the shadow of death the tidings of this universal and uncomprehensible love." He felt it incumbent upon him to lay before his father, with the utmost sincerity, the questions which were assailing him; and he strove to answer them now as he would have to answer them "when the trumpet of the archangel shall arouse the living and the dead, and when it will be demanded of me in common with all others, how I have kept and how employed that which was committed to my charge." But emphatically though he declared the desire of his heart, he submitted himself beforehand to the will of his father, in whose insight he had unbounded confidence. His father very sensibly advised him to postpone his decision until he had completed his studies, and at the same time he made it clear that he hoped that his son would think better of his resolve. In the course of the correspondence the son employed an argument which had almost a prophetic character. "I feel that my temperament is so excitable that I should fear giving up my mind to other subjects which have ever proved sufficiently alluring to me and which I fear would make my life a fever of unsatisfied longing and expectations." But when his father decided against the clerical vocation he not only submitted to this decision, but even justified it, by "his belief that a father's desire may be one of the appointed ways in which the will of God is made known to men." The correspondence concludes with a letter from Italy, which country he visited after his success at the University. He was anxious to study jurisprudence and history, and particularly those problems which most nearly affect the peace and happiness of humanity.

When fifty years later Lord Acton, who had studied Gladstone's character with the interest of the historian and the affection of a friend, was shown this great profession of faith, he exclaimed: "It shows how large a part of what we know and contemplate with wonder is an original gift and was born with him . . . there are almost all the germs of the power that rules the movement of half a world." The youth of one and twenty owed the deep and intimate piety which informed this letter neither to Eton nor to Oxford. At Eton only outward forms were considered, and from Oxford he wrote: "Here irreligion is the rule, religion is the exception." His own spiritual need and the example of his pious mother led him along this path.

But Gladstone was not conscious of this motive alone. At the close of the year 1831, on his twenty-second birthday, he wrote in his diary: "Politics are fascinating to me; perhaps too fascinating." To cherish his political inclination without being untrue to his religious and ethical convictions was a fundamental problem of his chequered life.

2. The Young Parliamentarian

Sooner than anyone could have expected, and at an earlier age than any other English statesman, with the exception of Pitt and Peel, those infant prodigies of Parliament, Gladstone took his seat in the House of Commons. While he was travelling in Italy, in the summer of 1832, he received a letter from his friend Lord Lincoln, who, on behalf of his father, placed the constituency of Newark at his disposal. True, the great Reform Bill had just successfully weathered the rocks, and had abolished the "rotten boroughs" and "pocket constituencies" of the wealthy gentlemen who disposed of them as their personal property. But anyone who had once possessed influence as great as that wielded by the Duke of Newcastle still retained so much of it, even after the most thoroughgoing reform, that he could speak the decisive word in this or that constituency. The electors of Newark, at the last election, which was fought in the heat of the Reform agitation, had dared to kick against the pricks and elect a Whig. The Duke, whose sense of property was affronted, was more than ever determined to get his way on this occasion. He therefore wanted a candidate who would pull his weight in the electoral contest, for the Whig elected for Newark, now Serjeant Wilde, was by no means a negligible figure. He had won fame and popularity in the most sensational trial of the period, by his defence of Queen Caroline against her unworthy husband, George IV, and later, as Lord Truro, he sat on the Woolsack as Lord Chancellor.

Gladstone felt some misgivings at first, especially as the Duke had been a bitter enemy of Canning, whom the young man revered as his political ideal. But his father's good advice, and the lure of ambition, overcame his scruples, and when in December 1832 the last Parliament to be elected under the old electoral law was dissolved, the young man of twenty-two presented himself to the honest and independent citizens of the little borough of Newark, in order to sue for their suffrages under the new Act. This, of course, was the age of the Eatanswill election, of which Dickens drew such an unforgettable picture a few years later in his *Pickwick Papers*. His account is a little highly coloured, but one notes many points of similarity on reading the description written fifty years later by Gladstone himself of his first electoral experiences:

"We started on the canvass at eight in the morning, and worked at it for about 9 hours, with a great crowd, band and flags, and innumerable glasses of beer and wine all jumbled together: then a dinner of 30 or 40 with speeches and songs till say ten o'clock; then we always played a rubber of whist, and about 12 or 1 I got to bed and not to sleep, for never in my life did I undergo an excitement to be compared with it." The young candidate had to stand a great deal of unpleasant heckling as "the nominee of the Duke." But it was soon evident that his rhetoric and dialectic were equal to such attacks, and with the help of the Duke's influence, to which many of the honest and independent electors were not immune, they were too much for the Whig and his forensic eloquence. Gladstone received 887 votes, while his opponent had to be content with 726. In an election in which the Tories suffered defeat in all parts of the kingdom this was a remarkable result.

And so began the sixty years of Gladstone's political career.

.   .   .   .   .

The Parliament in which the young member for Newark took his seat was not as yet sitting in the magnificent building whose lofty towers to-day rise like a landmark above the metropolis of the British Empire. It was the old House of Commons, with its badly lit and insufficiently ventilated Chamber, much too small for its purpose, in which the honourable Members, on occasions of importance, had to pack themselves together in a manner by no means befitting the dignity of the law-givers of a great Empire. But these same legislators were by no means always patterns of correct behaviour. If we can believe young Mr. Dickens, the House often presented an appearance that was anything but imposing. "Some members, with their leg on the back of the opposite seat: some with theirs stretched out to their utmost length on the floor; some going out, others coming in; all talking, laughing,

16

lounging, coughing, oh-ing, questioning or groaning; presenting
a conglomeration of noise and confusion, to be met with in no
other place in existence, not even Smithfield on a market day." It
cannot have been easy for the model scholar of Christ Church to
feel himself at home in this assembly.

He took his place among the Tories, who were now beginning
to call themselves Conservatives. Their leader was a man to whom
Gladstone felt akin inasmuch as he too owed his classical education to the beloved University. Oxford had manifested her high
opinion of this most distinguished son by electing him as her
representative in the House of Commons; but in 1829, when Peel,
who had formerly been regarded as the trusted champion of the
Protestant cause, had joined with the Duke of Wellington in
granting the Catholics the civil equality which had been so persistently denied them—for the great success of O'Connell's
agitation in Ireland had plainly shown them that the existing state
of affairs was indefensible—Oxford had repudiated him with
ecclesiastical zeal. Since then the more inflexible Tories had eyed
him with a certain distrust, and only his vigorous stand against
electoral reform had in some degree reconciled them. They had
no one to take his place; there was no one to equal him in Parliamentary experience and ability, in expert knowledge and eloquence.
Though he lacked the verve of his predecessor, Canning, and the
genius of his successor, Disraeli, he had a keen intellect, great
political insight, and a subtle understanding of the ideology and
the general temper of the politically and economically influential
upper middle class from which he himself had sprung.

Peel was much too intelligent not to see that the great advance
which had been made by the Reform Bill could never be cancelled
by reactionary legislation; that the Whig Party, to which the
country owed this decisive change, was for the moment riding
the crest of a wave of gratitude and popularity, and that the Tories
could not hope to return to power if they obstinately remained
what they had been up to 1831. He realized that they must gradually
adapt themselves to the spirit of the new age, and that therefore a
considerable time must elapse before they could again take the helm
of the ship of State. For this reason, as Leader of the Opposition,

he exercised the greatest caution, being always apprehensive lest some unforeseen development should compel him prematurely to resume his place on the Government benches.

When young Gladstone, from his seat on the back Opposition benches, looked across the table of the House to the Treasury bench, he saw a compact body of men who seemed to reveal all the qualities that make for political power and authority: the gift of eloquence, blue blood, Parliamentary experience, popularity, and the vigour with which a great success commonly endues the victor. There sat the scions of the great aristocratic Whig families: the Chancellor of the Exchequer, Lord Althorp, the heir of the Spencers, and Lord John Russell, the younger son of the Duke of Bedford. Althorp, indeed, was not intellectually brilliant, nor was he an able speaker, but he was a man of admirable character, for which reason he was the admitted leader of the Government party. The qualities which he lacked were possessed in abundance by Russell, the inspired and indefatigable champion of religious and intellectual liberty. It was true that his temperament often led him farther than was agreeable to his more prudent colleagues, but for the present he stood illumined by the light of the great victory.

Yonder, too, sat a younger man, from whose plump and prosaic person no one would have guessed that he could not only sway the House by an irresistible flood of the richest eloquence, but could also entertain the most intellectual gatherings of London Society, for hours at a time, by his discussion of any conceivable department of life or knowledge. But those who had read Macaulay's historical and literary essays in that famous Whig periodical, the *Edinburgh Review*, were not only impressed and delighted by his wealth of learning, and his intellectual power, and the plastic vigour of the descriptive passages; they knew also that in him the fundamental principles of Whiggism had found a prophet who had no equal for sincerity of conviction and persuasive force.

But the Reform Ministry included not only the born Whigs; there were also those who had formerly called themselves Conservatives, but had gradually, under the influence of Canning, outgrown the restrictions of the Party. Among them were two future Prime Ministers: the Foreign Secretary, Lord Palmerston, a man greatly distrusted in the chancelleries of the Holy Alliance, and the Colonial Secretary, Stanley, the son of Lord Derby, whose ready wit and eloquence in the battle for Reform had won him the title of "the Rupert of debate." No one as yet suspected that he would be the leader of three Conservative Cabinets!

The newly-elected Member for Newark, when he considered this group of experienced statesmen and Parliamentarians, was positively intimidated by their Olympian majesty. Only a few months earlier he had been a mere undergraduate; now he was theoretically the colleague of men who, like Palmerston, had been Ministers when England was waging war against Napoleon. To speak in the first Parliament of the world, in which the most famous orators competed for the palms of victory, was a very different matter from addressing the green undergraduates of the Oxford Union. In his old age it gave him pleasure to recall the shudder of reverence and the schoolboy timidity with which he had first entered this charmed circle. And the first time he himself was compelled to address the enthroned Speaker! "I remember," he said, "the revival in me bodily of the frame of mind in which a schoolboy stands before his master." But in spite of all such fears and misgivings, he knew that he must make himself heard as quickly as possible, in order to convince himself and others that he was deserving of the confidence which the honest and independent electors of Newark had reposed in him—and not they alone.

Gladstone owed the opportunity for his maiden speech to a circumstance which, from the considered standpoint which he then occupied, was extremely advantageous, though nothing could have been more harmful to his future reputation. In May 1833 Stanley introduced a series of resolutions for the gradual extinction of slavery in the British Colonies; a great step in advance along the path to which Wilberforce had pointed with such indefatigable zeal, and on which Charles Fox, in 1807, had entered with the prohibition of the slave trade. Unfortunately Gladstone's father, as the proprietor of great plantations in the West Indies, was personally interested in the question of slavery, and owing to his strong personality he was one of the leaders of the party opposed to abolition. As luck would have it, the champions of emancipation had severely criticized the administration of his plantations, and one of their most prominent spokesmen vigorously condemned it in Parliament. Naturally, young Gladstone had to reply, and he acquitted himself of his task in a manner that fulfilled the expectations of his well-wishers. He displayed a wide knowledge of the subject, a ready wit, and a great command of words, and was able to hold the attention of the House for fifty minutes. Experienced Parliamentarians were astonished by the effective arguments, the sonorous voice and the rich vocabulary of the political novice. His maiden speech made the best of possible impressions on friends and opponents alike. But that the man whose name was in later years a rallying-cry among the oppressed and the protagonists of liberty should have begun his Parliamentary career with a defence of slavery was something more than one of the bitter ironies of history; it was a token of the long path which Gladstone's development was to follow. His other speeches, also, in the first years of his Parliamentary career, were made in support of causes and institutions whose hour had long struck; for the unrestricted maintenance of the Protestant State Church in Ireland; the exclusion of the Nonconformists from the Universities, and the Jews from Parliament; and the retention of flogging in the Army.

But little as such speeches contributed to his future reputation, for the moment they gave him a position in Parliament. His earnestness, his scholarship, his wide knowledge, increased by incessant study, and his power of oratory, which quickly made an impression on the House, lifted him out of the ruck of the rising generation. He began to attract the attention of the House, and the man whose business it was to keep an eye on the rising generation of Conservatives—Sir Robert Peel—began to regard him with interest. After his speech on the proposal to open the Universities to Dissenters—a speech which Peel may have found particularly sympathetic, familiar as he was with the spirit of Oxford—he did the young man the honour of expressing, in the warmest terms, his personal appreciation. And this would be found to mean something if Peel should again be called upon to form a Government. But that, it was generally believed, could not happen for a long time to come.

Yet the unexpected came to pass, in this country so immune, as a rule, from surprises.

One evening in November 1834 the editor of *The Times* received, at a late hour, an unusual visitor: Lord Chancellor Brougham, the most gifted but also the most eccentric of Ministers, who told the editor angrily that Lord Melbourne, who had succeeded to the Premiership on the resignation of Earl Grey, had submitted to the King a choice of names for the Chancellorship of the Exchequer and the Leadership of the House—Lord Althorp having succeeded to his father's peerage—that the King had dismissed the Whig Ministry, and, further, that the Queen was at the bottom of the intrigue. Next morning the news was published—with the damaging but untruthful addition. The consternation and excitement aroused by this news in political circles was described, with satirical wit, by Disraeli in the pages of *Coningsby*. King William IV, who had often made things difficult for his Ministers during the campaign for Reform, now, in his desultory and unbalanced way, had become thoroughly weary of them. He took advantage of a purely fortuitous incident to rid himself of them. He sent for the Duke of Wellington, who advised him to entrust the Leader of the Conservatives in the House of Commons with the formation of a Government. But Peel was not in England at the moment; he had gone to Italy for his pleasure and refreshment, and was just then in Rome—which was, in those days, a very long way from London. The King had to send a special courier to call him home. Peel had to post across Europe, day and night, reaching the Court of the impatiently waiting King almost a month later. In those days of few railways the pleasure-trip of a party leader was a national inconvenience.

But finally the King had his way, and Peel his Premiership. On the formation of the Ministry Peel's fear that the attempt to form a Conservative Government might be premature was completely justified. Stanley and Graham, although they had parted company with the Whigs, were not inclined to enter his Ministry. He had to form it almost exclusively from his old friends and colleagues. But he wished to include representatives of the rising generation; and so it happened that Gladstone, only two years after his election

21

as a Member of Parliament, was summoned by the new Prime Minister, who, addressing him in the most flattering terms, offered him one of the subordinate posts—of course, without a seat in the Cabinet—in which the English Parliamentarian has an opportunity of gaining experience and learning the elements of Ministerial routine.

The office allotted to him—that of a Junior Lord of the Treasury —was, of course, not the essential thing. This was rather the fact that by this appointment, conferred upon him at the age of twenty-five, he was singled out from the crowd of Conservative members as one of the few who had a career before him. This was the more remarkable in that he was not a member of one of the great aristocratic families whose sons, in accordance with the custom of the eighteenth century—a custom not yet extinct—were commonly called to office when still young men. It meant much for his whole future that he came so early into close personal contact with Sir Robert Peel. For in Peel he saw the ideal statesman, and an administrative head whom he regarded all his life, with gratitude and reverence, as his greatest teacher. Lord Rosebery has called Peel, in his admirable biographical essay, "the pattern of all Prime Ministers." He not only led the Cabinet, but supervised the work of the individual Departments with a thoroughness which the enormously increased sphere of administrative activities made impossible in later days. But even then it was possible only for a man of the most exceptional intelligence and industry to master the whole range of problems with which such a method confronted the Premier. This was an ideal which Gladstone always upheld, and which he endeavoured to achieve at the summit of his political activity.

If Gladstone's reverence for Peel increased with every day of service under him, so also did the older man's estimation of the younger rise as rapidly as he watched him at work. Of this he gave substantial proof a few weeks later. In the elections which followed the change of Government the Under-Secretary for the Colonies lost his seat, and the Prime Minister offered the post which had thus become vacant to Gladstone. This was a much more important office; for since the Secretary for the Colonies, Lord Aberdeen, sat in the Upper House, it fell to the Under-Secretary to represent the Colonies in the House of Commons. Gladstone was as greatly surprised as he was delighted when Peel—at the end of January 1835—proposed this change of office. He made no secret of his doubts of his fitness for the post, nor of his overmastering urge to accept any responsibility that was offered him. This was the very tone most likely to delight Peel, so that he advised the other all the more warmly to accept the office and to realize the hopes that reposed on him. Gladstone accordingly proceeded to wait upon his new chief; not without a certain sense of misgiving; for Lord Aberdeen was an important personage, one of the most aristocratic of the Scottish peers, who had won his diplomatic spurs during the Napoleonic wars, and had taken part in the campaign of 1813 as the representative of the British Crown at the headquarters of the Allied armies. In the presence of this eminent gentleman Gladstone felt the timidity of the youthful scholar, the more so as he had been told that the Earl was cold and haughty. But after a few minutes' conversation all misgivings had vanished, for he perceived, behind Aberdeen's natural dignity, "a peculiar purity and gentleness," and Aberdeen, who had never before seen Gladstone, was delighted with his intellectual brilliance and his amiability. So this meeting was the beginning of a mutual affection and friendship which endured until Aberdeen's death, and assured him of a place next to Peel in Gladstone's memory.

As Under-Secretary for the Colonies Gladstone, of course, accomplished nothing of great importance; the administration was too short-lived. The elections which followed the change of Ministry confirmed Peel's belief that the majority of Englishmen still clung to the men who had introduced Reform. At the same time, Peel took pains to convince the voters that he was not by any means in favour of a premature resignation. This was evident from the manifesto addressed to his Tamworth constituents. In *Coningsby*, written ten years later, Disraeli derided this manifesto as an attempt to create a party without principles. As a matter of fact, it was an attempt to rid his party of an inheritance which would have delayed indefinitely its return to power; an example which

Disraeli himself imitated twenty years later, when he finally accepted the introduction of the principle of Free Trade, which he had formerly opposed with so much passion. For the Tamworth manifesto not only declared that a repeal of the Reform Bill was unthinkable: it even spoke in favour of "careful reform and respect for established rights." Peel had to say this, because he was convinced of the untenability of the old rigid Toryism, and the manifesto has justly been described as the transition from the antiquated Toryism to the new Conservatism. It was skilfully worded to appeal to the moderates, who stood between the two parties, and who now and again gave that party the victory which at a given moment approximated most closely to their political conceptions—a process which is described in political jargon as "the swing of the pendulum" —and of whom it may perhaps be said that they are really the determining factor in English politics. But in January 1835, although *The Times* was fighting for Peel, they were still under the influence of the great Reform victory, and still supported the Whigs so resolutely that Peel could not hope to win more than a *succès d'estime*.

Gladstone supported Peel's policy, praising the new Ministry, in his election speeches, as the government of a true party of reform, in contrast to the destructive Whigs. In this second election he had not to make any great effort. Conservatives and Whigs had peacefully agreed to share the two seats of the Newark constituency, so that he, and his former opponent Wilde, were elected without a contest. In the House of Commons he had still an opportunity, in a speech on the question of the Irish Church—which was later to absorb so much of his attention—to win the applause of his party friends, and the appreciation of the blackest of all reactionaries, the Duke of Cumberland, afterwards the King of Hanover. But a few days later Peel's Ministry was defeated on this very question of the Irish Church. On the 8th of April, 1835, Peel resigned office. His personal reputation had gained much by his behaviour during this brief Government, and he was now recognized on every side as "the first statesman in the land." But with his fall the last attempt of an English King to form a Government on the basis of his prerogative, without the assent of the House of

24

Commons, had miscarried. From this time forwards the Premier was what he is to-day, the trustee of the majority of the House of Commons. William IV, much as it went against the grain, had to recall Lord Melbourne, whom he had dismissed so hastily and inconsiderately, and put up with him for the rest of his life. When the Crown passed to a young girl of eighteen it was Melbourne who guided her first steps in political life, with all the adroitness of a cavalier of the old school.

So Gladstone's activities in the Colonial Office continued for only a little more than two months. But although in so short a time he was naturally unable to accomplish anything, yet this office gave him an opportunity of making an exhaustive study of the problems of the British Empire and its Colonies. In accordance with an early habit, he sought to elucidate his ideas by committing them to writing. Among his papers has been found a comprehensive though unfinished memoir which was apparently written shortly after his retirement from the Colonial office. It reveals his systematic mode of thought and his faculty of employing his wealth of general knowledge in the service of a concrete problem. Technically, it follows in the track of a Conservatism that was soon to appear superannuated. At this time he considered that the most necessary institutions of a British Colony were a State Church and a landowning aristocracy! On the other hand, now and for some years to come, he was opposed to the administration of the Colonies by freely elected legislatures.

3. Church and State

As regards his undisturbed evolution, it was well for Gladstone that his first term in office lasted only a few months, and that six years elapsed before he was again included in a Ministry. The interval, for him, was a period of indefatigable study. His Parliamentary activities gave him the opportunity of making himself intimately acquainted with the details of great problems, and with the institutions of his country. His friends were soon to discover that his earnest diligence enabled him to familiarize himself with the most intricate problems and completely master them. His

25

speeches were received with increasing applause, and confirmed the opinion that he had a great career before him.

But Gladstone never allowed himself to become absorbed by the general business of Parliament. There were too many other things that interested him, and his craving to read and study was too intense. He read, almost with the eagerness of a Lessing, everything that counted, everything of vital significance, in history and poetry, philosophy and theology: Tacitus and Bacon, Dante and Byron, Aristotle and Bolingbroke, St. Augustine and Bishop Butler. Many years later he was to describe Aristotle, Augustine, Dante and Butler as the four "doctors" who had been the guides of his speculative life.

In order to discipline and develop his political thought, he went back to his Burke, a writer who had made the greatest impression on him at Oxford. Like the Conservative Romantics of Germany, he learned much from the great Whig who under the influence of the French Revolution had become the champion of the historic past and the passionate critic of the untheoretical, purely rationalistic democracy; from the declared opponent of political theory who fertilized political thought as no other Englishman has done. He studied his doctrine of the State, which is indeed a partnership, but "ought not to be considered nothing better than a partnership agreement in a trade of pepper and coffee . . . to be dissolved by the fancy of the parties. It is to be looked up to with other reverence: because it is . . . a partnership in all science; a partnership in all art; a partnership in every virtue, and in all perfection . . . a partnership not only between those who are living, but between those who are living, those who are dead, and those who are to be born." He saw Burke's doctrine of the State as the bond between the visible and the invisible world. From his innermost conviction he agreed with Burke's exalted declaration that the English "do not consider their church establishment as convenient, but as essential to their State . . . consider it as the foundation of their whole constitution . . . Church and State are inseparable in their minds," and "the Christian statesmen of this land would indeed first provide for the multitude." For "the primary idea of my early politics was the church," as he wrote at the close of his life, and as he

26

declared in 1840, a political position "was mainly valuable as instrumental for the good of the church."

The central position which the Church and religion occupied in his thoughts at that time is manifest in the reflections upon all kinds of debatable questions which he was accustomed to put into writing, carefully numbering each link in the chain of argument— a habit which he extended to his political arguments, to the occasional annoyance of those to whom they were addressed. In this manner he examined the attitude of the pious Christian to money, to society, and to amusements, and while rejecting asceticism, he recommends the conscious performance of religious duties in worldly life. Such a course, indeed, is not without its dangers, "but our whole life is dangerous." At the same time he makes the characteristic remark that "conversation on religious principle in the midst of these parties is . . . an incongruity of the same kind, for example, as that of praying to God in the middle of a debate in Parliament."

"Politics would become an utter blank to me were I to make the discovery that we were mistaken in maintaining their association with religion," he wrote in April 1835, to a sometime fellow-undergraduate, with whom he was eagerly exchanging views on religion and the Church. This was Henry Edward Manning, at that time an Anglican clergyman, but one day to be a Cardinal and the Roman Catholic Archbishop of Westminster.

Manning is one of the most interesting of nineteenth-century Englishmen. At Oxford, like Gladstone, who was a year his junior, he distinguished himself in the Union. His great oratorical gifts, his unusual ability in dealing with his fellows and winning them to his own point of view, and his dexterity, which was equal to every difficulty, seemed to destine him for a political future; but this career, on which he had set his heart, was made impossible by the financial failure of his father. He accordingly turned to the Church, and here, as a matter of course, his career promised to be successful. But the peaceful unfolding of that career had been disturbed, since 1833, by the religious movement originating in Oxford, and by the *Tracts for the Times* published by another Anglican clergyman, John Henry Newman, which had attracted much public attention.

These were directed against worldliness in the Church of England, and also against what were really Calvinistic elements in the Church; and they inquired into the doctrines which it held in common with the Roman Church. After a long and despairing dialectical conflict as to the consistency of his ideas with his membership of the Church of England, in 1845 Newman took the decisive step of going over to the Catholic Church. This step was the most irrefutable evidence of the sincerity of his convictions, which he justified in his famous *Apologia pro vita sua*, but it naturally put an end to his influence as regarded the Church of England. Manning, who all this time had been in close touch with Newman, had not as yet the courage of his consistency. In his sermons he laid even greater stress than before on the Protestant elements of his faith, devoted himself to the duties of his clerical vocation, and won the reputation of a man who sooner or later would be one of the leaders of the Anglican Church. It needed the stress of many external events and inward struggles to bring him to the point at which he finally, in 1851, sought admission to the Church of Rome.

The Oxford Movement, according to Gladstone's own admission, did not directly influence him, nor did he pay special attention to Newman's *Tracts*. But although his actual contact with the movement was slight, the theological atmosphere in which he had his being was stirred by currents that had much in common with the early stages of the Oxford Movement. Nothing, indeed, was farther from Gladstone's thoughts than separation from the Anglican State Church—the step which Newman and Manning gradually saw themselves compelled to take. For him, on the contrary, in the course of his inward progress, the Church of England occupied an increasingly exalted position. He had grown to manhood in the Evangelical Movement, which in respect of its organization and its doctrines sought to base itself directly on the Gospels, laying the greatest stress on personal religious experience. But during the Italian journey which he made after leaving Oxford the idea of the Church began to take possession of his mind. As Gibbon on the steps of the Capitol, listening to the singing of the monks in Ara Coeli, was suddenly visited by the intuition that he must write the history of the decline and fall of the ancient world, so Gladstone, in St. Peter's, was overcome by his consciousness of the magnitude of the idea of the united Christian Church, which, of course, had been destroyed by the fault of Rome. The impression remained with him, and presently took shape in a new theological conviction, the central point of which was the Church with "its ministry of symbols, its channels of grace, its unending line of teachers joining from the Head."

For the young Gladstone, then, the Church was also the focal point of his political ideas. And inseparably connected with these ideas was the thought of the Church as an institution of the State, "the idea of establishment." The Anglican Church is a State Church. But what consequences follow for the State? What is the relation of the State to the Church? This is the problem which Gladstone and Manning discussed in their correspondence. And it was to this problem that he devoted his first book: *The State in its Relations with the Church.*

He was not only an intensive worker, but also a rapid writer. The words apparently flowed from his pen as they flowed from his lips. His literary productions did not gain by this facility, for they often wearied the reader by their prolixity. This fault appears in this first of his books, which would assuredly have profited by drastic abridgement. Prolixity is particularly dangerous in the treatment of a general and theoretical subject, which can be convincingly presented only by concise and abstract reasoning. This was realized from the outset by Macaulay, the first critic of eminence to notice the book. He complained that Gladstone "deludes first himself and then his readers." One has only to read Gladstone's book and Macaulay s criticism in conjunction to realize, almost palpably, the difference between an austere yet easy style, adapted to the subject, and a prolix, antiquated, unconvincing mode of treatment.

The book seeks to prove a thesis: the thesis that every State must concern itself with truth and error in religion, and that the English State in particular is pledged to promote and support only the religion of the State Church; which means, that it must regard as fully privileged citizens only the sectaries of this Church.

29

He finds the inner justification of this thesis in the conviction that the State has a conscience. Macaulay, with his keen logic and his wealth of learning, had little difficulty in confuting this thesis and its fundamental argument. But, what was much more important to Gladstone, the book found practically no response even in the circle of his own party friends. He could not avoid the conclusion— as he himself wrote a generation later—that he was "the last man on a sinking ship." The book was received with unqualified applause only by the orthodox thinkers of the German Protestant Church. Professor Tholuck of Halle, the militant adversary of rationalism, published a German translation to which he contributed an enthusiastic preface; and the Crown Prince Friedrich Wilhelm, whose romantic soul found it utterly impossible to reconcile itself with the modern conception of the State, expressed his delight in a cordial letter to Gladstone.

But even when divested of its theological content, the book expressed a fundamental conviction to which Gladstone was faithful all his life: that the activities of the State must be based upon the comprehensive idea of right and wrong; that the statesman who commits or causes to be committed an unrighteous action involves not merely the honour but the positive, subjective character of the State in dishonour, and indeed in sin! For what is expressed in this old-fashioned terminology is the outspoken protest against all Machiavellism, the expression of a conviction that was to plunge him into many a conflict.

Yet the actual rebuff which Gladstone encountered was accompanied by the most unqualified appreciation of his personality. Even Macaulay, whose personal acquaintance he had made in Rome in the course of the previous winter, prefaced his drastic criticism with a number of most flattering references to the character, the earnestness, and the self-denying zeal of the parliamentarian and politician. It was then that he coined the description whose aptness was so strikingly apparent that it was cited times without number; he called him "the rising hope of the stern and unbending Tories."

But the leader of the Tories himself—Sir Robert Peel—shook his head, and complained to his friends that he could not understand "why anybody with so fine a career before him should go out of his way to write books." Yet Peel was confident that at the given moment he could bring the wanderer back to the right path.

But before he could do so there was a great transformation in Gladstone's private life.

4. Marriage

On a July morning of the year 1839 there was a double wedding in the little parish church of Hawarden, in Flintshire. The two daughters of the late owner of Hawarden Castle, Sir Stephen Glynne, well known in Society for their beauty, were married on the same day: the elder, Catherine, to William Ewart Gladstone, the younger, Mary, to Lord Lyttelton. The whole village attended the ceremony, for the villagers were proud of their squire's family, which could boast of kinship with some of the most eminent names in England, and among them with the Earl of Chatham and his son William Pitt.

Gladstone had made the acquaintance of Catherine Glynne the previous winter, during his Italian tour, on which he had embarked with a view to resting himself and his overstrained eyes after the twofold strain of Parliamentary life and authorship. Catherine had only just recovered from an unhappy love affair. The story reminds one of Heine's pathetic poem, *Ein Jüngling liebte ein Mädchen*, except that the end was different. The young man, rejected by another, had paid court to her, not unsuccessfully; whereupon that other, who had at first been unresponsive, turned to him again and won him back; and at this he meanly jilted Catherine. The shock was severe, and to help her to forget her grief her mother resorted to the well-tried remedy of foreign travel. In Rome they met Gladstone, whose acquaintance Catherine had already made at a dinner-party, where he had been pointed out to her as a future Prime Minister. In Rome he paid court to the lovely and unaffected girl, and the fateful words were spoken amidst the ruins of the Colosseum. When he first spoke of his love she had not yet succeeded in forgetting her faithless admirer, and she told this new suitor that she had only half a heart to give him. "Give it to me and I will make it a whole one," he replied. And little by little he won it. She had first made an impression upon him in the course of a discussion of the contrast between the luxurious private life of the English and the slender endowment of their churches. "Do you think," she had asked him, "that we can be justified in all these luxuries?"

"I loved her for this question," he wrote in his diary. He had discovered in her a piety akin to his own. On their betrothal he quoted, as the lodestar of their common life, these lines from Dante's *Paradiso*:

> And in the will of God our peace is found
> And all the spheres of heaven are His floor.

On the first evening of their married life they read the Bible together, hoping and intending to do the same to the end of their married lives.

Nearly sixty years they lived together, and their common life brought them in full measure all the blessings for which they hoped. It was the expression of his deepest and sincerest feeling when Gladstone, at the close of his long life, said: "It would not be possible to unfold in words the value of the gifts which the bounty of Providence has conferred upon me through her." It was the greatest good fortune for him that in her he had found a life's companion whose relation to him was one of unchangeable love and enthusiasm, and who not only shared all the vicissitudes of his career with unfailing loyalty and devotion, but was also of inestimable help to him in matters of everyday life. In her manner she was absolutely natural and informal. Her personal charm did not desert her even in old age, and was hardly lessened by the fact that she treated such superficialities as her external appearance with an indifference that was not always consistent with the prominent social position which she was destined to occupy. Gladstone himself had a pedantic love of order, so that her careless insouciance often involved a startling derangement of his general routine. She was far from regarding this as a serious fault; jestingly, she one day said: "What a bore you would have been if you had married someone as tidy as you are!" She could make a jest of the matter, because she was well aware that in spite of these peculiarities

32

she was completely insulating him from all the little worries of everyday life, so that he might devote himself heart and soul to his great task, and she may well have realized that with her natural grace and her vital individuality she was no unfit comrade for an ambitious statesman: it was often easier to establish friendly relations with people when Catherine, in her careless fashion, had spoken words which her careful and deliberate husband would have found it difficult to utter.

There were seven children of Gladstone's marriage; twelve of Lord Lyttelton's. After the death of Mary Lyttelton in 1857 Catherine was in some degree a mother to her nephews and nieces, so that she had to watch over a young generation nineteen strong. There must sometimes have been lively doings at Hawarden. Naturally, Gladstone could not burden himself with the details of his children's education; that, after the fashion of the time, was left to their governesses and school-teachers. But he never lost touch with his children, and his son Herbert, when an old man, loved to remember how as a little boy he had ridden on his father's knee, who accompanied this procedure by singing a nursery rhyme. While the children were naturally taught at an early age to avoid disturbing their father when he was working, there were many hours when he joined in their play in a manner of which those w..o knew him only in public life would hardly have thought him capable. His letters to his wife show how attentively he followed their spiritual and moral development.

In the political world, and in London Society, Gladstone was regarded as having made a very successful marriage. The Glynnes belonged to the old aristocracy; Gladstone, the Liverpool merchant, did not. Further, they were believed to be wealthy, and the great castle and estate of Hawarden was bound to give a special cachet to the family. But it was fortunate for Gladstone that he had married without consideration of material advantages; for his connection with the Glynnes was for many years a source of financial anxiety and exacting care. His brother-in-law, Stephen Glynne, was the proprietor of an industrial undertaking of which great things were expected, and in which both Gladstone and Lyttelton were interested; but a few years later such a crisis arose

33

in its affairs that the family had to consider the possibility that Hawarden would have to be sold. That it was possible to avoid this extreme measure was due mainly to Gladstone, who, with his father's assistance, invested the whole of his fortune, and more besides, in the estate. The whole operation dragged on for thirty-five years, and necessitated the expenditure of more than a quarter of a million; at last, however, the goal was reached, and Hawarden, freed from debt, remained in the possession of the family. Through the death of Sir Stephen Glynne and his children it passed, in 1874, to Gladstone, who immediately conveyed it to his eldest son, reserving only the usufruct for life to himself and his wife.

Thus, during a period when he was dealing with the most difficult political problems, he was obliged to devote a great part of his energies to the worries and exactions of private business. For a time the strain was so great that he had serious thoughts of withdrawing altogether from political life. Nevertheless, he never grumbled or complained; as befitted his character and his conception of life, he regarded the burden as a dispensation of Providence. "It was evidently come to me by the ordinance of God; and I am rather frightened to think how light my lot would be, were it removed, so light that something else would surely come in its place"; and he added, "nor can our relation together be rendered in the very smallest degree less or more a blessing by the addition or subtraction of worldly wealth." Even those who do not accept this religious point of view must agree that this episode, with its far-reaching consequences, was not only an admirable test of character, but also a practical education which was of great advantage to his development as a statesman; for it compelled him to concern himself with the conditions and the cares of an industrial undertaking far more intensively than he would otherwise have done. And so it came about that when he came to fill—as he did before long—an important office in which both commercial and political experience were of equal value, he was able to speak out of his own experience.

PEEL'S CHANGE OF FRONT

1. From Theory to Practice

The autumn of 1841 saw the final fall of the long-tottering Whig Ministry of Lord Melbourne. To this Ministry had fallen the task of inducting the young Queen Victoria into the tasks and duties of a ruler. On the 20th of June, 1837, at the age of eighteen, she ascended the throne whose brilliance she was destined so greatly to enhance in her sixty years' reign. In the place of a capricious old man of limited capacity was a young girl, susceptible to the ideals of the new age, but requiring the guidance of an experienced statesman. It was the good fortune of the Whigs that their leader had all the qualities to win the Queen's confidence. An experienced man of the world, a pattern of good form, and highly cultivated, Lord Melbourne was as though created for the task, and in this introduction to practical statesmanship both teacher and pupil felt that they were equally fortunate.

When in February 1840 Queen Victoria married Prince Albert of Saxe-Coburg-Gotha, and the Prince, in the course of time, became the Queen's most confidential adviser, her relations with the leader of one of the parties contesting for power, which, from the constitutional standpoint, were too close and confidential, were gradually relaxed. Consequently, when Melbourne was defeated— mainly in respect of budgetary difficulties—Peel, as leader of the Conservatives, was able to take over the Government. In so doing he solemnly declared that he would remain in power only so long as he could retain it consistently with his own views. It was his tragedy, but England's good fortune, that during the five years of his Government these views underwent a fundamental transformation. For England Peel's Government of 1841–1846 constitutes one of the turning-points in her history, but for the Minister himself it meant the end of his political career and the cleavage of his party.

On forming his Government it was natural that Peel should give the first thought to his old fellow-combatants: the brilliant jurist and debater, Lord Lyndhurst, again took his place on the Woolsack; Lord Aberdeen became Foreign Secretary; Stanley and Graham, seceding from the Whigs, took the Colonies and the Home Office; and even the great name of Wellington gave its lustre to the new Government. But Peel was careful not to overlook new talent, and in this respect Gladstone was the first to be considered. What was to be done with this most promising young man, who had racked his brains over such a *démodé* problem as the relation between State and Church? Peel's answer to this question was evidence of his capacity as a teacher; he offered Gladstone the post of Vice-President of the Board of Trade.

Gladstone was taken completely by surprise when Peel made this proposal. If there was one department of Government remote from his own interests it was precisely the commercial administration which he was invited to take over. Commercial tariffs, railways, joint-stock companies—these were the province of the Board of Trade. Gladstone could assure Peel with a good conscience that he had never in his life had anything to do with them. But Peel gave him the considered answer: for such an office positive knowledge is of less importance than the inner qualities of a man. He explained that the most important problems of his Government were in the region of finance, and that it was here that he wanted Gladstone as his collaborator. Gladstone could not refuse in the face of such a proof of confidence; he accepted the post.

It was clear to him that he would have to find his way alone in his new office. His formal superior, the President of the Board of Trade, was Lord Ripon, very definitely a mediocrity; despite his rank, he was of no more importance than in the days when, as Mr. Robinson, he had been the colleague of Huskisson, or when, as Lord Goderich, he had succeeded Canning, and had resigned after a few months. Gladstone discovered, in the course of a few days, that he could learn nothing from his superior, and that he would not long have to put up with him. Although only Vice-President, he had to take over the actual control of the Department. That this was the case—that he had a formal superior who barred his way to the Cabinet—was of course a disappointment; for Gladstone, who did not underestimate his own capacities, had expected that he would at once be promoted to Cabinet rank. This state of affairs continued until 1843, when Peel appointed him President and called him into the Cabinet.

For the time being, however, he was only appointed Privy Councillor—an appointment which brought with it his first encounter with the Queen. The ceremony of kissing her hand was observed on the 3rd of September, 1841. Often, in the course of their fifty years of collaboration—a relation at first gratifying, and then only too often distressing—he looked back upon this first sight of her; how, "composed but dejected," a shy young woman, with her young husband beside her, she had presided over the Council of State. She had come to terms with Peel, but she still found the Conservative statesman, whose innate shyness was concealed by a stiff and formal manner, anything but sympathetic.

And now Gladstone had to set to work and familiarize himself with a thousand matters of which he had hitherto been ignorant. He likened himself to "a reluctant schoolboy meaning well." And his was a hard school. In the place of Burke's speeches or Butler's sermons he had now to pore over calculations and statistics, over commercial reports and the regulations of railway companies. Instead of discussing with Manning the dogmas of the Church he had to receive commercial and industrial deputations, which complained of grievances, or criticized his proposals, and endeavoured to prove, out of their long years of practical experience, that he was on a completely false track. But it was not long before he knew everything within the province of his office that was worth knowing. He knew every tariff-rate by heart, and all the important statistics of production, and was able to show the experts, not only that he knew as much about their subject as did they themselves, but also that there was a general interest to which their individual interests were subordinated. This, of course, required not merely a comprehensive knowledge of detail, but also an understanding of the fundamental principles of political economy. But for him the greatest of the classical political economists had not lived and thought in vain, and he quickly contrived to arrange the wealth

37

of economic data in accordance with Ricardo's laws. The facts that he came from Liverpool, and was a son of a mercantile family, may perhaps have contributed to his success; for he had assuredly brought with him something of the spirit of his father's house. And while it was afterwards said of him in jest, "Oxford on top, Liverpool underneath," he now showed that he could become a master in Liverpool's way of thinking, when his office made it impossible to take the Oxford way.

Peel saw with joy how completely his young friend was justifying the confidence which he had felt in his capacities, and before the new President had been a year in office the Premier wrote a letter to Gladstone's father in which he congratulated him in the warmest and most cordial terms on the success and the accomplishments of his son:

"Your paternal feeling must be gratified in the highest degree by the success which has naturally and justly followed the intellectual exertions of your son, and you must be supremely happy as a father in the reflection that the capacity to make such exertions is combined in his case with such purity of heart and integrity of conduct."

Peel had every occasion to congratulate himself on having secured so active a collaborator in the economic and financial labours of his Government; for it was in this province that the things were done that give his Ministry its great historical significance. To set the finances of the nation in order he resolved upon the bold step of reviving, in a different form, the income-tax, which Pitt had introduced during the Napoleonic war, and which had been hastily abolished after the peace. Gladstone objected that the tax was excessively inquisitorial, and that it threatened "credit, the pole of our commercial system." Peel had expressly requested him to explain his attitude to the project, although he was not then a member of the Cabinet. Considering the important part which the income-tax was to play in Gladstone's later financial policy, it is remarkable that his attitude towards this tax was at first critical and disapproving. But Peel, correctly judging the difficulties with which he would have to contend in Parliament, did not abandon his project.

For Peel, however, this was only one aspect of the projected financial reform. The surplus which he anticipated he proposed to employ in simplifying the extraordinarily complicated commercial tariffs, in order to lighten the burden of foreign trade. There were no less than 1,200 different tariffs for exports and imports, which had been imposed from time to time, and which were still in force, because no one had taken the trouble to examine the whole problem systematically. This was a task for which Peel needed a man like Gladstone, and for which no one was better qualified; for the difficulties of such a procedure became evident only during its execution, which called for a clear conception of the problem as a whole together with a complete mastery of the details. Here Gladstone displayed an unusual and astonishing faculty of mastering in a few hours a task which would occupy another man for days. Graham, who was in Peel's Cabinet, and was over and over again a colleague of Gladstone's, summarized his judgement of him by saying that "he could do in four hours what it took any other man sixteen to do"; and at that time—as he told John Morley when he was an old man—he was accustomed to working sixteen hours a day.

Before long Gladstone was so complete a master of his speciality that Peel was able to entrust him with not only the elaboration of the new tariff, but also with the task of laying it before the House. Here Gladstone was able to reveal yet another faculty—that of so dealing with the driest subject that it suddenly came to life and acquired the power of interesting his audience. Twice—in 1842 and 1845—he had to introduce such a tariff reform, on each occasion with complete success and lasting advantage to the economic life of the nation. Of this first reform of 1842, however, he admitted later that it had given him six times as much trouble as all the later reforms put together. No one, however, who heard Gladstone speaking on the exports of machinery, or the wool imports, could have imagined that only a few months earlier this man had been chiefly concerned with politico-religious problems.

Needless to say, he was not content with the assembling of the facts, but pondered them thoroughly and systematically. In so doing he was impressed by the contradictions between the actual

39

economic conditions and the existing laws. For example, there was an export duty on English machinery, which had originally been inspired by the notion that foreign countries should not be enabled to compete with England with the help of cheap English machines. Gladstone saw that English industry had long ago reached such a height that it was no longer in need of such timid protective measures. He therefore decided to abolish this export duty, thereby opening the world-market to the English machine industry, and initiating a period of dazzling and unprecedented development.

Peel's pedagogic intention was thus completely achieved. But something more than this was accomplished: Gladstone, as a result of this work, had opened his mind to the ideas of the new political economy. For this was the time when the campaign against the Corn Laws had reached its climax. Since the middle of the eighteen-thirties English industry had been in a critical state. The men who in 1838 had founded the Anti-Corn Law League in Manchester declared that the cause of this crisis was the rise in the price of bread due to the duties on corn. These duties had been constantly assailed since the peace of 1815, but the demand for their complete abolition seemed at first, to the overwhelming majority of politicians of both parties, to be little better than revolutionary insanity. How could one leave the "agricultural interest," when agriculture was still the greatest of English industries, without protection? But the adversaries of the Corn Laws were emphatic in their opinion, and they knew how to obtain a hearing for their views. The League began an organized agitation, such as had never been known before; and it had leaders who were capable of maintaining their agitation at a high moral and intellectual level: Richard Cobden and John Bright. Both engaged in the textile trade; they were both independent political thinkers whose ideas were strongly tinged with religion. Bright was a Quaker, with all the moral power of conviction that characterizes the sect. For both men the campaign against the corn duties was only one component of a great political programme, at the summit of which was the ideal of international understanding and peace between the nations. Lujo Brentano, the German economist who has, perhaps, best understood England, at the close of a long and militant career wrote of the co-operation of these two men, that nothing more flawlessly beautiful is recorded in political history. Both were indefatigable agitators, travelling from place to place, and winning innumerable listeners to the cause in which they believed with all their hearts. Cobden relied on the forcible exposition of the facts; Bright on the compelling power of his masterly speeches, whose simple and eloquent language was derived from Milton and the Bible. They were enormously effective, because the middle classes found in their words, in a more lucid and intensified form, the ideals and the tendencies of their own *élite*. But the effect of these speeches extended far beyond the limits of the middle classes, inspiring the working class, whose radical elements were disappointed by the failure of the semi-socialistic Chartist movement. The fight for cheap bread was quite obviously a battle for their most immediate interests. Cobden and Bright were thus able to speak as the spokesmen of a widespread and powerful popular movement, which recognized no class distinctions. In 1841 Cobden entered the House of Commons, and his political significance made itself felt immediately. Both parties saw that it was no longer possible simply to scamp the question of the tax on bread.

Lord John Russell, the actual political head of the Melbourne Ministry, had begun to tackle the problem of the Corn Laws a few months before its overthrow. When Peel took over the reins he had to follow suit. The existing system was undoubtedly unsatisfactory. What could be put in its place? The Board of Trade examined the problem. The President, Lord Ripon, could only repeat the current phrases of the landed proprietor, that it would be a disaster if England were to depend on the importation of foreign corn. This was no use to Peel, so the question was submitted to Gladstone. From him he could at least expect a thorough and objective and independent examination of the problem.

Gladstone accordingly set to work; at first, of course, in the spirit of his early education; that is, in the spirit of Toryism. The Tory Party was in the first place a party of landowners. The hale and hearty but not especially thoughtful squires of England and Scotland were its best supporters in the country and on the Parliamentary benches. The protection of their harvests by high duties against cheap foreign corn was one of the first principles of their programme, which was transmitted, without examination, from generation to generation. Gladstone, however, had now to inquire whether this protection was really so indispensable, and whether it was adapted to the current economic conditions, which had undergone great changes in the last three decades. Once more he had to immerse himself in the documents, study the usages of the corn trade, and examine the method of fixing prices.

He found, in the files of his department, a literal translation of a Chinese document. It was the report of a Chinese official in Canton to his superior in Pekin. He recommended that no foreign ship should be allowed to enter Chinese harbours without the exaction of a heavy duty. "But," he added, "the question of ships bringing food for the people was quite another affair." The letter was signed, with true Chinese politeness, "Your stupid little Brother."

This was very amusing. But it also made one think. This Chinese official, who was so submissive, accepted as a matter of course what the official wisdom of the British statesman had not yet grasped. Was it possible, after all, that he was not entirely mistaken? And the young Vice-President began to consider the problem from the beginning.

It was so that Gladstone, as a very old man, described to his intimates his first conversion to Free Trade.

We ought perhaps to allow something for the old man's love of giving an anecdotal point to a narrative; it may be that his intellectual development owed more in reality to the study of the actual data and the writings of Ricardo; but the fact remains that in a few months he had travelled all the way from protectionist prejudice to free-trade insight.

Peel himself could not at first keep pace with this rapid development, and for a time they were actually at loggerheads. He was gradually forced, by the development of current economic conditions, to adopt the same point of view that Gladstone had reached in 1842; but in the intervening years the younger man had to contend with fresh difficulties.

.   .   .   .   .

Of his other activities in his first important post one particular branch may be mentioned; that concerned with legislation affecting the railways. When Gladstone took office the idea of the railway had already taken possession of men's minds. The railways were already a power, even in Parliament. They had undergone a rapid though unsystematic development, and they thought far less of the safety and convenience of the public than of the height of their dividends. Gladstone found that serious grievances had occurred, in respect of which the Government had hitherto been helpless. By his indefatigable labours in the Select Committee which he himself had proposed, he was able to introduce great improvements. Opposition in the Cabinet—and especially from Peel, who was thinking principally of retaining his majority—prevented him from carrying out his entire programme of reform. Nevertheless, in one particular he introduced a reform which had far-reaching consequences. To the despised third-class passengers, hitherto so badly treated by the railways, it was of effective and lasting benefit. He carried through the House a statutory regulation by which the railways were pledged to run at least one express train daily which would carry third-class passengers at low fares in closed carriages with proper seating accommodation. Without exaggeration, this reform may be compared with the reform of the postal tariff by Rowland Hill. Just as on the introduction of the penny post the writing of letters ceased to be a privilege of the wealthy, so, thanks to Gladstone's reform, even the poor could travel by rail. It was therefore not without reason that this statute was nicknamed the "Poor Traveller's Charter."

2. The Paladin of Principle

So far Peel's pedagogic experiment had been a brilliant success. The political bookworm had evolved into a practical politician of the first rank, who, instead of wasting his time on theologico-political tracts, which in Peel's opinion were highly unnecessary things, now, more usefully, promoted the business of the Government by writing reports on railways and commercial tariffs, and by mastering the concrete details of the national economy with the same impeccable accuracy which he had formerly displayed in his citations of the works of St. Augustine or Bishop Warburton. And now, suddenly, it became evident that there had been much practical good sense in Peel's dry reception of Gladstone's book on Church and State, and that this work threatened to prove a rock on which Gladstone's brilliant career might be utterly wrecked.

This happened when for the first time in Gladstone's life he came into contact with the problem which was to leave its stamp on the closing years of his career: the Irish question. Throughout the whole of the nineteenth century Englishmen had to put up with the consequences of the fact that their forefathers, after centuries of conflict, had subjected Ireland by force, but had never succeeded in subduing or converting the Irish population. The north-eastern corner of Ireland, Ulster, was the only exception; here the English policy of colonization had succeeded in creating a closed caste of landowners and tenants, who clung to their Protestant faith as passionately as they declared their loyalty to the English Crown. But throughout the rest of Ireland the English and Scottish Protestants were only a thin upper stratum, beneath which there existed a compact mass of farmers and agricultural labourers who were absolutely Irish and Catholic. But the Irish State Church, for which the whole nation had to pay taxes, was a branch of the Church of England; that is, to the great mass of the Irish it was a foreign and heretical church. The State looked askance at the priests whom the Irish held in affection, and did next to nothing for their training and education. While the Protestant Trinity College in Dublin was richly endowed, the Catholic seminary of Maynooth had to be content with the shabbiest subsidy. If a Liberal Ministry attempted to treat the Catholics with a little more justice and generosity, the bigoted Protestants of England raised the dreaded cry of "No Popery"—a cry that had prevented the introduction of many conciliatory measures, and imperilled many a Ministry.

Now Peel, as the responsible Minister, had to confront this problem, and he realized at once that the situation was intolerable. He could not let it continue: he had far too high a conception of the duties of a Government. It seemed to him that the most urgent reform was to make better provision for the rising generation of Catholic priests. He therefore resolved to propose a considerable increase of the Government's contribution towards the upkeep of the Maynooth Seminary.

It was this proposal that involved Gladstone in a conflict between his loyalty to his political chief and his loyalty to his cherished and declared convictions. For in his book on Church and State he had expressed himself as opposed on principle to the idea that the State should give financial support to a heresy; indeed, he had dealt exhaustively with this very question of the Maynooth Seminary, as it revealed and determined the attitude of the State towards the Irish State Church: "articulus stantis aut cadentis Ecclesiae." And now, very shortly after the publication of his book, he had realized that he was a voice crying in the wilderness, "the last man on a sinking ship," and that there was not a single politician who dreamed of making his axiom of the conscience of the State, and its duty of presenting the truth—that is, the religious truth—the basis of a practical policy. He could no longer fail to realize that this was the case, and that his ideal, as he had developed it in this first book of his, had no place in modern life. When Peel informed him of his intention, Gladstone had to admit that he was right. But it was, he declared, quite impossible that he himself, as Minister, should advocate what he had condemned as a political writer.

Peel had the greatest difficulty in persuading him to abandon this view, which to him seemed a mere crochet. In order that he might not lose this youngest and most valuable of his collaborators he had to postpone for months the introduction of the Maynooth proposal. But the matter seemed to him so important that in the end he would rather have put up with the loss of Gladstone. And Gladstone, when at last the decision could be postponed no longer, wrote him exhaustive and complicated letters, in order to explain that he could not act otherwise, and why. These clearly reveal the battle of conflicting emotions and desires that was being fought in Gladstone's soul. It is not surprising that Peel wrote rather brusquely to his friend Graham, complaining that he found it extremely difficult to understand exactly what Gladstone really thought. That a politician could resign a seat in the Cabinet on account of a measure of which he actually approved must have seemed to Peel the very acme of unreason. As a matter of fact, for Gladstone there was very much at stake. He loved and reverenced Peel. Ought he to break with him at a moment when hotly-contested battles were impending, in which the older man had reckoned on his assistance, and in which, owing to his particular capacities, he could give the most effective aid? Ought he to fail and disappoint such a man? Was he not staking his whole career, a career which had only just begun? And all for the sake of an obsolete book, which was hardly accessible to the great public! Would not this be thought the merest quixotry, a comedy rather than a tragedy? All his friends advised him to change his mind: even Stanley, who, for other reasons, was himself on the point of resigning from the Ministry.

Nevertheless, he did not falter in his resolve; simply because he was convinced that his reputation as an honest man was in question. If he remained in the Ministry he would give people the impression that he had changed his opinion for the sake of office, that he had sacrificed his conviction to his career. He wished he could vote for Maynooth without exposing himself to such a suspicion.

The great majority of politicians could not understand such an attitude, and when, in the usual speech of the retiring Minister, he sued for their understanding, he failed to elicit a response. These were painful days and weeks for him, and at times his nerves rebelled.

When, in the debate on the Maynooth motion, Gladstone had concluded the speech in which he supported the Government from which he had resigned, amidst the pitying smiles of his friends and the scorn of his adversaries, another Member rose from the Conservative benches and derided him in the following words:

"I looked upon the right honourable gentleman as the last paladin of principle, the very abstraction of chivalry. . . . I never believed it would be the right honourable gentleman who would come down and give the House the small change of circumstances to settle this great account."

The Member who uttered these derisive words had first entered

Parliament a few years after Gladstone, although he was some five years his senior. He had made several unsuccessful attempts to secure election, and he had to contend against the suspicion that he had turned his coat from self-seeking motives, and on delivering his maiden speech he was shouted down by his opponents. But he soon showed the House that his energy and endurance were inexhaustible. His first failure did not deter him from speaking again at the appropriate moment; and not only had he always something to say, but he said it in a way of his own, expressing himself in the most polished style. His appearance unmistakably revealed his Jewish extraction, and although he had become converted to Christianity in his childhood, he emphasized the fact, both in speech and in writing, that he was proud of this descent. Even before he entered Parliament the name of Benjamin Disraeli was known as that of the author of a number of novels, which revealed unusual qualities of wit and intellect; and quite recently, in the years 1844 and 1845, he had created, in *Coningsby* and *Sybil*, the English political novel, which did not hesitate to portray the politicians of the day under a slight disguise, and which treated, with the greatest frankness, problems of the present and the future.

But political success did not come to him as soon as he had expected, and as he was quite justified in expecting, in view of his unusual gifts. Peel had grievously disappointed him when in 1841 he overlooked him altogether on forming his Ministry, and did not even offer him one of those subordinate posts with which it is usual to stimulate the zeal of talented disciples. Other grievances widened the breach, and finally Peel felt that he owed it to himself to break off all intercourse with him.

Before long he had reason to regret having taken this course. Disraeli made up his mind that what he could not achieve under Peel he would achieve in the enemy's camp, and that he would very soon make it clear that he possessed capacities which Peel had failed to recognize. These tactics suited him perfectly. No attack is so effective, and excites so much attention, as that which is delivered from the benches of one's own party, and no applause is so heady as that which comes from one's adversaries, across the table of the House. But if the assailant is a master of the weapons of wit and irony, of scorn and personal invective, which he wields with unprecedented ruthlessness and audacity, this attack becomes a Parliamentary event, and whenever he rises to address the House his fellow-members are filled with anticipation. Arrow upon arrow struck Peel in the most sensitive spots. Although he was an admirable speaker and a skilful debater, he was absolutely incapable of dealing with this sort of polemic, and he soon gave up the attempt to answer Disraeli. Even in the debate on Maynooth Peel had to submit to one of these pungent diatribes, although it failed in its ostensible object—namely, to induce the Whigs to reject the proposal. They applauded Disraeli when he attacked the Prime Minister, yet they did not vote with him, but with Peel. Great events had to come to pass before they found themselves voting with the Conservative rebel.

Disraeli could make little sense of Gladstone's behaviour in this crisis. After the unsuccessful speech in which the late Minister had sought to justify his behaviour, Disraeli told his friends that he could not believe that this man had any future before him.

3. Peel Victorious—and Defeated.

It seemed at first as though Disraeli was right. Gladstone was now once more a private Member; however, he could still speak in support of the Government, and he did so when the question before the House was one with which he was familiar. But he could no longer take part in the councils of the Government. Yet it was precisely now that the Government was on the point of taking decisions of the greatest consequence, not only for itself, but also for the whole course of English politics.

Peel had gradually but steadily come to the conclusion that the existing system of duties on corn was no longer tenable. His endeavours to follow a middle course, which would have enabled him to introduce a fiscal reform without splitting the Conservative Party, were wrecked by a natural event, the failure of the potato crop in Ireland (1845), which threatened the most vulnerable part of the kingdom with starvation. The Party was in an impossible situation, and Peel sought to save himself by resigning. But the attempt miscarried, and on the 20th December, 1845, he was once more Prime Minister.

A seat in his Cabinet was vacant owing to the final resignation of Stanley. Peel did not for a moment hesitate; he offered it to Gladstone. On the following day he was able, "with the greatest satisfaction," to announce to Her Majesty that Gladstone had accepted the office of Colonial Secretary. Thus, after a few months' interval, Gladstone was once more in the Cabinet. And now, for the first time, he encountered one of the greatest difficulties of political life. In accordance with the law, the acceptance of an office, even in the Ministry, meant the loss of the member's seat; so that he had to offer himself for re-election. But Gladstone's constituency of Newark was still in the hands of the Duke of Newcastle, and the Duke was beside himself over the change of front of Peel and his Ministry. If he could not prevent the change he could at least make things difficult for them. He immediately gave Gladstone to understand that he would now find his deadliest adversary in his former patron, if indeed he had the courage to face the electors of Newark. One cannot deny the Duke the virtue of consistency. His own son, Lord Lincoln, was in the same position as Gladstone, and his father did not hesitate to oppose his re-election. It may be that Gladstone would have succeeded in winning the Newark election without the support of the Duke. But he would have thought such a course improper and ungrateful, for he felt that he owed the Duke a debt of gratitude for his earlier patronage. To incite the electors against their landlord, one of the great landowners of the country, would have been incompatible with his Conservative views—for they were still Conservative. So, with a heavy heart, he bade farewell to his first constituency.

Under other circumstances it would not have been very difficult for a prominent Minister to find another constituency. But already the difficulties were gathering against which Peel's disciple would have to contend for many years to come. No Conservative member was prepared to make way for Gladstone, so that he remained without a seat until the General Election of 1847.

He had thus to watch, inactive, the great battle which Peel had to fight in Parliament for his policy and the life of his Ministry.

49

He could no longer stand beside Peel and defend him against the passionate attacks of Disraeli. For Disraeli now saw that his time had come. The Protectionists were still in the majority in the Conservative Party. But suddenly they saw themselves deprived of their leader, who now represented the cause which it had been, in the eyes of their followers, their duty to contest. With the adroitness of the born Parliamentarian, and the courage of a man conscious of his ability, Disraeli had been the first to express, in the House of Commons, the affronted Party's indignation with their renegade leader; opening the attack with a boldness of imagery and a brilliance of phrasing that suddenly restored the courage of the hitherto depressed and defeated ranks of the Conservative land-lords. From this time forward he was in the forefront of battle: indefatigable, ruthless, witty, emotional, and always effective. He was too intelligent to expect that the Conservative landowners, who distrusted him by reason of his origin and his earlier career, would formally regard him as their leader; for that office he found a suit-able figurehead in Lord George Bentinck, a son of the Duke of Portland. Bentinck was energetic and untiring, and honestly dismayed by Peel's betrayal of the Conservative Party. That he was not distinguished for exceptional knowledge or ability did not matter; Disraeli had more than enough of both, and he generously placed them at the disposal of his nominal chief. Nevertheless, no one who knew the facts could question who was the actual leader of the Conservative party now in process of transformation.

It must have spelt misery for Gladstone to follow all these debates in which he could play no part. He must have known that he could have encountered even a Disraeli successfully. How gladly he would have crossed swords with him! But that was impossible —for the present!

Disraeli's opposition, despite all his tactical ingenuity, failed to prevent the abolition of the Corn Law. Russell was determined to retain Peel until its abolition was secure, as much for the sake of the cause as because of the assurance which he had given the Queen at the time of the December crisis. But as soon as this goal was reached, Peel's fate was sealed. Now Disraeli was able to effect what he had so long been striving to accomplish: the union of the

Liberal and Protectionist votes in the House. On the 25th of June the Corn Bill, abolishing the Corn Law, was read for the third time in the House of Lords. On the same day the Commons voted on a Government measure—an Irish Coercion Bill. Eighty Protectionists voted against it with Bentinck and Disraeli. This was enough, with the votes of the Liberal opposition, to give a majority against Peel. Three days later he resigned, taking leave of the House in a speech which was worthy of so critical a moment. It concluded with a panegyric of the man who—as history has recorded—was more than anyone responsible for this victory of Free Trade— Richard Cobden. For himself, he could only hope that his name would be spoken with gratitude by those whose lot it was to earn their bread in the sweat of their brow.

PACIFICO AND POERIO

1. *Oxford, Döllinger, Gorham and Manning*

After the fall of Peel it was three years before Gladstone, by his speech against Palmerston in the famous Don Pacifico debate, took a great step forward in the consciousness of political England. And these were the last three years of Peel's life.

In these three years Gladstone's political situation was anything but comfortable. He had shared the fate of the rest of Peel's political followers. English politics, like the British Parliament, depend in principle on the existence of two parties. Supreme above all other differences is the one fundamental distinction: Government or Opposition; the right-hand benches and the left. This system is saved from the rigidity otherwise inherent in it by the fact that from time to time a group detaches itself from one or the other party, and after a period of wandering in the wilderness it merges, wholly or partially, in one of the two great parties, whose opinions and principles are often appreciably modified by this process. So it was with the Peelites in the middle and the Liberal Unionists at the end of the nineteenth century. The season of wandering in the wilderness is naturally always a difficult and depressing time. The severance of established bonds is painful, and the bygone conflicts are not easily forgotten. It is some time before the backsliders forget how completely they agreed, in fundamentals, with their old friends, and it is long before they are convinced that a reunion would be impossible.

For the first few years the attitude of Peel and his friends was decided by the realization that the reintroduction of the Corn Law was not at first impossible, and that the averting of this acute peril must take precedence of all other considerations. This meant that they must give their support to the Liberal Ministry of Russell, which had followed that of Peel. Outwardly the manner in which the divorce of the Protectionist and the Free Trade Conservatives had been effected—namely, by Disraeli's personal attacks on Peel—had still further widened the breach. Gladstone, to the end of his life, though acknowledging Disraeli's genius, could never forget this hurtful polemic. But the Peelites still regarded themselves as Conservatives, and this was especially true of Gladstone.

Moreover, since the General Election of 1847 he had been the Member for the University of Oxford. The right of the Universities to return Members to Parliament is one of those peculiarities of English politics which hardly finds its counterpart in any other country, and which has survived through the centuries, even in spite of the equalitarian tendencies of the nineteenth and twentieth centuries. The University electors have comprised, since the time of James I, all graduates of the University. In the first half of the nineteenth century the great majority of these graduates were theologians, who had acquired their spiritual orientation for life in this stronghold of Protestantism. For these electors the defence of the Protestant ascendancy against all the tendencies of the modern State was the first of all political aims. They had ceased to vote for Peel when he promoted Catholic Emancipation, and their first requirement of their Parliamentary representative was religious orthodoxy. In the eyes of many of them Gladstone had lost all claim to their confidence by voting in favour of the State allowance to the Catholic seminary of Maynooth. But in the majority the feeling that was uppermost was that no one then engaged in political life took religious principles so seriously as Gladstone; that he was a loyal and devoted son of the Church, and by far the most distinguished of Oxford's scholars. It is striking evidence of the respect which Gladstone had won in the fifteen years of his political activity that the majority of the exacting electors of the University gave him their suffrages in spite of Maynooth.

For him this was the realization of a dearly cherished dream. He had "desired with an almost passionate fondness" to become the elected representative of his own University, the object of his heartfelt devotion. Moreover, his success gave him a special position in the House. But election by any constituency is for the representative not only an honour, but also an obligation, and the Member for the University of Oxford in particular was compelled in respect of many questions to have regard to the special psychology of his electors.

But before long Gladstone was obliged, in a question of fundamental importance, to take up a position in conflict with the well-known views of his Oxford electors. The question of admitting Jews to Parliament was once more brought before the House. The City of London had elected, as its representatives, Lord John Russell and Lionel Nathan Rothschild. According to the law, Rothschild could be elected, but he could not take his place in the House, because every Member had to take an oath "on the true faith of a Christian." Russell, in the forefront of whose political convictions were liberty of belief and liberty of conscience, favoured the discarding of this formula. In the long and important debate on this proposal Disraeli, undeterred by the manifest disapproval of his party friends, championed, with the greatest energy, the race from which he himself had sprung. It was this speech that forced Russell to acknowledge Disraeli's political courage. But Gladstone was no less courageous in demanding equality of privilege for the Jews; for he could imagine what would be the effect of his speech in Oxford.

This speech represented another great advance in the evolution of his fundamental view of Church and State. Once more he declared his fidelity to the ideal of the Christian State. But this ideal had in practice been abandoned since Unitarians had been admitted to the House, while Jews were allowed to fill municipal offices and had been granted the suffrage. And if the ideal had been abandoned the exclusion of the Jews from Parliament could no longer be justified. "You first contended for a Church Parliament," he told the Tories; "you then contended for a Protestant Parliament; in both cases you were defeated. You were not defeated owing to accident. You were defeated owing to profound and powerful and uniform tendencies, associated with the movement of the human mind—with the general course of events—perhaps I ought to say with the providential government of the world." One is almost reminded of the well-known words of Hegel: "I hold that the World-spirit of the age has given the word of command to advance; that command will be obeyed."

This attitude was not calculated to meet with applause in Oxford. Many pious theologians, like Professor Pusey, whose religious principles were so akin to Gladstone's, protested vigorously. This disapproval found expression in many loud interruptions when he visited Oxford in the following year to receive the honorary degree of Doctor. But the majority of the electors were loyal to him.

The religious movements which constituted so marked a feature of the period claimed Gladstone's eager attention. The circle in which he discussed such matters now included a man with whom he was henceforth united by the closest ties of friendship—the great German Catholic scholar and polemist, Ignaz Döllinger. They had met when Gladstone had spent several months in Germany after his resignation from the Government in consequence of the Maynooth affair. In September 1845 he visited Döllinger in his home in Munich, and the two men conceived a strong liking for each other, though each was firmly rooted in the faith which he professed. Gladstone spoke with admiration of his friend's liberal views; and Döllinger introduced him to others who shared his opinions; for example, Görres. But the German society of those days was not such as to meet with the approval of a visitor accustomed to the refinements of English etiquette. Once, when Döllinger had introduced him to half a dozen Munich professors, it impressed him that these gentlemen did not really think it necessary to listen when one of their company was speaking. "Always . . . speaking at once, very loud, each not trying to force the attention of the others, but to be following the current of his own thoughts." So he told his wife in some dismay; and even the great Görres, it seems, was no exception.

Before his return from Germany Gladstone expressed his conviction, in a moving letter to his wife, that they were passing through a critical period. "What a crisis for religion at large is this period of the world's history!" For the Church of England, indeed, this crisis resulted in an explosion which most intimately affected Gladstone, and cost him two of his closest friends. It happened in

55

connection with a dispute over a matter of ecclesiastical law, which reached its conclusion in the spring of 1850. An elderly clergyman of Evangelical leanings, Gorham, was refused a benefice by his Bishop on the grounds that his views on regeneration through baptism were not in agreement with the binding and fundamental doctrines of the Church of England. Gorham took legal steps against this decision, which led him, in the final instance, to the Judicial Committee of the Privy Council. This was a purely secular authority, in whose deliberations the clergy could assist only in a consultative capacity. It decided in Gorham's favour, and also denied that his doctrine was incompatible with the dogmas of the Church of England.

This decision evoked a storm of indignation in High Church circles. Gladstone, as well as Manning, repudiated it emphatically. Its significance lay not only in the doctrine which it propounded, but above all in the fact that a purely secular State authority had decided a question of belief. The final result was very different in the case of the two men. Manning, together with Hope-Scott, a close mutual friend, came to the conclusion that there was no longer a place for him in English Protestantism. He took the course that Newman had already taken in 1845, and in April 1851 both he and Hope-Scott went over to the Roman Catholic Church, in which he was to reach such eminence. A generation later he gave a moving description of their last devotions in common. They knelt together in a little Anglican chapel. But when the Communion service began Manning rose to his feet with the words: "I can no longer take the Communion in the Church of England." He laid his hand on his friend's shoulder, saying: "Come with me!" But Gladstone remained. Their ways had come to the final parting.

Not for a moment did Gladstone consider the possibility of going over to the Roman Church. His place was and is in the Church of England. But he did once more, and for the last time, ask himself if he should not give up his political career and devote himself wholly to the Church. We cannot wonder that he decided against this course; he had immersed himself too profoundly in the problems of political life, and he was too clearly conscious of his abilities in this direction. Only an absurd under-estimation of his capacities could have prevented him from feeling that he had found his vocation. Here alone his courageous and militant intellect could find satisfaction. And—what was more important—he could tell himself that even as a politician he might be called upon to battle for the supremacy of the moral law.

And with this his politico-religious ideas underwent an important modification, which exerted a decisive influence upon his whole career. The perception that his original ideal of the relation of Church to State could not be realized, that the close union of the two might even be dangerous to the Church, made him an advocate of complete religious liberty. He emphatically repudiated "the servile doctrine that religion cannot live but by the aid of parliament." He came rather to the conclusion "that among us all systems, whether religious or political, which rest on a principle of absolutism, must of necessity be, not indeed tyrannical, but feeble and ineffective systems; and that methodically to enlist the members of a community, with due regard to their several capacities, in the performance of its public duties, is the way to make that community powerful and healthful."

So strong upon him already was the influence of the fundamental ideas of Liberalism, at a time when he still called himself a Conservative, and represented the most Conservative constituency in England!

This influence found unmistakable expression in a speech which he delivered in the following year, and which is rightly counted among his noblest and most significant utterances. It was delivered in opposition to a Bill laid before the House by the Liberal Government of Russell, though in fact it breathed the Liberal spirit which was not perceptible in the Bill. The Bill proposed, out of nervous dread of Papal encroachments, to prevent the erection of Roman Catholic sees in England. The Government had on their side the anti-Catholic feeling in the country and the House—a feeling always easily aroused—and the measure was accepted by an overwhelming majority. But this spirit—which, of course, was fully shared by Oxford—Gladstone courageously opposed, with all the fire of his eloquence and all his profound knowledge of the fundamental problems of political life. He invoked "the principle of religious freedom . . . which ultimately triumphed, after you had spent upon it half a century of agonizing struggle," and he reminded the House, in memorable words, that England had the reputation, all the world over, of taking a long time to resolve upon a progressive step, but that she held fast to what she had achieved. "They know that when you make a step forward you keep it."—"Have the courage to show the Pope of Rome and his Cardinals and his Church that England too, as well as Rome, has her *semper eadem.*" —"We cannot change the profound and resistless tendencies of the age towards religious liberty." He was conscious that he was speaking only for a small minority. But this small minority would be held together by "the conviction that we have on our side the principle of justice—the conviction that we shall soon have on our side the strength of public opinion."

This prediction was completely fulfilled. The law remained a dead letter. The Roman Church established her sees, and no English Protestant was a penny the worse. Gladstone himself repealed the Act in 1871, with the approval of the whole nation.

2. *Don Pacifico and Political Intervention*

The case that gave Gladstone his first opportunity of taking up a fundamental position in respect of foreign affairs was a true product of the policy which Palmerston, at the head of the Foreign Office, was pursuing with the enthusiastic approval of the English middle class. Its object was not only to represent British interests abroad, but also to combat anything that he regarded as despotic and arbitrary power in foreign countries. In the application of these principles he was not particularly fastidious. This was especially obvious in the case of Don Pacifico, a Jew, living in Athens, but born in Gibraltar—and therefore enjoying the privilege of British citizenship—whose house had been plundered by the Athenian populace. Palmerston espoused his immoderate claim for damages with the greatest willingness, and finally, as the Greeks would not consent to settle it, he promptly dispatched a British squadron to the Piraeus, to intercept Greek ships and blockade Greek ports.

This drastic policy brought England to the verge of a war.

58

Russia and France, who, like England, were Greece's guarantor Powers, intervened. Matters went so far as an extremely sharp exchange of notes, and even the temporary recall of the French Ambassador from London. The Queen and Prince Albert regarded Palmerston's reckless and dangerous proceedings with indignation. His colleagues were, to say the least, critical. *The Times* thundered against him, and the Opposition felt that this was an excellent opportunity for overthrowing Palmerston, and with him the Liberal Government. Lord Stanley, who was now the undisputed leader of the Conservative Protectionists, moved a vote of censure in the Upper House. In order to parry this blow the Radical, Roebuck, who, like so many Radicals, despite their opposition to the domestic policies of the Conservatives, was an enthusiastic supporter of Palmerston's foreign policy, moved a vote of confidence in the Lower House. This motion led to one of the greatest and most important debates—continuing for several days—which the English Parliament has ever known. Palmerston's assailants included a phalanx of the most prominent Parliamentarians of every shade of politics: Peel and Disraeli, John Bright and Graham, Cobden and Gladstone. Palmerston triumphed over them all.

Parliamentary eloquence was not, as a general thing, Palmerston's strong point. He was far more adroit with the pen than with the spoken word. As a rule he spoke carelessly, without much regard for style or construction, and often left it to the shorthand-writers to make wholes of his casual half-sentences. But this time he achieved an undisputed masterpiece. It was already late in the evening when he rose, but he spoke for fully five hours—from the late twilight of one day to the early dawn of the next, as Gladstone expressed it—amidst the breathless attention of the whole House. With the greatest skill he exploited a weak spot in the armour of the Upper House, and gave a description of the case of Don Pacifico which revealed such intimate and exact knowledge of the facts, and sounded so plausible, that those who heard him were forced to agree with him, and promptly proceeded to attack his critics. Did they consider that Pacifico must put up with everything because he was a Jew? And from this individual case he proceeded to a fundamental justification of his whole policy, which had

59

always served the justice, the honour, and the dignity of England. It was a magnificent survey of his whole work, which led him to Portugal, Spain, Switzerland and Italy: everywhere he had pursued a policy of peace and progress. Those who listened to this man of sixty-six, as with unclouded vigour and easy eloquence, with supreme mastery and perfect magnanimity he drew this historical picture, could not control their admiration, and a wave of enthusiasm broke at his feet as he concluded his speech with the now familiar passage: "Whether, as the Roman in days of old held himself free from indignity when he could say 'Civis Romanus sum,' so also a British subject, in whatever land he may be, shall feel confident that the watchful eye and the strong arm of England will protect him against injustice and wrong?" No one thought any more about Don Pacifico's doctor's bill; each of his hearers was conscious only of the glorious image of his mother country that these words conjured up in his mind.

The plaudits of Parliament were followed by the even louder applause of the people, and no one could flatter himself that he could sail against the tide of popular enthusiasm. Those who attempted to do so were forced to realize that wind and weather were against them, and that they were even in danger of being accused of lack of patriotism. Gladstone made the attempt.

The speech which he delivered in the Lower House on the 27th of June, 1850—twenty-four hours after Palmerston's speech —was the first which lifted Gladstone out of the ruck of gifted and influential Parliamentarians, and set him on a level with the few men who, like Peel and Palmerston, had already left their mark on the history of their time. It gave evidence—in the treatment of concrete instances—of his mastery of the facts, down to the smallest detail, and his great talent for presenting them in a convincing and illuminating form. It showed in every sentence that he had the courage to declare his convictions, no matter what the temper of the nation, and despite the manifest hostility of his hearers. And it revealed, more than any of his former speeches on the great problems that decide the fate of nations, leading ideas of great significance, which were rooted in strong moral conviction.

His encounter with Palmerston over the Pacifico case is a masterpiece of Parliamentary polemic. He willingly granted what was indisputable, or at least defensible. He declared, in moving terms, that he, like Palmerston, abjured all religious prejudice. "I say fearlessly . . . that no person could dare to stand up among us and allege his (Pacifico's) religion as a ground for mistrust or for the denial of justice, without drawing upon himself, from all quarters of the House alike, universal scorn and indignation." But he showed that the documents laid before the House, with which he was perfectly familiar, were themselves the source of mistrust, and that the Minister had infringed the principles of international law, inasmuch as he had supported, with the power of England, demands which no one had dared to bring before the Greek Courts. One by one he demolished the arguments on which Palmerston had based his triumphant concluding apotheosis. And all this in a tone of the highest respect and the most ungrudging appreciation of Palmerston's great speech, which he praised as a masterly performance, to which—he confessed—he had listened with delight and admiration.

But he rose to his full height when he declared himself as fundamentally opposed to the principle on which the whole of Palmerston's foreign policy was based. To the question of his opponents, what contrary principle its critics represented, he declared without circumlocution: "It is the principle of nonintervention in the domestic affairs of other countries."

With this statement, in fact, Gladstone had touched upon the conflict of principles that had left its mark on two generations of European politics. The period of the French Revolution and Napoleon I had seen the battle fought by two conflicting interventions. The Revolution sought to export its principle of liberty across the French frontiers—"War on the palaces, peace to the cottages!" And Prussia, with Austria, sought by a military invasion to impose her king upon France. Napoleon not only intervened on every side, but conquered on every side—and Hegel rejoiced, after the battle of Jena, that he had seen "the Emperor, this worldpervading spirit." When at last the nations had shaken off the yoke, the old-established Powers intervened, and not only in France, on the occasion of Napoleon's return; but they concluded "for all time" the Holy Alliance, in order to maintain the "legitimate" rulers everywhere, and to suppress liberalism and revolution, in whatever country they might show themselves. This system the great British statesman, Canning, deliberately opposed. To the claim of the Holy Alliance to meddle in the domestic affairs of other States he opposed the irrecusable right of nations to independent development, and his vigorous policy introduced a wholly novel feature into European history. Of course, it was really a sort of intervention when he decided the war of liberation which the South American colonies were waging against their Spanish fatherland by recognizing their independence, and, as he himself put it, "called the new world into existence to redress the balance of the old." It was *this* aspect of Canning's policy which Palmerston continued to develop, in intensified form, and frequently to apply, to the applause of his fellow-countrymen. It was this that had given the years 1830–1850, during which he returned—in spite of interruptions—again and again to the Foreign Office, their peculiar stamp.

Gladstone, therefore, with his profession of the principle of non-intervention, had attacked the very heart of Palmerston's policy. If Great Britain could influence the internal conditions of other countries consistently with the principles of international law, let her by all means do so, always, of course, in the sense of her own free institutions; here he declared himself in complete agreement with the Minister. But he definitely repudiated his method—a disposition "to go abroad and make occasions for the propagation even of the political principles which we consider to be sound. . . . I object to the propagandism even of moderate reform." In a striking figure he declared Palmerston to be "like some gallant knight at a tournament of old, pricking forth into the lists, armed at all points, confiding of his sinews and his skill, challenging all comers for the sake of honour." He did not deny that there were cases in which intervention in foreign affairs was unavoidable. But such interference "should be rare, deliberate, decisive in character and effectual for its end," such as Canning would have approved.

He dared even to confute the triumphant cry: "Civis Romanus

sum." He did not hesitate to point out that in the period to which reference was made the Roman citizen was a member of a privileged caste; and he denied that Englishmen occupied such an exceptional position. On the other hand, he acknowledged "that great code of principles which is termed the law of nations . . . in which I find . . . a great and noble monument of human wisdom, founded on the combined dictates of reason and experience." These were such words as were not often spoken, whether in the chancelleries of the nations, or in their parliaments. And in them he sounded a new note; not for his listeners alone, but also for the political world in general, when in conclusion he declared his adhesion to "the principles of brotherhood among nations, and of their sacred independence," in the words: "Let us do as we would be done by, and let us pay the respect to a feeble State, and to the infancy of free institutions, which we would desire and should exact from others toward their maturity and their strength." English supporters of the League of Nations might well invoke such passages when they claim that Gladstone was a precursor of their ideas.

But his contemporaries did not agree with him. The majority of the House decided for Palmerston, although Peel also had once more thrown the great weight of his speech into the opposing scale.

It was Peel's last speech. On the following morning, as he was riding in Hyde Park, he was thrown from his horse. Seriously injured and unconscious, he was carried home. During the night of the 2nd of July he died, in the sixty-third year of his life— a life of innumerable achievements, of battles innumerable. All England mourned him; and the Queen, in a letter to the King of Prussia, declared that the death of the man from whom she had so resolutely turned her face ten years earlier was "one of the hardest blows of Fate which could have fallen on us and on the country."

His death was naturally felt most grievously by his friends, among them Gladstone, who had never ceased to revere him as his great master and teacher. These friends formed only a small group, but everyone recognized that it was exceptionally rich in talent: Lord Aberdeen, who had been responsible for foreign policy under Peel, Sir James Graham, and Sidney Herbert—each would have been an ornament to any Ministry. But already many believed that the youngest of them all, Gladstone, had the greatest career before him.

3. The Prisons of Naples and Moral Intervention

For the Queen and Prince Albert, Peel's death was a blow of which they were all the more sensible in that there was now no one who could perhaps have rid them of Palmerston. Since his Parliamentary triumph he was even less agreeable to them, even less accommodating. He knew well enough that he was now the most popular man in England, and he continued to carry out his policy, regardless of the Queen's protests. Even her command that all important despatches were to be submitted to her before they were sent received only his formal agreement. A few months after the Pacifico debate, in connection with the affair of the Austrian General Haynau, who had made himself hated for his brutality in suppressing the Italians in their struggle for liberty, and who, during a visit to London, was thrashed by Messrs. Barclay and Perkins' draymen, Lord Palmerston behaved with an independence verging on insubordination. In the written apology which he had of necessity to address to the Austrian Ambassador on this occasion, he allowed a sentence to stand, against the express wish of the Queen, in which he declared that it was tactless of General Haynau to come to London at all. When the justly indignant Queen took him to task for this he replied in a letter which, as the letter of a Minister to his sovereign, is probably unique. For in it he explains that the draymen, much as their behaviour was to be deplored, had been inspired by a perfectly intelligible and indeed even praiseworthy feeling; their righteous and honourable indignation would be shared by all, not only in England, who knew of Haynau's cruel and inhuman treatment of the unfortunate inhabitants of Brescia and other Italian cities, in consequence of which he was generally spoken of as "General Hyaena."

However astonishing this letter, and however intelligible the Queen's indignation, yet, on the other hand, it shows one thing very plainly: namely, that Palmerston felt himself to be the repre-

64

sentative of humanity in the face of inhuman cruelty, and that his blood boiled whenever he heard of such cruelty.

Now it happened that Gladstone was presently a personal witness of such cruelty. And he too was unable to accept it in silence. And so it came about that these two men, who had lately been fighting so bitterly, were a few months later to come together in friendship.

In the autumn of 1850 Gladstone, for purely private reasons— one of his daughters was suffering from an affection of the eyes —paid a visit to Italy. He went as far south as Naples. Here, since the suppression of the revolution of the previous year, King Ferdinand had been subjecting the country to a reign of terror that earned him the name of "King Bomba." Gladstone had not the least intention of concerning himself with Neapolitan politics. Already, in his speech against Palmerston, he had expounded the doctrine of international law, according to which the existing government must be recognized, and adducing as one example the Kingdom of the Two Sicilies. But Gladstone was unable to close his eyes and ears, to refrain from seeing and hearing what might distress him. The men whose acquaintance he made in Italy told him of the conditions existing in Naples, and what he heard was so horrible that he determined to find out the truth for himself. He attended the trial of the former Minister Poerio and other political prisoners, and he visited the prisons in which the protagonists of the liberation movement were languishing. What he saw was terrible; it shocked him to the depth of his soul. To accept such things in silence seemed to him impossible. When he returned to England his friends remarked that he was full of this subject, that he could think of nothing but the tortured men whom he had seen in Naples. One must help them; but how?

Gladstone went to the man whom he had regarded as his leader since the death of Peel: Lord Aberdeen. He knew that he could rely to the full on his leader's humanity and nobility of character; and he could assume that Aberdeen, having once been at the head of the Foreign Office, was on good terms with influential persons on the Continent. Aberdeen too was anxious to help the victims, but he could not himself blazon their woes abroad, since it had been his policy to advocate the restoration of the Bourbons. He asked

65

Gladstone to describe the state of affairs in a letter, avoiding all exaggeration. This letter he sent to Prince Schwarzenberg, who after the collapse of the Austrian monarchy had helped to build it up again: a clever man, but as ruthless as he was unscrupulous. Schwarzenberg, after long delay, at last replied in an arrogant letter which virtually advised the Englishmen to mind their own business.

This was months after Gladstone's return, and every day he was forced to tell himself that in Naples, in the dungeons of King Bomba, in those horrible dens of filth and pestilence, men of blameless character and high breeding were languishing, chained to common malefactors. He could bear it no longer. He had to speak. To his first letter to Lord Aberdeen he added a second, supplementing it, and published them both in the Press.

The effect on the British public was tremendous. It simply devoured this thrilling description of terrible sufferings and infamies, which was all the more impressive in that the writer had evidently eschewed all exaggeration and had done his utmost to be perfectly objective. They read how venial courts, on the strength of the obviously perjured evidence of rascally hirelings, had sentenced honourable men to death, or, as in the case of Poerio, to twenty-four years of imprisonment in fetters. They followed the writer into underground dungeons, where hardly a ray of light entered, and in which Neapolitan patriots, formerly Ministers, were subjected to the worst humiliations, and all but starved. They shuddered when they read of the heavy irons with which they were riveted to the ground or fettered to common criminals. With all their hearts they agreed with Gladstone when he rebuked the government of King Bomba as "the violation of every moral law under the stimulus of fear and vengeance," and quoted the words that he had heard in Naples: "It is the negation of God erected into a system of Government."

All this was written and believed by a man who called himself a Conservative. But it was this very fact that had moved him to speak. "As a member of the Conservative party in one of the great family of European nations I am compelled to remember that that party stands in virtual and real . . . alliance with all the established Governments of Europe as such; and that . . . they suffer more or less of moral detriment from its reverses." It was only a moral pressure that he wished to exert. He was still faithful to the doctrine of non-intervention which he had pronounced in the House of Commons, and he stressed the fact that the matter must be regarded as the domestic affair of Naples, which the sovereign must settle with his subjects. But the public opinion of the world must compel him to do so.

The letters certainly influenced international opinion. They were translated; the liberal newspapers of Europe discussed them, and England's prestige as the champion of persecuted liberty was enhanced. Lord Palmerston welcomed the incident, for it seemed to justify his policy. Gladstone admitted, in a personal conversation, that he had been wrong to attack his Italian policy. In this case Palmerston could not contemplate political intervention, but he had a copy of Gladstone's brochure sent to every British Ambassador and Minister, requiring them expressly to bring it to the notice of the Governments to which they were accredited.

This, of course, did little enough to help Poerio and his companions in misfortune. King Bomba's Government, though its attempt to answer Gladstone's indictment was a pitiful failure, triumphed all the more over its helpless prisoners. The conditions of their imprisonment were worsened if that was possible. Not until 1859 were they "pardoned" and banished; but then it was not long before they were able to return to their mother country as free men. A year later Garibaldi landed in Sicily with his "Thousand," and the rule of the Bourbons pitifully collapsed.

For Gladstone this episode had a further significance: it caused him to concern himself more earnestly than ever with the Italian problem. Like all the Conservatives, he was on principle hostile to the notion of Italian unity. Even now, when he knew something of the horrors that would follow the restoration of the old rulers, he could not regard the ideal of unity with enthusiasm. He would have been satisfied with reforms within the individual States. But he gradually came to a better understanding of the elementary urge of the Italian people to achieve unity, not only as a people, but as a State. Distinguished Italians whose acquaintance he had made helped to bring about the change. Among these was the learned Antonio Panizzi, who had fled from Italy to London as far back as 1823, in order to escape arrest by the political police. In London, after years of poverty, he became Keeper of Printed Books in the British Museum; and the great Reading-room, in which so many scholars of all nations have worked, is his lasting memorial. But the man who afterwards exerted the decisive influence over Gladstone was Daniele Manin, the Italian Jew who had won undying fame as the liberator and defender of Venice in 1848–9. He too came to London a fugitive, and in 1854 he had various conversations with Gladstone, which convinced the British statesman that Italian unity was the indispensable prerequisite for all effective reforms in that beautiful country.

The lessons he had learned bore fruit in the year 1859.

THE FIRST ENCOUNTER WITH DISRAELI

1. Criticism

In the spring of 1852 Disraeli was appointed Cabinet Minister, thus reaching the first goal of his ambition. How this came about is one of the most curious episodes in English politics. Lord Palmerston, who in 1850 was the most popular man in England, for the people saw in him the representative of their own ideals of liberty, had suddenly lost their confidence, since he now appeared to be favouring a denial of justice and a tyranny. On the 2nd of December, 1851, Louis Napoleon carried out his *coup d'état* against the French Republic. The English Cabinet resolved, with the express consent of the Queen, to adopt an attitude of the strictest neutrality in respect of this incident. Palmerston, however, assured the French Ambassador, in unceremonious language, that he was delighted with the *coup d'état*, and he even said much the same in his instructions to the English Ambassador in Paris. The Queen and Prince Albert were beside themselves. The Cabinet was indignant. What was more important, the English people began to doubt their hero. Palmerston suddenly found that all parties were giving him the cold shoulder. When the Premier, Lord John Russell, who had hitherto acted as mediator between Palmerston and the Court, took the drastic step of informing his still powerful colleague that he must go, Palmerston had no alternative but to resign, with an ill grace. But while many politicians held that his career was ended, and while Disraeli sententiously announced: "There *was* a Palmerston," the latter waited, in complete silence, for the moment of his revenge. A Bill relating to the militia gave him his opportunity. Palmerston introduced a motion in the House of Commons which the Government would not or could not accept. The majority of the House voted for it, and a few weeks after his victory over Palmerston Russell and his Cabinet resigned.

The Queen, of course, could not be persuaded to send for Palmerston, so there was nothing for it but to make the attempt to govern with a Conservative Ministry. Stanley, who on his father's death had become the fourteenth Earl of Derby, was Prime Minister, and Disraeli became Chancellor of the Exchequer and leader of the Lower House. The Queen frankly confessed to Derby that she regarded Disraeli with the greatest distrust, and was reassured only when the Prime Minister undertook to be responsible for him.

Disraeli was then forty-eight years of age. If he compared himself with Gladstone, who had first taken office at twenty-five, and at thirty-five had achieved Cabinet rank, he had reason to rail at Fate for making him wait so long. And his satisfaction must have been clouded by the fact that in the House which he was expected to lead he had only a minority behind him, while his difficulties were greatly increased by the necessity of furling and laying aside the standard of Protection under which he had won promotion. He was far too keen-sighted not to realize that England, having achieved such prosperity under Free Trade, had no intention of abandoning it, and that his party must act accordingly if they hoped ever to be in power again. But to effect this change of front in the face of the rural Conservative constituencies and a suspicious and watchful Opposition was by no means easy.

And it gave him little satisfaction that Derby should appoint him Chancellor of the Exchequer. When the Prime Minister offered him the post, he justly objected that he had no knowledge of finance. But Derby cheerfully consoled him by assuring him that the Treasury officials would supply the requisite knowledge: "they give you the figures." The fact was that Derby felt that Disraeli was the only one among his colleagues who had the intelligence to master the difficulties of the office. The rest had just as little Ministerial experience, and considerably less intelligence. Disraeli never lacked self-confidence; and had not Pitt accepted the office of Chancellor although he had never filled any Ministerial post? So he accepted Derby's offer.

The most important of the Chancellor's tasks is to prepare the Budget. The first Budget, which he had to introduce very shortly after accepting office, was by general agreement framed on the old lines. Then came the General Election, which resulted in slight Conservative gains, while the Peelites suffered considerable losses; at the same time, it showed clearly that Protection was dead as a doornail. This became evident soon after the new Parliament had assembled, when the oldest protagonist of Free Trade, Sir Charles Villiers, introduced a resolution, in November 1852, which contained a categorical profession of Free Trade principles, and which was deliberately so framed that its acceptance would have led to the resignation of the Government. Disraeli combined, with his candid declaration that the Government had no thought of reversing its commercial policy, a *plaidoyer* which sought to show that his attitude in respect of this question had always been consistent. This naturally aggravated the bitterness of his adversaries, and the fall of the Government could hardly have been avoided if Palmerston had not come to the rescue with a conciliatory amendment and the soothing declaration: "We are here an assembly of gentlemen; and we who are gentlemen on this side of the House should remember that we are dealing with gentlemen on the other side." His amendment was accepted. The Government was saved and *finis* was written to the epoch of Protection.

Palmerston had framed this amendment with the help of Gladstone, who supported it in the debate. In so doing he was able to reconcile his veneration for his dead master with the rescue of the Government of his once bitter opponents. After all, "if Peel did look for his revenge," it was not by reviving an old quarrel; so "rather let them rejoice in the great public good that had been achieved." This attitude showed that Gladstone was by no means unconditionally anxious to overthrow Lord Derby's Government. It was, however, characteristic of his unsatisfactory position between the two parties. He still regarded himself as a Conservative—and in respect of many questions he was one. He did not wish to see the Liberals return to power, whether under Palmerston or Russell. Now that the conflict over the commercial policy had been settled there was no longer any insuperable obstacle to the reunion of the Conservatives. As a matter of fact, when on the day after the debate he attended a reception at Lady Derby's the Prime Minister definitely offered him a place in the Ministry. But Gladstone replied that in the mutual relations of the parties circumstances were often stronger than the human will, and he hinted at difficulties of a personal nature, which were an obstacle to a Ministerial coalition, and spoke of past and present conditions and individual defects of character. Lord Derby seems to have understood from these remarks that Gladstone was pointing to Disraeli, and in this he was probably correct. Peel's personal friends could not so soon forget the injuries which this very opponent had inflicted on him; and in debate this feeling was very clearly revealed by the unusually biting speech of another Peelite, Sidney Herbert. In any event, Gladstone explained, he would wait for Disraeli's first Budget. The fact was that he awaited it with the greatest misgiving.

He had not to wait long. On the 3rd of December, 1852, the Chancellor of the Exchequer introduced his Budget in a speech of nearly five hours before the packed benches of a tensely attentive House. As a rhetorical achievement it was brilliant; though such an expert as Macaulay, while acknowledging its brilliance, promptly added: "I could have said the whole as clearly, or more clearly, in two hours." But objectively considered, its proposals provoked the drastic criticism which Macaulay bluntly phrased: it was a question of taking money "out of the pockets of the people in towns and putting it into the pockets of the growers of malt."

Disraeli's task had certainly not been an easy one; he had to devise a Budget which was based on the principles of Free Trade, and which nevertheless satisfied the exaggerated hopes of the Conservative agriculturalists. These hopes had already been sufficiently disappointed by the fact that the party for which they had fought so stubbornly had bidden adieu to Protection when it came into power. Now they demanded that the redistribution of the burdens of the State should at least offer them something. Disraeli had still further increased their expectations by referring, in his electoral speeches, to "new principles," and a new policy, based on these principles, which he intended to introduce in Parliament. But a financial policy which should solve these objective difficulties necessitated not only a most profound knowledge of political economy and finance, but also a perfectly definite and completely planned system.

Disraeli could offer neither of these prerequisites; he had exceptional talents and wide knowledge, but in quite other spheres. In leading the Lower House with untiring endurance, persuasive tact, and unfailing readiness of repartee, and in reporting to the astonished Queen, in the most amusing style—the style of a novelist—on the proceedings of the House: in this he was incomparable. But he was not the man to immerse himself for days and weeks at a time in documents, statute-books, economic treatises and statistics, for which in any case he felt but a superficial interest.

Of his numerous proposals two stand out with some prominence: the halving of the duty on malt, which the farmers considered oppressive, and—in order to make up for the diminishing yield of this tax—the doubling and extension of the house duty, which would fall upon the urban population; and especially the poorer classes. Since it was based on the yearly rent it took but little account of the taxpayer's ability to pay, and its defects would be greatly aggravated by the proposed increase.

When the actual debate began in the Lower House Disraeli quickly realized the extent of the dangers now threatening him. They were all the greater inasmuch as he had agreed with Derby that he would resign if his motion relating to the house duty was defeated. On the morning of the day when he was to reply to his critics he received from Derby a very pessimistic letter, which made it fairly clear that the writer regarded defeat as inevitable. It is neither pleasant nor encouraging to speak with such a letter in one's pocket, and to tell oneself that within a few hours the result of many years' labour may be swept away after ten short months of success. What, after such a defeat, would be the attitude of the Party towards him? He had forced upon it this alteration of its programme, and the Party was going to lose by it. He was not despondent; the psychological tension of such a situation found an outlet in greater aggressiveness.

It was already late—after ten o'clock—when he rose. There was a glare of gaslight in the House; it was hot, and the atmosphere was tensely charged. Those who had anticipated that Disraeli would display his talents to the fullest advantage were not disappointed. Seldom had he shown a sharper and more resolute temper, whether he confessed that he was "not born and bred a Chancellor of the Exchequer," that he was "one of the Parliamentary rabble"; or whether he repaid the blows of his opponents with interest and compound interest. Certainly they had not spared him, but what they had to hear from him was a speech bristling with personal thrusts and strained antitheses that wounded their feelings and excited their wrath.

Gladstone listened with attention and with rising anger. He himself was too pugnacious a fighter not to appreciate Disraeli's tricks of fence. There were moments when he was so carried away by this brilliant speech that he quite forgot that he would have to reply to it. The hour grew late, and he considered whether he ought not perhaps to postpone his reply. But then Disraeli sharpened his personal polemic; "insolence," he said, "is not invective"; and he spoke of Gladstone's friend Graham as a man "whom I will not say I greatly respect, but rather whom I greatly regard." Gladstone could restrain himself no longer.

Hardly had Disraeli concluded, amidst the applause of his followers, when Gladstone sprang to his feet and caught the Speaker's eye. It was by now one o'clock in the morning, and the Government benches greeted the rising member with comprehensive ill-temper. This increased when Gladstone, in his opening sentences, repulsed Disraeli's personal attacks with anger, and indeed with indignation. Many of his sentences he was unable to complete, for the applause of his friends and the roars of his opponents drowned the concluding words: "I must tell the right honourable gentleman that whatever he has learned—and he has learned much—he has not yet learned the limits of discretion, of moderation . . . that ought to restrain the conduct and language of every member of this House, the disregard of which is an offence in the meanest among us, but is of tenfold weight when committed by the Leader of the House of Commons." And with this he proceeded to the objective criticism of Disraeli's proposals.

Verbal duels have always found appreciative listeners, ever since the days of Homer's heroes. But the true skill of the combatant is apparent only if he can succeed in holding the interest of his listeners even in the discussion of objective facts. Gladstone's speech withstood this test. When the storm of personal blows had abated the members found themselves suddenly drawn into a penetrating dissertation on finance and political economy, which they could but follow with the same intensity of interest; so clearly was each individual problem conceived, so systematically did one thing follow from another, so vividly was the effect of this and that tax described, and so convincing was the speaker's genuine mastery of his subject. They simply had to listen; not only when he declared his recognition of the Chancellor's high ability: "I pay to him the sincere respect that genius deserves"; but also when he proved that in actual fact the Budget was not balanced, and when he unfolded the fundamental ideas of his master, Peel, in five illuminating theses, and showed that the Budget proposals were gross infringements of one of these principles, and that they sinned against the others by their exaggeration. He deliberately invoked Peel as a Conservative politician and financier, for it was as a Conservative that he wished to speak; a Conservative who wished to establish the State securely on the basis of an ordered and balanced Budget, and so to distribute its burdens that the population would be content. The principal reproach which he brought against Disraeli was that "he had done more than any other man to revive and renew the war of classes," by casual promises which were not related to any definite plan. Once more it became evident that even the devising of a Budget was an emanation from a general ethical philosophy. Whatever one might think of Gladstone's theses, no one could fail to be impressed by the profound earnestness by which he was inspired.

Disraeli followed this drastic criticism with the imperturbable expression that he was wont to wear even in the heat of battle: his arms folded, his face stony and impenetrable. The more passionately Gladstone's phrases rang through the House, the more conspicuous was his unalterable calm. Only from time to time a brief interruption showed that he was following his adversary's arguments with strained attention. He had by now no illusions as to the fate of his Budget and his Ministry.

Out of doors there had been all night a December storm, with thunder and lightning. No one paid heed to it. The attention of all was given to the contest between the two great Parliamentarians, and the question was in the minds of all: which of them would be victorious?

About four o'clock in the morning the House voted on the motion. The votes appeared to be about equally divided. It was a moment of tense excitement when the tellers took up their position before the Chair. To whom would the Speaker hand the slip on which the result of the division was recorded? He glanced at it, and gave it to the teller of the Opposition. A deafening cheer ended the suspense. The Budget was thrown out by 305 votes to 286.

It had been a battle such as the House of Commons had hardly experienced since the debates of Pitt and Fox. Each side must have felt that it had been represented by a politician of the first rank. The newspapers were lavish of their praise, and Gladstone was able to send his wife a *Times* leader which was full of enthusiastic praise of Disraeli's speech. He himself wrote: "He by no means says too much in praise of Disraeli's speech. I am told he is much stung by what I said. I am very sorry it fell to me to say it: God knows I had no wish to give him pain, and really, with my deep sense of his gifts I would only pray they might be well used." These words bear the stamp of sincerity. But who can say whether under the threshold of consciousness a sense of rivalry was not at work, determining his attitude and the outcome of the conflict? No party can tolerate two men of the first rank, least of all in the English Parliament, where the party Leader, both inwardly and outwardly, is lifted above his party. The party Leader is the undisputed representative of his faction. He appoints a Whip who gives the party his directions. He agrees, with the Leader of the opposing party, how the business of Parliament shall be despatched. He has the preponderating voice in the choice of party speakers. Sessions of the party are very rare, being held on special occasions only. The accredited Leader therefore stands far above all other members of his party. To be second in the party is therefore to be in a particularly difficult position, especially if one man is a Disraeli and the other a Gladstone. However, this sharp debate was to have a pleasant epilogue. When it was clear that there was to be a change of Government, Russell suggested to the defeated Chancellor that

76

he should repair the defects which had so greatly damaged him. Disraeli did so with the grace of which, when he chose, he was as complete a master as of the most cutting diatribe, and his adversary replied in the same conciliatory tones. Prince Albert could not restrain his astonishment; it was surprising how well-bred all these gentlemen had suddenly become!

2. Construction

In the new Ministry the office of Chancellor of the Exchequer fel[1] to Gladstone. The Queen wrote to her uncle, King Leopold of Belgium, expressing her satisfaction in "the formation of so brilliant and strong a Cabinet. . . . It is the realization of the country's and our most ardent wishes." It consisted of a coalition of the Liberals with the Peelites, who now for the first time came together. Disraeli had declared in his last speech: "England does not love coalitions." It would now be seen whether he was right. The two leaders of the Liberals, Russell and Palmerston, who in the previous year had given each other so much trouble, now, after many changes of front, found it possible to serve under the Leader of the Peelites, Lord Aberdeen, who enjoyed the absolute confidence of the Queen. While in the late Cabinet Derby and Disraeli had stood high above a number of mediocrities, the new one had such high abilities at its disposal that, like Fox's Cabinet of 1806, it was called "the Ministry of all the talents." All the leading Peelites belonged to it: Sir James Graham, Sidney Herbert, Lord Lincoln, now Duke of Newcastle, and, of course, Gladstone. Aberdeen hesitated as to whether he should give him the Colonies or the Finances. The Queen wrote that "We (the Queen and the Prince Consort) argued the greater capabilities of Mr. Gladstone for the Finances"; and so England had to thank the Queen for the fact that the financial policy of the country was entrusted to the man who for half a century was to determine its direction.

Gladstone was now for the first time sitting in the same Cabinet with Liberals, and even with a Radical—Molesworth. For him this was a significant and not altogether easy step. Hitherto he had always called himself a Conservative, and only recently, in his attack on Disraeli's Budget, he had invoked the principles of Conservatism. Of course, he was not the only Conservative to enter the Cabinet; he was accompanied by the most distinguished of his party friends, one of whom gave the Cabinet its name. It was in the nature of the English Parliamentary system that anyone who, like Gladstone, had refused to enter the Ministry of the one party, was obliged to join the opposing party. He was now forty-four years of age, at the height of his powers—and his capacity for work. If he now stood aside he ran the risk of permanent exclusion from power. Now, undoubtedly, his decision was made easier by the nature of the work that awaited him. He had torn Disraeli's Budget to tatters; he must now produce another in its place. It is a wholesome provision of the English Parliamentary system that yesterday's critic may today be compelled to show that he can achieve something better. This task was one that Gladstone could not evade—nor did he wish to.

Hitherto the office of Chancellor of the Exchequer had been one among many; it was by no means usual that he should possess greater influence and be of greater importance than any other Minister. The change had come about at the time of Derby's Ministry, when the office of Chancellor of the Exchequer was combined in one person with that of the Leader of the House—and in the person of that Minister who was undoubtedly the most intellectual member of the Cabinet. In the Aberdeen Ministry this state of affairs was further accentuated. The Ministers of those departments whose expenditure was particularly heavy—such as the War Office and the Admiralty—would naturally be in some sense dependent on the Finance Minister, who has to plan the means at their disposal, and even the Secretary for Foreign Affairs soon finds that his policy is largely dependent on sound finances. This natural influence of the Chancellor of the Exchequer is of course increased when the financial situation is difficult, and all depends on the man who has to set it in order. Actually, the office of Chancellor of the Exchequer has become the most important in the English Cabinet since Gladstone filled it in 1853. A few weeks before the formation of his Cabinet Lord Aberdeen wrote to Guizot—with whom he had been on terms of friendship since the days when the latter was Minister to Louis Philippe—that he would look forward to the coming session of Parliament with entire confidence, if only the financial difficulties could be overcome. "These are great, notwithstanding the un-exampled prosperity of the country. Our friend Gladstone is most concerned in the solution of the problem."

Gladstone knew what was demanded of him. He had before him the example of Disraeli to show him that happy ideas and brilliant intuitions are not enough unless they are based on the most thorough and systematic labours. He was "the man for the job." This he had shown already at the Board of Trade. Now, once more, his working day was at least half as long again as that of any other Minister, and the amount of work that he was able to squeeze into a given number of hours astonished all his collaborators. The permanent officials of the Treasury were soon full of enthusiasm for their chief, who penetrated so rapidly to the heart of every problem, and after one conversation knew as much of any subject as his most experienced colleague. Such conversations were by no means easy. The Minister asked a great many very precise questions, and was never content with half answers. Those who came from his room took some little time to pull themselves together and recover. But those who knew their subject could not do otherwise than revere such a chief. The whole Department was gradually inspired by Glad-stone's spirit, which it retained even when another Minister stood at its head, and even when Gladstone had retired from the political stage.

But he did not content himself with listening to his official collaborators; he made use of every spoken, written and printed source of information at his disposal; City bankers, deputations from the provinces, petitions, official documents, books, and Par-liamentary reports. And such material was not mere lifeless in-formation; it was elaborated by systematic criticism in accordance with his own point of view.

But with all these titanic labours he had still time and energy to give one of his sons a daily Latin lesson.

The time at Gladstone's disposal for the preparation of his Budget was very short measure. On the 28th of December, 1852, he received the seal of his office, and on the first day of April he submitted his financial plans to the Prince Consort. Then came the Cabinet meetings, at which many doubts and objections had to be overcome; for here sat men who had already collaborated in many Budgets, and had their own ideas on the subject. But they soon saw that the Chancellor of the Exchequer was their superior at every point of the discussion, and as the Prime Minister admiringly declared, in the art of continuing an opponent's argument *ad absurdum* there was no one to match him. It was always evident that he had considered every point in all its bearings, and that he had completely mastered the material facts. Naturally, in addition to the practical problems, questions of political expediency had to be given full consideration. The Government's majority in Parliament was neither large nor homogeneous. Was there not some danger of upsetting some section of this small majority by this or that proposal, so that the Ministerial majority would become a minority? But Gladstone unrelentingly defended the standpoint that by weakly making concessions beforehand they would endanger their whole achievement. The close texture of his plan considered as a whole must, he believed, overcome opposition.

In the end the whole Cabinet was won. On Saturday evening, the 16th of April, it gave its assent to the Budget. On Monday the 18th the Chancellor had to introduce the Budget in the House of Commons. Some part of the intervening Sunday he was obliged to devote to preparing his speech on the Budget. This concession he was forced to make; it was a breach of his pious custom. Nevertheless, as a matter of course, he went twice to church that Sunday. And he still found time to read a little Dante and Shakespeare.

Gladstone's Budget speech was no shorter than Disraeli's. The verbatim report filled eighty large pages of newsprint. Judged by the German Parliamentary standards, this would seem excessively long. A German Minister of Finance would previously have laid before Parliament a printed memorandum containing an exhaustive exposition of the principles underlying his fiscal proposals, and in his oral address he would content himself with elaborating a few leading points of view. The English Chancellor has to communicate both his proposals and their justification by word of mouth.

Only from his lips may Parliament learn what expenditure is proposed, what revenues are to be anticipated, what taxes retained, or repealed, or modified. This makes great demands both on the speaker and on his audience. Nothing is so tedious to listen to as figures, and a statement of the Budget without figures is unthinkable; nothing is so dry as fiscal problems, and the speaker has continually to deal with problems of taxation; nothing so quickly excites criticism as proposals to impose taxation, and the Chancellor must deal with such criticism then and there. Gladstone, during the whole of the five hours of his speech, was severely practical, yet the attention of his audience never flagged for a single moment, and no one could have said of his speech, as Macaulay said of Disraeli's, that the same thing could have been said in less time.

It was precisely his unconditional objectivity that very largely explained the secret of his success. Even the bitterest opponent had to concede the claim that he himself made at the close of his speech —"that we have not concealed our difficulties either from ourselves or from others." On the contrary, he deliberately drew attention to every possible objection, and then explained why nevertheless he believed his point of view to be correct. The very style of his speech proved that his chief concern was not to persuade, but to convince. There were none of the Ciceronian periods in which his other speeches were so often delivered: but only concise and purposeful propositions. At the same time, the speech was constructed with such supreme art that the principal question, which was on the lips of all, was answered only near the close, after the ground had been so carefully prepared, by progressive stages, that the final conclusion seemed to follow of itself.

The principal question was: Would the Chancellor retain the income-tax? Nowadays, when it has become the most important base of the fiscal system in almost every country, it is difficult to imagine how violently it was opposed in 1853. But one must realize that England was then the only country in which this tax was imposed, and that nearly forty years were to elapse before such a country as Prussia introduced it. In England it originated as a war tax. It was one of the greatest achievements of William Pitt that he had succeeded in inspiring England to what was then, according to the notions of the period, this unheard-of willingness to make sacrifices, in order that the terrific struggle against Napoleon I could be continued. When the war was over the tax was repealed. Then, in 1842, Peel had the courage to revive it, so that he might set the shaken finances of the country in order. But he too had been careful to emphasize the fact that it was only an exceptional and temporary expedient, which the Government would not hesitate to repeal so soon as the Budget could be balanced by other means; for he knew that the temper of the English people was opposed to the interference of the State in the private affairs of the individual, and such interference was unavoidable in the case of the income-tax. How far Parliament shared this refractory temper was shown in 1851, when it restricted the operation of the tax to one year. When Gladstone introduced his Budget in 1853 he had to inform the House: "The income-tax has at this moment legally expired, and it will be for the Committee to consider whether or not they shall revive it." It had, therefore, to be introduced anew: that is, each individual Member was urged to assume the responsibility for its reintroduction in the face of a hostile electorate.

It speaks volumes for the greatness of Gladstone's achievement in his Budget speech that he not only persuaded the majority of the House to assume this responsibility, but he also convinced the influential strata of the population that for the time being the income-tax must remain in force. The agitation against it practically ceased. So complete was his success that in respect of one particular point —though here his opinion is, as a matter of fact, highly contestable—in respect of the question of the unequal taxation of earned and unearned incomes, he determined public opinion for decades to come.

It was soon seen how right had been his judgement when during the discussion of the Budget in the Cabinet he had insisted on the unconditional retention of his whole plan. Both Parliament and the nation received the very definite impression that England had now a Chancellor of the Exchequer who had mastered the *whole* of the financial problem; who was working not for the moment only, but for time to come—for example, he had the courage to propose the income-tax, with a predetermined and diminishing rate, for a period of seven years; a Chancellor who did not here make a little concession and there impose a trifling tax, in order to win here a group of Members and there a complex of interests, but who proceeded in accordance with an objectively considered plan, in which every section was intimately connected with the next, in order to realize a great and definite aim. Even those who, going further than the Chancellor, would have liked to see the revenue from funded investments taxed at the source, had to concede that he had to a large extent achieved the same purpose by the bold imposition of a probate duty which for the first time was extended to real property. Here Gladstone had originally had the whole Cabinet against him—Palmerston had indignantly spoken of "a positive confiscation"—but it had to give way to him, for he conclusively countered all its objections. In view of the extraordinary complexity of the English laws of inheritance the elaboration of this tax called for juristic abilities of no mean order. The Cabinet found that here the Chancellor was a match for the Attorney-General, Bethell, who was regarded as one of the most eminent lawyers of his time.

One of the leading ideas of this budgetary system was that it was designed to promote the greatest possible economic and industrial productivity. Whatever taxes or duties stood in the way of increasing production must be repealed. As in 1842 and 1845, Gladstone swept away some hundreds of inexpedient duties, thus taking a further step on the path of Free Trade, on which he had entered a decade earlier in the wake of Peel. But this procedure had its most important results in the domain of public expenditure. The whole of his financial activities were governed by the purpose: by the greatest frugality to guard the national economy against the exaction of a shilling more than the State positively required for its just occasions. This maxim, to be sure, was on the lips of every Chancellor; but very few actually put it into practice. Gladstone not only did so, with the utmost consistency: he created a tradition which was a determining principle of the administration of the public revenues for the rest of the century.

In the long run it was a matter of comparative indifference whether the Chancellor of the Exchequer was a Conservative or a Liberal. In this connection even the Conservative Chancellor was a Gladstonian, and if he was not one at the moment of entering upon the office he slowly but surely became one, thanks to the senior permanent officials of the Treasury, who were unanimously faithful to this tradition.

Gladstone's reputation as a financier was established once and for all by his Budget of 1853. Prince Albert sent him his congratulations, saying: "I have just completed a close and careful perusal of your speech which I admire extremely." The Chancellor could accept expression of the Prince's admiration as something more than a few polite phrases. But of all the congratulations which he received, those of Peel's widow touched him most profoundly. In his reply he once more acknowledged in heartfelt terms his debt to his "great teacher and master"; that he was walking in Peel's footsteps had been the thought that had inspired him in his work. With proud humility he wrote: "I was inspired by the thought of treading, however unequally, in the steps of my great teacher and master. . . . It was one of my honest anxieties not to do . . . injustice to the patriotic policy with which his name is for ever associated." Peel might indeed be content with his pupil.

ERA, PALMERSTON

1. A Reluctant War

The great success achieved by Gladstone's Budget conferred a lustre upon the Aberdeen Ministry. In May 1853 the Prime Minister was able to write to his friend Princess Lieven: "The Government is infinitely stronger and better than I myself had anticipated. The truth is, that Gladstone has raised himself to the highest pitch of financial reputation and has given a strength and lustre to the Government which it could not have derived from anything else." But it was written in the stars that Lord Aberdeen and his Government would not long enjoy this reputation. In the next paragraph of the same letter he had to report that London was full of forebodings of an imminent European war. And the more desperately he fought against the spectre, the closer it came.

The Crimean War, which Great Britain, at the side of Napoleon III, waged against Russia from 1853 to 1856, for "the independence and integrity of the Turkish Empire," and which cost the country 25,000 lives and £50,000,000, is regarded today, by most English historians, as a blunder. But at the time the English people were almost passionately eager for war, inspired by their abhorrence of the Tsar, who in 1849 had suppressed the revolution in Hungary. The exponent of this warlike temper in Parliament was once again Palmerston, who, supported by the people, finally compelled the peace-loving Aberdeen to proceed to the declaration of war.

Gladstone, in respect of his fundamental ideas, was undoubtedly nearer to Aberdeen than to Palmerston. He was quite immune from the comfortable tendency to veil the horrors of war by a romantic ideology. "The way of Peace and negotiation is undoubtedly devoid of that romantic interest which attaches to heroic achievements in war. But if the result is the saving of the effusion of human blood and the averting of that calamity which would disturb the operations of industry and deprive small nations of their subsistence, surely the sacrifice is small and surely the reward is adequate. When we speak of general war we do not mean real progress on the road of freedom, the real moral and social advancement of man, achieved by force. This may be the intention, but how rarely is it the result of general war. We mean this—that the face of Nature is stained with human gore; we mean that bread is taken out of the mouth of the people; we mean that taxation is increased and industry diminished; we know that it means that burdens unreasonable and untold are entailed on posterity; we know that it means that demoralization is let loose; that families are broken up; that lusts become unbridled in every country to which war is extended."

This assuredly sounded more like John Bright, the leader of the pacifists, than Palmerston. And Gladstone refused to allow himself to be bewitched by the formula according to which Palmerston and the public opinion of England were proceeding: that "the independence and integrity" of the Ottoman Empire must be preserved. He told his audience that this Empire represented a monarchy "full of anomaly, full of misery and full of difficulty," and reminded them of the "twelve millions of our fellow-Christians," whose very existence was "a political solecism of the Mohammedan faith." But this did not prevent him from declaring that England could not tolerate that Russia should become the predominant Power in the East. And this point of view made it impossible for him, despite all his horror of war, to declare himself in favour of peace at any price.

When the declaration of war was about to be signed, the unhappy Aberdeen once more unbosomed himself to Gladstone. "How could he bring himself to fight for the Turks?" he cried in despair. And Gladstone: "I said we were not fighting for the Turks, but we were warning Russia off the forbidden ground. That if, indeed, we undertook to put down the Christians under the Turkish rule by force, then we should be fighting for the Turks; but to this I for one could be no party."

This would seem to be an unreal and purely pedantic distinction.

For how could England fight against Russia without at the same time fighting for Turkey? And would not the support of the Turks by England inevitably subject the Balkan Christians to a heavier yoke? Here, as a matter of fact, we have the problem of British policy in the Balkans, with which Gladstone was to concern himself so seriously half a century later. He then answered it in a very different sense. Nevertheless, he insisted all his life, not only that he shared the responsibility for the Crimean War, but also that he could bear this responsibility with a clear conscience.

A decade after the Russo-Turkish War of 1878, during which he had so passionately opposed the intervention of England, he seized the opportunity offered by the publication of Greville's journals for the period of the Crimean War in order to explain his attitude, in the leading historical review, by appealing to the contemporary judgement of the Crimean War. The argument with which he justified England's participation in the war hardly explains the motives of the English people or of their leading statesmen. But it sounds like a premonition of later conceptions. England, he says, acted at that period as a member of a great league of the leading European Powers. This league had represented the general interest; that is, the interest of the small Powers; for these would become the booty of any aggressor unless the whole community of Powers opposed him. Russia had wilfully offended against this community, inasmuch as she wished to fall upon Turkey. England, as a morally responsible and leading member of the community, was bound to oppose Russia. In this sense the old statesman, looking back on the political life of 1853, saw there "a European protest against the wrong-doing of a single nation"; and he even ventured in this connection to declare: "We are prepared to argue that this policy represented an advance in civilization, and a method of action favourable in itself to peace." Of course, he found in 1887 that the world had altered greatly since 1853. In those days the Great Powers had not been so hostile to one another, and "the pest of militarism, one of the greatest that afflicts humanity, had not attained anything like its now portentous and ever-increasing development." Although these considerations are more characteristic of the Gladstone of 1887 than of the Gladstone of 1853, it is nevertheless true that in 1853 he already regarded England's attitude from the standpoint of a great universal principle.

If we apply this principle to the concrete, individual case, the question still remains: did the Turks justify the confidence that they would of their own accord introduce the reforms that Russia wished to enforce by brutal violence—and, as the other Powers assumed, for her own special benefit—by a direct intervention in Turkey's domestic affairs? In 1853 Gladstone had not yet made this question the object of personal study. He believed that he could follow the authority of others, such as Palmerston, and the eminent but also very obstinate British Ambassador in Constantinople, Stratford Canning. That in spite of this confidence he was most bitterly disappointed by the actual evolution of Turkey after the Crimean War was the principal conviction that evoked his behaviour in 1876.

"War, war, that is the excitement and turmoil of the moment, and I fear it will swallow up everything good and useful." So Gladstone wrote on the 28th of March, 1854, the day on which war was declared, to his wife. His dark foreboding did not deceive him.

To begin with, as Chancellor of the Exchequer it was his duty to provide the means required for the conduct of the war. There have always been two alternative methods at the disposal of the Chancellor: he could borrow, or he could tax. Pitt had financed the long war against Napoleon mainly by means of loans in the first place; afterwards he had proceeded to tax income. Gladstone, in his great Budget speech of the 18th of April, 1853—that is, before the war-cloud had appeared—had dealt exhaustively with Pitt's financial policy, and had professed his belief that if Pitt had resorted to the income-tax at an earlier stage there would have been no burden of debt. He now, consistently with his belief, proposed to double the income-tax. Characteristically enough, he adduced a justification for so doing in which moral arguments played at least as large a part as fiscal theories:

"The expenses of the war are the moral check which it has pleased the Almighty to impose upon the ambition and lust of conquest that are inherent in so many nations. There is pomp and circumstance, there is glory and excitement about war, which, notwithstanding the misery it entails, invests it with charm in the eyes of the community, and tends to blind men to these evils to a fearful and dangerous degree. The necessity of meeting from year to year the expenditure which it entails is a salutary and wholesome check, making them feel what they are about, and making them measure the cost of the benefit upon which they may calculate.

"The system of raising funds necessary for wars by loan practices wholesale, systematic and continual deceptions upon the people. The people do not really know what they are doing. The consequences are adjourned into a far future."

This view was violently opposed by contemporary and by later critics. Disraeli countered it by a panegyric on Pitt and his financial policy—but a later generation, familiar with the finance of the Great War, is better qualified to realize its wisdom.

The Budget of 1854 was for the time being the last introduced by Gladstone. When the Budget for 1855 was on the order of the day in the House of Commons, another man sat on the Treasury bench. Gladstone had resigned in the meantime, accepted the office again, and again resigned. The maelstrom of the war had engulfed him.

The grievous abuses in the military administration which the Crimean War had revealed, and which the Press had vigorously condemned, evoked a storm of public indignation which naturally had its repercussions in Parliament. Possibly the Government could have defended itself had it been united; but it was not. Lord John Russell not only shared the conviction of the public, that Aberdeen was not fitted to lead a War Cabinet; he was also convinced that the man who was really qualified to lead it was himself. Russell, in other periods of his life, had rendered the country great service, as history proudly records. What he did in the period of the Crimean War cannot be justified and is difficult to explain.

When Parliament assembled the Radical member Roebuck—the same who in the Pacifico affair had thrown Palmerston a resolution by way of lifebuoy—moved the appointment of a committee to inquire into the state of the Army and the military administration. On the same day Russell, without a word to his colleagues, submitted his resignation to the Prime Minister. "I do not see," he said, "how this motion is to be resisted. But as it involves a censure of the War departments . . . my only course is to tender my resignation." Naturally, his colleagues felt this to be a stab in the back. Gladstone exclaimed, indignantly, that Russell "to escape punishment, ran away from duty." And the Queen sent Russell a letter of four lines in which she expressed "her surprise and concern at hearing so abruptly of his intention to desert her Government."

Of course, under these circumstances it was hopeless to oppose Roebuck's motion. It was, in reality, opposed only as a point of honour; and it is characteristic of Gladstone's position in the Cabinet that not only Aberdeen, but Palmerston also decided that the prickly task of replying to Russell in suitable tones should be allotted to him. But the majority of the Cabinet considered that Palmerston should have replied; since he had succeeded Russell as Leader. However, he refused to do so, and when Gladstone spoke on the second day of the debate the battle was already lost.

Palmerston himself, in a despatch to the Queen, described his younger colleague's speech as masterly; it must have convinced any listener who had not made up his mind beforehand. The Saxon Minister, Count Vitzthum von Eckstädt, who, at a late hour, had hastened from the dinner-table to the House, in order to hear the debate, described Gladstone's defence of the Cabinet as "brilliant." He certainly succeeded in unhorsing Russell. With a lavish wealth of argument he defended the thesis that the proposed Commission of inquiry was unconstitutional, an inadmissible invasion by Parliament of the executive powers reserved to the Government. "I for my part shall ever rejoice, if this motion is carried tonight, that my own last words as a member of the Cabinet of the Earl of Aberdeen have been words of solemn and earnest protest against a proceeding which has no foundation either in the constitution or in the practice of preceding Parliaments . . . and which . . . is full of danger to the power, dignity and usefulness of the Commons of England."

But the majority of the House was concerned only to dismiss a Ministry which was already tottering, and which was apparently too weak to conduct a great war. By a two-thirds majority it accepted Roebuck's motion.

This was the end of the Aberdeen Ministry. But what was to follow it? Public opinion declared unhesitatingly for Palmerston. But the Queen found it hard to overcome her mistrust of the self-willed Minister. First of all, she attempted every thinkable constitutional alternative. She summoned, in succession, Lord Derby as the official Leader of the Opposition, the aged Lord Lansdowne as the most respected and, by her, most highly valued spokesman of the Whigs, and finally, even Lord John Russell, the real contriver of the overthrow of the Aberdeen Ministry. All failed to form a Government, but all sought to win Gladstone for themselves, so high an opinion had all parties of his eloquence and his significance. Derby's invitation once more confronted him with the question of returning to the Conservative Party. He still regarded this as an open question, on which negotiation was possible. He did not share Lord Aberdeen's view, that the Peelites, by the coalition of 1852, had definitely gone over to the Liberal Party. But he declined Derby's offer at this decisive moment, and in so doing he dealt the Conservative Party a blow from which it did not recover for a decade.

Derby considered that without Gladstone and Palmerston he could not undertake to form a Government. He returned his mandate; to the chagrin of Disraeli, who was convinced that this was the moment—never, perhaps, to return—for the Conservatives to seize power with the prospect of retaining it permanently. That Derby had allowed the moment to pass mortified him profoundly; the more so as he was forced to realize that Derby's lack of confidence in him had played a disastrous part in his refusal to take office. It was years before Derby fully realized Disraeli's ability.

But Disraeli was guilty of an even more disastrous error in his judgement of Palmerston, whom he described, with a sigh, as "the inevitable." In a private letter he wrote, venomously: "He is at the best only ginger-beer, and not champagne, and now an old painted pantaloon, very deaf, very blind, and with false teeth, which would fall out of his mouth when speaking, if he did not hesitate and halt so in his talk." Disraeli was certainly a judge of men, but in this instance how completely he was mistaken! As a matter of fact, the "blind and deaf pantaloon" who now became Premier remained—apart from a short interruption—in this high office until the end of his life; for a decade longer, during every session of Parliament, he sat on the Treasury Bench from four o'clock in the afternoon until late at night, and then, as an astonished German observer wrote: "at night, and often in the early hours of the morning, he walks home—almost half an hour's walk—in order to replace the carbon dioxide inhaled in Westminster Palace by a little oxygen"; and once home, he had still to write with his own hand his letter to the Queen. It was not surprising that the British newspaper-reader, or, as Palmerston used to call him, "the fat man with a white hat in the twopenny omnibus," regarded this Minister with pride and affection. Palmerston was so exactly what he imagined a British statesman ought to be: combative, proud that he was an Englishman, capable at need of striking the patriotic note as no other man could do, good-tempered and witty, and with all this amazingly industrious, and perfectly at home in every office that he filled. At a time of violent Party strife an embittered Tory told Disraeli that he knew of something that would ruin Palmerston; he had an affair with a certain lady. "Good God!" cried Disraeli: "if the English learn that Palmerston, at the age of eighty, still has his affairs, they'll make him Dictator!" As a matter of fact, everyone knew that the old gentleman was most happily married.

Hardly had Palmerston received the Queen's mandate when he offered Gladstone the office of Chancellor of the Exchequer in his Cabinet. Gladstone was thereby confronted with a difficult decision. On the one hand, it was impossible that the formation of any Government should be nipped in the bud by his refusal, and that of his friends—Graham and Herbert—to take office. The elementary fact that "Her Majesty's Government"—especially in time of war—must be carried on in one way or another, controlled the situation after a ten days' crisis. On the other hand, he saw that the Cabinet planned by Palmerston was an Aberdeen Ministry without Aberdeen, but with Palmerston at its head. This prospect filled him with serious misgivings, especially in view of the question, which for him stood in the foreground, whether this Government would seize every opportunity of ending the war by a negotiated peace. For in respect of Palmerston he harboured a feeling which Palmerston himself did not hesitate to describe as mistrust, while he regarded Aberdeen as the most solid and indispensable guarantee of a policy that would lead to peace. "I have acted with Lord Aberdeen all my life," he wrote in a letter to Palmerston: "I am deeply attached to him. I feel with him more nearly than with any other man on the one great question of the hour."

It was Aberdeen himself who finally decided the matter, and persuaded Gladstone to take back his initial refusal. Gladstone asked him frankly as a matter of conscience: "When we have joined the Cabinet, will you rise in the House of Lords and say that you give the Cabinet your confidence with regard to the question of war and peace?" Only when Aberdeen had answered this question in the affirmative did Gladstone declare that he was prepared to enter the Cabinet, thereby making it possible to form a Government. The Queen, who deplored in the most moving tones the loss of "so kind and dear and valued a friend" as Aberdeen, greeted the adhesion of his friend with a sigh of relief; it "would tend"— so she wrote to her uncle, the King of Belgium—"to allay the *alarm* which his (Palmerston's) name will, I fear, produce abroad."

Her satisfaction was unhappily short-lived. In the heat of negotiation the three Peelites had forgotten to ask as plainly as they should have asked a question which immediately obtruded itself. What of the commission of inquiry proposed by Roebuck and voted by the Lower House? The Peelites considered that the matter was closed, since the motion had achieved its political purpose— the fall of Aberdeen. They had also every reason to suppose that Palmerston shared this view. It was certain that he too would gladly have allowed this troublesome commission to sink into oblivion, and he attempted to influence Roebuck in this direction. But there was another who had made up his mind that the Government was not going to get off so easily. Disraeli's perspicacity had realized how much trouble this commission might give the Government; possibly he saw, too, that Gladstone, who had especially annoyed him by his repeated hesitation to join the Conservatives—"this is the third time he shies at us"—could hardly agree to the inquiry after his former speech and his solemn declaration. He therefore insisted on the appointment of the commission —and Palmerston gave way.

Gladstone blamed him greatly for this surrender; perhaps he was thinking precisely of this when in after years he declared that Palmerston was not among the few statesmen—such as Peel, Russell and Disraeli—who possessed real courage. But we may perhaps find it intelligible that he had no particular desire to stake the supreme position which he had at last, in his old age, achieved, and the possibilities of great political activity, for the sake of a matter of principle, which to him, like all matters of principle, was actually indifferent; what with questions as to what was and what was not constitutional, he would soon dispose of the commission.

But for Gladstone a principle to which he had once confessed was a flag which he could not desert without staking his honour. As he explained to Prince Albert, he regarded the path on which the Lower House was proceeding "a most unconstitutional, most presumptuous, and most dangerous course." The Prince was not very far removed from sharing this opinion, for he was put in mind of the French National Convention. Nevertheless, he urgently advised Gladstone to remain in the Cabinet. But neither Gladstone nor his two friends, Graham and Herbert, could resolve to do so; their consent to the appointment of a commission would have seemed to them an act of disloyalty toward Aberdeen and Newcastle. Accordingly, all three tendered their resignation.

The impression hereby created was the worst conceivable. What was the public to think of Ministers who within three weeks took office and then resigned? Their colleagues, comprehensibly enough, were greatly dissatisfied. Lord Clarendon, the Secretary for Foreign Affairs, unamiably declared that Gladstone had resigned out of punctilio, Herbert out of sentimentality, and Graham out of fear. In the Parliamentary session of 23rd of February they attempted to justify their attitude. They made no impression on the House. Gladstone, indeed, had no better fortune than ten years earlier, when he sought to justify his resignation over the Maynooth affair.

In the same session there rose from the same bench on which the three ex-Ministers had taken their places that experienced fighter, the Member for Manchester: John Bright. With his friend Cobden he had been the leader of those who had fought to the last moment for the preservation of peace. In this battle he was defeated, and the man who had worsted him was now Prime Minister of England. But no ill-success could break his courage and his sense of duty. Peace must be restored as soon as possible; if it could not be re-established in opposition to Palmerston, then the attempt must be made to restore it with his co-operation. In moving terms he now conjured the Prime Minister and the House to make an end of the unspeakable misery which the war had already caused. Once more, of course, the temper of the House was against him; but even the most reluctant were affected by the incantatory power of his virile speech, and when he cried: "The Angel of Death has been abroad throughout the land; you may almost hear the beating of his wings," the House sat spellbound, friends and enemies alike, and it was almost as though they were listening for that dread sound, as though the speaker's words had described a palpable reality. Even the cool, sarcastic Disraeli had to confess to him: "Bright, I would give all that I ever had to have made that speech you made just now." And the pious Quaker replied, with flashing eyes: "Well, you might have made it if you had been honest."

But Palmerston was not the man to be diverted from his course by a speech, however moving. He went his way, heedless of Bright, heedless of the Peelites. He soberly weighed the profits and the disadvantages, and he came to the conclusion that his Cabinet, the gaps in which were quickly filled, was more easily to be managed without these all too independent colleagues.

For Gladstone began the days of which it is written "they delight us not." He was in much the same position as on his resignation over the Maynooth affair. But while Peel had then regarded him as a strayed yet valued follower, whom he intended as soon as possible to help out of a *cul de sac*—as he actually did—Gladstone was now isolated, equally remote from all the parties, supported only by a few friends who had no sort of power behind them. Even observers who were not ill-disposed to him might have thought that he had played his part, that his day was over; and this in spite of his great achievements. In the Englishman's estimation, the Parliamentarian who cannot become a Minister slowly but surely drops out of the ranks of the men who count.

This time, as a matter of fact, it was four and a half years before he resumed his place on the Ministerial bench; years that were priceless in the life of a man of forty-five, and who had proved to himself and the world that he was now at the full height of his power.

At this period it was well for Gladstone that there were other things which meant as much to him as politics. Such leisure as political life now afforded him he could employ by immersing himself in the world of Homer. The fruit of this occupation was a work in three volumes and 1,700 large pages, *Studies on Homer and the Homeric Age*, which was published in 1858.

This is not a scientific work in the philological sense of the term. No modern philologist would think of citing it. The application of the modern philological methods calls for critical faculties which Gladstone did not possess, nor had Oxford done anything to awaken and develop them. The notion that the Homer who was supposed to have dictated the *Iliad* and the *Odyssey* never existed was to him a sort of sacrilege. He read his Homer not as a *savant*, but as a lover. Its beauties filled him with enthusiasm and his imagination was kindled by them; and Gladstone's imagination was unusually vivid, and at times excessive, when it was not controlled by the hard data of reality. It was not an imagination that liked to play, as Disraeli's did, with the future of Europe and the East; but it was wholly in control when he interpreted the Homeric fables or the Greek mythology. Perhaps his incapacity for purely scientific treatment was not unconnected with his tendency to treat even the Homeric epos as a source of moral edification.

He calls the study of Homer a "'palace of enchantment" and likens the spells of the enchanter to "a remedial specific, which, freshening the understanding by contact with the truth and strength of Nature, should both improve his (the reader's) vigilance against deceit and danger, and increase his vigour and resolution for the discharge of duty."

The second volume of the work, in which the author dealt with the religion of the Homeric age, was a complete failure; so that one can understand the derision of the great philologist, Jowett, Master of Balliol, who declared that a man who discovered the doctrine of the Trinity in Homer must be crazy. But though this work is of so little scientific value, it is convincing proof of Gladstone's real and complete absorption in the world of Homer, of his intimate knowledge of Greek poetry, and his understanding of its beauty. He was, indeed, not the only English statesman of his generation who in the study of the Greek classics sought relief from the heat of the political struggle. Lord Derby also thought himself happy when he could go back to his Homer and polish his translation of the Iliad.

His Homeric studies, however, did not prevent Gladstone from following with critical attention the course of English politics. The war with Russia followed its bloody course, and the fears which he had expressed on Lord Aberdeen's resignation from the Cabinet were soon justified. Palmerston displayed no inclination to conclude peace before his war-aims were completely achieved. Russia, after the death of the Tsar Nicholas I (2nd March, 1855), was more disposed to meet the demands of the Allies, but on one point she refused to submit: the banning of Russian warships in the Black Sea; and because of this ban and this refusal the war continued. Naturally, the peace party were opposed to its continuance. Yet the reasons which John Bright gave in justification of his point of view were not the products of a sentimental pacifism, but would hold their own—as the experience of 1870 was to show—against the criticism of the most bigoted political realist. "Russia," he said, "is a great power, as England is, and in treating with her you must consider that the Russian Government has to consult its own dignity, its own interests, and public opinion." Russia could never permanently submit to such a limitation of her sovereignty. These are fundamentally the same arguments as those which Bismarck adduced in his significant conversation with Odo Russell at Versailles on the 21st of November, 1870. To squander more blood and gold on such an imaginary war-aim was against Bright's conscience. It was also against Gladstone's conscience, and so for the first time the two men found themselves in agreement. In later life they were to become comrades in arms: a connection that was to leave its mark on English history, and to be for the men themselves a source of inner strength and support. At first, of course, it hardly added to Gladstone's reputation that he, who had been a member of the Cabinet when war was declared, now sided with the man who had most vigorously attacked the Cabinet, and who was decried as an apostle of "peace at any price." Nevertheless, in Parliament he was unreservedly in favour of refusing to neutralize the Black Sea, a proposal which he declared to be unjust, as it was restricting the defensive powers of a free nation to the advantage of its neighbours. But in principle he found it deplorable that England should wage war for the sake of mere victory, for the sake of prestige. "It is hideous," he said, "it is anti-Christian, it is immoral, it is inhuman . . . you tempt the justice of Him, in whose hands the fates of the armies are as absolutely lodged as the fate of the infant slumbering in its cradle; the moral sense of mankind would not permit the promulgation of such a doctrine." Such words, of course, were not likely to be applauded in an England infected with the war-fever. But few critics were as malicious as Karl Marx, who for years had eaten in England the bitter bread of exile, and who honoured Gladstone with an especial hatred. He said of this speech that while it brought conscience into diplomacy, it introduced even more diplomacy into the conscience. Another German observer, who stood on the opposite wing of German politics, could see in the co-operation of Gladstone and Graham with Cobden and Bright merely a proof of their lack of principle. But it did not say much for the perspicacity of this observer that he should declare that England had already passed the summit of her greatness, and that one looked in vain for men who had not yet fallen victims to *marasmus senilis*. One must not hold Disraeli, from whom Count Vitzthum was wont to derive his information concerning English politics, responsible for the grotesque errors of judgement with which the Saxon Minister adorned his despatches. Of greater weight than the views which the radical-revolutionary German journalist published in a Silesian newspaper, and those which the reactionary German diplomatist expressed in his letters, were the opinions of English politicians and newspapers. Of these the great majority agreed with Palmerston, and only a few thought, like young Lord Ripon, of contrasting Gladstone, as the pattern of an honourable man, with "a self-seeking political adventurer" like Palmerston.

Gladstone himself was conscious at first of this opposition to Palmerston as the determining motive of his position. He believed as firmly as his friends—Aberdeen, Graham, Herbert—that their group could not continue to lead an isolated existence, and that sooner or later it must be absorbed by one or the other of the two great parties. But by which? Here they were unable to agree, and yet they were resolved that they would take this last step together. Gladstone wrote to Graham that he decidedly preferred Lord Derby to Lord Palmerston, but Graham vigorously protested. Gladstone, however, so completely identified the Liberal Party with the Prime Minister that he declared it to be dead to all that he valued in Liberalism. Moreover, Derby, whom he still privately preferred to Disraeli, had been making fresh advances to him since the spring of 1856; advances which led, in February 1857, to repeated explanations. But again no agreement was arrived at. What prevented it, perhaps, apart from Gladstone's regard for his friends, was the insoluble problem of Disraeli. Derby could neither drop Disraeli nor propose that Gladstone should serve under him. Still, as before, there were many causes of difference. They were agreed mainly on one point —in their repudiation of Palmerston's foreign policy. But they were soon to learn that in this connection he was stronger than all of them together.

2. "Civis Romanus Sum" in China

The Crimean War was finally terminated by the Peace of Paris on the 30th of March, 1856. By the English people, the war and the peace were both placed to the credit of Palmerston. The strength of their attachment to him was shown in the following year by a case in which his method was almost more irresponsible than in the Pacifico affair, and in which he had Derby and Russell, Gladstone and Cobden against him. All the greater was his triumph.

In October 1856 some Chinese officials on the Canton River seized a small vessel, the *Arrow*. This vessel (a *lorcha*) was the property of some Chinese merchants, and she had once enjoyed the privilege of flying the British flag. Her crew were accused of piracy by the Chinese authorities, and arrested. The British Consul in Canton requested the Chinese to hand them over, alleging that an insult had been offered to the British flag, and as the Chinese Governor Yeh refused to comply, the diplomatic representative of Great Britain in Hong Kong, Sir John Bowring, a Radical and a friend of Cobden, caused Canton to be bombarded by British ships, and its forts to be destroyed.

Of the illegality of this procedure there cannot be the slightest doubt, but for Palmerston this was no reason for condemning it. The lawyers could argue the matter. He palliated the behaviour of his officials, which suited his purpose, this being to break down China's resistance to the admission of British goods. But there were British politicians for whom questions of right or wrong were not of subsidiary importance. Richard Cobden felt that he must in conscience protest against the fact that England should make such lawless and ruthless use of the right of the stronger over a helpless adversary. That the principal culprit was a former friend could not, of course, affect his judgement. He moved, in the House of Commons, a vote of censure against the Government. The official Opposition joined him. Of the two leaders of the Conservatives, Disraeli, who remembered Palmerston's triumph in the Pacifico debate, recommended caution. But Lord Derby was as indignant as Cobden, and it was he who determined the attitude of the party. For Gladstone, Palmerston's procedure in this case was only another instance of his method of using England's superior power against weak peoples, a method which from his Christian and ethical point of view he could only condemn. He was true to himself when he protested against the ill-treatment of the Chinese. Fifteen years earlier, as a young Member, he had uttered a passionate protest against the "Opium War," and had accused Palmerston of protecting an infamous contraband traffic under the British flag, which had formerly been unfurled in the cause of righteousness. And in his speech in the House of Commons he referred to the violent means which the British had taken against Canton as an offence against justice, once more uplifting the isolated instance to the level of an exposition of principles. He invoked "that justice which binds man to man; which is older than Christianity, which is broader than Christianity . . . and which underlies Christianity, for Christianity itself appeals to it."—"As he spoke the thunder of his voice rolled, and he raised his arm to his full height, as an appeal to Heaven itself, and then it moved majestically across as if to the full breadth of the world, and then dropped it to that which underlies everything, and binds man to man."

This speech made a profound impression on the House, and its arguments were seconded by Russell and Disraeli. Palmerston's defence was feeble, and the House accepted Cobden's resolution by a majority of sixteen votes. Many said of Gladstone's speech that it was one of the rare cases in which a speech has influenced a division. But Palmerston was not the man to admit defeat on account of such an adverse majority. With admirable self-confidence he immediately assured the Queen of "his own firm belief . . . that the present Government has the confidence of the country in a greater degree than any other Government that could now be formed would have." Whether or no the Queen sympathized with her Prime Minister, she could not, under the circumstances, refuse to dissolve Parliament, and the new elections showed that his judgement of his fellow-citizens had once more been perfectly correct. Palmerston knew just how to deal with them, and he consciously simplified the problem, inasmuch as he roundly declared that "an insolent barbarian had violated the British flag." The British elector was not in the least degree concerned as to whether the Chinese Governor was really a barbarian, or whether he had been insolent, and whether the British flag had been in any way insulted. It was enough for him that Palmerston had told him that these things were so, and he voted for Palmerston. We cannot be surprised that he should have done so when we know that even Macaulay bade his nephew conclude a set of Latin verses with a panegyric of Palmerston, for "the name of Palmerston at once procures the prisoners their liberty." The British voter gladly took advantage of the election to show Cobden, Bright and their friends what he thought of their attitude during the Crimean War. One and all, they lost their seats. Even John Bright, who had gone abroad after a serious illness, and had taken no part in the debates on the Chinese war, was defeated in Manchester, though a few years earlier the city had been proud to think that it had given the Free Trade party its name. The peace party was overwhelmed by an absolute catastrophe, and Palmerston's triumph was complete.

Gladstone, indeed, was re-elected by the University of Oxford without opposition. Nevertheless, he was bound to regard the result of the General Election as a grievous defeat of his policy. The appeal to justice found no echo in the heart of the British electors—or in other words, of Englishmen of the upper and middle classes, who in the then state of the law were alone privileged to vote. His antipathy to the Liberal Party, which was, after all, merely a Palmerston Party, was intensified; with a certain premeditation, and to Graham's dismay, he reaffirmed the fundamental Conservative principles which formed the bond between him and his Oxford electors.

That he did so with some reason became evident in the course of the same year, in respect of a proposal that quickly made him abandon the thought of retiring from Parliament, which he had entertained for a time after the General Election. The Government introduced the draft of a genuinely liberal and reasonable Bill which would provide for the dissolution of marriage by civil process. Hitherto divorce could be obtained only by means of a special Act of Parliament for each individual case; a means, of course, which was available only to the wealthy. The unspeakable misery which this state of affairs inflicted upon persons of limited means had been depicted, some years before this date, by Dickens in his *Hard Times*. But Gladstone did not and would not realize this, because he saw the whole problem in the light of an ecclesiastical dogma, which in his opinion was the matter at stake. A law directed against the indissolubility of marriage was for him an infringement of the Divine ordinance, and for this reason he opposed it with passionate obstinacy, and also with such ingenious sophistry that malicious tongues declared, some years later, that Gladstone was the inventor of obstruction. It took all Palmerston's energy, and all the dexterity of his quick-witted Attorney-General, Sir Richard Bethell (afterwards Lord Chancellor Westbury), to pass the Bill in the face of Gladstone's opposition. But although, as far as this question was concerned, Gladstone was behind his age, in one respect he was far in advance of it; for he insisted that the husband and wife should be equal before the law, whereas the new Act was very far from admitting such equality. Nevertheless, it would not have been surprising if all progressively-minded Englishmen had regarded Gladstone as a hopeless case.

But the very next year there was again a call from the Conservative side of the House. For in 1858 something happened which in 1857 no one would have thought possible. Palmerston fell, and Derby became Prime Minister for the second time. This change of Government was an episode in a drama of great historical significance. On the 14th of January, 1858, the Italian Orsini attempted to assassinate Napoleon III by means of a bomb. This shocking atrocity was intended to punish the Emperor for breaking the promises of his revolutionary youth. Napoleon was unhurt, but a month later Palmerston fell. Orsini had manufactured his bomb in England, which had provided him with an asylum when he had escaped from his Mantuan prison. The French Foreign Minister, Walewski, complained, in a Note which erred on the side of excessive bluntness, that the British Government encouraged "conspirators outlawed by humanity." But this annoyed the English; they had not backed up Palmerston in defending England's honour against the insolence of the Chinese only to allow the French to insult them unrebuked. The "Civis Romanus" faith found spontaneous expression, and since the Conspiracy Bill which Palmerston introduced gave rise to the impression that he himself had relapsed from the faith, he was swept aside. The majority of the Lower House accepted an amendment proposed by a Radical member, which censured Palmerston for not giving Walewski the fitting answer. Gladstone was among those who spoke in favour of the amendment. Precisely because he had so often criticized his fellow-countrymen, he felt that he was all the more justified in defending the honour of England, which had been grievously and unjustly aspersed by the French accusation that the English had encouraged murder. Palmerston realized, with astonishment and dismay, that his opponent, when it was necessary, could sound this note in a masterly fashion, and Count Vitzthum reported that Gladstone, whom he called "the first orator of the House," had lifted the debate to the level of statesmanship. "Last year," wrote Gladstone to his wife, after the amendment had been voted, "we struck one stroke for humanity—this year for honour: God be praised"; and he added: "In hours of great joy as well as great sorrow it is very sad to be away from you."

With the change of Government he was again confronted with the problem of choosing between the Right and the Left. After this speech of his Lord Derby, who was then making up his Cabinet, believed that he could count on Gladstone's co-operation. But Gladstone again declined the invitation. The letter in which he stated the reasons for his refusal did little more than make it clear that he did not wish to break with his friends. More can be gathered from another exchange of letters written on the same day. For John Bright, when he heard that Lord Derby was inviting Gladstone's co-operation, sent him a friendly and candid letter, warning him against joining the Conservative Cabinet. This letter betrays the intense sympathy with which the Radical leader was following Gladstone's development, and shows that his judgement of it was actually more confident and more accurate than Gladstone's own. While Gladstone was not yet fully aware of the direction which he was taking, Bright, in spite of the other's divagations, was not only certain that he would end by joining the Liberals, but was confident that sooner or later he would become their leader. "If you remain on our side of the House, you are with the majority and no government can be formed without you. You have many friends here . . . and I know nothing that can prevent you being Prime Minister before you approach the age of every other member of the House who has or can have any claim to that high office." Gladstone was then in his forty-ninth year, and before he had completed his fifty-ninth year he had fulfilled Bright's prophecy. But at this time he knew what he disapproved of more definitely than what he was striving for. In his cordial letter of reply he explained that he was divided from the Conservative Ministry by matters of conviction: "The opinions . . . that I hold on many questions of government and administration are strongly held; and although I set a value, and a high value, upon the power which office gives, I earnestly hope never to be tempted by its exterior allurements, unless they are accompanied with the reasonable prospect of giving effect to some at least of those opinions and with some adequate opening for public good. On the present occasion I have not seen such prospect; and before I received your letter . . . I had made my choice."

But this was not the end of the matter. A few months later this —to outward appearance—completely isolated member was again confronted with the same problem. The occasion was connected with the alarming Indian Mutiny of the years 1857–1858. Lord Derby's Secretary for India, Lord Ellenborough, was obliged to send in his resignation in May 1858, on account of a conflict with the Governor-General, and this incident forced not only the Prime Minister, but also Disraeli—his Chancellor of the Exchequer and the Leader of the Lower House—to realize how poor in political talent the Cabinet was, and how urgently it was in need of intellectual reinforcement. As far back as January Disraeli had boasted to Vitzthum that his party was prepared to readmit the "renegade" Gladstone, but only if he made an unconditional surrender. Yet now it was Disraeli who literally implored Gladstone to return.

Shortly before this Disraeli had made an offer which we can but describe as magnanimous and unselfish. He was willing to resign the Leadership of the House to Graham, an older man, and to serve under him as Gladstone's colleague. Now he went even farther: he wrote a personal letter to Gladstone. This letter is a most remarkable and characteristic document. To begin with, its outward form is remarkable; for it contains neither the usual form of address, nor the complimentary formula which commonly precedes the signature. He comes to the point at once, and without further ceremony he addresses himself to the difficulty: "Our mutual relations have formed the great difficulty in accomplishing a result which I have always anxiously desired." He then briefly enumerates the steps which he has taken to achieve this result.

"I have been, at all times, actively prepared to make every sacrifice of self for the public good, which I have even thought identical with your accepting office in a Conservative government." And then the cool objectivity of his proposal is interrupted by the appeal: "Don't you think the time has come when you might deign to be magnanimous?" He assures Gladstone that he will find "some warm personal friends and admirers" in the Conservative Cabinet: "You may place me in neither category, but in that, I assure you you have ever been sadly mistaken."

No one can read this letter without being impressed. Was Gladstone an exception? His answer seems to show that he was: for in respect of his personal attitude to Disraeli it is marked by a reserve which even its voluble phrasing cannot conceal. "I pray you let me say that I have never known you penurious in admiration towards anyone who had the slightest claim to it, and that at no period of my life, not even during the limited one when we were in sharp political conflict, have I either felt any enmity towards you or believed that you felt any towards me."

Morley, who knew Gladstone as few knew him, and who, on the other hand, felt for Disraeli the admiration of the literary connoisseur and the historical biographer—an admiration unaffected by political differences—finds in this letter "the same accents of guarded reprobation" in which the aged Gladstone was wont to speak of the work and the personality of his dead antagonist. Later on, it is true, in the conflicts of the 70's and 80's, the reasons for such inner reprobation were multiplied. But even then he must have been secretly influenced by a feeling that prepossessed him irresistibly against the thought of collaboration. Disraeli's uncommon abilities, the range of his thought, the width of his intellectual horizon, the brilliance and richness of his oratorical style, and his power of prompt resolution were things that he could not and did not ignore. But it seemed to him that this rare and singular personality was lacking in the ethical sense which he held to be indispensable in public life. What form would the collaboration of these two men have assumed? Would Gladstone, as his friends believed, have won the leadership by his actual superiority, or would Disraeli, as his biographer imagines, have won over even his great rival by the personal irresistibility which triumphed, sooner or later, over the aversion of Derby, and Salisbury, and Queen Victoria herself? One thing alone is certain: the Conservative Party may congratulate itself that this interesting experiment was never made. It would have paid dearly for it, as the Liberal Party had to pay, for twenty years, for the rivalry between Palmerston and Russell. Even William Pitt and Charles Fox could exist only as opponents.

Nevertheless, Gladstone came very near to venturing on the experiment. His position was irksome to him. He likened it to that of a man at the bottom of a well, waiting for someone to throw him a rope so that he could climb out. The prospect of important practical work was enormously attractive, especially as he was offered what was, at the moment, the most important post in the Cabinet, namely, the office of Secretary for India. Were there any fundamental reasons why he should not accept it? What fundamental principles divided Lords Derby and Palmerston? If Gladstone resisted the temptation that would have diverted him from his predestined path, this was mainly due to his friends Aberdeen and Graham. Both had now now retired from active politics; for which reason they were all the more anxious that their younger friend, who so admirably embodied the tradition of Peel, which they so dearly cherished, and who had the greatest future before him, should continue on the right path. Graham, whose advice Gladstone sought, made it clear to him that if he went over to Derby he must go alone. This decided him; for Gladstone was willing to go over to Derby only if the latter "could rally the old materials which were at Peel's command." This was evidently impossible, so Gladstone bade farewell to an unrealizable dream.

And this time he had really spoken the last word. Derby's second Cabinet had only a short existence. Gladstone kept his promise that he would give it his "independent support"; and for this reason he felt justified in accepting a very singular mission, with which it entrusted him in 1858.

The seven Ionian Islands—Corfu, Ithaca, Zacynthos, etc.—had been since 1815 under a British protectorate. The good administration which they enjoyed did not prevent the population from making active efforts to achieve union with Greece. Since 1848 the islands had been in a state of continual unrest. The British Government decided that a special commissioner must be sent out to the islands. The Colonial Minister was Bulwer-Lytton, the author of *The Last Days of Pompeii*. He regarded the matter from a literary point of view. To the isles of Odysseus and the Phaeacians they must send a man who was familiar with the world of Homer. That is, they must send Gladstone. In a despatch addressed to the Governor of the Ionian Islands Bulwer-Lytton described him as "a statesman who belongs to his country rather than to any party in it, whose mind has grasped foreign as well as domestic questions with equal vigour and success, and whose renown as a Homeric scholar will justly commend him to the sympathies of an Hellenic race." Disraeli agreed: he too was quite capable of taking the literary point of view. But perhaps he regarded this mission of Gladstone's much as Caesar regarded the honourable mission of the earnest Cato to Cyprus, which removed him from Rome at a critical moment. Accordingly, in November Gladstone proceeded to Corfu. His wife and daughter accompanied him. An Englishman who had personal experience of the people of the Ionian Islands explained that "one could only deal with the Ionians through the women." "On that account," replied Gladstone, "he would take with him some of the ladies of his family." As his secretary he took the Italian patriot Giacomo Lacaita, who had once opened his eyes to the state of affairs in Naples, and who, having fled from Naples during King Bomba's reign of terror, had migrated to London, where with the help of Gladstone and certain eminent Whigs he had achieved a good position. Gladstone felt under a special obligation to him, because he had been victimized in consequence of his letter to Lord Aberdeen on the prisons of Naples.

Gladstone spent several weeks in the Islands with which his imagination had busied itself for so many years. It was certainly a fascinating experience. He was able to astonish the Ionians by the faultless Italian of his extremely eloquent addresses; he heard himself greeted as a Philhellene, and—what was more important —he was able to expound the principles of British politics. "I really do not know," he wrote to Lytton, "for what it is that political life is worth the living if it be not for an opportunity of endeavouring to redeem in the face of the world the character of our country wherever, it matters not on how small a scale, that character has been compromised." But practically nothing much came of his mission. The problem was insoluble. In 1863 it was Palmerston who ceded the Islands to Greece. Palmerston was certainly not the man to decide with a light heart to abandon anything on which the British lion had once laid his paw. But in this case even he felt that he must recommend renunciation. Bismarck was of another opinion. He described the cession of the Ionian Islands as a grievous mistake, and a manifest symptom of British decadence.

On the homeward voyage from the land of Homer, when Gladstone looked back on the last ten years of his life, he could not feel entirely satisfied. Until the 18th of April, 1853, the day when he introduced his first Budget, the curve had steadily risen. But since then? The hopes which he had aroused in the nation had been only to a slight extent realized. A few brilliant speeches, a few meritorious essays in the reviews, a bulky volume that was, after all, a subordinate achievement, and a rather romantic mission —this was all that the world knew of him. To be sure, his Catherine had brought him untroubled domestic happiness, which was increased by the little flock of growing children. But he was now in his fiftieth year, and his Catherine too was fully convinced that life had by no means offered her William all that his gifts, his character, and the fire that burned within him had deserved.

What would he find on returning to England? With what problems would he be confronted?

His homeward journey led him through Turin, the capital of the kingdom of Sardinia. Here was Count Cavour, the Prime Minister of King Victor Emmanuel. Gladstone took the opportunity of making the personal acquaintance of the man who, he was confident, was destined to play a great part in the near future, and Cavour was delighted to be able to speak openly to an English statesman for whom he, in common with all Italian patriots, had cherished the greatest reverence since his protest against the scandalous government of Naples. What Gladstone was told of Cavour prepared him to expect great things of this man. Was the dream at last to be realized that Panizzi and Manin had revealed to him in their inspired and patriotic utterances? Was it possible that the hour of judgement for the abomination of the Neapolitan dungeons was at hand? Even while Gladstone was in Turin, Poerio and sixty-six other former inmates of those dungeons landed on English soil. Fearing the approaching storm, King Bomba had banished them from his dominions. He died a few months later, before the storm had broken.

3. *Italy, and the Great Budget*

Europe had been unquiet ever since that fourteenth day of January, 1858, when Napoleon III, pale with terror, had barely escaped assassination by Orsini's bomb. He was possessed by the fear that this might not be the last attempt upon his life to be made by the sometime comrades of his youthful days in the Camorra, so long as he failed to keep his promises to help in the liberation of Italy. Cavour was the man to exploit, with supreme ingenuity, resolution and resource, the Emperor's fears and his still surviving enthusiasm for nationalistic ideals. The result was the alliance between France and Sardinia, their war upon Austria, and their victories at Magenta and Solferino.

For England, the result was the resurrection of Palmerston. The sympathies of the British public were entirely on the side of Italy, and again the public took it for granted that Palmerston would be in agreement with it. And rightly so; for the statesman of seventy-five wrote in his best manner: "I am very Austrian north of the Alps, but very anti-Austrian south of the Alps. The Austrians have no business in Italy, and they are a public nuisance there."

In this matter Gladstone was in complete agreement with Palmerston. His whole heart was in the struggle of a long-oppressed people for liberty and unity. In his great speeches on matters of foreign politics he had spoken in support of the self-determination of even the weak nations: as in the Pacifico case and the war with China. This had become one of the leading ideas of his foreign policy. Now he saw that in Italy one of the great problems of the time was pressing for solution. It was pressing for a solution in the Liberal sense, and he was no less fervent in his support of this solution than were the Liberal leaders, Palmerston and Russell. He had cause to remember now that he had once found an ally in Palmerston, when he had roused the public conscience against the atrocities of the Neapolitan prisons. What he had seen and heard in Italy had convinced him of the fact that the outbreak of war was imminent. But if the war did really break out, he would much rather see the control of England's foreign policy in Palmerston's hands than in those of the Conservative Foreign Minister, Malmesbury, who was generally believed to sympathize with Austria. The Conservative Government fell when an electoral reform proposed by Disraeli was rejected, and the ensuing General Election failed to give it a majority. Palmerston and Russell and Bright came to a mutual understanding. The result was a vote of censure which compelled Lord Derby and Disraeli to resign.

Gladstone had voted for the Government, just as he had voted for the proposed electoral reform. But with this he felt that he had fulfilled his obligations to Derby. He did not feel that he was pledged to refuse a post in the Government that was now in process of formation.

At the head of the new Government was Palmerston. But there had been difficulties in the way of his Premiership. The Queen found it difficult to choose between Palmerston and Russell, for which reason she first of all entrusted young Lord Granville, the leader of the Liberals in the Upper House, whose amiable and tactful personality was much to her liking, with the formation of the Government. Only when Granville had failed did she turn to Palmerston. He, it was true, was now in his seventy-sixth year; but age, it seemed, was powerless to subdue him. The London correspondent of the *Preussichen Jahrbücher* reported, with admiration: "One can still see him walking down Piccadilly to the House, with the same firm step, the same erect and almost elegant bearing, and in his speeches one notes the same quickness of repartee." In a few days he had formed a Cabinet—of Liberals, Radicals, and the remnant of the Peelites.

And thus it was that he approached Gladstone with the request that he would once more assume the office of Chancellor of the

Exchequer. Gladstone accepted the invitation, and in so doing took a decision which was to determine his whole future career. It meant a final parting from the Conservatives—and this was soon followed by his resignation from the Carlton Club—and a co-operation with the Liberals which was bound, before long, to lead to complete union. There was no longer a Peelite Party; what Aberdeen had said years ago had become an indisputable reality. Those of Peel's friends who were still in political life were fighting in the ranks of the Liberals: Sidney Herbert, who went to the War Office, the Duke of Newcastle, who was Secretary for the Colonies, and even Sir James Graham, who felt that he was now too old to serve in the Ministry.

But outwardly, of course, their case was quite different from Gladstone's. They had not voted for Derby up to the last moment; they had not published articles in the periodical Press which attacked the former Palmerston Government. It was, therefore, not astonishing that the Conservatives were grievously disappointed, and that even on the Liberal side there were many who envied him his high office. He himself, in a later letter to his friend Lord Acton, declared that it was the Italian question which had finally decided his action. But, of course, the consideration that he must not continue to stand aside, if he hoped ever again to hold office and wield political influence, was of equal importance. His personal reluctance to serve under Palmerston was swept aside, not only by their agreement in respect of foreign policy, but also by the Prime Minister's earnest endeavour to bury the hatchet and forget their bygone differences. Further, he did his utmost to secure for his Cabinet the man who had opposed him most bitterly during the Crimean War, and had led the attack against him on the occasion of the war with China: namely, Richard Cobden. It was no fault of his that Cobden was unable to overcome his aversion to taking office, and persisted, after friendly negotiations, in his refusal.

Gladstone was able to convince himself that in entering Palmerston's Cabinet he would not be surrendering any of the principles for which he had been contending for the last decade. But he could not be surprised that many of his past electors should think otherwise. To them the gradual transformation which their Member had

112

undergone in the twelve years during which he had represented Oxford was revealed by his sudden step to the Left. They naturally opposed his re-election, and he had to be content with a majority of 200. This was the last time he represented Oxford. When he was next a candidate he had already advanced so far along the path of Liberal politics that he could no longer find grace in the eyes of the ancient University.

When the result of the division which overthrew Derby's Government was known in the Lobby, where the diplomatists were waiting for the figures, the Piedmontese Minister, in his jubilation, threw his hat into the air and embraced the French chargé d'affaires, to the amazement of the correct and conventional gentlemen by whom he was surrounded. Palmerston's return to power was regarded as a victory no less significant than that of Magenta, where the Piedmontese and the French had defeated the Austrians only a week earlier. For the same reason the Pope was greatly dismayed. Pius IX, who had long abandoned the liberal ideas which he had professed at the beginning of his pontificate, unbosomed himself to young Odo Russell, the nephew of Lord John Russell, the representative of the British Crown at the Vatican. There were three men who were causing him the greatest anxiety: Palmerston, Russell and Gladstone. He had read Gladstone's pamphlet on the prisons of Naples with all the greater displeasure inasmuch as after the troubles of 1848 he had appealed to the King of Naples for protection. If the man who had written these glowing words was now, in these critical times, responsible, with others, for British policy, it was a bad lookout for the Pope and the other sovereign princes of Italy, whose sovereignty was based on the treaties of 1815. He assured Russell that the pamphlet could only be the result of a misapprehension; "he does not know us and Italy."

The Pope's apprehensions were well founded; he knew very well who it was that threatened his sovereignty. The three Ministers whom he had named did their best, during the next few years, often in opposition to the Queen and the rest of the Cabinet, but supported by the public opinion of England, to enable the Italians to achieve their great object. In two stormy years the Italian patriots made such headlong progress—exceeding all expectations, and holding all Europe breathless—that against the will of Napoleon, and in opposition to the whole of monarchical Europe, they achieved the unity of almost the whole of their native country. This result was made possible only by the concurrence of three things: the statecraft of Cavour, the heroic deeds of Garibaldi, and the strongly benevolent neutrality of the British Government. But the whole of Palmerston's and Russell's Italian policy would never have been achieved if Gladstone had not given his vigorous support to the Prime Minister and the Foreign Secretary. The opposition in the Cabinet was considerable. Lord Granville—who in later years was twice Gladstone's Foreign Secretary—wrote to a friend of his, referring to the state of affairs within the Cabinet: "Johnny and Pam (are) like twins, too much united on foreign affairs, for with Gladstone as their ally they are inclined to meddle too much in Italian affairs." When the Cabinet had to take a decision the matter was often decided by the attitude of the member who was superior to all the others in debate, as much by reason of his dialectical talent, as because of the thoroughness with which he mastered every question in which he was interested. He furnished a proof of both qualities in the Lower House, when in August 1859 the Opposition endeavoured to deter the Government from any participation in a conference to settle the terms of peace between France and Austria. He was able to refute every argument brought forward by the Opposition by reference to the transactions of the Tory Government itself, and to the Blue book which they had published, and his ability in adducing historical precedents aroused the astonished admiration of his opponents. Even Disraeli, after listening to this speech, could not refrain from complimenting the Chancellor on its extraordinary brilliance.

The speech was unusually impressive because Gladstone did not fear to call things by their right name; and in particular, in contrasting Piedmont and Austria, he expressed himself—though in measured terms—with perfect frankness. Disraeli, in a private conversation with Count Vitzthum, described Austria, "despite all its defects," as "the centre and nucleus of all Conservative endeavours in the field of European politics." But Gladstone, in moving phrases, pointed out that "wherever liberty reared its head in Italy, wherever there was the slightest and most moderate attempt to procure even the hundredth part of those franchises which as Englishmen we hold so dear, there the iron hand of Austria has interposed, and has re-established in all their vigour the abuses of the actually existing Governments." In questions of foreign policy Gladstone thus very definitely severed himself from all that styled itself Conservative. While Disraeli was able to rejoice in the approval of a German reactionary like the Saxon Minister, Gladstone was in complete agreement with patriotic German democrats like Ferdinand Lassalle and Ludwig Bamberger, who saw, in the Italian Risorgimento, the prelude to a struggle for the liberty and unity of the German nation.

With special emphasis he censured the attempt to give a one-sided and Conservative interpretation to the principle of non-intervention, which he himself had professed in his speech on the Pacifico case. This question, moreover, played a prominent part in the correspondence between the Queen and her Ministers. Napoleon III, in the armistice of Villafranca, had advocated the revival of the Middle Italian principalities of Tuscany and Parma. To this the Italians could not possibly agree, and the policy of the British Government encouraged their resistance. The Queen reproached it with "reversing the principle of non-intervention" which had hitherto been rigidly observed. Russell replied that giving good advice was not intervention. "If intervention were to mean giving friendly advice . . . (then) if we refrain from doing so we may ultimately be obliged to have recourse to intervention . . . against the ruthless tyrant of Austria, or the unchained ambition of France." Gladstone, however, speaking in the House of Commons, asked whether the Governments which the Italian people had expelled were "to be restored by force." "If this was the meaning of Villafranca, then the British Government would wish to be in a position to protest with all the energy that the Government of a free State can command against a doctrine that would treat the inhabitants of the territories in question . . . as the property of so many ducal houses, who might dispose of them, their families, their fortunes, and those of their posterity as they pleased, without any regard to that independent will and judgement which as human beings they are entitled to exercise."

In this speech of Gladstone's we may discover the fundamental idea of the policy which found conclusive expression in Russell's Note of the 27th of October, 1860. In plain and unmistakable terms this Note took the part of the Italian people, "a people building up the edifice of their liberties and consolidating the work of their independence amid the sympathies and good wishes of Europe." This Note, which was received by the Italian people with passionate enthusiasm, and which moved Cavour to tears, while a diplomatist of the old school bluntly described it as *une polissonerie*, was entirely after Gladstone's heart. It must above all have delighted him in that it reproached the Government of the King of Naples in plain terms for its "failure . . . to provide for the administration of justice, the profession of liberty, and the general welfare of the people," so that his subjects were longing for the overthrow of their ruler as the necessary prelude to any improvement of their condition. King Bomba's son, who ascended the throne in 1859 and lost it in 1860, had an opportunity of considering in exile whether his father would not have done better to listen to Gladstone's warning, instead of driving his supposed informant, Lacaita, out of the country. It was Lacaita, now an English citizen and a knight, who persuaded Russell, at a decisive moment, to decline Napoleon's offer of intervention in the Straits of Messina, thereby making it possible for Garibaldi to cross to the mainland, and to deliver the *coup de grâce* to Bourbon rule in Naples. Poerio himself, whose ill-treatment had once incited Gladstone to take up his pen, was now a deputy in the North Italian Parliament, and from the tribune he refused alliance with Naples, when the King sued for it in his need, on the grounds that "the Neapolitan Government has the tradition of perjury, handed down from father to son . . . I trust that the Ministers of Victor Emmanuel will not stretch out their hands to a Government which certainly is the most declared of the enemies of Italian independence."

Before Italy was able to complete the work of union by the inclusion of Venice and Rome, she suffered a grievous and irreparable loss, which could never be made good. On the 5th of June,

1861, Cavour died in the fifty-first year of his short but infinitely momentous life. "All the enlightened thinkers of the world," wrote Treitschke, in the brilliant essay which in 1869 he dedicated to the Italian statesman, "felt the blow as a common loss to the great community of liberty; the Puritans in England lamented: a prince has fallen in Israel." Gladstone, too, was profoundly aware of the gap made by Cavour's death. Towards the close of his life he spoke of the two "nation-makers" whom he had lived to see: Bismarck and Cavour. But he "put Cavour rather above Bismarck . . . having effected as much with smaller means." No one can doubt for a moment for which of the two great statesmen he had the greater admiration.

.   .   .   .   .   .

Napoleon's reputation in England had not gained through his Italian policy. When in May 1859 he declared war upon Austria in a manifesto which upheld the causes of nationality and humanity, he was generally acclaimed. But when at Villafranca he left his ally in the lurch the world was disillusioned, and when he compelled Piedmont, as the price of his services as ally, to cede Nice and Savoy, the world was indignant. Palmerston's attitude to the French Emperor was completely transformed by the incidents of 1859 and 1860. He spoke with unrestrained mockery of the Emperor's mind, which, he said, teemed with ideas as a rabbit-warren teems with rabbits, and whose ideas took flight as rabbits do when they think they are observed or pursued. He passed on, speaking coolly enough, but for that reason all the more incisively, to the suspicion inspired by the Emperor's armaments, and finally touched on the apprehension that he might be planning a sudden attack on England; after all, he was a Bonaparte, and England had not forgotten his uncle's long considered and never realized plans of a landing on English shores. This feeling could easily have been fanned into a blaze that might have been disastrous to both countries.

British pacifists beheld with keen anxiety this gathering cloud. Was there no means of dispersing it before it became dangerous? Bright was the first to make a suggestion which led to a genuinely Free Trade train of thought. Free Trade, for Cobden and Bright, was the means which would lead not only to the exchange of the nations' goods, but would also tend to a mutual interchange of their virtues. Bright suggested that close relations between Great Britain and France should be promoted by facilitating the exchange of their products.

That this suggestion found concrete realization in a commercial treaty was due, in the first place, to Richard Cobden. He resolved to take advantage of a protracted visit to Paris; he would persuade the Emperor to conclude a commercial treaty with England. But in order to do this he must have the approval of the British Government. There were three men whose consent must be obtained: the Prime Minister, the Foreign Secretary, whose duty it was to watch over the relations of the two countries, and the Chancellor of the Exchequer, who would have to advocate a trade agreement and explain its fiscal and economic results.

Palmerston and Russell regarded Cobden's plan with cool approval: it was not to be expected that these two old gentlemen would feel any great enthusiasm for such political innovations. And then, in September 1859, Cobden went to Hawarden.

He was by no means prejudiced in Gladstone's favour. He could not forget that the statesman had been responsible, with others, for the Crimean War, and—what was still worse—did not appear to feel any remorse, or seem in the least inclined to admit that the war had been a mistake. As early as 1857 he had written to a friend that he had the highest opinion of Gladstone's abilities. He was the most eloquent and the most impressive speaker in the House. His influence was to be explained mainly by the earnest conscientiousness which stamped his utterances. But his conscience had not yet led him in the direction of Cobden and his friends, or, if it had, he had ignored its admonitions. As a matter of fact, Cobden was afraid that his conscience was sometimes ensnared by his intellect.

Consequently, on that journey to Hawarden, he may well have been conscious of misgivings. But Gladstone's acceptance of his idea was very different from anything he had anticipated. In a moment the Chancellor had realized the full scope of the proposal. Here, he perceived, was a means, not only of continuing the work of his master, Peel, but of serving the cause of peace at a time when a war was being waged, and when other wars were threatening. Accustomed to regard all political tasks in the light of historic experience, he thought of the tariff war which had brought about and confirmed the estrangement of France and England in the days of the French Revolution and the first Napoleon. In order to achieve the opposite result one must employ antithetical methods, as he afterwards explained in Parliament, on the occasion of his great Budget speech. "If you desire," he cried to the House, "to knit together in amity those two great nations whose conflicts have often shaken the world, undo for your purpose that which your fathers did for their purpose, and follow, with the same intelligence and perseverance, a far more beneficial aim."

Cobden was delighted with the understanding and the offers of active help which he found at Hawarden. "Gladstone," he confided to Bright, "is really almost the only Cabinet Minister . . . who is not afraid to let his heart guide his head a little at times"; and in these words he exactly described one of the ruling traits of Gladstone's political character. "It is God's own method of producing an *entente cordiale*"; so the project was entirely after Gladstone's own heart.

In spite of serious difficulties, Cobden succeeded, thanks to his powers of cool and convincing argument, and his personal superiority, in persuading Napoleon to accept his ideas. The Emperor's attitude was largely determined by the fact that he did not want to lose the friendship of England at a critical juncture. After protracted negotiations, in which Cobden was finally given an official status, while Gladstone remained his most effective support, he achieved his aim. A treaty was concluded which would essentially facilitate, for a period of ten years, the importation of French products—especially of French wines—into England, and the exportation of British manufactures to France.

And now came the second part of the task. The treaty had to receive the suffrages of the British Cabinet and the Houses of Parliament—in France, of course, Napoleon was not dependent on the consent of Parliament—and this task naturally devolved upon the Chancellor of the Exchequer. The Cabinet was not without its misgivings. "It is no small thing," the Chancellor wrote to his wife, "to get a Cabinet to give up $1\frac{1}{2}$ or 2 millions of revenue at a time when all the public passion is for enormous expenditure." But these misgivings were overcome. Russell definitely supported Gladstone, while Palmerston remained neutral. But the principal thing, of course, was to win the approval of Parliament. Gladstone resolved to make the commercial treaty the starting-point of the entire fiscal policy which he would expound in his Budget for 1860.

He wished to introduce his Budget earlier than usual; in fact, at the beginnning of February. All England awaited it with tense anticipation. And then came a delay—the Chancellor fell seriously ill. His doctor absolutely forbade him to speak for at least ten days, and threatened him, if he disobeyed this prescription, with the fate that had carried off Canning so prematurely. The speech on the Budget had to be postponed. But only five days later Gladstone rose to his feet in the tensely listening House. Would he achieve his end? He spoke for nearly four hours, triumphing by sheer force of will over the effects of his illness. He resorted, at intervals, to a restorative which was to serve him well for many years to come—an egg beaten up in wine, with which his anxious wife had provided him. This elixir afterwards became famous, and facetious journalists would humorously speculate on the mysterious contents of the glass which Gladstone unobtrusively raised to his lips when a thundering salvo of applause gave him a momentary breathing-space.

The Budget of 1860 was Gladstone's fiscal masterpiece. Lujo Brentano speaks of the "undying fame" of this manifestation of his "incomparable financial genius." It was a milestone on the path of British financial history, for it developed the principle of Free Trade to its last financial and political consequences, and established it so firmly that for two generations it was able to weather every storm. It repealed the recent protective tariffs and contented itself with financial duties, imposed mainly on such wares as were not produced in England. In so doing, of course, it ran counter to many individual interests, but Gladstone succeeded in making it clear to his listeners, and to the nation, that here a higher and communal interest must be given precedence. Once more, he achieved his great success by the manifest courage with which he attacked the most difficult and politically thorny problems, and also by the fact that he rose to the height of a fundamental standpoint, by which he justified both the commercial treaty with France and his tariff reforms. For example, in vindicating the surviving duties on tea and sugar, despite his purpose of bettering the lot of the working classes by his financial policy, he said:

"It is a mistake to suppose that the best method of giving benefit to the labouring classes is simply to operate on the articles consumed by them. If you want to do them the maximum of good, you should rather operate on the articles which give them the maximum of employment."

He showed that the principal benefit derived from the great financial change of front was not that bread had become a little cheaper, but "that you have set more free the general course of trade . . . that you have put in action the process that gives them the widest field and the highest rate of remuneration for their labour."

Naturally, the speech comprised many ideas which today are superseded or defunct. But how many financial speeches could stand the test of being read ten or twelve years later? Yet in Gladstone's Budget Speech of 1860 we still find much, after the lapse of three-quarters of a century, that impresses us by its factual content and its perfection of form. Its general sense and its significance were summed up in the following peroration, which reveals his individual manner of conceiving the problem—a mixture of sober fiscal policy and moral earnestness: "Our proposals involve a great reform in our tariff, they involve a large remission of taxation, and last of all, though not least, they include that Commercial Treaty with France which . . . we confidently recommend, not only on moral and social and political, but also, and with equal confidence, on fiscal and economical grounds. . . . By pursuing such a course as this it will be in your power to scatter blessings among the people, and blessings which are among the soundest and most wholesome of all the blessings at your disposal, because in legislation of this kind you are not forging mechanical helps for men, nor endeavouring to do that for them which they ought to do for themselves; but you are enlarging their means without narrowing their freedom, you are giving value to their labour, you are appealing to their sense of responsibility, and you are not impairing their sense of honourable self-dependence. There were times, now long gone by, when Sovereigns made progress through the land, and when, at the proclamation of their heralds, they caused to be scattered heaps of coin among the people who thronged upon their steps. That may have been a goodly spectacle; but it is also a goodly spectacle, and one adapted to the altered spirit and circumstances of our times, when our Sovereign is enabled through the wisdom of her great Council assembled in Parliament around her, again to scatter blessings among her subjects by means of wise and prudent laws; of laws which do not sap in any respect the foundations of duty or of manhood, but which strike away the shackles from the arm of industry, which give new incentive and new reward to toil, and which win more and more for the Throne and for the institutions of the country the gratitude, the confidence, and the love of an united people."

The success of the Budget speech of the 10th of February, 1860, was great and uncontested. Once again Prince Albert expressed himself as one of his enthusiastic admirers; writing to his friend and mentor Stockmar—anticipating the course of events by a few years—he declared that "Gladstone is now the real leader of the House and works with an energy and vigour almost incredible." Bulwer Lytton, who recognized literary merit even in a political opponent, prophesied that this speech would be a monument of English oratory so long as there was an English language, and from across the Channel the French Emperor sent—most correctly, through the British Ambassador—a message of thanks, clothed in the most respectful and flattering phraseology. It gave the British people the feeling that Gladstone's firm and considered leadership could be trusted without misgiving in matters of finance, and many were already beginning to feel that they could also entrust other matters to him when once the old generation had retired, whose two aged representatives were still as yet in the foreground.

But this general admiration and recognition did not, of course, mean that there were no sharply-contested Parliamentary conflicts. As far as his adversaries' attacks were directed against the commercial treaty with France the Chancellor could easily repel them. It was approved by a large majority in the Lower House, and even in the Lords its opponents were defeated. People were speaking— so Vitzthum recorded—of "the Magenta and Solferino of Conservatism." But with this, of course, the victory was not won all along the line. Other portions of the Budget met with a stormier reception.

Among those who congratulated and complimented the Chancellor on the day after his great speech was the Prime Minister himself. In his letter to the Queen he was lavish of the most flattering adjectives. He described the speech as admirable, detailed, lucid, comprehensive and eloquent. To the Chancellor himself Palmerston sent a brief note: "I hope," he said, "you are none the worse for that Triumph . . . for which the Government is much the better." Gladstone thanked him for the compliment with a warmth which its brevity seemed hardly to justify. It was, perhaps, to a certain extent of a diplomatic nature. The Chancellor was not quite certain of the Premier's concurrence with all the points of his Budget.

Already, indeed, during the preparation of the Budget, a difference had cropped up which threatened to prove disastrous. Palmerston, in his distrust of Napoleon's murky plans, regarded the fortification of the English coast as essential, and wanted to raise a loan for this purpose.

This struck at the most important and fundamental principle of Gladstone's financial policy: to avoid all expenditure that was not absolutely necessary. He could see no evidence of its necessity; and at the same time, he put no faith in Palmerston's assertions in respect of Napoleon's aggressive intentions. He therefore informed the Prime Minister that he could not agree to his proposal. To do so, he said, "would be on my part, with the views I entertain, a betrayal of my public duty." Not until just before the introduction of the Budget was the difference composed; Palmerston agreed to the postponement of his plans. Yet this, of course, did not dispose of the difficulty. It was bound to come to the fore again sooner or later. But now, unexpectedly, another difference emerged, which was not confined to Downing Street, but was at once exposed in the full glare of publicity.

A special feature of Gladstone's Budget was the abolition of the tax on paper. This had been demanded for years past by the Radicals, who called it "a tax on knowledge." According to them, the increased cost of paper resulting from the tax prevented the production of cheap books, and, above all, so added to the price of newspapers as to make them inaccessible to the less prosperous classes of readers.

A threefold burden had been imposed on the English newspapers by the Inland Revenue Department. To begin with, for every advertisement a tax of one shilling and sixpence was imposed. Gladstone had proposed a great reduction of this tax in his first Budget of 1853; but the House of Commons, incited by the Radicals, went farther than he had intended, and had abolished it entirely. Secondly, each sheet of a newspaper had to bear a penny stamp. It was not surprising that the price of a newspaper had risen to a level inconceivable to us to-day. A copy of *The Times* cost originally 7d., and from 1836 onwards 5d. A year's subscription to the paper cost £6 10s. 0d., at a time when the franchise began with the £10 freeholder. This state of affairs did *The Times* no harm, as it constituted a protection against cheap competition. In the fifties its circulation of 50,000 to 70,000 was three times as large as that of its five chief competitors put together. Not one of these could boast of a circulation exceeding 7,000. The paucity of these figures gives one a tangible idea of the very small number of persons who were able to take any serious interest in political events, and so constituted the nucleus of what one could call "public opinion." With all the more reason, therefore, the democrats were compelled to press for a reform. In 1855 the newspaper stamp duty was abolished. The result was very considerable. *The Times* reduced its price, first to 4½d. and then to 4d. And now for the first time it had a competitor of which it was sensible, as it gradually made its way into circles in which *The Times* had hitherto enjoyed a monopoly. In 1855 the *Daily Telegraph* was founded, and sold at the price of twopence. But a few months later it was acquired by a man whose mercantile genius enabled him to read the signs of the times more closely than his fellows. Joseph Moses Levy not only reduced the price of his paper to one penny; he also increased its size. Under his brilliant control, inherited by generation after generation of his family, the newspaper gradually achieved such a large circulation and such wide popularity that the monopoly of *The Times* was broken.

Now only the third burden weighed upon the Press, the tax on paper, and it was this that Gladstone now intended to abolish. True, this would mean a loss to the revenue of more than a million, but this he believed he could obtain in other ways. He took special pains to explain the reasons for this proposal in his speech, and he did not forget to emphasize its bearing on popular education. Expensive books for the wealthy hardly suffered from the tax. But "on books brought out in large quantities by enterprising publishers for the middle and lower classes it is a very heavy and a very oppressive duty." He considered it "a most desirable and legitimate object to promote the extension of cheap literature." At the same time, he hoped to see the further extension of the cheap newspapers, which had greatly increased their circulation since the removal of the newspaper stamp duty, and whose character since that reform did great credit to their publishers.

At first it seemed as though this proposal would be accepted without more ado. But for various reasons the final decision was in the balance until May. Russell had once more introduced a Bill for electoral reform, which did not get through the House. Then came the popular excitement caused by France's annexation of Nice and Savoy. War had broken out again with China. In the sphere of foreign policy the tension had increased. Those interested in the tax on paper began to bestir themselves; it seemed to the Conservatives that the Budget had suddenly become unpopular, and they hoped that the conflict over this tax would provide them with a useful weapon; even Disraeli, at other times opposed to the "tax on knowledge," collaborated with them. The result was that the motion was accepted by only a bare majority of nine votes.

But worse was to follow. The Prime Minister was not in favour of the abolition of the paper duty. The surrender of such a source of revenue sorted ill with his costly plans for rearmament. He was not interested in the reduction of the cost of newspapers. He relied on *The Times* and his devoted friend Delane, its shrewd and able editor, a popular and influential figure in the political *salons* of London. A great expansion of the newspaper-reading public was as little desired by him as a great expansion of the electorate. He had already spoken against the lifting of the tax in the Cabinet. He had a perfect right to do so. But he was guilty of a really incredible and irresponsible action when in writing to the Queen he declared that if the Lords, encouraged by the small majority in the Lower House, were to reject the proposal they would "perform a good public service," and that the Government would be glad to see this settlement of the matter.

Gladstone first learned of this letter, which sheds such an ugly light on Palmerston's character, only some decades later, when it was published in the biography of the Prince Consort. But he was well aware that certain members were working against him, and the agitation caused by this knowledge made him ill. His fears were realized. The Upper House not only rejected the motion, but the Leader of the Opposition, Lord Derby, called the Chancellor "a desperate and improvident gambler." The Prime Minister did not fail to report to the Queen, who quite approved of the attitude of the Lords, as evidence of the popular temper, that "the people in the gallery of the House of Lords are said to have joined in the cheers which broke out when the numbers of the division were announced." As a matter of fact, Lady Palmerston was sitting there and she loudly expressed her delight in the result of the division. Less than nine months earlier, on reading in her boudoir Gladstone's speech on the Italian question, she had cried aloud in her enthusiasm.

Lady Palmerston's jubilation was her own affair, but if the Lords were delighted over the result of the division they had soon cause to ask themselves whether they had not made a great mistake. For their adverse vote gave rise to a serious political controversy. In every State where Parliament consists of two chambers the constitutional control of financial business is a problem. In Prussia this problem was the juristic nucleus of the constitutional conflict which broke out a few years later between Bismarck and the Chamber of Deputies; and this conflict, and its final issue, exerted a decisive influence on the subsequent history of Germany. The problem is always the same: whether the popularly elected chamber has the sole right to control the finances of the State, or whether it must concede to the upper chamber the right of more or less effective collaboration. In England, in the course of five hundred years, the financial centre of gravity had been displaced further and further in the direction of the Lower House, which was elected by the taxpayers, and which claimed, with increasing success, the sole right to vote on supplies. The Lords did not dispute the fact that they had not the right to vote on taxation, nor to amend a finance Bill passed by the Lower House. But what of their right to withhold their assent to a fiscal measure accepted by the Lower House? In the decisive session of the Upper House the aged Lord Lyndhurst, a former Lord Chancellor—who had left his warm fireside on his eighty-eighth birthday in order to address the House—rose from his seat and proved, to the satisfaction of the Lords, in a speech in which he manifested all his famous juristic perspicacity, and a fabulous vivacity, that they were justified in rejecting a motion to impose a tax, and also a motion to abolish a tax.

Palmerston was naturally inclined to accept not only the adverse vote of the Lords, but also its constitutional justification. Not so Gladstone, however! "This proceeding of the House of Lords," he explained to the Cabinet, "amounted to the establishment of a revising power over the House of Commons in its most vital function, long declared exclusively its own." He demanded "action founded on the principle that the Lords are not to tax the people without their consent." As a matter of fact, a Chancellor of the Exchequer cannot serve two masters, and a Budget would be an impossibility if an Upper and a Lower House with equal rights were to take different sides. Palmerston had finally to give way to some extent. It was agreed that the question should be examined by a commission, and this produced three resolutions, which the House accepted without opposition, but whose full scope only the Chancellor of the Exchequer may have understood.

While Palmerston believed and hoped that these resolutions had settled the whole business, Gladstone regarded them as a beginning only, so that it is not surprising that the unity outwardly apparent in respect of the negotiation of these resolutions was immediately followed by a rupture. As Prime Minister, Palmerston was obliged to introduce the resolutions; but from the manner in which he acquitted himself of his task all could see that he was in complete agreement with the Upper House. Gladstone could contain himself no longer. Even before the debate he had informed the Prime Minister that while he assented to the resolutions he "did not desire in the debate to bind himself to that course" if either side of the House should call for more drastic action. And since Palmerston went too far in the other direction, he too spoke his mind: passionately and eloquently attacking the Lords and their "gigantic innovation." It was a brilliant speech, but it was almost an open revolt against the Prime Minister, and Count Vitzthum, in his despatch to Count Beust, was pleased to speak of a "tactless outburst" and "the lamentable role of Gladstone." But the aged Palmerston knew better than the Saxon diplomatist what Gladstone meant to his Government, and he refrained from making any sort of capital out of the episode.

Even so, the results were sufficiently far-reaching; above all, for Gladstone's inner development. Only a little before this the Conservatives had still been courting him. But this time Derby and Disraeli sent Lord Malmesbury to Lady Palmerston, to whisper to her that if the Premier was willing to part company with Gladstone and Russell they were ready to ally themselves with him against the Radicals. When the altercation had occurred in Parliament they were convinced that their time had come, and Malmesbury remarked with evident discomfort that after all Gladstone had not resigned. The report that reached him soon afterwards, that "Gladstone is now quite enthusiastic about negro melodies, singing them with the greatest spirit and enjoyment," cannot have given him equivalent satisfaction.

These party intrigues were merely a symptom of the change that had taken place in Gladstone's attitude during the months of his collaboration in Palmerston's Government. He had entered it from the right; now suddenly his place was on its left wing. His speech had been greeted with tempestuous applause by the Radicals alone, and John Bright was now his declared ally in the attempt to instigate a popular movement against the Upper House. His success, however, was small. So at least *The Times* asserted, and the witty cartoonists of *Punch*. This made Bright more than ever anxious to shatter "the unwholesome supremacy of the wretches who direct *The Times!*" Whether they had rightly interpreted the temper of the people may be doubted in view of the popularity which Gladstone achieved when in the following year he won a triumphant victory over the Lords.

But before this happened his position was more sharply defined.

Palmerston insisted that the ports must be fortified; Gladstone did not consider that this was necessary; he held that the expense of such a proceeding could be avoided, and from his standpoint, which was one of the greatest frugality, he regarded it as indefensible. There were sharp altercations in the Cabinet, in the course of which the Chancellor threatened to resign. Palmerston reported this to the Queen, with the consequential comment that "however great the loss of the Government by the retirement of Mr. Gladstone, it would be better to lose Mr. Gladstone than to run the risk of losing Portsmouth or Plymouth." Despite this unamiable remark, he finally made it up with the Chancellor. But when he laid the proposal before the Lower House he accompanied it with a patriotic fanfare, and an attack on his sometime friend Napoleon: Heavy storms, he declared, were on the horizon, and the most immediate danger threatened from our powerful neighbour, the Emperor of the French. Palmerston's speech was highly provocative, and entirely directed against France.

Neither Gladstone nor Russell was in the House at the time. But next morning Gladstone sent the Prime Minister a few lines of protest. The controversy continued for months, on paper and by word of mouth. Palmerston demanded further considerable and costly reinforcements of the Navy, in view of the alleged French plan of attack. Gladstone put up a strong defence. Just how inconvenient the Prime Minister was finding his all too conscientious and frugal Chancellor is shown by the New Year's letter which he wrote to the Queen at the beginning of 1861. He spoke of Lord John Russell's wish to retire to the Upper House, and ventured the comment, in the half serious, half jocular manner that was one of his characteristics, that "he would think himself doing better service by recommending the House of Lords for Mr. Gladstone than for Lord J. R." Gladstone himself, at this same New Year, received a letter from Bright, who treated of the same theme in a rather different manner: "The men," he wrote, "whose minds are full of the traditions of the last century, your chief and your foreign minister, will still cling to the past, and will seek to model the present upon it—but the past is wellnigh really past, and a new policy and a wiser and higher morality are sighed for by the best of our people, and there is a prevalent feeling that you are destined to guide that wiser policy and to teach that higher morality." Such a letter from such a man might console Gladstone for the frequent want of appreciation of his colleagues, and strengthen him in the battle for what he believed to be right.

This battle very soon reached a critical stage. In February 1861 Gladstone wrote an exhaustive memorandum, in which he asserted, without circumlocution, that Palmerston's declarations in Parliament, which had related the plan of fortification with the alleged French plans of attack, had been productive of highly prejudicial, not to say dangerous consequences. In equally plain terms Palmerston replied that "no doubt a full Exchequer is a good Foundation for National Defence, but if the superstructure is wanting, the Foundation would be of small avail . . . (and) likely to lead to disaster or humiliation." This was evidently a preliminary for a very considerable demand for naval expansion.

On receiving this letter Gladstone had the feeling that the Premier wanted to get rid of him. If it came to their parting company he himself would resign. He therefore wrote a perfectly courteous but very definite letter in which he tendered his resignation, but—he kept it until he could give a verbal explanation of his position. As a result of this conversation he was able to pigeon-hole the letter, for Palmerston renounced his naval programme.

In the matter of armaments Gladstone had to proceed with the greatest caution. He knew well enough that public opinion was entirely on Palmerston's side. Once again one of those panics had broken out which attack the British people from time to time, and which Cobden described and criticized in a well-known pamphlet. Gladstone had to take into account the fact that his words would find no echo in the minds of the majority of the electorate if he had to resign office on account of increased expenditure on armaments. He saw himself threatened with the fate that thirty years later was to overtake Lord Randolph Churchill, as the penalty of deficient foresight. His position in the Cabinet was by no means comfortable. He himself has characterized it exactly in a phrase contained in a letter to his colleague, the Duke of Argyll: when he thought of the Cabinet he was always reminded of Jacob and Esau, who contended even in their mother's womb. But he accepted the vexations connected with his office because he had a task in which his heart and his conscience were involved. And the first thing to be done was to settle the conflict with the Upper House.

He had found a way which must bring him to victory, and which would also lead to great financial improvement. Hitherto the kind of finance Bill obtaining in most of the Continental States, by which the revenue and expenditure for one year were summed up in a single measure, was alien to English practice. On the contrary, each individual tax had to be sanctioned by a special Act. Gladstone now conceived the notion of comprising at least the whole of the taxes for the financial year in a single Bill, the Finance Bill. In the light of the controversy excited by the paper duty, this meant that the Lords were no longer in the position to vote against a single tax sanctioned by the Commons, or the abolition of a single tax, but were confronted by the problem of rejecting the Finance Bill as a whole—that is, the Budget—and of withholding from the State the means for a year's subsistence. So the Chancellor understood the third and most important of the resolutions which the Lower House had unanimously accepted the year before, that "the right of granting aids and supplies to the Crown is in the Commons alone, as an essential part of their constitution; and the limitation of all such grants as to the matter, manner, measure, and time, is only in them."

The innovation which Gladstone proposed to the Cabinet was regarded with little approval. After the first discussion his brief and eloquent comment was: "Chaos." Palmerston was least of all inclined to approve of it. During the debate on the Budget he lost control of himself for the first and only time. His objection to the measure was all the greater in that Gladstone combined the renewed proposal to abolish the tax on paper with a further proposal, whose tactical cleverness was equalled only by its practical importance: he wanted to take a penny off the income-tax. This not only made it all but impossible for the Lords to throw out the Bill; it also frustrated Palmerston's costly armament schemes. But all resistance was in vain: Gladstone had his way.

Palmerston was obliged to surrender: but not without resentment. On the day before his Budget Speech the Chancellor received a letter in which the Prime Minister announced in plain terms: "As far as I am concerned, I do not intend to make the Fate of my administration depend upon the Decision which Parliament may come to over your proposal." Gladstone, putting the best face on the matter, contented himself with a non-committal and amiable reply. All that mattered to him now was the cause, which he did not wish under any circumstances to imperil.

He was victorious all along the line. Disraeli did his very utmost to defeat the Budget, and especially the removal of the paper tax. He felt his defeat all the more keenly in that it came about by the secession of distinguished Conservatives, who could not avoid seeing that the homogeneous Finance Bill constituted a very real progress. The excitement of the contest frayed Gladstone's nerves. Previously, thanks to his vitality, he had always been able to put the subject of Parliamentary warfare out of mind as soon as the session was ended; but now, for the first time, he found himself unable to do so.

With grief and anxiety Catherine Gladstone saw how her adored husband was suffering as the result of this continual excitement. Was there no way in which she could help him? She could not, like Lady Palmerston, pull strings and manipulate the political barometer, but perhaps she could speak a word in confidence to an old friend. So she summoned up her courage and wrote a letter to Sir James Graham. He was now nearly seventy years of age, and weary of the endless struggle. Nowadays he rarely spoke in the House which he had adorned for forty years. But when he received Catherine Gladstone's letter, which referred in moving words to his old friendship for Gladstone, saying how happy her husband would be if he would speak in support of his Budget, he could not resist the appeal. Her husband, she said, did not know that she was writing to Sir James. But because she knew that Graham loved him, and took a cordial interest in his career, she made bold to speak to him. She well knew with what affection he looked back on the old days, and how great was his veneration for Sir Robert Peel and the dear friends with whom it had been his pride and his joy to collaborate. Such a letter, no doubt, was unconventional, but Catherine Gladstone was never conventional, and she knew the man to whom she was addressing herself. Graham spoke in support of the Budget —it was his last speech of any importance—and his support contributed not a little to its successful passage through the Lower House.

With the victory in the Commons the battle was won. The Lords did not dare to repeat the trial of strength of the previous year. They could not fail to realize that their attempt to meddle with taxation had subjected them to a serious defeat. It was fifty years before they forgot it. Not until 1909 did the Upper House venture to throw out a Budget—Lloyd George's. This time the conflict ended with an even more serious defeat of the Lords. The Parliament Act of 1911 is its lasting memorial.

Gladstone had won this great success almost exclusively by his own personal efforts. He had the Conservative Opposition, his own Prime Minister, the Queen, *The Times* and *Punch* against him, and he obtained support only from those who did not dare to express their opinion too loudly lest they should imperil his cause. But not only was he more than a match for all his opponents—he even won over the recalcitrant by the power and magic of his eloquence. "He talks shop like a tenth Muse," wrote a critical observer: no small compliment, when the "shop" was taxation!

The sharper the conflict, the greater the impression produced by it, especially in those who reaped the immediate harvest: for it brought to the citizen's door, not indeed his daily bread, but the daily newspaper. A later age, which has seen how often the expansion of the Press has served to excite men's passions, may think more sceptically of the utility of the cheap newspaper. But Gladstone's period, rejoicing in education and having faith in the blessings of enlightenment, had a hopeful and admirable confidence in the progress of civilization; for such progress there must be if everyone, even the humblest, were in a position to learn, day by day, what was happening in the world about him. It was the firm conviction of Bright and Cobden that the Press would promote peace and good will between men of different nationality and religion, and the British artisan and petty bourgeois began to name in the same breath with Bright and Cobden the Chancellor of the Exchequer, though only a few years earlier they could not have said whether they were to regard him as a Liberal or a Conservative. The prophetic words which Bright had addressed to him at the New Year were beginning to come true. Many considered that in this conflict he had revealed a quality of which not every politician can boast: the passionate earnestness with which he devoted himself to his cause. The groundlings on the floor of the House might smile occasionally at the burning zeal which he displayed in debate; but the simple folk became aware of the ethical fire that blazed in the heart of the pious Chancellor.

And their perception of this moral fire could not fail to affect Gladstone's way of looking at things. In obedience to the law of mutual attraction, which operates between every politician and his supporters, he felt more and more drawn to the people who flocked to hear him whenever he spoke in public, who surrendered themselves with delight to the spell of his eloquence, and rewarded him with enthusiastic applause.

But it was not in the first place his rhetoric that won him his great popularity; it was rather the great and indisputable benefit which his financial and commercial policy had bestowed upon the whole country, and especially upon those of whom Peel had said, in his farewell speech in 1846, that they earn their daily bread by the sweat of their brow. For seven years, on this occasion, from 1859 to 1866, Gladstone was in charge of the country's finances, and with every year his success became more evident. In his Budget speech of 1863, with which—as he wrote in his diary—he "wound up . . . a chapter in finance and in his life," he gave a survey of the progress effected, and it was a record to gratify the nation and fill the Chancellor with pride. It was enough to mention that the national income, in the years 1853–61, had increased by 20 per cent. "But," he added, "I should look with some degree of pain upon this extraordinary and almost intoxicating growth, if it were my belief that it is confined to the class of persons who may be described as living in easy circumstances. . . . It is a matter of profound and inestimable consolation to reflect that while the rich have been growing richer, the poor have become less poor. . . . If we look to the average condition of the British labourer, we know from varied and indubitable evidence that, during the last twenty years, such an addition has been made to his means of subsistence, as we may almost pronounce to be without example in the history of any country and of any age."

This was not the rhetorical exaggeration of an optimistic Chancellor. Expert inquiry has confirmed it, and Froude, an enthusiastic admirer of Disraeli, sums up the blessings of Free Trade in England in the exultant phrase: "Amalthea's horn of plenty was full to overflowing."

But in this same year of 1863 Gladstone showed that the wine of increasing popularity had not gone to his head; that he had not forgotten how to swim against the tide, and that he refused to sacrifice the convictions won in strenuous labour to popular prejudice, however strong and widespread. In the Budget of 1863 he proposed to extend the income-tax to charitable institutions. In no country do such foundations play so important a part as in England, so that nowhere could such a proposal encounter more vigorous opposition. The deputation to the Chancellor which gave expression to the protest of the institutions affected was headed by a royal Prince and two Archbishops, and included all the most respected personalities in religious and social life; as, for example, the indefatigable pioneer of legislation designed to protect labour, Lord Shaftesbury. It was a protest which might well have made a man fear for his reputation among right-thinking people, had he not possessed, in the highest degree, the courage of his own convictions. On the very day on which he had received these distinguished visitors in the Chancellor's office, he rose from his seat on the Treasury bench, and for three hours spoke exhaustively and frankly in defence of his proposal, without surrendering an inch of ground. The disputed point is merely a fiscal detail, and to-day it is buried under the dust of seventy years. But what gives this speech of Gladstone's an undying interest is not the cause for which he contended, but the manner of his defence. The unprejudiced acuteness with which he stated the problem, the various standpoints from which he considered it, and the data by which he illustrated his argument, were outweighed by the courage with which he unveiled the self-seeking spirit that lurked behind many a seemingly benevolent action; and in particular he showed up "death-bed" benevolence in its true light. This he could do with the clearest conscience, and he had no need to fear that anyone would contrast the private man with the Chancellor of the Exchequer. For he himself gave generously to the utmost of his ability, and his carefully-kept accounts show that he gave for charitable objects very much more than he retained for his own use, quite apart from the large sums which he distributed among members of his family during his lifetime.

That he lost his case—perhaps his only great financial defeat—does not in any way diminish the value of his performance, even though his speech was to be no more than a contribution to Schopenhauer's doctrine of "that which a man is" and "that which a man represents."

On the other hand, an outwardly inconspicuous but highly beneficial achievement shows that the Chancellor was most earnestly mindful of the welfare of the less prosperous classes of the nation. In his old age Gladstone once summed up the five or six pieces of legislation for which he was responsible on which he looked back with especial satisfaction. Among them was the founding of the Post Office Savings-Banks, which he established in 1861, and which achieved the most stupendous development even during his lifetime. It gave him peculiar pleasure to think that he had done something for those who wished to help themselves by thrift.

In the contest with Palmerston over the question of disarmament Gladstone was finally victorious. The dreaded French attack was never delivered. The English coastal defences were never utilized, and the panic subsided as it had arisen. Yet this did not mean that his differences with Palmerston were things of the past. But they assumed a milder form after Palmerston, in the summer of 1861, had replied to an offer of resignation—evoked by a dispute on a question of secondary importance—with the words: "I should consider the Termination of our official connection as a real misfortune to myself, to the Government and to the public Service." But the disputes over the armaments question continued until 1865, and almost every Budget was prefaced by a correspondence in which the letters of the two Ministers often assumed the dimensions of actual negotiations. Gladstone wished to reduce the Budgets, and wrote to the Prime Minister stating that their exaggerated dimensions could be attributed only to Palmerston's extraordinary popularity. Palmerston replied: "You misplace Cause and Effect . . . it has been because they think that I have endeavoured to maintain the Dignity of the Country and to uphold it abroad, and to provide for its security at home. You may depend on it that any Degree of Popularity that is worth having can be obtained only by such means and of that Popularity I sincerely wish you the most ample share."

But in the end the Chancellor had his way to a certain extent. The expenditure on armaments was no greater when he resigned office than when he entered the Cabinet; it had even been reduced by a few million pounds. This, as against a fatalistic conviction that such expenditure is bound, by an inherent tendency, to rise incessantly, and that no financial skill can alter the fact, was no negligible achievement.

One of the enduring successes of this period of Gladstone's financial activities was the commercial treaty with France. It lasted for twenty years, outliving Napoleon's government. How far it contributed to the maintenance of peace, which in Palmerston's imagination was threatened by the dark schemes of the Emperor, it is difficult to estimate. As a matter of fact, the danger of international complications threatened from quite a different direction. On the 9th of January, 1861, the guns of Fort Sumter, on the other side of the Atlantic, fired the first shot that heralded the secession of the Southern States of the North American Union, and marked the beginning of four years of a bitter and bloody civil war.

4. *A Singular Error*

It is one of the most singular circumstances of Gladstone's development that his most indubitable blunder was his error of judgement
in respect of a great historical event that did more to advance
the political movement which he was following at the height of
his political achievement than any other event of the nineteenth
century. The great war of the Northern States of the Union
against the seceding Southern States not only put an end to slavery,
but it also won the final victory of the democratic over the aristocratic conception of the State. And not only for North America.
The democracy of the Northern States, based on the equality of
all its citizens, had proved itself capable of carrying on an arduous
four years' campaign, in which all the military talent was at first
on the side of the enemy, and of evolving out of itself the forces
which gradually counterbalanced all its disadvantages, and finally
gave it the victory. This it did under the leadership of a man
who united in his person all the qualities which the imagination
would confer on the democratic politician only; emerging from
the humblest circles of society, simple, kindly, and human, full of
political shrewdness, and inflexible in misfortune, devoid of
arrogance, and conciliatory when victorious. This great example
had the greatest influence on the political evolution of Europe as
well as that of America. But while the great war was being waged
only a very few people in England had any insight into its character.
One of these few was John Bright, whose clear and straightforward
mind was not confused or misled by any subtleties. Everywhere
he told the workers, for whose right to vote he was contending,
that the cause of the Union was their cause, that they must take the
side of those who were liberating the slaves, and that they must
not be led astray by the serious economic distress which the
American Civil War had brought upon them.

For the blockade which the Union had imposed on the ports of
the cotton-exporting South was disastrous to the English textile
industry. In the centre of the industry, in Lancashire, as a result
of the dearth of cotton, hundreds of thousands of spindles were
still and tens of thousands of workers were unemployed. Despite

their distress, the British workers were loyal to the cause of personal liberty, and Lincoln spoke only the truth when he wrote to the working-men of Manchester, who had spoken loudly and decisively in support of the abolition of slavery, that their attitude was "an instance of sublime heroism which has not been surpassed in any age or in any country."

But Gladstone, at this time, was far from taking this clear and simple view of the matter. He naturally sympathized with the campaign against slavery, but to his thinking the question whether the Union should use violent means to compel the States which desired to go their own way to return to it was a very different matter; and he spoke very critically of "the freaks, pranks and follies" by which the Northern States had reacted to the secession. Above all, the military successes of the Southern States during the first years of the war convinced him more and more that it would be quite impossible to subdue them.

In the beginning he preserved, better than any other member of the Ministry, an attitude of cool deliberation. At the end of the year 1861 the *Trent* affair brought England to the brink of war with the Union. Two commissaries of the Southern States, Mason and Slidell, had taken passage for Europe on the *Trent*, an English vessel. The captain of an American warship had forcibly removed them and had taken them as prisoners to an American port. The two nations concerned reacted as is usual in such cases. The Americans fêted their captain as a national hero, and the English were furious because their national honour had been insulted.

Palmerston and Russell proposed to the Cabinet that the American Government should be requested, in a strongly-worded Note, to make reparation—that is, to release the prisoners forthwith. But it was evident that the refusal of this request must lead to war. It was Gladstone who objected to this course; let them first hear what the Americans had to say in justification of their action. But he was voted down.

Then another man intervened; and this was his last opportunity of placing his keen and far-sighted intelligence at England's service. The Note was sent to Windsor, in order to receive the Queen's approval. Like all documents of decisive importance, it was laid before the Prince Consort. Albert was at this time already seriously ill; but his unfailing sense of duty made him study the Note with meticulous attention. He realized that prudence demanded that the American Government should be offered an easy and dignified means of retreat. With a hand that could hardly hold the pen he wrote the draft of a letter from the Queen in which she requested her Ministers to express the hope in their Note that the American captain had acted without instructions from his Government. The Cabinet followed this sensible advice. Lincoln too was accessible to good advice, and so before long the matter was settled; Mason and Slidell were released, and the storm blew over.

But on Albert's draft these words are written in the Queen's hand:

"This draft was the last the beloved Prince ever wrote."

A fortnight later, on the 14th of December, 1861, Prince Albert died, and Queen Victoria, at the age of forty-two, was left a heartbroken widow, despairing of the future, whose thoughts for many years were centred on her loss and the memory of her beloved dead. She was grateful for every word that was dedicated to his memory, and when Gladstone, at Manchester, spoke with respect and affection of the dead Prince, the Queen poured out her thanks in a letter whose broken phrases are moving evidence of her tempestuous grief. It closed with the sentence: "Mrs. Gladstone, who, as the Queen knows, is a most loving wife, may have some faint idea of what the Queen is suffering." In Gladstone's letter of reply the profoundest human compassion and the noblest piety are joined with the reverent devotion which he always felt for the Queen. The Queen was grateful for his words, and in the following years she often spoke to him of her bereavement. For Gladstone, too, the untimely death of the Prince Consort was a real loss. His objectivity, his honesty, and his moral earnestness had endeared him to the Prince, who was conscious of possessing the same qualities. It is possible that if the Prince had lived longer he would have enabled the Queen to understand many particulars of Gladstone's policies, and of his way of looking at things, which in after years were causes of dissension. Albert's eldest daughter, the

140

Princess Victoria, always cherished for Gladstone the sympathy which her father had felt for him.

But life continued—and so did the bloody civil war beyond the Atlantic. And the longer it lasted, the more grievously did England suffer from the dearth of cotton, and the more anxiously did Ministers ask themselves whether there was no means of ending the war, and the more obstinately did they persist in the delusion which had seized upon the upper middle class, that the North had no prospect of winning the war. In September 1862, when the war had continued for eighteen months, and almost every action had been decided in the favour of the South, the Prime Minister wrote to Gladstone "that he himself and Lord Russell thought the time was fast approaching when an offer of mediation ought to be made by England, France and Russia." Gladstone was in complete agreement with them. He thought that such a step was urgent for two reasons; firstly, because of the sufferings of the people of Lancashire, and secondly, because the Confederate Army was making such rapid progress that the Southern States might very shortly be able to claim recognition as an independent nation.

He was fully possessed by this erroneous judgement of the situation when, a little later, he had to speak of it in public. The Liberals of the great industrial city of Newcastle, who stood in the foremost ranks of the Party, had begged him to visit them. They gave him a reception marked by unprecedented enthusiasm. It was the first time that he had come into direct contact with a great industrial population; the first time that he had had a chance of realizing that the enthusiasm of the people had lifted him high above his political contemporaries. Mrs. Gladstone, in her naïve admiration for her husband, told one of his followers, twenty years later: "I shall never forget that day. It was the first time that he was received as he deserved to be."

If Gladstone himself was bound to recall this occasion, in later years, with a sense of regret, it was because he had allowed himself to be carried away, and to utter words concerning the American Civil War which had proved almost disastrous. Of Jefferson Davis, the President of the Confederate States, he cried: "He has made an army; he is making, it appears, a navy; and he has made what is more than either, he has made *a nation.*"

Such words on the lips of the Chancellor of the Exchequer, one of the most important and influential members of the Cabinet, were interpreted by the whole world to mean that England was on the point of recognizing the newly-created State, when she would throw the whole weight of her authority into the balance. On the cotton market prices came tumbling down from the heights to which the blockade had driven them. The American Minister in London calculated that he would soon be homeward bound; the further consequences were past reckoning. Fortunately it speedily appeared that Gladstone was not in this case the spokesman of the Cabinet. The majority regarded the question of recognition with misgiving; even Palmerston finally spoke in favour of postponement; and when they reverted to the question a few months later the military situation was very different, and all were thankful that they had not burned their fingers.

Gladstone's premature and ill-considered sally was severely criticized, and by no one more severely than by himself. A generation later he was to call it not only "an undoubted error," but also "the most singular and palpable error . . . the least excusable."

5. Schleswig-Holstein

While across the Atlantic a great nation was battling to preserve its political unity, and on the shores of the Mediterranean another was waiting for the moment to complete a unity half achieved, a third nation, in the heart of Europe, was seeking the path that would lead to the unity long desired. Like the United States and Italy, Germany found the great statesman who crowned her efforts with success. Like Lincoln and Cavour, Bismarck had made the outer world aware of his existence only just before he set his hand to his historic task. But neither his manner nor his appearance was calculated to find understanding among British statesmen. They knew that he was in violent conflict with the Parliament of his own country, in which he had dealt with questions of legal

142

procedure in a somewhat arbitrary fashion. They found it difficult to understand that in 1863 he had assisted the Tsar in suppressing the Polish insurrection, and had even permitted him to arrest Polish refugees on Prussian soil.

He had become a European figure when on the death of King Frederick VII of Denmark on the 15th of November, 1863, the Schleswig-Holstein question entered upon its acute stage.

Of this question Palmerston is reported to have said that there were only three men who had understood it; one of them, Prince Albert, was dead; the second, a German professor, had gone crazy; and the third—he himself—had forgotten it. The fact is that it was one of those questions whose actual crux is as simple as its historic and juristic structure is complicated. The actual cause of the dispute was this: the German population of the former Duchies of Holstein and Schleswig were anxious to break loose from the connection with the kingdom of Denmark, which was too close to satisfy their national aspirations, and not close enough to assure the Danes of permanent sovereignty. Holstein belonged to the Deutscher Bund; Schleswig did not. But both Duchies asserted their claim to remain for all times "undivided." Consequently any constitution that might be devised or applied must infringe either the German or the Danish ideals and demands. Further, the law regulating the succession to the throne was different in the two countries. The fact that Bismarck succeeded, with equal skill, in exploiting the juristic difficulties, the political desires of the German people, and the rivalry of Austria, to the benefit of his Prussian policy, and in emerging as the undisputed victor and master from the wars of 1864 and 1866, will always evoke the astonished admiration of the historians. That his contemporaries often took a very different view of him is, of course, not surprising. In England, when Germany and Austria took up arms against Denmark, the majority were very definitely on the side of Denmark. One thing that contributed to this was the fact that in this same year the Prince of Wales was married to the very popular daughter of the new Danish king. But the principal cause of this attitude was the thought that little Denmark was in danger of being overwhelmed by the great Germanic Powers, and the Englishman's lack of understanding for the political ideals and objects of the Germans.

No one stressed this lack of understanding more sharply than Queen Victoria. She felt that in respect of this question she had the advantage of all the English politicians, for Prince Albert had explained the matter in every detail. For her his opinions were a sacred legacy. Prince Albert had always remained a good German, and he had a clearer and more sympathetic understanding of the German movement towards unity than any English statesman. Consequently the Queen was now in opposition to Palmerston and Russell, whose policy she followed with alarm and anxiety. She felt more grievously than ever the loss of her husband. Again and again in her letters—especially in those to Lord Granville, her confidant among the Cabinet Ministers—the complaint recurs that she is "alone and unaided. . . . The Queen suffers much and her nerves are more and more totally shattered." In Parliament Palmerston had permitted himself to make a declaration which seemed to go altogether too far. In July 1863 he spoke most emphatically in favour of maintaining the independence and integrity of Denmark, and he continued: "We are convinced—I am convinced at least—that if any violent attempt were made to overthrow the rights and to interfere with the independence of Denmark, those who made the attempt would find in the result that it would not be Denmark alone with which they would have to contend."

Whatever Palmerston meant by this, the whole world accepted his words as a declaration that in the event of war England would take up arms in defence of Denmark. In Denmark, more particularly, this belief was general, and this is one of the principal reasons of her otherwise unintelligible obstinacy, which prevented a timely understanding.

Everybody was bound to assume that the Prime Minister had discussed the matter with his Cabinet before making such an important declaration. As a matter of fact, he had done nothing of the kind. Gladstone, in particular, was taken completely by surprise. Nor was the Queen questioned, and before she started on her journey to Coburg in August 1863 she had expressly forbidden the Prime Minister to take any steps whatever in the domain of foreign affairs without her previous approval, especially in respect of Schleswig-Holstein, "about which the shameful bad faith of the Danes may lead to serious mischief." When at the close of 1863, on the approach of the outbreak of war, Palmerston brought the matter up before the Cabinet, the latter refused to consider itself bound by his hasty declaration. The majority declared that it was out of the question that England alone should intervene in the war; France, at least, must also take part in it.

Gladstone, who was becoming more and more definitely the leader of the peace party in the Cabinet, was largely responsible for this resolution. As the march of destiny irresistibly closed in upon Denmark, Palmerston was once more confronted by the question whether England alone, without allies, was to take up arms against the great Germanic Powers. Both he and Russell were inclined to answer the question in the affirmative, and risk the consequences. The Queen was definitely, and indeed passionately opposed to such a course. Unfortunately her views were known to the public, and a member of the Opposition, distinguished by a peculiar tactlessness, permitted himself to make an attack upon her in the House of Lords which absolutely infuriated her. She therefore felt it all the more essential that she should apprise the Cabinet of her views and her reasons for holding them. She even appealed to Gladstone, and in him she found the support that she needed. He confronted Russell with the convincing proof that England was in no position whatever to intervene with success. Her land army, compared with the German forces, was quite without significance. She could not send more than 20,000 men into the field, while the German troops numbered hundreds of thousands. "The country had no wish whatever to go to war, and their excitement arose entirely from misapprehension of the question."

The great majority of the Ministers supported Gladstone. Palmerston, who had followed the argument with bowed head in silence, wound it up with a single sentence: "I think the Cabinet is against war"; and with that the Schleswig-Holstein question was a closed chapter as far as British foreign policy was concerned.

145

The Queen drew a sigh of relief. To Gladstone, with whom she had discussed the matter exhaustively, she was especially grateful.

There was a domestic epilogue to all this. The Government's policy had been so full of contradictions, and the public was so taken aback by its results, that the Opposition could not allow the opportunity of a frontal attack to go by. Disraeli, in a great speech, ruthlessly reproached the Government with all the errors of its Danish policy, and challenged the House to pass an unequivocal vote of "no confidence." Palmerston had taken the precaution of writing to Gladstone: "We shall want a great gun to follow Disraeli. Would you be ready to follow him?" Little as Gladstone could approve of all that Palmerston and Russell had done and left undone, he as willingly accepted the task, and acquitted himself as brilliantly. Vitzthum, who was wholly on Disraeli's side, paid Gladstone the doubtful compliment of declaring that the worse the cause which he represented, the greater his eloquence.

The praise of his other listeners was more unconditional. An independent Member, and a witty and vivacious critic of the Cabinet, who described it as "a museum of curiosities," expressly excepted the Chancellor as "a very great and able Minister." But his greatest triumph came when Palmerston himself rose to speak. The octogenarian Prime Minister was far too quick-witted not to realize that an apology for his Danish policy would find no echo in the House. With the greatest adroitness he treated the attack of the Opposition as a pretext for putting up a defence of his whole conduct of the Government. But what he adduced in justification of his Government, and deserving of praise, was—Gladstone's financial policy, to which no one had opposed so many obstacles as he himself. If there is more joy over a repentant sinner than over a hundred of the righteous, the Chancellor could indeed rejoice over this "effective repentance" of his chief—though this, of course, did not in the least prevent him from again making all sorts of difficulties in the following year.

At all events, the move was successful. The Government obtained a majority. The decision rested with Cobden and his friends. Little as he cared for Palmerston's foreign policy, as little did he anticipate any improvement if Derby and Disraeli should take the helm. It

146

seemed to him that one thing had been achieved: the principle of non-intervention, which he had upheld all his life, had triumphed, and for this reason he voted for the Government.

And so it came about that Lord Palmerston was able to remain Prime Minister of England for the brief term of life that was still vouchsafed to him.

THE SECOND ENCOUNTER WITH DISRAELI

1. *Leader of the House*

On the 18th of October, 1865, Lord Palmerston died, two days before the completion of his eighty-first year. With his death there disappeared from the stage of British and Continental politics an imposing figure, despite all his weaknesses; the last European statesman who had been a Minister when Napoleon was at the zenith of his career, and who had played his part in what for others was merely history.

But however men might marvel at his astonishing vitality, they could not but realize that there must be new laws to fit the new age, and this Palmerston would not recognize. "What am I to say about internal political reforms?" asked a by no means Radical supporter, the clever and cool-headed banker Goschen, Member of Parliament for the City of London, in 1864, when he called on the old Minister in connection with the reply to the Address. "Oh, there's nothing to be done," he replied, comfortably rubbing his hands; "we cannot go on adding to the Statute Book *ad infinitum!*" Such quietism was not made more tolerable by the fact that he called himself a Liberal. John Bright wrote, at the news of his death: "We are breaking with the old generation, and I hope we shall see the rise of newer and better principles and policies." So thought many others who were not accounted as radical as Bright.

Of course, there was still another old man who for the time being must fill Palmerston's place. But Lord Russell had been sitting for some years past in the House of Lords; in the Cabinet, and above all, in the House, he could only play the part of an elder statesman, presiding by virtue of seniority. The question to be answered was this: who would undertake the leadership of the Lower House, where the decisive battles for England's future policies must be fought? Formally the choice was in the hands of the new Prime Minister, but Russell knew, as did everyone else, that there was only one choice possible: Gladstone. Even old King Leopold, who still continued to favour his niece with his advice, described him as "the natural leader." Palmerston had foreseen this, but the thought had not cheered him. "Gladstone," he said, "will soon have it all his own way, and whenever he gets my place we shall have strange doings." He could never get over the feeling that this indispensable colleague was cast in quite a different mould to his own. It was perhaps against his will that he himself, before all the world, appointed Gladstone his successor, when in defending his political existence he invoked the work of his Chancellor of the Exchequer as the only thing that had crowned his Government with fame and success.

That Gladstone was by far the most distinguished Minister in the Cabinet was a matter of unanimous agreement. No one doubted that his gifts and his achievements completely justified his appointment as Leader of the House of Commons. Many even considered that he might have laid claim to a still higher post—even *The Times* adopted this standpoint for a day or so—and that in justice he should have been Prime Minister. Yet there were a few who feared that his fiery temperament unfitted him for the post of Leader. That temperament of his delighted many, but as many were repelled by it. Sceptics shook their heads and murmured: he will be more hated than loved!

So, in his fifty-sixth year, Gladstone was at the head, if not of the Party, at least of its most important nucleus. The old friends who had always been convinced that he would reach a great position were no longer there to see the fulfilment of their prophecies. Lord Aberdeen had died in 1860, unreconciled with the destiny which compelled him to declare "the most senseless and superfluous war in all English history"; Graham had followed him a year later, and a younger, more hopeful and highly gifted friend, Sidney Herbert, succumbed in the same year to a painful illness. In the year 1864 the Duke of Newcastle died, who once, as Lord Lincoln, in the unforgettable Oxford days, had attached himself to Gladstone, and had been the first to foretell his fame. Of the whole circle of Peel's friends hardly one was left, and that man, too, was gone to whom Peel, in the greatest and most onerous hour of his life, had with noble self-denial awarded the wreath for their work in common. Richard Cobden had died a few months earlier. Fate did not permit him to see the day whose advent he had confidently foreseen after Palmerston's death, and for which he had worked with such indefatigable energy. That Gladstone would help to build up the new age was the hope of his last years; and the purport of many letters in which he sought, with his utmost powers of persuasion, to influence him.

Yet another tie was broken which for Gladstone had been a bond with his past. He was no longer Member for the University of Oxford. In the General Election of the summer of 1865, which had awarded Palmerston his last popular triumph, Gladstone had been rejected by Oxford. Or, to be more exact, the country clergymen who had graduated in Oxford, and who now, in virtue of a new statute, were able to record their votes by post, had rejected him. The scholarly ornaments of the University, even those who were every inch Conservatives, had remained faithful to him. For they still realized that it added to the fame of their University that their most brilliant scholar should represent them in Parliament. And yet the country clergymen were right if they no longer regarded Gladstone as their trusted representative. The never-resting development of his intellect had borne him too far away from them. True, in the acutest question of University politics he was still following the old track; he had always voted against the Liberal members who wished at last to liberate the acquisition of a University degree from the traditional and antiquated requirement of a formal profession of the doctrines of the Church of England. But in their eyes he had committed the unpardonable sin: he had supported a Bill which was to abolish the inconveniences to which Dissenters were subjected in respect of their funeral rites; and his attempt to tax charitable foundations was bound to excite their reprobation. And apart from all such details, they felt that a man who had identified himself so closely with the Liberal movement could not possibly be their representative. As a matter of fact, moreover, they had parted ways in the region of religious policy also.

For faithful though Gladstone himself had remained to the High Church convictions which he had acquired in his youth, he was perfectly ready to admit that other men had the right to their own convictions, however divergent from his own. In private letters of the year 1865 he speaks with striking candour of the change in his opinions in this respect:

"I have no mental difficulty in reconciling a belief in the Church and what may be called the high Christian doctrine, with that comforting persuasion, that those who do not receive the greatest blessings (and each man must believe his religion to be the greatest) are notwithstanding the partakers, each in his measure, of other gifts, and will be treated according to their use of them. . . . I was myself brought up to think otherwise, and to believe that salvation depended absolutely upon the reception of a particular and very narrow creed. But long, long have I cast those weeds behind me."

A man who had attained such heights of intellectual liberty and tolerance had no longer sufficient in common with the zealous country clergymen to whom, long before this, young Lord Robert Cecil had spoken from his very heart when he cried: "Only he who is a good Conservative can be a good Churchman."

For Gladstone this forcible separation from Oxford was a profound grief. He speaks in a letter to the Bishop of Oxford of "two great deaths" in his political career, his gradual divorce from his old party, and the "very short and sharp" rupture of the bond that tied him to Oxford. But for his future development this breach was a piece of great good fortune. It liberated him from a hundred considerations which he must always have borne in mind, and for this reason Bright welcomed it as "a national gain." Palmerston also had foreseen this, though with less benevolent feelings. "Keep him in Oxford," he told his friends, "and he is practically muzzled." But now Gladstone could present himself to his new constituents in Lancashire "unmuzzled," and *Punch*, who knew his Schiller, depicted him on the back of a Pegasus liberated from the traces of the Oxford chariot, and soaring heavenwards on his pinions—"Free Thought" and "Free Trade." In his native Lancashire, a year earlier, he had addressed the people in a series of speeches which made high claims on their intelligence as well as their moral feeling, and for this reason were regarded, by many of his hearers, as a great mark of confidence. Now they gave him their votes, so that he was elected, although two Conservative members obtained a larger number of votes. But many politicians took great objection to the novelty of Gladstone's appeal to the people.

This liberation from the bonds of the ancient University was an advantage to Gladstone when he assumed the leadership of the Party. But what of the Party, what of the faction of the House of Commons whose banner he was now to uphold? To begin with, there were the old Whigs, to whose ranks he had never belonged, and who for the first time in centuries saw at their head a man who had not sprung from one of the great aristocratic families. They could not regard him with unrestricted satisfaction. On the terrain in which their liberalism was most positive—in the fight for intellectual freedom and liberty of conscience—Gladstone had but recently and gradually drawn closer to them. In respect of internal politics he was—with the exception, of course, of Russell —far in advance of them. On the left wing of the Party were the men on whom Gladstone could rely for any progressive legislation; and here, above all, was Bright, who now hoped that it would be possible to get a move on the electoral reform for which he had so long contended. But the great majority of the Members inclined rather to the Right than to the Left; they had been elected as Palmerston's henchmen, and Palmerston, in questions of domestic policy, signified: "Quieta non movere." That witty man of the world, Monckton Milnes, whom Palmerston had sent to the Upper House as Lord Houghton, and whose genuine Liberalism was far in advance of most of his contemporaries, gave, in a letter to a French friend, an apt description of the General Election of 1865: Without Conservative reaction, and without Liberal enthusiasm. "The Radicals on the whole are the losers, which I am not glad of as I foresee a danger in our bourgeoisie becoming too exclusively an aristocracy."

But a very different tendency made its entry into Parliament with the election of John Stuart Mill for the hotly-contested constituency of Westminster. The prophet not merely of Utilitarianism, but also of liberty in Humboldt's sense of the word, he was the revered leader of a group of young men—not numerous, but intellectually active and vigorous—who were eager to attack all problems of political, intellectual and religious life with completely unprejudiced minds, and without swearing allegiance to any party, with the result that they contributed very largely to the elucidation and the propagation of liberal ideas. The most influential of them was a young scholar who had but recently left Oxford: John Morley, who, towards the close of the 'sixties, had begun to edit the *Fortnightly Review* in the spirit of this movement. These young men were by no means unconditional disciples of Gladstone's, but he could count on their support in respect of what was then the question of the day.

This question of the day was Franchise Reform. Fully a generation had elapsed since the Reform Bill of 1832 had retraced the main outlines of the distribution of political power. Behind the class which had then acquired influence by the granting of the franchise—the propertied bourgeoisie of the commercial rather than the industrial centres—new social classes had emerged, which could not be permanently denied the exercise of political rights: the urban middle classes and the industrial workers. They were not in the least revolutionary or socialistic in temper. The Chartist infatuation was an old story now, and it had left but few traces behind it, and the circle of those whom Karl Marx and Friedrich Engels were able to influence was and remained small and insignificant. In the working classes their influence could not be compared with that of John Bright, the special apostle of Reform.

The most fundamental difference between Russell and Palmerston was this—that Lord John had for many years admitted the justice of the demand for reform. He had been the hero of the Reform Bill of 1832, and he was conscious of the obligation which this great memory imposed upon him. He had repeatedly made the attempt to bring about a further reform. Again and again he had introduced a Bill in the Lower House, but after some months it had always been held up for some reason—to the barely concealed delight of Palmerston—who regarded all this activity as a well-intentioned but not altogether harmless hobby of his right honourable colleague. Disraeli's own elaborate attempt of 1859 had failed. John Bright had done his utmost to excite a popular movement by his powerful oratory, with very meagre results. It seemed as though the British lion, as *Punch* represented him in a very amusing cartoon, had no intention of allowing himself to be startled out of his majestic calm, however Russell, Disraeli and Bright might prod him with their several spears.

Palmerston had the same notion of the British lion as *Punch*, so that he felt that he had good reason to rub his hands and smile his condescending smile: "We cannot go on adding to the Statute Book *ad infinitum*." But in the same session which had been prefaced by the interview between Palmerston and Goschen at which these words were spoken, something happened that entirely upset the old gentleman's ideas. Once again, of course, this self-willed Chancellor of the Exchequer was responsible! In May a Radical Member proposed a measure of reform, and Gladstone had to answer it. Palmerston, who was kept at home by an attack of gout, felt uneasy, and warned the Chancellor that he must not commit himself and the Government too far. But—"Tell the silkworm that it may not spin!" Gladstone's reply contained a sentence which immediately caused the greatest sensation: "I venture to say that every man who is not presumably incapacitated by some consideration of personal unfitness or of political danger, is morally entitled to come within the pale of the Constitution."

This, again, was followed by several sentences full of Gladstone's favourite limitations and parentheses, and it was possible to read all sorts of limitations even into this main sentence. But here it was again—this combination of politics and morals, which to Palmerston and his like seemed so strange, and here again a general principle was enunciated which one could interpret in quite a number of ways that were thoroughly opposed to the senile caution of Palmerston. What wonder, then, that the Prime Minister promptly and emphatically protested, so that a correspondence followed in which a dozen letters—most of them long letters— were exchanged, by which neither of the correspondents managed to convince the other? What wonder that *Punch*, the faithful mirror of the opinions of the propertied middle class, illustrated the conflict between the two Ministers by drawing them as jockeys, riding a race in which the Chancellor was obviously the loser? Who can say how the conflict would have ended, had not the Conservatives' motion of "no confidence" intervened, so that it became impossible for Palmerston to withdraw his "great gun" from the line of battle?

Gladstone's declaration caused such a sensation because it seemed to consider the question of the franchise from the standpoint of a principle, an attitude which was quite foreign to the manner in which the problem had hitherto been considered. The historical British view was that the franchise was a kind of property, and above all incidental to real property. Even Lord Brougham, the great champion of the Reform Bill of 1832, had described it as "incident to property." The basing of the franchise in natural law on a universal human right was regarded as quite un-English, and more or less a French speciality. Hence Disraeli, listening to Gladstone's speech, was reminded of Rousseau's *Contrat social*, which according to English notions was quite enough to condemn it. Palmerston was expressing an essentially British notion when he admonished Gladstone, in flat contradiction to his thesis: "What every man and every woman too has a right to, is to be well governed and under just laws." However, Gladstone always denied that he had stated a legal maxim. He emphasized the fact that he had spoken only of a "moral" claim; but it was this very word that gave his speech its special resonance. Bright was delighted. "It makes a new era in the reform question, and shows what he is looking towards in the future . . . he will be more than ever the dread of the aristocratic mob of the West End of London."

The effect of his speech, of course, was far in excess of his original intention. His statement, so far from being the result of previous consideration, had arisen out of the course of the debate in which he had intervened. Yet the idea itself was no passing thought, but the final link in the deliberation of years and the careful elaboration of deep and lasting impressions. His political activity, his speeches to the public, his visits to industrial centres had given him a new conception of the working class as it had

155

evolved in the last few decades of economic development, for which he himself was mainly responsible. He had found that the traditional conceptions of the parliamentary bourgeoisie were inadequate and unjust, that the working class was developing qualities for which he had the greatest respect, and which they shared with other groups of the British people. In his speech, which recognized the workers' fundamental right to the vote in terms that caused such a sensation, he asked the rhetorical question, what qualities fitted a man for the franchise?—and he described the typical qualities of the ideal Englishman: "Self-command, self-control, respect for order, patience under suffering, confidence in the law, regard for superiors." But as the great example that illustrated and united all these qualities, he described the attitude of the working class of Lancashire under the suffering caused by the cotton famine of the winter of 1862. This was a moral achievement which, precisely because morality and politics were intermingled at its very core, could not fail to influence his political conceptions.

But their evolution in the direction of democracy was related also to his experience of foreign politics. A man of his active intellect, sensitive to every impression, could not for months encourage the struggle of a foreign nation for liberty without considering whether his own people also should not demand an enlargement of their rights. The convenient divorce between foreign and domestic political tendencies in Palmerston's style was impossible to Gladstone; and perhaps Palmerston was not mistaken when he ascribed the enthusiasm with which Garibaldi had recently been received in London as due in some degree to Gladstone's sweeping declaration. With his constant readiness to learn from events, he could not fail to note the fact that the American democracy had revealed powers of resistance with which no one would have credited it. It was only a few months since Abraham Lincoln, at the foot of the memorial to those who had fallen at Gettysburg, had clothed his profession of the democratic faith in words as imperishable and unforgettable as those which Thucydides put into the mouth of Pericles at the funeral rites of those Athenians who had fallen in the Peloponnesian War. His proclamation that "the government of the people, by the people, for the people, shall not perish from the earth" cannot have failed to impress Gladstone. It was a long way from that undergraduate address in the Oxford Union by which he had begun his political career to the programmatic announcement of 1864. Many professional politicians found his development hardly comprehensible, and they deduced from it the objection that he was not qualified for the position of Leader of the House. But for the people outside Parliament the future goal to which he pointed was far more important than the path which he had followed to reach his present position. It would soon be seen which impression was the more consistent with the facts. In any event, Gladstone had succeeded in doing something which—according to *Punch*—neither Disraeli nor Russell nor Bright had been able to do: he had awakened the British lion from his comfortable sleep.

2. *Gladstone's Franchise Reform Defeated*

Russell was already past seventy when after Palmerston's death he filled for the second time the office of Prime Minister. He did not possess the robust imperturbability of his predecessor, and he could not reckon on a long-continued term of political activity. He must make haste if he was to accomplish the only thing that he still desired to achieve—namely, the reform of the franchise. Nevertheless, it was some months before the Cabinet could deal with the matter, for important happenings had intervened. The mood that prevailed in the Cabinet was nothing short of tempestuous. It included only two real supporters of Reform: the Prime Minister and the Chancellor of the Exchequer. The other members were, to say the least of it, sceptical. They had seen so many miscarriages in this domain that they felt that it was better to pour plenty of cold water on the enthusiasm of the two supporters of Reform. The result of these tactics was that only the most moderate proposals were put forward, which, it was hoped, would not meet with any great resistance.

This temper of the Cabinet communicated itself even to the speech with which Gladstone, on the 12th March, 1866, introduced the Bill in the Lower House. The speech was marked by nothing of the contagious impetuosity, the passionate emotion which commonly lifted him far above all other speakers. It was his object to show—paradoxically enough, since he was a friend of Reform—not how extensive, but how modest was the reform proposed by the Government. Certainly, they wanted to include more working-men in the franchise, for the proportion of the workers who had hitherto possessed the right to vote was altogether too low. But the increase in the number of electors was to be strictly limited. The roll would not be increased by more than 400,000 voters, of whom about half would belong to the working class, and half to the "new middle class." The principal means of achieving this end was the lowering of the property qualifications in the urban constituencies. Hitherto the franchise was extended to occupiers of houses of a yearly value of £10; but now a value of £7 would suffice. This would mean that a working-man earning a weekly wage of twenty-five shillings or so might be granted the franchise. However, the qualification was still high enough to prevent the transference of the balance of political power in the urban constituencies to the working class. Only at the close of his speech did Gladstone arouse himself to greater enthusiasm, when he declared that "liberty is a thing which is good, not merely in its fruits, but good in itself," and admonished the House that they must not regard the question of extending the franchise as though they had in one way or another to compromise with dangerous people, but rather in the sense of a gift which would be abundantly repaid in "a feeling of grateful attachment" to the Constitution and the Throne, which was more valuable than gold and silver, or than fleets and armies, being "at once the strength, the glory and the safety of the land."

But there was little trace of such a way of looking at the matter in the debate that immediately followed. That the Conservative speakers, and among them Lord Cranborne (Lord Robert Cecil), should condemn it most violently, as dangerous and democratic, was to have been expected. With this opposition the Government had no difficulty in dealing. But on the second day of the debate there rose from the benches behind it a Member with whose finely chiselled face, with its blinking, myopic eyes, and whose snow-white hair, betraying the albino, the House had been familiar for more than a decade. Robert Lowe had joined Palmerston's administration as Vice-President of the Committee of Council on Education—but without Cabinet rank—and had been driven to resign by an adverse vote in Parliament—which, as a matter of fact, was certainly unjustified. Russell had not felt it possible to include him in his Cabinet, because in May 1864, during the debate on Gladstone's sensational declaration of his views on electoral reform, he had expressed opinions which were quite irreconcilable with the Prime Minister's plans. The House had long known that Lowe was a brilliant speaker and writer—he was for years a leader-writer on the staff of *The Times*. But no one had credited him with such powers of eloquence as he now unfolded. At one step he took his place in the front rank of Parliamentary speakers. Sentence after sentence was greeted by the Opposition—and also by many who called themselves Liberals—with delighted applause, and even those members of the public who read the exhaustive report of the speech in the next day's issue of *The Times* were fascinated by a speech which summed up, in sparkling and incisive phrases, all the arguments against the advancing democracy; a speech instinct with the classical culture of the English Universities, and excelling even the Chancellor's speeches in the effective application of quotations from Virgil. Every fresh speech which he made against the new Franchise Bill—and he made many—added to his fame, so that he was finally regarded—though only for a while—as a man who was "the equal in oratory and the superior in intellect to Gladstone and Bright." Lowe's speeches represented the last and most brilliant stage of the fight which an intellectually distinguished but obsolete form of Liberalism was putting up against the slow but inexorable advance of democracy. For he was a Liberal; he had been a Liberal all his life, as he justly insisted, and it was for this reason that his attitude excited such an extraordinary sensation. He felt the most extreme distrust of the uneducated or badly educated mass of the people, and of the pressure which their organized strength might bring to bear on the political life of the country. "If you wanted venality, ignorance, drunkenness," he cried, "if you wanted impulsive, unreflective, violent people—

where do you look for them? Do you go to the top or the bottom?"
No one could accuse Robert Lowe of timidity.

The task of replying to this first speech of his fell to John Bright, and he accomplished it not merely with the passionate earnestness of which he was such a master, but with a sparkling and memorable wit. He could not rival Lowe in his familiarity with Virgil, but he knew his way about the Bible better, and the laugh was on his side when he accused the renegade Liberals of taking refuge, like David of old, in the cave of Adullam: "And he had called about him every one that was in distress and every one that was discontented." The name "Adullamite" stuck to Lowe from that time onwards. "Lowe and Horsmann"—Bright continued—constituted "a party perfectly harmonious and distinguished by mutual and unbroken trust. But there is one difficulty. . . . This party of two reminds me of the Scotch terrier, which was so covered with hair that you could not tell which was the head and which was the tail of it."

Unfortunately, however, the "party of two" really comprised some dozens of members. This was not astonishing in a Parliament which only a year before had been elected in the name of Lord Palmerston, and in which there were many who had not yet realized that a new era had begun since Palmerston's place had been filled by Gladstone. A clever and essentially Liberal observer like Lord Houghton realized it well enough; and once, after he had been sitting beside Gladstone at table, and conversing with him, he wrote: "This is indeed a contrast to Palmerston's ha ha and *laissez faire*." He knew, too, how to judge Lowe's political wisdom: "It is against 1688, and it is all for a wise despotism." The passion with which the Liberal secessionists fell upon the Bill was a godsend for the Conservative Party, and especially for their leader Disraeli. He was glad to leave them to play the part of protagonists and to content himself with a tactical rather than a positive opposition.

The burden of defending the Bill fell above all on Gladstone's shoulders. Bright's speeches were brilliant enough, and Mill's were the fruit of careful deliberation, but it was the Chancellor who bore the brunt of the attack, and it was to him that all those looked whose future rights were being contested. When he reminded the opponents of Reform, who spoke of the working classes as of a hostile army preparing for attack, that they were "of our own flesh and blood," the indignation aroused by such demagogic utterances, which smacked of the French Revolution, knew no bounds. And when Gladstone, who was very well aware that he had a much stronger backing in the country than in Parliament, went to Liverpool, where he expounded his policy to a monster meeting, to be greeted by the most enthusiastic applause, the exasperation of his opponents rose to its maximum, more especially as he declared that the Government would stand or fall by the Bill; they had crossed the Rubicon and burned their boats behind them. Now indeed every effort must be made to reject the unwelcome measure before the people saw fit to take a hand.

Of Gladstone's appearance in the House at this time an able and sometimes enthusiastic journalist gives a living portrait in his reminiscences:

"In these days was Gladstone a tall, slightly made man with pale face, sharp classical features and piercing eyes, across whose countenance, as he spoke, were constantly fleeting shades of expression. . . . There were in his voice fine deep impressive notes, reminding one somehow of the effect produced by a church organ. Unlike many speakers he never fixed his eyes upon any particular part of his audience to address only them. He would speak all round. At one time he was persuasively addressing his opponents opposite: at the next speaking in a deprecating tone to censorious supporters behind him; or again would give encouragement to his admirers farther down. He had very little action. With his right forefinger he would emphasize certain statements and occasionally his hand would fall sharply on the table in front of him; sometimes he would drop both hands at his sides, or for a second or two fold his arms, but whatever the movement it was always in harmony with the spirit of his words, and often gave them increased effect. As an orator he was not that faultless monster the world never saw. Persons who listened to him for the first time not infrequently felt apprehensive. It seemed impossible that a speaker who hurried into such mazes of words could extricate himself with safety—that is, grammatically. The more intricate Gladstone was, the greater the need of caution. He would half-rouse the most startling fears, and then, by a sheer plenitude of words allay them. Good heavens! What is he going to say now? one asked one's self, as he began to speak of the exceptions to the rights of property or approaching changes in society, but in a second or two he had so surrounded his words with such conditions or explanations that the most timid were assured. On he would go with his marvellous vocabulary and his unrivalled power."

The debate in Parliament on the second reading of the Bill continued for a week. The most brilliant combatants on both sides of the House entered the arena and delivered speeches of intellectual power and vigour. Following them, the two Party leaders had the last word. Disraeli spoke with the adroitness that never deserted him, though without very great effect. He avoided the adoption of a positive attitude, and confined himself to acrid criticisms of the Bill and its advocate, the Chancellor of the Exchequer. He objected to it that it savoured of the spirit, not of the British but of the American Constitution; which sounded well, but which might with equal justice have been said of any Franchise Bill.

Naturally, Gladstone had no difficulty in disposing of this argument. Disraeli was no more than an insignificant opponent in the battle of ideas into which he entered with his speech. The more serious, because more dangerous and thoroughgoing adversary, was Lowe, and with him he had an encounter which forced even his enemies to accept him as the greatest master of Parliamentary eloquence. With supreme facility he sounded every note, from passionate earnestness to easy humour. His honourable friend reminded him of an anecdote of Lieselotte of the Palatinate, who said of her son, the Duc d'Orléans, "he shall have all the talents except one, that of knowing how and for what end to apply them." Or he informed him that his gloomy prophecies resembled those of the great Burke, in that they were false, and formed "admirable material of declamations for schoolboys, and capital exercises to be translated into Greek." He countered them with a single word: Lancashire, and referred once more to the heroism of the masses, who during the years of the cotton famine had endured the most grievous suffering without betraying the cause which they believed to be just. With ruthless energy he attacked those who concealed their aversion to any enfranchisement of the working class under all sorts of elaborate technical objections, and he did not hesitate to take his stand upon the basis of still remote ideals. To the present anxieties of his adversaries he opposed the firm conviction of inevitable future development. Even if they succeeded in throwing out this Bill they would have won no more than a brief intermission. And this—as he had already said in one of his Liverpool speeches —would be no interval of rest, but as an interval of fever and expectation. They would never abandon the problem until it was solved. "You may drive us from our seats—" he said—"you may bury the Bill that we have introduced, but we will write upon its gravestone for an epitaph this line, with certain confidence in its fulfilment:

Exoriare aliquis nostris ex ossibus ultor."

This was a quotation that Lowe could not make the object of his wit, and one of whose truth he was all too soon to be convinced. But who the avenger was to be was hidden from him and from Gladstone alike.

A reply made in the course of this speech to a personal attack of the Conservative leader's is of great biographical interest. In the deluded belief that he had found a weak spot in his opponent's defences, Disraeli so far departed from his usual good taste and intelligence as to employ, as a weapon against Gladstone, the speech opposing Reform which he had made as a young undergraduate in 1831. The well-earned rebuff which he received exhibited Gladstone at the full height of his human superiority. In words whose echo has not died out in two generations, Gladstone spoke of the errors of his boyhood, which he had repented long and bitterly. "I was bred under the shadow of the great name of Canning; with Canning I rejoiced in the removal of the disabilities from the Roman Catholic body, in the free and truly British tone which he gave to our policy abroad . . . under the shadow of that great name, and under the shadow of the yet more venerable name of Burke. I grant my youthful mind and imagination were impressed with the same idle and futile fears which still bewilder and distract the mature mind of the right honourable gentleman . . . the only

163

difference between us is this . . . that having those views, I moved the Oxford Union Debating Society to express them clearly, plainly, forcibly in downright English, while the right honourable gentleman does not dare tell the nation what it is that he really thinks. . . . I envy him not one particle of the polemical advantage which he had gained by his discreet reference to the proceedings of the O.U.D.S. in the year of grace 1831."

After administering this rebuff to his Conservative opponent Gladstone turned to the Liberal Party of which he was now the Leader. In sharp contrast to Lord Russell, for whose position and whose career he had the sincerest respect and appreciation, he described himself as one who had no claim to such acknowledgment:

"I came among you an outcast from those with whom I associated, driven from them . . . by the slow and resistless forces of conviction. . . . I had nothing to offer you but faithful and honourable service. You received me, as Dido received the shipwrecked Aeneas: *Ejectum littore egentem accipi.* I must ever be in your debt."

The storm of applause which followed these words, and which must have made Disraeli keenly aware of his blunder, sounded in the ears of countless listeners all over the country, and so strengthened the bond that tied them to Gladstone that it outlasted his temporary defeat and the triumph of Disraeli.

For the success which Gladstone achieved by his brilliant speech was but short-lived. It is true that he succeeded in procuring the second reading of the Bill; but his majority was distressingly small: it was only five. And a few weeks later the Opposition, under the leadership of the Adullamites, outvoted the Government on a matter of detail. 315 voted for the hostile amendment, and only 305 for the Government. In the fierce rejoicing with which the Opposition greeted this victory Lowe and his friends were foremost. Had they possessed the prophetic faculty of looking only a year forward into the future they would have covered their heads, as did Cassandra when she entered the city of Mycenae.

The victorious amendment referred to a mere detail: the difference between an assessment of £7 and a rent of £7 is to-day a matter of no special interest. But it clearly showed the Government that they could not pass their Bill in the face of the renegade Liberals and the Conservatives acting in conjunction. They would have to make concessions, but these would not avert the final defeat. They had no stomach for this cat-and-mouse game. Their fate was so intimately involved—especially since Gladstone's solemn declaration—with that of Franchise Reform that they could not continue as a Government if they withdrew the Bill.

They therefore decided to resign.

There was, of course, another alternative: to dissolve Parliament and appeal to the nation. This would have been more agreeable to Gladstone's militant temper. But the party Whip, Brand, who was afterwards Speaker of the House, a man of deserved reputation, was afraid that an electoral contest would result in a serious defeat. In vain Bright assured him that he was underestimating the moral factor. The Cabinet resolved on resignation, and Gladstone was in agreement with it.

In later years he inclined to the opinion that this had been a blunder, and that it would have been better to risk the electoral contest. He assuredly would have decided on this course had he suspected what use Disraeli would make of the power which the resigning Government was placing in his hands.

3. Disraeli Reforms the Franchise

The Queen did not at all approve of the resignation of the Cabinet. Especially in view of the external situation she felt that it was ill-advised. Two days before the defeat of the Government in Parliament the British Ambassador in Berlin reported his conversation with Bismarck, in which the latter informed him that at that very hour the Prussian troops would have entered Hanover, Saxony and the Electorate of Hesse. Three days after the new Derby–Disraeli Government had been formed the Prussian Army inflicted a decisive defeat on the Austrians at Königgrätz, and a few weeks later Hanover and the Electorate of Hesse had been wiped off the map, and the victorious Prussian King stood at the head of a powerful Federal State, the North German Confederation. But this Confederation conferred upon itself a Constitution which instantaneously realized what in England not even Bright had dared to demand, nor any but the most extreme Radicals: the universal, equal, direct and secret franchise. Apparently Count Bismarck, who had hitherto been regarded as a stronghold of the blackest reaction, knew nothing of the fears that possessed the anxious heart of Robert Lowe, and in drafting the new Constitution of his new kingdom he did not shrink from profiting by the American example, with which Disraeli had thought to strike at the heart of his adversary. But England was so strongly rooted in the tradition of her centuries of political evolution that it would not have occurred to any British politician to follow Bismarck's example. And after all, there was a difference between the right of electing members to a Reichstag which on principle was invested only with powers of control, and the right of electing members to a Chamber which was actually a governing body.

If the enemies of electoral reform had believed that after Gladstone's defeat they would now—despite his prophecy—be left in peace, the events were soon to make them wiser. The popular excitement, far from abating, was intensified. *Punch* could no longer depict the British lion as drowsy and immovable. A few weeks after the formation of the new Cabinet the demonstrating masses violently asserted their right to hold meetings in Hyde Park in support of a radical Reform Bill, and the shattered railings of the Park, which had fallen before their onset, were the sign that further resistance was useless. Throughout the country, and above all in the great cities, the advocates of Reform conducted an intensive agitation, and Bright, in particular, was able to impose his rousing eloquence on meetings many thousands strong.

Gladstone took no part in this agitation; he was still far from seeking to mobilize the nation against a refractory Parliament. He believed that he had said all that he could find to say on this important question. But even though he did not address the meetings, his name was on all men's lips; for by his advocacy he had set the great movement on its feet.

He himself profited by the recess to take a holiday in Italy. He was urgently in need of rest. Even the Queen, at his farewell audience, noted that "Gladstone looked ill and harassed." He had cause enough to do so. Even more than by the exceedingly strenuous and exciting labours which the fight for the extended franchise had imposed upon him, he was depressed by his defeat. This was the result of his first attempt to lead the Liberal Party. He was defeated because he had not succeeded in holding the party together. Before he had embarked on the franchise reform he had been leader of a safe majority. During the fight for the Bill the majority had gradually become a minority. It was not surprising that many held him responsible for their defeat, and an increasing number of critics began to question his capacity as Leader. They reproached him with increasing the majority against the measure by employing arguments which by far overshot the immediate aim. From the standpoint of the Parliamentary tactics of the moment they were justified, and the Whip responsible for the division may have wrung his hands in despair at some of the forecasts and discursive passages in Gladstone's speeches. But in respect of further developments the case was altered. The broad foundation of his arguments gave a lasting impetus to the movement. People saw that he was no mere tactician, but that he was passionately in earnest in his advocacy of the cause; and they did not forget this.

In Rome Gladstone applied himself, by way of recreation, less to the consideration of the marble memorials of a great past than to attentive observation of the present, and listening to Italian preachers. Their political differences did not prevent Pius IX from receiving him twice in audience, when the Pope had long conversations with him. Afterwards he summed up his impressions of Gladstone and three other English Ministers in the witty epigram: "I like but I do not understand Mr. Gladstone. Mr. Cardwell I understand but do not like. I both like and understand Lord Clarendon; the Duke of Argyll I neither understand nor like." On his way back to England Gladstone interviewed yet another sovereign. In Paris the Emperor was eager to invite to his table the man who had negotiated the Anglo-French commercial treaty, when he distinguished him by the greatest attention. But this, of course, did not prevent Gladstone from entering into friendly relations with the members of the French Opposition.

From Rome he followed the progress of the Reform movement

in England, but what he read of Bright's speeches gave him little pleasure, and he felt that their different ways of looking at the matter were beginning to create a gulf between them. Here he was completely mistaken; and later on he had no closer collaborator in the great contest than Bright.

Not only the Opposition, but the Government also was groping in the dark. When Gladstone returned home for the opening of Parliament, at the beginning of February 1867, he was quite in the dark as to the Reform Bill about to be introduced—but the Ministers were no less so.

Lord Derby, when forming his third Cabinet, had endeavoured to secure for it the men whom he had to thank for the overthrow of the Russell–Gladstone Cabinet. But Lowe refused to join it. He regarded himself as too much of a Liberal to serve under the leader of the Conservatives. This spoke well for his character, but it deprived him of all possibility of influencing in any way the course which events were now bound to follow—a course which from his point of view could only be regarded as disastrous. Derby therefore had to form a purely Conservative party Cabinet. The principal figure was of course Disraeli, who was once more Chancellor of the Exchequer. The most important of the new members were Lord Cranborne, now thirty-six years of age, formerly known as Lord Robert Cecil, and soon to be the third Marquess of Salisbury; and Lord Stanley, the son and heir of the Prime Minister. While Stanley inclined to hold Liberal views, Cranborne, with all the powers of his remarkable intellect, defended his firmly founded and inexorably Conservative convictions, to which he had given unvarnished expression in opposing Gladstone's Franchise Bill.

The Ministers were agreed as to the necessity of a franchise reform, but they approached the matter from very different standpoints, and exhibited very different tendencies. Lord Derby, who had been one of the champions of the Reform Bill of 1832, was not, even now, on principle, opposed to reform. Lord Cranborne regarded himself as bound by what he had said in the contest with Gladstone, and he insisted that a Conservative reform should be less extreme than Gladstone's measure; that is, it should proceed more cautiously than the Liberal measure with the admission of new voters of the working class. Disraeli, on the other hand, did not feel tied to any former declarations, nor was he so fearful of the extension of the franchise. He did not want to see it extended, but he did not believe that so much depended upon it as Bright believed, on the one hand, and Cranborne on the other. "There is something to be considered beyond forms of government— national character. And hereon mainly should we repose our hopes," he had written more than twenty years earlier, in *Coningsby*, and even now he was not afraid that the national character would be altered by a modification of the franchise. He had only one real anxiety—that this franchise reform, which had already embittered the lives of so many Ministers, might shorten the life of his Government. How the reform was effected was to him, if not a matter of indifference, at least a matter of secondary impor- tance; the point was, who was to effect it. He was resolved that it should be effected by no one but himself. In this neither Gladstone, nor Bright, nor Lowe, nor Cranborne should hinder him. He might have to throw a few principles, and even a few colleagues overboard. Well, that must just be taken as part of the bargain!

He went to work very cautiously at first. The Parliamentary situation was so confused that one could not see just where the line of least resistance lay. Disraeli therefore induced the Cabinet to begin by laying before the House, not anything so definite as the draft of a Bill, but merely resolutions, so that they could slowly feel their way. At first these resolutions were to culminate in the proposal for a commission of inquiry to examine the details, but this idea he dropped even while the Cabinet was deliberating, so that the resolutions might appear to be the preliminary stage of a future Bill. At this point there were difficulties with the Cabinet, for one Minister, General Peel, threatened to resign; but Disraeli persuaded him to change his mind.

On the 11th of February, 1867, began the first act of this incom- parable Parliamentary drama. The Chancellor of the Exchequer informed the House that the Government intended to follow a course which, without relieving it of its responsibility, would assure it against a repetition of former defeats. They would therefore move certain resolutions, on which the House would have the opportunity of voting on the 25th of February. The House was dumbfounded. Gladstone, as the Leader of the Opposition, declared himself, despite great misgivings, in agreement with this procedure, provided the resolutions were not confined to mere generalities which would leave the real question of dispute open.

The reservation was only too completely justified. When the resolutions were made known all saw that they were full of non-committal generalities. It was soon made clear that the House was by no means inclined to accept them, and so save the Government the trouble of elaborating a Bill in their place. The Queen was distressed; Derby and Disraeli had given her cause to believe that all would be settled without a contest, by mutual concessions, and now they were faced with the danger of the Party warfare that she so dreaded. Disraeli saw that the Government must after all resign itself to making concrete proposals. But how could this be done without splitting the Cabinet?

The two short weeks that elapsed between the first announcement and the actual debate were filled with the most singular vacillations. Disraeli made proposals which in principle were very far-reaching, but he burdened them with numerous parentheses and countervailing clauses which were designed very largely to restrict their effect. Hardly had his more cautious colleagues accepted them, when he discarded one safeguarding clause after another, and finally, two days before the fateful 25th, they were confronted with a projected measure whose scope they could not estimate, as the Chancellor had been careful to omit all statistical details. The whole of the following Sunday—which was the one day remaining—Lord Cranborne spent in calculation; and the longer he calculated, the more clearly he saw that the small boroughs, on which the strength of the Conservative Party depended, would one and all, in future, be controlled by the new working-class electors. He felt as though he were being asked to assist at the suicide of his own party. "If I voted for this measure," he wrote to Lord Derby on Sunday evening, "I could not look in the face those whom last year I urged to resist Mr. Gladstone." He therefore declared that the life of the Cabinet was at stake, and two influential and respected colleagues, General Peel and Lord Carnarvon, did the same.

Disraeli was furious. "This is stabbing in the back," he cried, when Lord Derby showed him this letter. At 2.30 there was to be a meeting of the Conservative Party, at which Derby had undertaken to expound the Government's programme. At 9.30 Disraeli would have to address the House. At last, at two o'clock, he succeeded in getting the Cabinet together. Were they to go forward or retreat? It was decided that they must retreat a little, in order to hold their refractory colleagues in check. There were just ten minutes left in which to devise a new measure on this basis. It was accordingly known as "the Ten-Minutes-Bill." But its actual life was almost as brief.

If the House had been dumbfounded on the 11th of February, it was even more amazed on the 25th, when Disraeli expounded his programme of the moment in greater detail but with less enthusiasm. Working on rather different lines he came to much the same result as Gladstone: the electorate would be increased by about 400,000 voters. So it was for this that a Ministry had been overthrown! Moreover, the new proposals literally invited criticism, both from the Right and the Left. But Lowe realized immediately that he was deserted by all parties. So long as it had been a question of attacking Gladstone there were those who were glad to make use of his eloquence, his wit, his arguments. But now, when the life or death of the Conservative Government was at stake, no one was less inclined than Disraeli to follow him along the path that must needs lead into the wilderness. There was something pathetic about the manner in which Lowe set himself to wage a desperate battle against that which he believed would be the ruin of England, but which was now approaching with irresistible force. With bitter derision he cried that Disraeli's whole policy could be summed up in a few words: "Say what you like to us, only, for God's sake leave us our places." Both parties, he cried, were conducting "a Dutch auction, in which the country was to be knocked down to the one who proposed the swiftest element for its destruction."

This voice of one crying in the wilderness cannot have greatly

171

troubled Disraeli; his mental comment was probably: "Well, you poor devil! What have you got to offer us?" He was more greatly impressed by the obvious intention of the House to go beyond his proposals. And it was soon evident that Cranborne's supporters in the Conservative Party were by no means so numerous as had been supposed. Disraeli, accordingly, hastened to drop the curtain on the second act.

When it went up for the third time, Disraeli had got rid of his hostile colleagues. He had induced Derby to accept their resignation, in order that he might propose, unhindered by their opposition, the more radical measure which they had declared to be unacceptable. Cranborne felt bitterly that Disraeli had played him a dirty trick. But Disraeli was considering only the necessity of keeping his vessel afloat, and of getting rid of every obstacle to his intention; no matter who or what. A year later, when he became Prime Minister, he got a third person to ask Cranborne whether he would not return to the Cabinet, but Cranborne told the go-between that he had the greatest respect for all the members of the Cabinet with one exception, and in that man's hands his honour would not be safe. It was seven years before the two men were reconciled. But for the moment it made things easier for Disraeli that he should be the only member of the Cabinet with a political will of his own.

When on the 18th of March the Chancellor of the Exchequer rose for the third time, and this time to introduce the expected Government Bill, he had an even greater surprise for the House. For the measure comprised something that only Bright had demanded hitherto: household suffrage. Every head of a household who was a ratepayer and had lived at one address for two years was to be granted the franchise. As a counterweight to this plurality of votes was proposed. But even with this countervailing measure the Bill was a step in the direction of democracy which went far beyond that which had brought about Gladstone's defeat. And with it Disraeli had placed the Opposition in a 'difficult tactical position. They could not deliver a frontal attack on such a measure as this; they could only indulge in skirmishes. For the moment, Gladstone was inclined to move the rejection of the Bill, but on his calling a

172

Party meeting it was immediately clear to him that the Party was unwilling to follow this course. He must therefore confine himself to proposing amendments.

The most important point in dispute was the provision that the voter must pay the local rates. Now, it was a general practice that the householder paid a rent in which the rates were included, so that the owner of the house paid them out of the rent. The upshot of this provision would therefore be that by this arrangement the tenant would lose his vote. This was the point at which Gladstone proposed to deliver his main attack. But now he experienced the greatest disappointment of the whole campaign. A fraction of the Party—and this time it consisted principally of members of the left wing—refused to support him. This group, which assembled in the tea-room of the House, and was therefore known as the Tea-room Party, was afraid that such an attack might lead to the rejection of the Bill, or that Disraeli would advise the dissolution of Parliament. This secession led to Gladstone's public defeat. His amendment was rejected.

Such a mishap to the Leader of the Liberal Party in a House which had a Liberal majority was a serious personal defeat. Gladstone felt it as such, and was terribly depressed. He called this defeat "a smash without example," and thought of "retiring to a back bench"; but the consideration that the great majority of the Party was still loyal to him restrained him from such a course. Yet it was a fact that his position was badly shaken. He no longer enjoyed the confidence so essential to the leader of a party. Many Liberal Members had voted against his amendment because they did not want to see a change of Government, which would have meant Gladstone's return to power. Disraeli's situation was all the more brilliant: the third act ended with his complete success.

Then came the Easter recess. The country bestirred itself again, and it was once more apparent that here Gladstone enjoyed far more powerful and enthusiastic support than in the House. Bright, with incomparable zeal and effect, once more took his part, for he had got to know him, in the course of their common labours, far better than the malcontents who deliberately criticized his every action. Bright's question :"Who is there who equals Mr. Gladstone in earnestness? Who equals him in courage and fidelity to his convictions?" found an echo in thousands of hearts. Gladstone was able to throw off his mood of heavy depression and to take up the fight again, though he refrained henceforth from lending his name to amendments.

But now, in the fourth act, in the debates on the separate provisions of the Bill, he won success upon success. But these successes were not so many defeats for Disraeli, for he, with an adroitness which Gladstone beheld with an aversion that was mingled with admiration, was in most cases able to evade an open defeat. If he felt that the majority of the House was against his proposals, he made a concession which put his opponents completely out of countenance. A Liberal Member contributed to the problem of the incidence of rates an amendment drafted by Bright, which obtained on other lines the result that Gladstone had tried to achieve with his defeated amendment. Suddenly Disraeli rose to his feet, and declared, to the general amazement, that he would not oppose the amendment. Gladstone could hardly trust his ears when his Whip informed him, as he entered the House, that Disraeli was on the point of giving way. Never, he wrote thirty years later, had he experienced such a complete surprise! As a matter of fact, with this concession one of the most important safeguards of the Bill was swept away without ceremony. And the same thing was done with the other safeguards. What was left was a householder's franchise without any important restriction, without any stipulation as to length of domicile, and without plurality of votes.

Lord Cranborne, who opposed the measure most bitterly to the last, summed up, on the occasion of the third reading, no less than ten important modifications of the Bill which had been demanded by Gladstone and conceded by the Government, and he congratulated the Conservative Party with biting irony on the triumph which they had achieved by the acceptance of Gladstone's demands, and the principle laid down by Bright. A Liberal Member, too, described Bright as the true father of the Bill, and compared Disraeli with a gipsy woman who has stolen a child and disguised it in order to pass it off as her own. "But immense credit attached to him for the tact and the temper he had shown on the conduct of the measure."

The fifth act was played in the Upper House. If a Liberal Government had introduced a measure whose democratic significance was so incalculable, the Lords would undoubtedly have thrown it out. But since it came to them with the sign and superscription of a Conservative Cabinet, the case was very different. They passed it without serious opposition, and Lord Derby, after the third reading had been unanimously voted, expressed his gratitude for their impartiality. But he added a few words which were not so soon forgotten: "No doubt we are making a great experiment and taking a leap in the dark!" With this curious confession of a leading statesman the curtain fell for the fifth and last time. Franchise Reform was now a fact, and it was Disraeli who had made it so.

If after the conclusion of this exciting drama the British politicians asked themselves, after calm consideration, what they had done, and what they had witnessed, they must have given themselves some singular answers. Robert Lowe had become a truly tragi-comic figure. He, whose fame had filled the clubs and the newspapers only a year earlier, was now regarded as the chief culprit, who had defeated a harmless Bill in order to make way for a much more radical measure. Instead of the 400,000 new voters, whose admission to the franchise he had opposed as an unspeakable misfortune, the register was now increased by three times as many. This time he quoted not the Aeneid of Virgil, but Bürger's *Leonore*, for after the Bill was passed into law he began a letter to a friend of his, a lady of the same way of thinking, with the German quotation: "Hin is hin, verloren ist verloren." (Gone is gone, lost is lost.) Many of the Conservative Members who had constituted the Government ranks agreed with the young aristocrat who bluntly declared that "he did not see how he could meet his constituents after having refused a moderate measure from a good Christian and taken an extreme measure from a bad Jew." Lord Cranborne, however, published in the leading Conservative periodical, the *Quarterly Review*, an article entitled "The Conservative Surrender," which expressed the most merciless judgements of the Party leaders, reproaching them with betraying all that the Party held sacred, and forecasting an irresistible descent into democracy. Even more dismal was Carlyle's prophetic comment: "Shooting Niagara!"

But all this could not alter the fact that Disraeli had won an unexampled success. What all others had failed to do he had done; not at the head of an overwhelming majority, but as the leader of a definite minority. He had to fight, not only against the greatest Parliamentarian and the most brilliant speaker in the House, but also against the lack of confidence in his own ranks. But he now dominated the Conservatives so completely that he could openly boast that he hoped "to educate his party."

How different, on the other hand, was Gladstone's position in his party! He bitterly complained that if he spoke a word against Disraeli someone would get up on the Liberal side to oppose him. Gladstone's failure was the most brilliant foil to his success.

Each of these adversaries expressed his opinion of the other in characteristic terms. Lord Houghton met Gladstone in May 1867: "He seems quite awed with the diabolical cleverness of Dizzy, who, he says, is gradually driving all ideas of political honour out of the House, and accustoming it to the most revolting cynicism."

Disraeli, however, was in a rejoicing mood: now "he would hold him down for twenty years!"

But what a delusion! Not a year had passed, and Gladstone stood higher than ever before. Yet before this Fate had awarded Disraeli the highest prize within his reach, of which he had been dreaming for thirty years. He became Prime Minister.

4. Gladstone's Triumph

In February 1868 Lord Derby retired from the head of the Government. The greatest enemy of the British politicians of the eighteenth century, the gout, had not spared him; a particularly severe attack, which gave him reason to fear the worst, compelled him at last to resign the high office which he had filled no less than three times. As his successor he recommended to the Queen the Chancellor of the Exchequer, as the only Minister who could count on the warm support of all the other Ministers; and the Queen had already anticipated this advice in a conversation with Disraeli. If she looked to find in him a Prime Minister who would be ready to accommodate himself to her peculiarities his very first letter showed her that she was not mistaken. He tendered the request that Her Majesty would "deign not to withhold from him the benefit of Her Majesty's guidance," and praised "those great abilities," that "rare and choice experience," and spoke of "an advantage in judgement which few living persons can rival." She had not been accustomed to such a tone as this from Palmerston, and she gladly paid the new Premier the compliment of informing him that he might be assured that only "his own talent and successful labours in the service of his Sovereign and country had earned for him the high and influential position in which he was now placed."

And in saying this she was not exaggerating. No one had smoothed Disraeli's path; no influential family connections had set his foot on the ladder. Step by step he had made his own way, relying only on his great gifts, his indomitable energy, and his unfailing endurance. Neither his descent—which he was wont to proclaim aloud, regardless of the prejudices of most of his party friends—nor his adventurous beginnings could keep him down. His rise to power was a triumph of personality which had not its like even in the England of the nineteenth century.

Now, at the age of sixty-four, Disraeli was Prime Minister. But—he was a Prime Minister without a Parliamentary majority. He could count on a majority in the Lower House only so long as the Liberal Party was divided. Was he in a position to pursue a policy which would make this division permanent? Whether or not he was in that position he had no opportunity of testing. For this time it was Gladstone who took the initiative and prescribed to Disraeli the course that he must follow.

It was no mere chance that the domain which Gladstone chose for his offensive was that of Irish policy. The Emerald Isle had once more become most unpleasantly actual. Twice already in this century it had determined the course of British policy; once in respect of Catholic Emancipation, once in the abolition of the Corn Laws. Then it was Peel who heard Ireland's cry of distress; now it was his great disciple.

Irish history in the nineteenth century was controlled by an incident that occurred at the beginning of the century; the union of Ireland with Great Britain by Pitt's Act of Union of 1800. This union, which abolished the separate Irish Parliament in Dublin, and brought the Irish representatives to Westminster as Members of the Parliament of Great Britain and Ireland, was brought about only by the bribery and purchase of the Irish Members by the English Government. The Irish people had never ceased to regard it as a high-handed act of injustice, to which they ascribed every misfortune that befell them. The rural population of Ireland, which —with the exception of the inhabitants of Ulster—was exclusively Roman Catholic, and which consisted mainly of the tenants of the Protestant and English landlords, was suffering, about the middle of the century, the greatest economic distress, which was shockingly intensified by the land laws, as these were heavily weighted in the landlords' favour. The people's reaction to this state of affairs was an emigration that amounted to some hundreds of thousands yearly. Between 1849 and 1854 one and a half million emigrants left the Emerald Isle. A great proportion of these sought a new home in the United States. They took with them their hatred of England, and the great cities of the Eastern States and the Middle West became the nurseries of revolutionary movements against British rule. In the 60's a secret society was founded in Chicago, which named itself the Fenian Brotherhood, after the legendary national hero, Finn, and whose object was the foundation of an Irish Republic.

In 1867 the Fenians made themselves felt in England by a series of outrages which caused public alarm. In September, in Manchester, two Fenian prisoners were liberated by their fellow conspirators, and an English policeman was shot. The execution of three Irishmen who took part in the affray, and who were found guilty of murder in the English courts, was regarded in Ireland as a tyrannical act of terrorism, and the "Manchester Martyrs" became the objects of a national cult. In December 1867 there was a bomb outrage at Clerkenwell gaol, where a Fenian was awaiting trial. The Fenians failed to achieve their object, but twelve innocent persons were killed and some hundred and twenty wounded.

Dreadful as these crimes were, they had one wholesome consequence. The English people began to ask themselves seriously why the Irish should be so lawless and discontented, and it was found that the latter had many just causes for complaint. In the foreground was the settlement of the ecclesiastical question. Seven-eighths of the Irish were Catholic. But by the Act of Union of 1800, the Established Church of Ireland, which was richly endowed, was Protestant and Anglican. There were fewer than 700,000 members of the Established Church in a population of nearly six millions.

Just and open-minded politicians had already taken objection to this state of affairs, and as long as thirty years before this Lord John Russell had declared it to be indefensible. But he was not strong enough to cope with the then overwhelmingly Protestant prejudices of the House. Now, however, a stronger man took the matter in hand.

Gladstone had for many years been preoccupied with the problems of the Established Church of Ireland. In his younger days he had championed it unconditionally, as was shown by his book on State and Church, and also his resignation of account of the Maynooth affair. But the sacrifice which he had then offered to his convictions signified also a move in the direction of greater freedom of thought. "By this act," he claimed, "my freedom was established," and the unprejudiced consideration of his earlier point of view convinced him more and more fully of its untenability. Even when, in 1847, he was standing as candidate for the University of Oxford, he had distinctly refused to pledge himself to stand by the Irish Church. Now, since the question was being continually brought to the fore by the motions of independent Members, he was obliged, as Minister, to define his attitude towards it. In 1865 he declared that he was opposed to a proposal to disestablish the Irish Church, simply saying that "he did not believe that the time had come for actively dealing with the question," but that it was the question of the future; and this declaration did not fail to make the most unfavourable impression, both on the Conservatives and on his clerical electors in Oxford.

Now, however, it seemed to him that the time had come. He happened to be on a railway journey when he read the report of the violent rescue of the Fenian prisoners in Manchester. At that moment, as he afterwards told the Queen's confidential adviser, General Grey, it became clear to him that the question of the Irish Church would now have to be dealt with. He doubted whether it would be advantageous, as a matter of party politics, if he were to proceed with the matter then; indeed, he rather expected to meet with opposition in the ranks of his own party; but he had soon made up his mind that he must seize the first opportunity of taking the initiative.

The opportunity occurred a few days after Disraeli had formed his Cabinet. A Catholic Member moved that the House should now proceed "to consider the state of Ireland." This motion resulted (in March 1868) in a four days' debate, which showed how the Irish question was preoccupying the minds of the English. The new Government threw out some hints as to its future policy, but these were vague, hesitating and unsatisfactory. All the more prominent Members, including Lowe and Bright, took part in the debate. But they said nothing between them that had anything like the significance of Gladstone's speech.

He rose on the last day of the debate. He had now to speak with the authority and responsibility of the Leader of the Liberal Party, for Russell, by declaring that he would never again accept office, had practically abdicated. Gladstone's very first sentences gave the House the feeling that the speaker had a powerful grasp of the problem, and that he was lifting it out of the region of unfruitful discussion into that of practical politics. The programme of the Government, he insisted, showed that "they had failed to realize the great fact that we had reached a crisis in the Irish question. Ireland had an account with this country that had endured for centuries . . . we had not done enough to place ourselves in the right." He went on to examine the problem from every standpoint, and at last, on coming to the question of the Church, as the most urgent matter of all, he declared categorically: "The Irish Church as State Church must cease to exist."

Such a declaration, at such a moment, from the lips of such a man, was a political event of far-reaching importance. The Liberal Party in the House accepted it with vigorous and unequivocal applause; sweeping away any doubts which Gladstone may have harboured as to their attitude. He had actually re-established, at a single blow, the unity which of recent years had, to his distress, been destroyed. His declaration was the war-cry to which the Liberals reassembled, in the House and throughout the country.

In his speech Gladstone had announced that he would take the initiative if the Government did not anticipate him. This Disraeli could not or would not do. Although he himself, some decades earlier, had coined the slogan of "an alien Church," he was now all for tactics and for temporizing. Apparently the full political significance of this step of Gladstone's had escaped him. "Mr. Gladstone has mistaken the spirit of the times and the temper of the country," he wrote to the Queen, who was at once filled with anxiety.

Gladstone now proceeded with the greatest energy. A few days after the debate he gave notice of a group of resolutions which contained his solution of the problem. The first and most important formulated the principle of the disestablishment of the Irish State Church with due regard for all properly acquired personal rights. Naturally, there was a prolonged debate on this resolution. But the debate showed from the first that the Government had lost with one stroke all the tactical advantages which it had won in the preceding year. This time the rift appeared on the Government side of the House. Disraeli did not dare to assert that the existing state of affairs was worthy of continuance; but he got Lord Stanley to introduce a motion—once more of a purely tactical nature—requesting that the decision should be postponed until the General Election. But this by no means satisfied the pronounced Churchmen of the Conservative Party. Lord Cranborne was not the only one to come forward with a drastic criticism—he had foretold that in this matter Disraeli would attempt the same diversion as in connection with the question of franchise reform—for a prominent member of the Government declared, in an impassioned speech, which was steeped in the spirit of indomitable Toryism, that he would never agree to Disestablishment. The division showed for the first time the restored unity and therefore the superior strength of the Liberal Party in the House. Gladstone was victorious, with a majority of some sixty votes, and Disraeli, in his letter to the Queen, had to content himself with the poor consolation: "Mr. Disraeli does not believe that there is any substantial power in this display."

As a matter of fact, with this division, though formally speaking it was concerned with a merely preliminary question, the issue was decided. When after the Easter recess the first of Gladstone's resolutions came up for debate, the division gave him the victory, and with an increased majority, for Disraeli was not in a position to oppose his demands by any positive proposals. By this Disraeli was compelled to take a momentous decision. The result of the division had really the same significance for his Cabinet as Gladstone's defeat of June 1866, which led to his resignation. Several of the Ministers took the view that they must now follow Gladstone's example. For Disraeli this would have meant that after two short months he would have to renounce the prize for which he had fought and laboured all his life. There was one constitutional alternative: the dissolution of Parliament. But the new electoral registers required by the recent franchise reform were not yet completed, and considerations of public policy were against allowing the old electorates to vote again. In this dilemma Disraeli thought it proper, without previously consulting the Cabinet, to go to the Queen, and with her assistance to come to an agreement in respect of further proceedings. She gave him permission to dissolve Parliament "at the proper time," which, as matters then stood, meant after the new registers had been completed.

If this procedure did not meet with the unanimous approval of his own Cabinet colleagues, it appeared, as seen from outside the Cabinet, even more objectionable, owing to the manner in which it was communicated in Parliament. The affair was badly stage-managed; Disraeli's statements in the Commons did not agree with those of his colleagues in the Lords, and Gladstone, of course, did not fail to draw attention to this lack of agreement. The impression of the Opposition was that Disraeli had, in an unconstitutional manner, drawn the Queen into the debate, and indeed, that he was trying to prejudice her, in his own favour, against the future Government. As in many a previous instance, Disraeli showed his lack of self-control by pelting his opponent with sarcasm and invective. This angered Bright, with whom he had always been on good terms, despite their political hostility; for he was convinced that Disraeli's private opinion of the problem of the Irish Church was totally different from the view that he openly professed; and he reproached him, in an exasperated speech, with giving the Sovereign advice which he knew was not correct; and Disraeli, in great indignation, replied with equal acerbity. The incident did nothing to mitigate the bad opinion which Gladstone had formed of his adversary's lack of conscience.

In the end the Opposition agreed that Disraeli should remain at the helm, and that the election should be postponed until November. In the meantime the virtual Leader of the House was Gladstone, whose resolutions were one by one adopted. Disraeli made no attempt to influence the country by a widespread agitation. But with every day that passed he became more sympathetic to the Queen. His almost daily letters, "in his best novel style," fascinated and amused her, and made her feel that he was keeping her informed of everything. The dedication of his novels pleased her all the more in that when conversing with her he liked to speak of "us authors," thus placing her occasional writings on the same level as his own. Who could have resisted this bewitching art of conversation, which was able so to present even difficult subjects that nothing was dry or tiresome? She had never thought of sending flowers to Aberdeen; no, nor even to Palmerston. But she sent them to Disraeli, as a sign that he found favour with her. And when he visited her at Balmoral she wrote in her journal: "He certainly shows more consideration for my comfort than any of the preceding Prime Ministers since Sir Robert Peel and Lord Aberdeen."

It was easy to understand that she found it difficult to part with such a Prime Minister. But the hour of parting came, when the nation had spoken its mind in the General Election.

The election constituted an overwhelming triumph for Gladstone, an unequivocal vote of confidence. In the urban constituencies, which comprised the great majority of the new voters, the Liberals were victorious to an extent that exceeded their own expectations. It did not help Disraeli that the reform of the franchise which had created these new voters bore his name; for they saw in Gladstone the man to whom they owed this reform. In the rural constituencies the Conservatives did better. But the final result was a Liberal majority of 112. Gladstone himself suffered the chagrin of defeat in his rigidly Protestant constituency, South-West Lancashire. But he could console himself with the fact that he had already been returned by Greenwich (having been doubly nominated).

Confronted by the accomplished fact, Disraeli recovered his dignity and self-control. He accepted the verdict of the country with admirable composure, and proceeded to act in accordance with it. Without waiting for Parliament to assemble he tendered his resignation to the Queen, which she immediately accepted, in complete appreciation of his point of view. He declined the honour of a peerage for himself, but accepted it for his wife, thereby giving yet another proof of his lifelong and unchanging solicitude and esteem for her.

Who was to follow him as Premier? The question answered itself; the verdict of the country had pointed to Gladstone as the chosen leader.

On the 1st of December, 1868—the day on which the Queen accepted Disraeli's resignation—she sent her private secretary, General Grey, to Hawarden.

THE GREAT MINISTRY

1. Prime Minister

"This birthday," wrote Gladstone in his diary, on the 29th of December, 1868, "opens my sixtieth year. I descend the hill of life. It would be a truer figure to say I ascend a steepening path with a burden ever gathering weight. The Almighty seems to sustain and spare me for some purpose of His own, deeply unworthy as I know myself to be. Glory to His name."

This was the spirit in which William Ewart Gladstone assumed the highest office. It was the same spirit which had inspired him as a young man, when he turned to politics from the dream of a spiritual vocation, in order to devote himself to questions "of the greatest consequence for the peace and happiness of humanity." The profound piety and devotion which filled him during his daily study of the Bible, or when he attended Divine service in the little church of Hawarden, did not desert him in the House of Commons, or at the door of the small house in Downing Street from which, since the time of Robert Walpole, the First Lord of the Treasury had endeavoured to guide the destinies of the British Empire. They had inspired him when he had protested in the name of justice against Palmerston's Chinese War, and when he recognized the moral right of his fellow-citizens to share in the government of the country, and when he declared that the maintenance of the Irish State Church was incompatible with England's duty to her neighbour island. This continuity of spirit and of character was unaffected by the fact that now his aims were very different from those which he had envisaged thirty-five years earlier; for he had never, for reasons of personal advancement, abandoned a conception to replace it by one more convenient. He had always wrestled with every subject until he had mastered it, and more than once, as the result of such investigation, he had given his support to the less popular cause. But this deliberate relinquishment of popularity for the time being had gradually won for him the affection of the people, because they were convinced of his integrity and his earnestness. Nothing is more significant in this connection than the veneration which was felt for him, the High Churchman, by the Nonconformists, whose religious opinions were so widely divergent from his. Their spokesman was able to assure Gladstone, in a critical hour, that they were praying for him, and to express their thankfulness that he was "educating this nation to believe in conscience and truth." But the same veneration was felt by many Catholics, who were able all the more highly to value his impartial acceptance of their claims because they knew that he had attained this impartiality only at the cost of severe inward conflict.

"My mission is to pacify Ireland," was his first words when he knew that the Queen was about to send for him. He was in the park at Hawarden, felling a tree with the axe, when the telegram arrived in which General Grey announced that he was on his way to him. "Very significant!" he remarked, after glancing at the telegram. Then he resumed his occupation, to stop a few minutes later; and then, leaning on his axe, and speaking with profound earnestness and great emphasis, he made avowal of his task in Ireland.

Gladstone had been sufficiently informed of the Queen's frame of mind to understand that not everything that General Grey would have to say to him would be gratifying. He knew well enough that any intercourse with the Queen would be very difficult just now, and that he himself had many peculiarities which would not make it easier. "I," he wrote, with disarming self-criticism to a clerical confidant of the Queen's, "am a man so eager upon things as not enough to remember always what is due to persons—and I have another great fault in the unrestrained manifestations of first impressions." He knew that the Queen had most unwillingly consented to the disestablishment of the Irish Church, and that she did not approve of his way of attacking the problem. He therefore frankly explained to General Grey the reasons for his procedure.

There were certain personal problems that were even more

186

ticklish. Lord Clarendon, than whom few were believed to possess a more intimate knowledge of the Continent, had repeatedly been Foreign Minister in Liberal Cabinets, and it went without saying that Gladstone would choose him again. But he had earned the Queen's disapproval, not only on material but also on personal grounds. He had reported the proceedings of the Frankfort Diet of Princes in 1863 in a tone which she regarded as unfitting, and he had made no secret of his dislike of the unification of Germany, which she regarded as a bequest of Albert's. Further, it seemed that certain extremely outspoken utterances of Clarendon's had been repeated to her; he let his tongue and his pen run away with him, and had been known to refer to her as "the Missus." But here Gladstone could make no concession; he had spoken to Clarendon months earlier in connection with his position in a future Cabinet. If we were to exclude him from the Cabinet now, his absence—so Gladstone explained to Grey—would give rise to suspicions of a Court intrigue. This the Queen would naturally wish to avoid, so she submitted, with a sigh, only making the stipulation that her personal relations with the unwelcome Minister should be restricted to the minimum.

But there was something else that Gladstone wanted, something incomparably more important: he wanted John Bright in his Cabinet—a man of whom fashionable Society had said, only a few years earlier, that it would gladly "go twenty miles to see John Bright hanged." People, of course, felt differently now, for they had seen how often he had won his cause, and a Conservative Prime Minister had already executed a good part of his programme. But he was still the extremest Radical in English politics. He was the idol of the mob which had torn down the railings of Hyde Park, and he was a Quaker, a Nonconformist. In every way he was unlike the men who had hitherto been members of the Cabinet, irrespective of party. His appointment was a sign to the whole political world that a new era had begun, that the Liberalism which Gladstone had established in power was something very different from the Whiggism which had been embodied in Melbourne and Palmerston, and even in Lord John Russell. Fortunately the Queen, as she told Gladstone, had no objection whatever to Bright;

for once, at a public meeting, when someone had referred in a tactless manner to the Queen's seclusion, he had spoken of her bereavement in such human and moving terms that she had never forgotten the incident. She even made allowance for his religious scruples, and exempted him from kneeling to her, as other Ministers did, in accordance with the etiquette prescribed on assuming office. His spontaneous character made the best of impressions on the Queen. But apart from this his office—he was President of the Board of Trade—gave him little satisfaction. In dealing with documents, as in Cabinet meetings, he was out of his element. But slight as was the practical value of his collaboration, its symbolical significance was great, and for this reason his appointment was a historic action on Gladstone's part.

His other proposals were accepted by the Queen without much discussion, and she was able to describe her first interview with the new Prime Minister as "satisfactory"; he was, she said, "most cordial and kind." One has the impression, on reading her memorandum, that she had looked forward to their first conversation with great anxiety.

On forming his Cabinet Gladstone allotted a high proportion of offices to the old Whig aristocracy. He had never belonged to it, but he regarded it as indispensable to the interests of the Liberal Party. His closest friend among the Whigs was Lord Granville, whom he made Colonial Minister and Leader of the House of Lords; Granville had been his most enthusiastic disciple since he had listened to his Budget speech in 1853, and his loyalty to Gladstone was lifelong. Great things were expected of young Lord Hartington, the son and heir of the Duke of Devonshire; his aristocratic connections, his disinterested character, and his lucid intelligence seemed to mark him out for a leading rôle.

But Gladstone sent for another man who not only did not belong to the Whig aristocracy, but had given proof that he was very much less progressive. Robert Lowe became Chancellor of the Exchequer. No appointment could have been more magnanimous. If anyone had forfeited all right to consideration, that man was Lowe. It was to him that Gladstone owed his overthrow in 1866. With his sharp tongue he had eagerly seconded every criticism of Gladstone's leadership. But Gladstone believed that Lowe, with his pre-eminent intellectual powers and his great knowledge of affairs, should make a successful administrator of the nation's finances, and in view of this belief he thrust all personal considerations into the background. As a matter of fact, by this appointment he was doing his Cabinet no service. Lowe was as little of a success as the very differently-minded Bright, and at a critical juncture his financial policy greatly increased Gladstone's difficulties. On the other hand, the Prime Minister made a good choice when he appointed Cardwell, one of the last Peelites, to the War Office; and Goschen, as President of the Poor Law Board, was a great acquisition. On the whole, the Cabinet comprised a very respectable capital of political ability, and its rapid formation was greeted with applause by the public.

But in addition to his Ministers the Prime Minister had to find collaborators who for him were frequently even more important; his private secretaries. Gladstone had said of the relation between a Minister and his private secretary that it was "impossible . . . for a Minister and his secretary adequately to perform their respective duties unless there was established between them such an absolute confidence as in a happy domestic life between a man and his wife." He acted up to this maxim, so that in respect of his Ministerial activities the importance of his private secretaries must not be too lightly estimated. A man of his incomparable capacity for work naturally expected the utmost from his secretaries, and he was never the man to waive, out of mere good nature, any services which he felt that he must demand in the interest of his cause. To be his private secretary was never an easy occupation, but all those who had ever filled this post regarded this time as the best and most precious period of their lives, and were inspired with an enthusiasm for their chief that was not diminished by even the most critical observation. The proverb that no man is a hero to his valet may be applied also to the secretary of a politician. But it was not true in Gladstone's case. Three of his secretaries —Algernon West, Arthur Godley (later Lord Kilbracken) and Sir Edward Hamilton have written their reminiscences of him, and their books are not only among the most intimate, but also among the most affectionate and enthusiastic tributes to his memory. These were all men who were afterwards appointed to high official positions; the capacities which qualified them for these positions had recommended them to Gladstone, and again, it was under his guidance that these capacities were developed.

In 1868 he chose for his private secretary an official of the India Office, Algernon West, who had already filled the same position under Lord Halifax. He has described his first meeting with Gladstone in his memoirs:

"He was sitting . . . at his writing-table, wearing a dark frock coat, with a flower in a buttonhole, a pair of brown trousers with a dark stripe down them, after the fashion of twenty years earlier, a somewhat disordered neck-cloth and large collar, the never-ending subject of so much merriment in contemporaneous caricature; and I noticed the black finger-stall which he invariably adjusted over the amputated finger of his left hand before he began to write. An upward and almost annoyed look at the interruption caused by my entrance melted into a kindly smile as Mrs. Gladstone told him who I was. He at once in a flattering way asked me to be his secretary. I cannot describe the delight with which I accepted his offer." And at once they set to work. In a few minutes West had in his hands the entire correspondence relating to the formation of the Ministry—human documents which permitted him profound and often surprising revelations of persons and events. Out of their common labours developed a friendship which lasted until the hour of Gladstone's death. It was not disturbed by the fact that West often had the feeling, when some problem of scholarship was discussed at Gladstone's table, that the conversation was above his head; or that an essay on Homer which the Minister once dedicated to him, as a particular token of gratitude, was put aside unread.

All Gladstone's intimate collaborators were amazed by his energy, his capacity for work, and the quickness of his decisions, and, above all, by his incomparable power of concentration. They likened his brain to a vessel with watertight compartments, which were hermetically closed when he passed on to another subject. If his official business allowed him a few minutes' leisure he was at once absorbed in a book, over which he forgot all his cares, whether it was his beloved Homer, or a novel of Sir Walter Scott's, or a theological treatise. With the same promptitude he would return to his work if a secretary appeared with an official document. For dealing with his enormous correspondence a special system was devised, so that he was obliged to write only the most important letters himself. Naturally there were letters that even a Prime Minister overwhelmed with political affairs had to write himself, apart from the letters to the Queen, which had, of course, from the first word to the last, to be written by his own hand. He dispensed with the assistance of a stenographer until, in extreme old age, his failing eyesight compelled him to accept this innovation.

He naturally demanded of his secretaries the unconditional execution of his orders. But when he knew them intimately and had come to trust their judgement he would invite their candid criticism and would discuss a question with them as with equals. He often found it difficult to realize that anyone could form an opinion of any question that differed from his own, because he so often regarded it as an ethical problem, a matter of right or wrong. But nothing could be more untrue than the legend that he could not bear to be contradicted. Among those who helped to spread this legend was Prince Bülow. He related in his "Chapter of Autobiography" that a diplomatist who contradicted some statement of Gladstone's at the dinner-table was handed a slip of paper from Mrs. Gladstone, on which were written the words: "We never contradict Mr. Gladstone." The story is delightfully told, but it is certainly untrue; not only because the opinion which Bülow's informant attributed to him was one which he could never have expressed —for he was naturally the very last man who could have disputed the existence of Bulgaria—but all those observers who were acquainted with Gladstone's family life are agreed that the tone in which he was addressed was refreshingly and sometimes even embarrassingly spontaneous. John Morley could hardly keep his countenance when on one of his visits to Hawarden he heard one of the children exclaim, in reply to an assertion of their father's: "That's a lie!"—which in the idiom of the Gladstone family "meant merely that the speaker disagreed with him."

It is true that Gladstone had a passionate and fiery temper, and that it made itself felt now and again, especially when it was aroused by such personal matters as disputes within the Cabinet. But in general, as all his secretaries agree, he was perfectly self-controlled, and he never allowed a word to pass his lips that would have hurt his collaborators' feelings. He knew that he was zealously and affectionately served by one and all, and this he never forgot, even after the official bond was dissolved.

Among the Members of like political principles who gathered about him in the House, one with whom he was especially intimate, was John Acton, a stepson of Lord Granville; connected, through his mother, a Princess Dalberg, with the German aristocracy, and intellectually as much at home in Germany as in England. He was a pious son of the Catholic Church, but also a convinced Liberal, who sought in History, which he made his life-work, the idea of liberty. His great work on the *History of Liberty*, for which he collected a library of sixty thousand volumes, was never written; though sometimes, late at night, when conversing with a learned friend, he would discuss the plan of the "History" in persuasive and profoundly thoughtful words. His productive powers were not, unfortunately, equal to his ability to collect an enormous mass of material and to imbue it with his own ideas. But few men have ever had a more actual conception of the world-historical process as a whole, and few have regarded it from so firmly established and exalted a standpoint. This standpoint was that of absolute veracity and the ethical duty of efficacious justice. For him the principles of public morality were just as definite as those of private life, but they were "not identical." In Gladstone he saw the states-man who was inspired by these principles; the two men met on the basis of this common conviction, and in later years Acton favoured Gladstone's growing daughter, Mary, with his stimulating friendship.

Acton sat in the Parliament elected in 1868 until the Queen, on Gladstone's recommendation, raised him to the peerage. But another ornament of the intellectual life of England was absent from the Lower House: John Stuart Mill had not been returned to the House by the Westminster electorate. The defeat of a man distinguished by an idealism so pure and a selflessness so complete seemed to his friends an evil omen, especially as the Radical working-class candidates had likewise been defeated. This mood of depression was expressed, in the most pessimistic temper, by John Morley, in an article published in his *Fortnightly Review*. The article bore the significant title: "The Chamber of Mediocrities." Gladstone's return to power was welcomed, of course, because he brought with him his capacity for work, his consummate administrative experience, a rare financial genius, and a noble devotion to progress. But he would not be able to effect much with a House which differed in little from its predecessors, and which did not seem inclined to make any serious effort to abolish the defects of existing institutions.

The next few years were to show whether the disgruntled Morley was right in his gloomy forecast.

2. Ireland

The first task of which Gladstone had to acquit himself was prescribed by the previous history and the issue of the electoral contest. He had to accomplish the disestablishment of the Irish Church. The principles of the disestablishment had been firmly outlined. They were comprised in the resolutions which Gladstone had introduced in the previous Parliament, and piloted through the House. They had been the chief subjects of debate during the electoral contest. Gladstone himself had made a singular contribution to this discussion. He had published a "chapter of autobiography" in which he expounded, with great sincerity and earnestness, his own inner development from the time of his writing his book on *The State in its Relations with the Church*. The issue of the elections meant that the country had accepted the solution which he had proposed. According to this, not only was the Irish Church to be disestablished, but it was also to be divested of the rich benefices which it had hitherto enjoyed.

So far, of course, no one had doubted that a Government measure based on these fundamental principles would be accepted by the newly-elected House of Commons. But there was the House of

Lords to consider, and the Queen, and it was not to be expected that either would greet the measure with cheerful approval.

In the House of Lords, for some decades past, the Conservative and the Liberal peers had more or less balanced each other. It was one of the glories of the English aristocracy that a considerable proportion of its most distinguished members had always been in favour of progressive and liberal development, and that the great tradition of the "glorious Revolution" had always been preserved by their families. Bitterly though Disraeli might deride what he chose to call the "Venetian oligarchy," the nation had benefited by it greatly, since it had saved England from the many conflicts that had shaken other countries. But the new era which had begun with the death of Palmerston and Gladstone's Government had brought with it new problems, which did not fit into the traditional frontiers, and the new solutions were just as unwelcome to many of the peers who had hitherto described themselves as Whigs or Liberals as they were to their Conservative colleagues. So it was that about this time the Liberal phalanx in the Lords was attacked by a steady crumbling process, which the great adroitness and personal popularity of their Leader, Lord Granville, could only delay, but could not wholly check. Granville was almost ideally qualified for the task to which Gladstone had appointed him. By his unfailing affability and his perfect tact he was able to avoid all unnecessary conflicts, and to lead the House as successfully as it could be led by the spokesman of a small minority. He was the inevitable mediator in the event of any troubles inside the Cabinet and the Party, and also in the case of difficulties with the Opposition, and—the most important and most difficult task of all— with the Queen.

The Queen, in her earlier years, under the guidance of Melbourne and Prince Albert, had inclined to be liberal in her views, so far as this was consistent with the impartiality prescribed by the Constitution. But these mentors were gone, and her own inclinations were rather for the permanent and conservative, even though she was anxious to have it known that her fundamental outlook was liberal. Her Liberalism, however, fought shy of innovations, which she preferred to call "Radical," especially if they seemed

194

likely to excite violent party strife, or even to give rise to the public agitation which she so detested. In reality her mode of thought was that of the Palmerston era, in which the differences between the parties were so attenuated as to be almost imperceptible, and a change of Government was usually brought about by a few dozen votes, which would group themselves differently again when another question came up for consideration. It did not escape her that now causes of dispute were arising which went very much deeper, and which, for that reason, she found much more displeasing. She could not see the necessity of tackling such a ticklish question as the disestablishment and disendowment of the Irish Church, and she was annoyed with Gladstone for having done so. She could not get rid of the suspicion that he might have been led away by ambition, untenable though this theory seemed after the explanations which he had given through her confidential secretary, General Grey. At all events, she had no hesitation in giving him to understand, and repeatedly, that she was dissatisfied with his conduct. Further, his proposals were necessarily highly complicated, and he could not manage to explain them so clearly and comprehensibly that she was able to feel that she had mastered them.

At first, however, she refused to allow these differences to lead her astray from the constitutional path, and it could hardly be said that she was prejudiced against her chief adviser, whose great earnestness and peremptory sense of duty made a deep impression on her. But there were, unfortunately, difficulties of a more personal nature. The Queen was not only a woman, but a wife heavily stricken by Fate, and she expected special consideration to be paid to her in both capacities. Disraeli was a master in this respect, and he had sunned himself in the full glow of her favour. Gladstone, indeed, was not lacking in consideration, and he certainly did not fail in reverent devotion, but there were times when he felt that the matter in hand required that he should disregard her sensibilities. The Queen had never yet emerged from the retirement which she had imposed upon herself after Prince Albert's death, and Gladstone was too well acquainted with the general opinion of the people not to know how greatly their feeling for the monarchy was diminished by the fact that the average Englishman never caught a glimpse of his Queen. Even when a foreign potentate visited the country Victoria was not prepared to show him hospitality. When in May 1869 the Viceroy of Egypt—who was certainly a person of importance, regarded from the standpoint of British interests—wished to pay a visit to England, and Gladstone called the Queen's attention to an article in *The Times*, which spoke of his staying in Buckingham Palace, the Queen replied, in a most agitated manner, that she would, of course, under certain circumstances, see the Egyptian, but that she must "strongly protest against the pretension raised, that she should— at her *own expense* and in the *only* Palace of her own which she may come to at any time . . . entertain all the Foreign Potentates who choose to come here for their own amusement. If the country does wish . . . these Royal personages to be received and entertained, let the Government buy a house, which may be called a Palace, and give the Sovereign the means of entertaining or at least maintain them in it." But Gladstone, the apostle of frugality, was the last man to look kindly on such a demand. Even more serious was the Queen's dislike of being disturbed by the cares of government or political crises when she was staying in one of her usual country residences—at Osborne or Balmoral. Her medical attendant was always ready to declare that a sojourn in the country was indispensable to her health, but even Grey, her faithful secretary, was more sceptical in this connection, both in his thoughts and in his words. When the Irish Church crisis was at its height Gladstone begged her insistently, in the most tactful and respectful language, to remain at Windsor, where she could be reached immediately in case of necessity, for a few weeks longer. She could not disregard his urgent request, especially as only a few weeks earlier she had expressed her gratitude for his invariable readiness to enter into her views and understand her feelings. But she impressed it upon him that this must absolutely remain an isolated instance; so great was the sacrifice that she was making of her health and convenience. These fancies and peculiarities of the Queen's must have made things very difficult for Gladstone. But it is only just to admit that the Queen, when it came to the point, fulfilled her duties as sovereign in a loyal and conscientious manner.

She soon had occasion to do so in respect of the Irish question. After Gladstone had overcome her objections by oral representations and written explanations, he was able, on the 1st of March, to bring forward his Bill. One may justly call it "his Bill," for not only the basic ideas, but the extremely complex details were his own work, and in its final form it corresponded almost exactly with the first draft in which he had set his ideas on paper. In a speech of more than three hours, in which, as Disraeli acknowledged, there was not a word too much, he explained the projected measure, its motive, and its aims to a House which, without distinction of party, was spellbound by his art of lucid and comprehensive exposition. That he had the great majority behind him was shown by the first division, when the motion was accepted by 368 votes to 250. It was years since the House had known such a majority; and this, again, was significant of the changing era. The majority remained of much the same order during the whole of the debate, so that within three months the Bill had passed through the Lower House in a practically unmodified form.

This was a triumph, but it was not unexpected. The real problem began with the debates in the Upper House. It was said that Lord Derby, who had once more recovered from his malady, intended to move the rejection of the Bill, lock, stock and barrel. This would have meant open conflict between the two Houses of Parliament. The Queen was so worried by the prospect that she took the unusual step of writing a letter to Lord Derby, in which she warned him of the "most disastrous results" of such procedure. As a matter of fact, the worst was avoided. But the Lords amended the Bill in such a way that neither Gladstone nor the Lower House could accept it. When for the second time it came before the Upper House the Queen redoubled her efforts to bring about an understanding at the eleventh hour. Her mainstay was Granville, who conducted the negotiations with untiring patience and imperturbable good humour, exploiting every remotest possibility of an understanding. Nevertheless, it looked, for the time being, as though the whole measure would be wrecked by the defiance of the extreme Tories, and Gladstone, who was confined to his room by illness, was apparently on the point of withdrawing the Bill and thereby declaring open war. Then, at the last moment, Granville succeeded in effecting a compromise with the leader of the Conservative Peers, the eminent jurist and politician, Lord Cairns, whom Disraeli had made Lord Chancellor. Cairns was statesman enough to foresee the grievous results of further intransigence on the part of the Upper House, and thought better of it. Lord Derby was so indignant that he ostentatiously withdrew from the session. This was the last time he engaged in the political struggle; a few months later he was dead.

With this understanding between Granville and Cairns the battle for the disestablishment of the Irish Church was ended. In all essentials Gladstone had imposed his point of view. That it was the correct one is no longer doubted by thinkers of whatever party.

Many zealous Protestants had feared that the disestablishment of the Irish Church would be followed by the worst consequences. Gladstone had likened them to the blind Gloucester in *King Lear*, who imagines that he is about to fall from a height of "ten masts," but who actually does not fall at all. Time has shown that the comparison was perfectly just. The fears of the Protestants were unfounded.

But neither were the hopes for the future which some had based on the Bill fulfilled. Beneficial as it was in itself, Disestablishment was by no means enough to pacify Ireland. Only one of Ireland's grievances was abolished. There were others, which were not less urgent.

For the first time Gladstone now approached the question which occupied so much of his later life: Could legislation do anything to improve the unhappy situation of the Irish peasants? These peasants were, for the most part, tenants; the soil did not belong to them, but to landowners of English extraction. The law which regulated their relations was extremely defective, and it favoured the landlord. The defects of the law, and the need of reform, had been recognized as early as the 40's by a Parliamentary Commission. Nevertheless, nothing efficacious had been done. The landowning interest in Parliament, which was still very powerful, was against reform. Here again Palmerston represented the average opinion, which he formulated in the epigram: "Tenants' right is Landlords' wrong." The leasehold system was very widespread in England also, where it worked excellently; for a reason which was very creditable to the English landlords, but which, unhappily, did not apply to Ireland. The English landlord, in his relations with his tenants, was guided by the motto: *Noblesse oblige*. For him, reasonable consideration for the economic needs and requirements of his tenants was regarded as a matter of course. It was not fair or fitting that he should exploit them to his own advantage. But such ideas were unknown in Ireland, where landlord and tenant were not united by any common bond.

It is Gladstone's historic merit that he was the first English statesman to recognize that here it was England's duty to repair an injustice, and that he devoted himself to this task with his utmost energy. This stimulus to reform may have been given by the Secretary of State for Ireland, but Gladstone made it his own business directly he had recognized the full extent of the problem. He was not contented with approving what the Irish Secretary recommended; he felt that it was his duty to master the problem himself, and he was not afraid to make the Socratic confession: I know that I know nothing. Just as when a young man he had studied the tariff problem, so now he studied the Irish land question until he understood it as well as any English politician or political economist could. One source of knowledge, however, he did not utilize. He never went to Ireland to see things for himself on the spot.

Nevertheless, when he brought up the subject in the Cabinet, he was once more better informed than any of his colleagues, and it was owing simply to his superior knowledge that he was able to carry his plans into effect; for here he met with great opposition. After all, a large proportion of his colleagues were great landowners, and found it difficult to approve of proposals to subject the rights of landowners to quite unprecedented restrictions. Equally strong was the doctrinaire opposition of the champions of the economic principle of the free play of forces, with which, of course, many of the Prime Minister's proposals were incompatible. Lowe, in particular, was in his element here, and was not sparing of dismal prophecies. Gladstone, he wrote, would run the vessel on the rocks. But Gladstone was no doctrinaire. He was, indeed, an individualist to the backbone, and a zealous advocate of the free play of forces. But he was realist enough to realize that this doctrine presupposed a fundamental equality of forces, and such equality was absolutely lacking in the relation between the Irish tenant and his English landlord. It would have been against his political conscience had he failed to remedy a condition of extreme distress, under which a whole population was groaning, merely because he would thereby be going against a doctrine which, beneficial as it might be elsewhere, could find no application in the present case.

Compared with what the legislature of Great Britain did afterwards in the domain of the Irish land question, Gladstone's Land Law is tame and feeble. But compared with the earlier passivity of Parliament it was a bold step; astonishingly bold, and of far-reaching consequence. He recognized for the first time the tenant's right to demand compensation for the improvements which he had made on leasehold land. Even more important fundamentally was the injunction that a landlord who gave his tenant notice must compensate him for this disturbance of his peaceful economic development. By this Gladstone wanted to prevent the arbitrary termination of tenancies which had become a serious vexation to the Irish agriculturalist.

How right he was in adopting his line of action was shown by the fate of his draft Bill. The greatest difficulties were encountered in the Cabinet. After these were overcome the victory was as good as won. The Queen allowed herself to be convinced, and wished to see only a few isolated modifications. In Parliament the Opposition did not venture to move the rejection of the measure, even when Disraeli objected vigorously to the State's "interference with the freedom of contract, one of the greatest safeguards for the progress of civilization." The second reading was accepted, only eleven votes being registered against it. The first serious conflict was in respect of compensation for arbitrary eviction, but here again the Government was victorious. Nevertheless, the Bill did not go through Parliament easily. About three hundred amendments were proposed. The defence of the Bill was left almost entirely to Gladstone. No one had mastered all the problems, great and small, as he had done. The only man who could have stood beside him on a footing of equality, Bright, was then suffering from a serious malady which finally compelled him to resign his office. Indefatigably Gladstone fought for each individual paragraph, the debates lasting for three months in all, until at last the Bill had passed through all stages. The Upper House, the situation being what it was, could not raise serious objections to the Bill, and those which it did advance were soon disposed of.

To come to the help of Ireland with the Land Act was for Gladstone an obligation of justice. England had hitherto failed in justice, he declared in Parliament, and for this reason her Irish policy had been a failure. The new policy was to be just to the majority as well as the minority. "Justice," he cried, "is no respecter of persons, and she will not take advantage of a favourable moment to oppress the wealthy, for the sake of flattering the poor, any more than she will condescend to oppress the poor for the sake of pampering the luxuries of the rich."

This faith in the healing power of justice did not desert him, even though Ireland had interminable difficulties and disappointments in store for him.

3. Reforms

Gladstone's first Ministry was epoch-making, as the Ministry of the great administrative reforms. More than any other Ministry of the nineteenth century it may claim the credit for sweeping aside the survivals of the past, which had persisted with characteristic tenacity, and making way for a modern conception of the State and its functions. For, far as England was in advance of the great European States as regards the active participation of her citizens in the government of the country, she was equally behind the times in respect of many other problems which had long been solved on the Continent.

As yet education was not compulsory in England, though in Prussia, for example, it had been established in principle by the

Prussian General Code of 1794, and actually introduced, by decades of diligent and thorough administrative work, after the Napoleonic wars. But in England the notion prevailed until well after the middle of the century that the enforcement by the State of attendance at school was in some way incompatible with the national character. Nothing was so remote from the English mode of thought as the idea which had already been expressed by the Prussian General Code, that the school is a political organ, and a department of the State, or even the notion that the State ought to exercise supervision over all its schools. The State should rather leave the care of the schools to such persons as are inclined to give voluntary help in looking after them. This meant leaving them in the first place, and indeed almost entirely, to the Established Church. The greater proportion of the schools were Church schools, maintained by the Church and guided by its spiritual ideas. The result of this system was that a great proportion of the nation's children grew up without any education at all. It was reckoned that about one and a half-million children were regularly attending school, while nearly twice as many were receiving no education.

It was characteristic of the State's passivity in respect of popular education that there was no such thing as a Ministry of Education. It was already a sign of progress when in 1836 the Lord President of the Privy Council, who sat in the House of Lords, was given a collaborator in the shape of a Vice-President, who was a Member of Parliament, and was supposed to concern himself with educational questions in the Lower House. But this Vice-President was not a Cabinet Minister, so that he had to appeal to the Lord President to advocate his proposals in the Cabinet; and the Lord President, as a rule, was not in any way an expert on educational questions.

Gladstone had given the office of Vice-President to W. E. Forster, a retired manufacturer from Bradford, who was regarded as one of the leading men of the Radical wing. He had originally been a Quaker, but had been excluded from the Friends' community on account of his marriage with a daughter of Dr. Arnold of Rugby, who was herself a member of the Church of England. Forster was a man of upright but rigid character, who applied himself to his task with the greatest energy and self-sacrifice, but who could not tolerate opposition or contradiction; so that it happened more than once that he gave the most serious offence to his political friends.

Forster had the most lively compassion for those unfortunate children who grew up without any schooling. He therefore applied himself to introducing, without delay, legislation which would eradicate this evil. The public opinion of England was now ripe for such a reform. Now that a great proportion of the less prosperous citizens had received the vote, people's eyes were opened, and they saw that the existing state of affairs was indefensible. Their new slogan was: "We must educate our rulers!" Also, they had learned something of political events on the Continent. Prussia's victory over Austria was ascribed to her superior system of national education; and the familiar saying that the Prussian schoolmaster had won the battle of Königgrätz was repeated in England. The Liberal advocates of a sweeping reform of the system of national education had organized themselves in a league which was called, after its place of origin, the "Birmingham League." Birmingham, which was Bright's constituency, was considered the most Radical city in England. Its mayor was a young manufacturer of screws who was regarded as a Radical of Radicals: Joseph Chamberlain. It was in the fight for educational reform that Chamberlain made his first entry into national politics. Like Chamberlain, most of the Parliamentary representatives of the League were Radicals and Nonconformists. Their object was not merely the extension of the schools, but the general introduction of the secular school with free instruction, and the abolition of all confessional schools, especially of those which had hitherto been maintained by the State Church.

It may be doubted whether public opinion was ripe for a programme which broke away in such a radical fashion from the line of development hitherto followed. Forster was decidedly of this opinion, and he felt that he could not postpone his Bill until opinion had evolved thus far. He therefore proposed a measure which would leave t' existing Church schools untouched, and would establish new schools only where those hitherto existing were insufficient. Gladstone supported this proposal. He was then so taken up with his Irish Land Bill that he had to leave Forster a free hand in matters of detail—both Bills were introduced at an interval of only two days—but even if he had applied himself more intensively to the question of education he could hardly, in view of his ecclesiastical standpoint, have agreed to the abolition of the Church schools. He also had to leave the duty of the Bill in Parliament almost entirely to Forster. However great and meritorious the zeal with which Forster performed this task, he was by no means the man to compose differences. In the end Gladstone himself had to intervene, in order at least partly to satisfy the wishes of the Radicals in respect of the bitterly contested question of religious instruction. They were less ready to agree to the financial amendments which Gladstone considered to be necessary. The Radical wing made no secret of its displeasure, and the spokesman of the Nonconformists, Edward Miall, even threatened Gladstone that they would proceed to move a vote of no confidence. But he had the worst of the encounter. "I hope," replied Gladstone, vehemently, "my honourable friend will not continue his support to the Government one moment longer than he deems it consistent with his sense of right and duty."

These encounters, which did not cease even when the Bill was passed, had very undesirable consequences as regards Gladstone's position in the Party. The Nonconformists, who had been among his most devoted supporters, were disappointed. The enthusiasm of many of them waned, and some deserted Gladstone altogether. This defection had disastrous results at the next election. Even Bright, who had been deterred by illness from taking part in the debates in the Cabinet and the House, was not sparing with his criticisms. These disputes did much to prevent the recognition of the extraordinary advance which the Act represented. Few pieces of legislation have proved such a blessing to England, and all the criticisms which were launched against this or that feature should be silenced by the millions of children who at last, and only by virtue of this Act, were given a proper schooling. The number of pupils was doubled and trebled, the whole intellectual level of the English people was raised, and although it is less easy to give evidence of moral progress, such progress there undoubtedly was. Anyone who reads the autobiography of Lord Snowden will obtain a vivid impression of the profound transformation effected by the Education Act of 1870.

The Universities, too, were no less urgently in need of reform than the schools. Here a problem was awaiting solution which Gladstone had been considering for decades. He himself, in 1854, had drafted the great measure of reform which completely modernized the mediaeval constitution of Oxford. He had then been guided by the perception that a change was inevitable, and that it was in Oxford's interest that it should be effected by someone who was bound to the University by ties of affection. The Oxford University Act admitted to matriculation candidates who were not members of the Church of England. But this particular innovation was resolved upon by Parliament against his wish, for he would have left it to the University itself to abolish this restriction. He had then coined the formula, that the teaching and the administration should remain, as of old, ecclesiastical, but that in all other respects freedom should prevail. The Act of 1854 had allowed one very important restriction to stand. The final examinations, at Oxford as at Cambridge, were still to be taken only by those who subscribed to the Thirty-nine Articles. In all other domains of public life this confessional limitation had been gradually abolished; but the conservative *genius loci* of the old Universities defended this last position with the utmost obstinacy, and it had hitherto proved itself stronger than the spirit of the nineteenth century. Gladstone himself had until a few years ago supported the maintenance of this restriction. But for some years now the battle was joined again. The Member for the City of London, Goschen, had shown that he was not interested merely in financial and commercial problems, for since 1865 he had been advocating a Bill to abolish this test. And Gladstone's own Solicitor-General, his friend Coleridge, had given attention to the matter, though not in his official capacity. For a long time Gladstone's ecclesiastical prejudices and his respect for the Oxford tradition were too strong to permit him to co-operate with Coleridge, and as long as he held aloof success was impossible. At length, in 1871, he broke this last tie that bound him to the Oxford of his youth, and placed the abolition of tests on the Government programme. With this the passage of the Bill was assured. It was quickly accepted by the House of Commons, and even the House of Lords finally gave way, much against the will of Lord Salisbury, whom the University of Oxford had significantly elected as its Chancellor; but this time, in the Lords, the reins slipped out of his grasp. Henceforth the Universities and the liberal professions were open to all seekers after learning, without distinction of faith. Those who guarded the Holy Grail of tradition, like the great theologian Pusey—and hitherto Gladstone had been regarded as his special disciple—lamented the end of the old Oxford, but the more modern spirits, like the Master of Balliol, Jowett, who was training the next generation of politicians, rejoiced in the new and fertile spirit that must now make itself felt in the University.

And so, in the domain of University education, so important for the nation, the Reform Ministry swept away a fossilized relic of the seventeenth century.

In the same year Gladstone repealed the Ecclesiastical Titles Act, which he had opposed so vehemently on its passage through the House. For twenty years it had led the sorriest existence a law can lead; it had been constantly infringed and ignored, and no one had lifted a finger in its defence.

Not only the children whose path to the national schools had been smoothed, and the undergraduates who were now able to enter the learned professions, had reason to be grateful to Gladstone's Ministry, but also those young people who wished to qualify as Government officials. Here, too, certain vestiges of the past had to be cleared away—relics that had persisted with extraordinary obstinacy. In the England of the eighteenth century a public office was not an opportunity of serving the interests of the State, but a source of income and a means of rewarding political or personal services. If it happened to be a sinecure, or if the work was done by another person, this did not in any way trouble the conscience of the gentleman who drew the emoluments of the post. How many such offices, in respect of which he never lifted a finger, did not the critical Horace Walpole adorn! The great historian

Gibbon thought it by no means beneath his dignity to accept such a sinecure in return for the silent support with which he favoured Lord North's Ministry in Parliament. Thanks to the indefatigable reforming zeal of Burke the worst of these abuses were eradicated. But even in the nineteenth century Greville, the celebrated diarist, filled the office of a secretary for the island of Jamaica, on which he never set foot, and for which he never did a stroke of work. And readers of *David Copperfield* were not in the least shocked when the faithful Mrs. Micawber expected her family to use their "local influence" to obtain for her husband, who was only just discharged from the debtor's prison, a post in the Customs. Such "local influence" was harmless enough, but it was less harmless that the political influence of Members of Parliament should be decisive in the matter of filling official positions. The Members asked the Government of the day to grant certain appointments, not indeed to themselves, but to their dependants and helpers, and saw in this "patronage" one of the most important advantages of the Parliamentary system. Only a few more farseeing men realized that it was, on the contrary, most vitally necessary to its permanence that the administration should be freed from political strife and the influence of party politicians. Gladstone was one of the first to realize this. As Chancellor of the Exchequer in Aberdeen's Ministry he set up a commission, in 1853, which was to inquire into the conditions of admittance to the Civil Service, and as chairman and vice-chairman of the commission he appointed his former private secretary Stafford Northcote and Macaulay's brother-in-law, Charles Trevelyan. Accepting the findings and recommendations of this commission, he proposed to the Cabinet that in future all offices should be thrown open to all candidates in accordance with the results of an examination for which one and all would have to sit. At that time he was not able to get his way; the opposition of Parliamentarians who felt that their influence was threatened, and of the aristocracy, who regard the Civil Service and the Army as the rightful preserve of their sons, was too much for him. Macaulay, who entirely approved of his brother-in-law's scheme, found, to his distress, that in the leading Whig club everyone was passionately opposed to it.

But Gladstone, despite all hostility, held fast to his standpoint. In 1870, as Prime Minister, he was at last in a position to realize his plans. In the Cabinet he was supported by most of his colleagues; to name one of them, by Lowe. Lord Clarendon, however, obstinately defended the right of the Foreign Office to choose its officials for itself, and to ignore the persuasions of any examining board. Here, nevertheless, Gladstone found the way out of the difficulty: to hold competitive examinations for all candidates approved by the competent Minister. At his request the Queen, who in 1854 had considered Gladstone's plan to be "not without serious objections," issued an Order in Council to this effect. By this Order all appointments, with the exception of those to the Foreign Office and the diplomatic service, ceased to be filled by patronage. They were now, without distinction, accessible to every candidate whose learning and ability were adequate.

In one branch of the public services, however, an abuse still existed which excelled all the rest in absurdity. Commissions in the Army were acquired and disposed of by sale and purchase. This custom was introduced by an order of King Charles II in the year 1683. William III had the good sense to take steps to remedy the abuse, but after his death the system was reintroduced, since it suited well enough the aristocratic and plutocratic views of the eighteenth century. But it was quite unsuited to the age of Liberalism and the rise of democracy. Gladstone had entrusted the War Office to his old colleague Cardwell, an administrator of the first rank. Cardwell was of course a civilian, but his knowledge of every department of military affairs was exhaustive. It was clear to him that the experience gained in the war between Prussia and Austria, soon to be followed by the Franco-Prussian War, could be profitably applied by England, and that the British Army, which had revealed numerous defects in the Crimean War, would become quite useless if it did not learn by this experience. Cardwell became the reformer of the British Army; but if the soldiers of later generations have been eager to give him credit for his reforms, those who were his contemporaries were equally zealous in putting obstacles in his way. The political *chef d'œuvre* of his reformation was the abolition of the traffic in commissions. He proceeded with all due consideration of a prescriptive right, but this did not prevent the beneficiaries of the existing system from opposing the reform in the most vehement manner. People asked what possible justification there could be for a system which prevented the competent authorities from appointing to a post the person best qualified to fill it, and under which the aspirant was commonly required to pay not only the officially sanctioned purchase price, but a large sum in excess of this. Nevertheless, the Opposition contrived to drag out the debate on the proposal by endless speeches and motions, so that Gladstone, in his despatches to the Queen, had to speak of "the unparalleled obstruction" in favour of a class interest. Disraeli was much too clever not to realize the indefensibility of such a system. But this, of course, did not prevent him from exploiting the difficulties of the Government. In the end the Government had to restrict its proposal to the one decisive point, the abolition of purchase. In this form it was accepted by the Lower House.

Now, however, the Government was to learn what obstacles the Upper House could place in the way of a Liberal Ministry, even in the case of a reform which was long overdue. There sat the heads of families who had hitherto regarded commissions in the Army as their own perquisite, and they experienced no moral or intellectual difficulty in equating their own interest with the interest of the State. It is astonishing to look back on the arguments with which a man with the pre-eminent intellectual powers of Lord Salisbury defended this most indefensible of abuses. The Government had reason to assume that the Opposition was drawing support from the Commander-in-Chief of the Army, who regarded the reform with the same suspicion as the majority of its officers. The Commander-in-Chief was a royal prince, the Duke of Cambridge, over whose privileges and interests the Queen watched with a jealous regard. Gladstone was therefore compelled to enter into an exhaustive and difficult correspondence with Her Majesty on the subject of the Duke's position. However, in respect of the abolition of purchase the Queen entirely approved of the attitude of the Ministry.

She had soon occasion to show this in a surprising fashion.

209

When on the 17th of June, 1871, the Lords blocked the progress of the Bill by a dilatory resolution, Gladstone resorted to an expedient which the Opposition had not foreseen. Purchase was not based on a statute, but on a Royal decree. Such a decree can be annulled by another decree. It was this course that Gladstone now proposed to the Queen, and she did as he advised, without raising any objections. In this way the ancient privilege for which the Lords had fought so stoutly was abolished from one day to the next.

Naturally, the first shock of amazement was followed by a tremendous outburst of disapproval. Disraeli spoke of a "shameful conspiracy of the Cabinet against the Upper House." The Conservative Leader, whose Governments the Upper House had always supported, found it easy to regard the Liberal Prime Minister's emergency measure with indignation; and certainly Gladstone could not be acquitted of the charge of inconsistency, however ingenious the arguments with which he defended himself. But the conflict in respect of this question of method was of ephemeral interest, whereas the actual improvement which he effected belongs to history.

Here were four great, lasting reforms in the most important domain of the national administration. Further, we must not forget a political reform, which was a considerable advance, in the direction which Bright had advocated, on the Franchise Act of 1867: the introduction of the ballot, of the secret vote, by the Act of 1872. Gladstone had never been among the most enthusiastic advocates of the ballot, and it was only after some hesitation that he included it in the Governmental programme. But when in this case also the Lords repeated their performance, and rejected the Bill which had passed through the Lower House, Gladstone attacked them with such decision that they finally gave way. The Lords and the Conservative Opposition feared that the introduction of the secret ballot would mean the final destruction of all Conservative institutions; of the House of Lords to begin with, and perhaps even the Monarchy. However, the elections of 1874 convinced them that their fears were unfounded. But the Liberals were no less deluded, for they had firmly believed that, once protected by the secret ballot, the English people would always vote for liberty and progress.

Lastly, mention must be made of an Act whose significance for the social evolution of the English people cannot be over-estimated: the Trade Union Act of 1871. Its origin is one of the most characteristic examples of the English method of legislation. Certain disorders which had occurred in 1866, especially in Sheffield, occasioned the appointment of a commission of inquiry. This, however, had a result very different from what had been anticipated; namely, the complete justification of the Trade Unions and the recognition of their valuable work. This was especially emphasized in the minority report from the pen of Frederic Harrison, a leader of the English Positivists. The Cabinet decided to base its legislative measures on this minority report, and the Trade Unions were granted their long-overdue legal basis. Although Gladstone was not particularly interested in these questions, he must be given full credit both for the responsibility for this decision and for its consequences.

Such were the reforms of this first Gladstone Ministry, which assured it of a place of honour in the English history of the nineteenth century. England, after this Ministry had done its work, was no longer the same country. An historian who has not refrained from criticizing Gladstone's political activities, G. M. Trevelyan, summed up his career in the following words: "Gladstone did more than any other man to adapt the machinery of the British State and the habits of the British politicians to modern democratic conditions without a total loss of the best standard of the older world." There are not many statesmen of whom this can be said. But there were not, of course, many countries which enjoyed, in the nineteenth century, so long a period of untroubled peace as England.

4. The Franco-German War

"Never has the news of a death rejoiced me more than the news of your father's death." With these astonishing words Bismarck is said to have greeted Lady Emily Russell, the wife of the British

Ambassador in Berlin and the daughter of Lord Clarendon. When Lady Emily expressed her very natural stupefaction at this speech, the Chancellor continued: "Pray don't misunderstand me; I mean simply that if your father had lived he would have prevented the war." Even though one may doubt whether Bismarck would have expressed his actual thought so candidly at the dinner-table, these words show the significance which the world attributed to the fact that Lord Clarendon, the British Foreign Minister, died on the 27th of June, 1870. He was undoubtedly a man of great ability and experience, and, above all, he enjoyed in a special degree the regard and confidence of Napoleon III.

As his successor, Gladstone appointed the Secretary for the Colonies and Leader of the House of Lords, Lord Granville, who had once already been Foreign Minister in 1851—though only for a little while—and who, in several Liberal Cabinets, had played a leading part in questions of foreign politics. The Queen, who indeed liked Granville best of all her Ministers, gave her willing consent to the appointment. On the 5th of July, 1870, Granville paid his first visit to the Foreign Office, in order to obtain information as to the state of affairs from Hammond, the Permanent Under-secretary. Hammond, who had then been forty years at the Foreign Office, was rightly regarded as one of the most competent of experts, but he was an expert for whom the world was identified with his documents. A few months before this interview one of the most eminent of British diplomatists, who more than any other had furthered the work of Cavour, had exclaimed, in despair: "So long as a Foreign Secretary is hampered by office rules such as those concocted in the last twenty years by Hammond there is no such thing as diplomacy in the British service." And this was the wise advice which Hammond vouchsafed to his new Chief on the 5th of July, 1870: "He had never during his long experience known so great a lull in foreign affairs." These words were barely uttered when the first rumble was heard of the earthquake that was very soon to shake the very foundations of the Continent. A few hours later Granville held in his hand the telegram which informed him of the choice of Prince Leopold of Hohenzollern as the candidate for the throne of Spain.

212

The Queen cannot have been so surprised as Lord Granville, for as far back as March her daughter, the Crown Princess of Prussia, had warned her in the strictest confidence of the impending candidature. She had also stated that neither the King nor the Crown Prince was in favour of the Prince's candidature, but the Queen, on Clarendon's advice, had declined confidentially to define her own attitude, as her daughter had requested. Hammond, of course, could know nothing of this, as no hint of the matter had reached the Foreign Office.

Gladstone, a few months after taking office, had given a systematic explanation of the leading ideas of his foreign policy in a letter to General Grey (dated the 17th of April, 1869) which was intended for the Queen's perusal. A remark of Clarendon's had occasioned the Queen to ask whether in future England would be in a position to give no more than a *moral* support to a righteous cause. To this he replied that England would never be unfaithful to her great tradition. "But her credit and her power form a fund, which in order that they be made the most of, should be thriftily used. . . . Is England so uplifted in strength above every other nation, that she can with prudence advertise herself as ready to undertake the general redress of wrongs? . . . But do not . . . allow it to be believed that England will never interfere. . . . It is dangerous for her to assume alone an advanced and therefore an isolated position, in regard to European controversies . . . she should seek to develop and mature the action of a common, or public, or European opinion, as the best standing bulwark against wrong." In phrases that plainly allude to Palmerston's unadvised policy, but which now had acquired actual significance, he wrote: "It is better for her to promise too little than too much; that she should not encourage the weak by giving expectations of aid to resist the strong, but should rather seek to deter the strong by firm but moderate language, from aggressions on the weak." Now the time had come to put these principles into practice.

Even a leading statesman can do no more than base his actions on the knowledge at his disposal. What scientific research has unearthed from the archives during the last few decades was hidden from contemporaries. Here, then, the great controversy as to

Bismarck's aims, motives and methods in supporting the Hohen-zollern candidature—one of the most difficult and most interesting of historical problems—need not be considered. Gladstone had already described the development of the crisis, as seen from the English standpoint, in an article contributed to the *Edinburgh Review* in 1870. In the October number of this periodical appeared an anonymous article on "Germany, France and England." The veil of anonymity was quickly rent, and very soon politicians and journalists knew that the author was none other than the Prime Minister. Gladstone had been naïve enough to believe that his authorship of the article could remain a secret. Such an expression of opinion by a responsible politician in office was contrary to all tradition. But for the historian it constitutes a valuable and authentic source.

Gladstone and Granville knew only what the English diplomatists reported and the newspapers published. They saw the stupendous excitement which this candidature had aroused in Paris, and the danger which it threatened to the peace of Europe. They therefore wished to see the candidature withdrawn, although Gladstone, when the first news of it arrived, had declared that "he was not disposed to interfere with the liberty of the Spanish people to choose their own sovereign." When the French Ambassador begged the British Government to use its influence in Berlin and Madrid to procure the withdrawal of the candidature, the Government willingly did what it could, however greatly it disapproved of Gramont's menacing speech in the French Parliament. Queen Victoria, who seconded the Government's efforts, complained of "the conduct of the French . . . most preposterous and insulting to Spain." The statement of the King of Belgium, who had good reason to fear for the peace of Europe, that "it would seem that it was Bismarck who urged Leopold to accept," seems to have made little impression on the Queen. When Leopold's father, Prince Anton von Hohenzollern, withdrew the candidature in his son's name, it was Gladstone's opinion that France had now obtained all that she had the right to ask, and must not under any circumstances make further demands. And when the French Cabinet actually did make further demands he had no hesitation in declaring to the

Prussian Ambassador, on the 13th of July, that Prussia, in his opinion, had gone to the utmost limit of conciliation, and that France would be flagrantly in the wrong if she should none the less declare war. He also informed him that Granville had immediately telegraphed to the British Ambassador in Paris, Lord Lyons, instructing him to make emphatic and cautionary representations to the French Minister *before* the Ministerial Council which had been convoked. Gladstone would have had Granville use even more incisive language.

Gramont was already in the Ministerial Council when Granville's telegram reached Lyons. The Ambassador therefore wrote him a letter to the desired effect while the Council was sitting. But Gramont disregarded the warning, and sent forth his Ambassador, Benedetti, to that fateful interview with King William on the promenade at Ems, by which he placed himself hopelessly in the wrong, and delivered himself into Bismarck's hands. The publication of the Ems telegram on the evening of the 13th of July made the decision irrevocable, and it also deprived of all purpose the British Government's final attempts to act as intermediary. On the 14th of July the Cabinet met and resolved to make, to both parties, a proposal for the settlement of the dispute, in order, as Gladstone wrote to the Queen, to avert "the guilt and horror of war." He proposed to Berlin that the King, in the interest of peace, should "communicate to the French Government his approval of the Prince's withdrawal," if France would waive her demand of a guarantee for the future. He informed Paris that the French claim was indefensible, that he had given the above advice to the King in the interest of peace, and that France should on no account proceed to extremities. Bismarck refused to place this proposal before the King; he was not yet aware of the fact that in the meantime the King had actually made it known to Benedetti that he approved of the withdrawal of the candidature. In any event, the attempt to negotiate failed, both in Berlin and in Paris, and destiny followed its course.

Both the French and the Germans have reproached the British Government for not having done all that lay in its power to prevent the war. Naturally, both countries have entirely contrary ideas as to the steps which England ought to have taken. In the opinion of the French Premier of that day, Ollivier, England ought to have explained that Prussia's behaviour was a violation of an internationally recognized rule; according to the German view, England should have informed Paris that in the event of war France would find her orf the side of the enemy. This view was supported also by an English diplomatist, Sir Robert Morier, then chargé d'affaires in Darmstadt, a man distinguished by great determination and a sharp tongue, who, as he himself wrote, at this international crisis was heart and soul on the side of the Germans. "One whisper," he wrote to Lord John Russell, "would have sufficed to make war impossible." But subsequent research has revealed nothing in support of this view. Gladstone, in any case, would have regarded the application of such pressure as an instance of partisanship far in excess of anything that was permissible to the representative of a neutral State, and in this the public opinion of the country supported him. In Germany, of course, this neutrality was severely censured, and Treitschke spoke in bitter scorn of the possibility that "the Queen of the Ocean" would sell "that useless plaything, her battle-fleet," to the highest bidder.

How difficult it was to maintain a strict neutrality was shown to Gladstone by the example of the royal family. The Queen's personal sympathies were definitely on the German side, in which, as she wrote to Gladstone, two of her sons-in-law, her only brother-in-law, and other near relatives and friends were fighting. But the Prince of Wales, as was generally known, took quite another view of the matter. The Prussian Ambassador wrote to Berlin that the heir to the throne had informed the Austrian Ambassador that he was glad to think that Austria wished to ally herself with France, and the Queen, who at once heard of this from her daughter Victoria, told Gladstone, with a sigh, that the Prince was unhappily very incautious. Gladstone could not do otherwise than urgently remind the Prince, who flatly denied the impeachment, that he must rigorously refrain from any expression of his private feelings.

It is probable that on this occasion the Prime Minister made no attempt to conceal from the Prince—as he had not attempted to conceal from the Queen—his opinion of the attitude of the French statesmen. "Whatever may be said of the prior conduct of Prussia," he wrote to the Queen on the 16th of July, "France has entirely failed to show, in the circumstances of the present crisis, any adequate warrant for breaking the peace of Europe. This failure is accompanied, in the Ministerial statement of yesterday of Paris, with a hardihood of assertion which it is painful to witness." This drastic judgement he never modified. In his article in the *Edinburgh Review* he spoke of folly, inconsistency and foolhardiness, of blunders and follies which were unexampled in history. What must have filled a man of his views with peculiar indignation was the frivolity with which the French Ministers, "with a light heart," as Ollivier said, delivered sentence of death on thousands of human beings. The tragic expression of his face when he received the news that war had been declared was never to be forgotten by those who witnessed it.

Ten days after the declaration of war Bismarck published in *The Times* Benedetti's draft of a Franco-Prussian treaty which would have given Belgium to the French Emperor. He had already acquainted Gladstone and Granville with the content of the treaty through the intermediary of Bernstorff, apparently in order to compel them to make it known; but they had not agreed to do so. The publication of the draft had not quite the effect that Bismarck had intended, for the English doubted whether Benedetti would have been prepared to make such a proposal if Bismarck had not previously given him reason to believe that he was ready to proceed on the lines laid down in the projected treaty.

Gladstone concluded, from its publication, that England would now have to obtain from both nations a new and explicit pledge and covenant that they would safeguard the neutrality of Belgium, and would at need defend it, in co-operation with England, against the aggressor. With this demand of the English Cabinet Bismarck complied with the greatest promptitude, which Gladstone regarded as a fresh and convincing proof of his political judgement. The long hesitation of the French Cabinet, which was cut short only by the defeat of Worth, naturally produced the contrary impression. Gladstone drew attention to the conclusion of the treaty by a speech in the House of Commons, in which he stigmatized an eventual usurpation of Belgium as "the direst crime that ever stained the pages of history," and made it clear that in case of need England would intervene by force of arms. The objections which John Bright raised to his policy he refuted conclusively by appealing to the people's right of self-determination. The treaty proved to be effective: Belgium's neutrality was not infringed. Gladstone always counted the conclusion of this treaty as one of his most significant achievements, and in one of his Midlothian addresses he emphatically declared that he would readily have gone to war in the defence of Belgian liberty, passionate as was his abhorrence of war.

The lightning rapidity of the German victories, which surprised the whole world, the fall of the French Empire, and the institution of the French Republic, soon confronted even the neutral States with a completely novel situation. At the beginning of the war the English people were entirely friendly to Germany, but as the war continued their feelings gradually underwent a change, and in many circles were transformed into actual hostility as the German claims to Alsace and Lorraine found more definite expression. The revulsion of feeling was most apparent among the Radicals, who sympathized with the French Republic. The most outspoken representative of this tendency was Frederic Harrison, who said of himself that at the beginning of the war he had been definitely on the side of Germany, but that now he was just as definitely opposed to her designs; and in working-class circles there was an intensity of feeling that did not recoil even from demanding war against Germany.

Gladstone also was greatly perturbed by the proclamation of the annexation of Alsace and Lorraine. True to his fundamental standpoint, he did not presume to form an opinion on Germany's claim that she required a safeguard against future French aggression, and he made no secret of the fact that he regarded the declaration of Jules Favre: "Not an inch of our soil, not a stone of our fortresses!" as absolutely futile. What distressed him was the fate of the inhabitants of the two provinces. Once more, he was actuated by ethical reasons. As in 1859 he had protested against the fact that at Villafranca Napoleon and Franz Joseph disposed of the population of Central Italy as a feudal seigneur disposed of his property, so he now deplored that anyone should have relapsed into "the old and cruel practice of treating the population of a civilized European country as mere chattels."

Gladstone was even disposed to proceed to the practical corollary of this standpoint. He proposed to the Cabinet that England should invite the other neutral Powers to join her in requesting Germany to allow the population of the two provinces to decide their future nationality by the vote. Here he encountered the most resolute opposition from Granville, and after a long and excited discussion his proposal was rejected. "Quite exhausted after the longest fight I ever had against Gladstone," wrote Granville to his wife. "The losses were great, the killed and wounded innumerable: but I remained in possession of the field and of the Cabinet."

Granville and the rest of his colleagues approved of the annexation as little as Gladstone, but they believed that the step which he proposed would have been completely ineffective; that it might even have prolonged the war, and that it would certainly have meant that a victorious Germany would have cherished an enduring grudge against England.

Gladstone was so convinced of the correctness, and indeed of the necessity of the measure which he had proposed, that he explained to the Queen exactly where his views diverged from those of the Cabinet, and he went very thoroughly into the reasons which had prompted him to make the proposal. A general principle was involved, whose violation "has caused much disturbance and much bloodshed in subsequent times to Europe. . . . The opposite rule of action is favourable to future peace. . . . A matter of this kind cannot be regarded as in principle a question between two belligerents only, but it involves considerations of legitimate interest to all the powers of Europe. . . . It cannot be right that the neutral Powers should remain silent while this principle is trampled down." This made little impression on the Queen, who regarded the French as "quite crazy."

Further, Gladstone repeatedly laid memoranda before the Cabinet which carefully explained his point of view, but they did no more than elicit a somewhat ironical compliment from Granville: "an excellent argument, the more so as it is what Thiers ought to have said, but did not say." It was then that he took the unusual step of appealing to public opinion, under the cover of anonymity, in the pages of the *Edinburgh Review*.

When Gladstone saw that he could not carry his plan against the opposition of the Cabinet he had to submit to *force majeure*. But he was not persuaded. He not only held to the opinion that it would remain as a lasting reproach to England that she had not made her voice heard in Europe, but he regarded the future with dark misgivings. "While I more and more feel the deep culpability of France," he wrote to Granville on the 20th of December, 1870, "I have an apprehension that this violent laceration and transfer is to lead us from bad to worse, and to the beginning of a new series of European complications." And when Germany's final conditions of peace became known in February 1871, he wrote in the same tone of anxiety to Professor Max Müller at Oxford, whose love for his German fatherland was unabated: "I am afraid . . . that Germany, crowned with glory and confident in her strength, will start on her new career to encounter the difficulties of the future without the sympathies of Europe; which in my opinion no nation, not even we in our sea-girt spot, can afford to lose." Even at the outset, then, Gladstone's repugnance to the *Realpolitik* of Bismarck was manifest. And the great German statesman was quite aware of his opposition.

Before the war between France and Germany was ended Gladstone was to have yet another experience which not only showed him that even treaties of peace are not concluded for eternity, but also that neutral states, in time of great conflicts, are less concerned to co-operate in order to put an end to bloodshed and prevent future conflicts than to exploit the situation to their own advantage. On the 31st of October, 1870, the Tsar declared that he no longer considered himself bound by the terms of the Treaty of Paris of 1856, which closed the Black Sea to Russia.

This unilateral abrogation of an international treaty aroused a storm of passionate indignation in London. The spirit of the period of the Crimean War seemed to have been resurrected, and the newspapers were soon speaking of war with Russia as of an imminent event. Not only the Queen, but even John Bright was infuriated. Gladstone entirely shared the popular opinion that

Russia could not possibly be allowed to renounce her pledges without the consent of the other parties to the treaty. This fundamental conception found immediate expression in a vigorously worded Note of Granville's. On the other hand, the Prime Minister was not by any means convinced that the determination of the Paris treaty denounced by Russia was permanently defensible. How could England go to war in order to uphold a proviso which sooner or later would have to be annulled?

Gladstone therefore strove—and with success—to avoid over-hasty action, without neglecting such steps as were necessary. For here the saying of Goethe was peculiarly relevant, that the difficult secret of our age lies between undue haste and omission. Gladstone could not allow himself to be guided by the outcry in the Press, nor yet by the adjurations of Bright—now a sick man—who warned him that his might be Ollivier's fate if he allowed himself to be persuaded to a declaration of war. Granville's words were more statesmanlike: "Promising peace is as unwise as to threaten war." To safeguard the principle of the sacredness of international treaties, which Granville had upheld in his Note, Russia must be induced to negotiate over what she had annulled by her unilateral action.

Of the guarantors of the Treaty of Paris who were pledged to uphold by force of arms the closing of the Black Sea, France was evidently unable to act. As for Prussia, who was not pledged to go to war in support of the Treaty, it was assumed in London that she had given her assent beforehand to Russia's denunciation of the Treaty in return for the latter Power's benevolent neutrality. In any case, since Prussia's relations with Russia were believed to be so close, and her interest in maintaining peace between the guarantor Powers so great, it was decided in London that it would be best to approach Petersburg through Versailles, for the Chancellor of the North German Confederation was now at the headquarters of the victorious Army. The mission to Bismarck was entrusted to young Odo Russell, who was justly credited with the needful capacities for so difficult a task. When Bismarck first read Granville's Note he had cried, contemptuously, to his friends: "Future complications! A Parliamentary orator! They daren't do anything!" Russell realized, in the course of his conversation with

Bismarck, that the important thing was to make him understand that if the worst came to the worst the English would "dare do something," and he resorted—on his own responsibility—to the dangerous expedient of declaring that if he could not induce Russia to withdraw the offending circular Note, this would "compel us with or without allies to go to war with Russia." This was a high card, but it won the trick. Bismarck (who made no reference to this declaration of Russell's in his official Note) was finally convinced that the Englishman was speaking the truth, and undertook, without in any way binding himself, to persuade Russia to resort to negotiation. And since the self-confidence of the Russian Chancellor, Gortschakoff, had been considerably shaken by the excitement caused by his temerarious Note, Bismarck was successful. The Conference was held in London, after Gladstone had expressly stipulated that there must be no question of a "conference which should assume any portion of the Treaty to have been already abrogated by the discretion of a single Power."

The Conference had no easy time of it, but when its work was concluded, in March 1871, Russia had in all essentials obtained her liberation from the fetters of the Black Sea proviso. But this result had been reached without the shedding of a drop of blood, and without the creation of a dangerous prejudice. So far Gladstone might well be content with the outcome of the Conference. But he could not bring himself to approve of the daring expedient employed by Russell, which had contributed very largely to the success of the negotiations.

5. Fighting for Peace

By 1872 the popularity of Gladstone's Ministry was beginning to wane. But the first cause of this diminished popularity was a political achievement which history must regard as one of Gladstone's greatest titles to fame: namely, the peaceful settlement of the dispute with the United States over the privateering exploits of the *Alabama*.

The story began like a comedy, but it afterwards threatened to develop into an international tragedy.

On a fine summer morning of the year 1862 a newly-built ship was launched from the world-famous ship-building yard of Lairds in Birkenhead. There were all the ingredients of a pleasant trial trip: a cheerful company, a band, and fluttering pennants. But the ship was hardly beyond the three-mile limit when the scene underwent a sudden transformation. Armed men, whose expression was anything but festive, appeared on deck, and in a twinkling the yacht was converted into a privateer, which forthwith proceeded to harry the shipping of the Federal States of North America, plundering and burning her captures, until the *Alabama* became the terror of the Atlantic. For close on two years the ship continued to work havoc, until at last, in June 1864, a Federal warship succeeded in capturing and destroying her.

In the conflict between the Union and the seceding States the North had profited by its naval superiority to blockade the ports of the South, which were soon choked with cotton. The Southern States revenged themselves by despatching privateers which harried the overseas trade of the Northern States, and since their own ports were blockaded they had these vessels fitted out and replenished by the ship-building yards of the greatest seafaring nation, which were very ready to undertake such business. The representatives of the Northern States in England naturally kept a watch on the suspected yards, and appealed to the British authorities with the request that they would put an end to this practice, as it was inconsistent with the duties of neutrality.

The United States Minister in London was Charles Francis Adams, a worthy scion of the distinguished family which had already furnished two Presidents to the United States. When he was told of the singular vessel which had been built at Lairds' he requested Lord John Russell, the Foreign Secretary, to intervene. Russell was not convinced by the information laid before him, and a long correspondence ensued. At last, on the 29th of July, 1862, the Attorney-General, Sir Roundell Palmer (later Lord Selborne, and Lord Chancellor), after examining all the documents, expressed the opinion that it was the Government's duty to order the seizure of the vessel. Lord Russell at once complied—but the ship had already put out to sea.

The cause of this fateful delay was of a singular nature. One of the Government's legal advisers, Harding, to whom the documents had first been submitted, had suffered a nervous breakdown which presently developed into mental derangement. His wife, anxious to conceal his true condition, kept the documents by her for three days before she finally sent them on to Palmer. These three days, thanks to the spies of the Southerners, assured the ship of a start which saved her from capture. Such trifling contingencies have before now tipped the balance between peace and war.

In England there were many who considered that Russell should have intervened very much earlier. John Bright, in particular, who had passionately supported the cause of the Abolitionist Union, complained bitterly of the mischief that had been caused by this procrastination—a mischief which he described in unforgettable words in the course of one of his most impressive Parliamentary speeches. But on the other side of the Atlantic the exploits of the *Alabama*, and of other privateers built in English yards, were evoking a feeling of intense exasperation with England. Each fresh report of the destruction of an American merchant vessel by the *Alabama* resulted in a renewed outburst of wrath. It was said that she was a British ship, manned by British sailors, equipped with British guns and ammunition, and that she had slipped out of the Mersey because the British Government had closed one eye. So long as the Civil War continued nothing could be undertaken against Great Britain, but when once the South had been completely subdued the Union demanded full compensation for all the damage which the privateer had committed. The British Government's original attitude of complete repudiation was abandoned by Derby's Cabinet, and when Gladstone took office in 1868 he was faced with the task of finding an acceptable settlement of this dispute, which had long envenomed the relations between the two countries.

For a long while the negotiations made no progress, and the longer they continued, the more incisive the tone and the greater the claims of the Americans. An agreement to submit the matter to arbitration, which had been negotiated with the American Government by Lord Clarendon, was repudiated by the Senate in April 1869. At the same time Senator Sumner, the energetic champion of emancipation, accused England, in an extremely violent speech, of prolonging the Civil War by years by her building of privateers. For this, too, she must indemnify the Union. These "indirect damages," which could be reckoned at n million dollars, were to play a fateful part.

The sudden crisis evoked by Russia's unilateral denunciation of the Treaty of Paris, as far as the closure of the Black Sea was concerned, made the British Government more than ever conscious of the necessity of retaining the friendship of the United States. It was therefore urgently necessary to get rid of this bone of contention, and Lord Granville now applied himself with energy to the task. Since the usual diplomatic methods had failed, he agreed with the Americans, at the beginning of 1871, that a commission consisting of delegates of both countries should be appointed in Washington, which was to conclude a treaty for the settlement of the whole dispute.

As chief of the British delegation Gladstone appointed a Cabinet Minister of tried discretion—Earl Grey, later the Marquess of Ripon—but he prudently arranged that the Opposition too should be represented on the Commission, and again by a man who was no Hotspur—Sir Stafford Northcote, once his own private secretary. The members of the delegation proved to be happily selected, inasmuch as they succeeded in negotiating an arbitration treaty with the Americans. And this was a task of the greatest difficulty. In an age which has become accustomed to the notion that the diplomatists do much of their work by travelling from country to country, and when long and complicated treaties are concluded in places which are hundreds of miles distant from the capitals of the countries concerned, one can hardly form a just idea of the technical difficulties which confronted the delegates at every step, for they had to consult their Government beforehand in respect of every move, so that there was a constant exchange of circumstantial telegrams. There was no telephone in those days; no question of a Foreign Secretary at one end of a wire and an Ambassador at the other. The British delegates declared, derisively, that before they could respond to the "good morning" of their American colleagues they ought by rights to ask permission of London, and the frugal

Northcote lamented, when all was over, that the telegrams alone had cost £5,000! But the technical obstacles were as nothing to the practical difficulties. When at last it was agreed that the whole question was to be submitted to a court of arbitration, nothing, unfortunately, was said as to the juridical principles which were to inspire the verdict of the court. For the international law on the point was completely obscure and inadequate. Were the arbitrators to be left to excogitate these principles for themselves? The risks of such a course were tremendous. Or were they to be formulated in the arbitration treaty? In that case they must be invested with retroactive efficacy, if they were to be applied to counts which had preceded the treaty. And this, strictly speaking, was contrary to all juristic logic. How could a State be held responsible for infringing, in the year 1862, juridical principles which were first declared in 1871?

Despite all these objections, Gladstone decided for the subsequent agreement as to principles of international law which should possess retroactive efficacy. This seemed to him better, at all events, than the renunciation of any firm foundation for the court of arbitration, whose composition was not yet determined, and whose mental operations no one could foresee; this was, after all, a first experiment with an institution as yet entirely untested. Further, the absurdity of retroactive juridical principles was by no means as great as it seemed in theory; for they must, on the whole, have the same content as the English law on the subject—the Foreign Enlistment Act—except that a law which had hitherto been national in its application must now be given international validity.

That this policy was practically justified may be seen from the fact that the legal principles enunciated in the Treaty of Washington have remained ever since, and practically undisputed, as part of the generally recognized stock of international law, and thirty-five years later they were included by the Hague Peace Conference in a great general agreement as to neutrality in time of naval warfare. But from the standpoint of contemporary politics the matter had a very different appearance. A Government which agreed to make the country amenable to juridical principles established after the act was likely enough to be accused of possessing a defective sense of national honour and of feebly yielding to a foreign Power, especially as it was obliged, if it hoped for the conclusion of the treaty, to express its regret that the *Alabama* had escaped from a British port.

But there was worse to come. The British delegation had returned from Washington, the treaty having at last been concluded. The arbitration court on which the parties had agreed had assembled in Geneva, had been formally constituted, and had requested the parties to submit their pleas in writing. Everyone believed that at last the old dispute would be settled without further friction. The United States submitted their plea and their proposals to the court. But as soon as these were known in England a cry of indignation went up from the whole country; for the Americans had extended their claims to include compensation for "indirect injury," and this on the most comprehensive scale imaginable, including indemnity for the prolongation of the war.

Even Gladstone was infuriated. In letters to the Queen he declared that it was "wholly incompatible with the national honour to admit, or to plead to before a tribunal" such claims as these, and he declared that "the conduct of the American Government was the most disreputable he had ever known in his recollection of diplomacy." The Queen asked, as she well might do under the circumstances, whether the English delegates in Washington had perhaps allowed themselves to be deluded into believing that they were dealing with gentlemen. The English delegates declared most positively that the Americans had agreed to drop the question of "indirect injuries"; the Americans denied this just as positively.

How was such a thing possible? The explanation is found in a psychological fact with which many post-bellum conferences were to familiarize a later generation. The men who sit together round a table as representatives of their nations think, as a rule, much more objectively and are capable of a much more reliable estimate of what is possible and attainable than the public in either country, which tries, as it were, to look into the court room through the windows, and whose expectations have previously been roused to impossible heights. The American delegates at the Washington Conference knew very well that England could never enter into an arbitration treaty which would include the question of "indirect injuries," and·they had, therefore, made it sufficiently plain that they would claim for such only if no peaceful agreement could be reached. But they had been very careful not to put this into writing; for then it must have been laid before the Senate, and the domestic opponents of President Grant might have made capital out of it.

There was to be a Presidential election the following year, and Grant was anxious to be re-elected. The English delegates had accepted the situation, because otherwise no treaty could have been concluded, and because they were confident that the American Government would feel itself bound by the declarations of its representatives. But when it came to the point the American Government had not after all the courage to renounce beforehand claims which the Americans themselves can hardly have taken seriously. Gladstone considered, quite correctly, that they were actuated by considerations which arose out of the sphere of their own domestic politics.

If Gladstone had chosen to behave after the same fashion, the only thing to do would have been to withdraw from the arbitration treaty. In this case he would have taken his stand as the unbending champion of the national honour, and his popularity would have been supreme. In his own Cabinet there were many who expressly recommended such a step. But after recovery from his first reaction of anger he resolutely sided with the prudent minority—Granville, Forster and Ripon—who wished to continue negotiations. In the House of Commons, of course, there had to be plain speaking, and Gladstone spoke plainly enough; he was able, also, to approve of Disraeli's attitude: "Nothing could be more equitable and considerate or more conducive to the public interest." But he would not allow relations with Washington to be broken off, and he himself refused to be disconcerted, although old Lord John Russell, who, as a matter of fact, was more than anyone responsible for the whole affair, beat upon the national drum and insisted that England must retire from the court unless America withdrew her claim to compensation for "indirect injuries." But Gladstone knew very well what was at stake: the future of Anglo-American relations, and a great principle, full of promise for the future. It was probably

228

an exaggeration to say, as some did, that the breakdown of negotiations would lead to war. But the lasting hostility of the United States, which might make itself felt on the occasion of any foreign complications, and which would disturb the peaceful intercourse between two nations meant to understand each other, might certainly be anticipated, and no one could say whether it might not one day have even more disastrous consequences. And there was also something else to be considered. Was there really no better means of settling disputes between States than a bloody war, such as a horrified Europe had only just witnessed? Was it really impossible to employ such peaceful methods as men had resorted to for thousands of years in the settlement of their private differences? If the experiment of a court of arbitration failed in the case of two nations that spoke the same language, no second attempt could be anticipated for many years to come.

It needed a firm conviction of the righteousness of the purpose for which he was striving, and an untiring patience, in order to continue the negotiations with America notwithstanding the increasing restiveness in England. Here Gladstone was supported by the sangfroid and adroitness of Granville, who, rather than give vent to his exasperation with American "cuteness" in diplomatic Notes, preferred to express it, epigrammatically, in private conversation, by referring to the "Americoquins" or "the more or less United States." But the progress of the negotiations was very, very slow.

In the meantime the 15th of June, 1872, was approaching, the date on which the court of arbitration would commence its deliberations. This was the last moment for an understanding for which both Governments were equally anxious. The American Government was secretly prepared to renounce its claim in respect of "indirect injuries," if only matters could be so arranged that it did not appear to be renouncing them.

The credit of finding the way out of this dilemma belongs, in the first place, to the former American Minister in London, Charles Francis Adams. He was now the American member of the Court of Arbitration, and he resolved to do, in this capacity, what his Government could not. For if the court could be induced to declare beforehand that it declined to deliberate on the question of "indirect claims," the rock would be safely avoided. England would then have attained her material object, and the American Government would be in the enjoyable position of being able to shrug its shoulders and ruefully explain that it certainly had not renounced the claims, but if the court really would not consider them . . .

On Saturday the 15th of June the Cabinet assembled in Downing Street. The subjects down for discussion on the order of the day interested none of the Ministers; they were one and all simply waiting for the news from Geneva. It was known that the English representative would move that the court be adjourned; it was known that Adams would do his utmost to induce the court to declare its decision, and that the English representative would support him in this, but no one could foresee with any certainty what attitude the other members of the court—an Italian, a Swiss, a Brazilian—would adopt in this connection. The Cabinet had completed its deliberations, but yet no news had come from Geneva. The Ministers decided to wait on the terrace; but hour after hour went by, and all subjects of conversation were exhausted. A chess-board was brought out; Granville and Forster sat down to play; there was still no news. In the end the Ministers had to separate without having learned what was happening. News travelled slowly sixty years ago.

Meanwhile, however, in Geneva, the car had been set rolling on the right track. The members of the court soon reached a unanimous conclusion, and finally the President, the Italian Count Slopis, announced that the arbitrators had "individually and collectively" decided that the "indirect injuries" did not, according to international law, justify any claim for compensation, and therefore could not be considered by the arbitrators. By this decision the "indirect claims" were finally set aside, and the arbitration treaty was saved. *Tantae molis erat* . . .

Gladstone's policy, then, was justified; at all events, before the tribunal of history. For his fellow-countrymen, at the time, thought otherwise. They grumbled over the 3½ million pounds which the Geneva court finally declared that England must pay. They thought it a monstrous sum. They had had no experience of a world-war which would deplete the treasury daily by twice that amount. The man in the street could not see the imponderable advantages—infinitely greater, in the long run—which both England and America would derive from this cancellation of "unprofitable memories and futile strife"; he regarded the decision of the court as a national defeat, and he blamed the Government for it. He accordingly began to look with more sympathy on the Opposition, and in 1872 Disraeli was for the first time cheered by the London public. At the same time, he had maintained a perfectly-correct and objective attitude. With all the clearer conscience, therefore, could he reap the political harvest.

But Gladstone had stood the test of the statesman: he had staked his popularity in order to serve a just cause and a great ideal.

6. Decline

On a foggy October afternoon of the year 1871 there was great excitement in Greenwich. From the banks of the Thames, from which the ancient Greenwich Hospital so peacefully greets the ships faring Londonwards, passing the world-famed Observatory, and coming also from the neighbouring wharves of Woolwich, thousands of people were pouring through the streets to Blackheath, where the Member for Greenwich intended to address his electors under the open sky. The Member for Greenwich was the Prime Minister of England, and many of his electors considered that he had urgent need to justify his political actions and omissions. A section of them had even challenged him, earlier in the year, to resign his seat. Especially refractory were the workers from the Woolwich Arsenal, for their activities had been restricted by measures of economy, and frugality, though highly prized in a general way, was no less disagreeable to those who had to suffer its results as individuals.

So now the sixty-three-year-old Minister stood bareheaded before a vast assembly whose numbers were estimated at from ten to twenty thousand. When had the Minister who held the highest office under the Crown ever come into such close touch with the masses? And this in an environment, and under circumstances so little in correspondence with the lustre and the outward dignity of his office! Every churlish proletarian in overalls and choker could interrupt him, and if many did so simultaneously they could shout him down. There were many who obviously took pleasure in doing so, and after the clapping of hands and the hissing had abated almost every sentence of the speaker's was interrupted by a more or less angry interjection from a political opponent. But one by one the interrupters were silenced by the imperturbable amiability and the genial wit of the speaker, and the longer he spoke, despite the wind and the rain, the more triumphantly emerged the British sense of fair play, and soon his opponents were silenced by the desire to lose not one of those virile and pithy phrases which the speaker's powerful and sonorous voice carried to the outermost fringes of the crowd. And as he spoke—and his address was no apology, but a deliberate exposition of his doings—the anger in the hearts of his opponents was appeased, and they began more and more to feel that the veteran statesman had acted rightly, that he had been inspired by a deep sense of responsibility, that he felt for the humblest of his listeners, and that he had done them a great service. What made the greatest impression on the crowd was the feeling that he was not flattering them or seeking to influence them by tricks of oratory, but that he was explaining all the problems of which he spoke with the utmost objectivity and lucidity, and that in so doing he was expressing his trust in them. They followed him, too, when he warned them against the quacks who sought to delude them with the promise of unattainable social panaceas, and when he expounded the unassailable principles of his own social and political standpoint: that human happiness and misery depended, first and foremost, not on law and Governments, but on the intelligence, the conscience and the character of the individual. This he told them with such earnestness and such power of conviction that by the close of his two hours' speech opposition was silenced, and all those who had come to hear him—some as friends, some as enemies—broke into unanimous and enthusiastic applause.

It was not merely the eloquence of his speech that elicited this applause; it was rather the magic of his personality, before which even the rebellious had to bow.

232

But Gladstone could not be everywhere, could not address the people in every constituency, and so the slow and at first almost imperceptible decline of his popularity continued. Many things contributed to this decline. The passive rôle of England during the great European conflict was felt as a humiliation by those who had grown to manhood under the traditions of Palmerston's active policy. The *Alabama* affair intensified this feeling. The fruits of the political reforms introduced at home were not perceptible as quickly as many had expected. The Irish reforms, from which Gladstone and his followers had hoped so much, did not prevent the recurrence of agrarian troubles which again compelled the Government to resort to coercive legislation. A fiscal experiment of the Chancellor of the Exchequer—Lowe—had given rise to much dissatisfaction. In 1871 Lowe had to meet a deficit; it would have been easy to cover it by increasing the income-tax. But this was too simple and ordinary for Lowe. Instead, he proposed a duty on matches; but this was greeted by the populace with such resentment that it had to be repealed. And this, of course, did not add to the Government's reputation. It goes without saying that all those whose interests were affected by the reforms were up in arms. And the greater proportion of the Nonconformists, who could not overlook the fact that the Church was unduly favoured by the Education Act, now joined in the chorus of the discontented.

Further, Gladstone had made a few bad mistakes in the choice of persons to fill certain offices. For example, he appointed as a member of the judicial committee of the Privy Council the Attorney-General, Sir Robert Collier, who possessed all the desirable personal qualifications for this office with one sole exception: the law prescribed that he must previously have been a judge, and he was not a judge. In order to fulfil this condition Gladstone appointed him to another judicial function, and a few days later transferred him to the Privy Council. Such a sophistical method aroused a good deal of bad feeling, the more so as Gladstone obstinately defended it with arguments that were unintelligible to the simple mind.

For years Disraeli had restricted himself to the attitude of an observer, without very actively assailing his opponent. He knew that so long as Gladstone was at the height of his popularity he would only be the gainer by any attack. Supreme tactician that he was, he waited quietly until the tide began to ebb, intending then, with redoubled force, to take the offensive. Now, it seemed, the moment had come. No one understood better than he how to strike at his enemy's more vulnerable spots and give his criticism a form that assured it of lasting effect. In his first great speech in the spring of 1872 he depicted the Reform Ministry and its embarrassments with such biting wit and such plastic skill that his words were repeated from mouth to mouth and were still remembered decades later.

"As I sit opposite the Treasury Bench," he said, "the Ministers remind me of one of those marine landscapes not very unusual on the coasts of South America. You behold a range of exhausted volcanoes. Not a flame flickers upon a single pallid crest. But the situation is still dangerous. There are occasionally earthquakes, and ever and anon the dark rumblings of the sea." These were phrases which could be quoted with delight in every club and drawing-room, and at which even the victims had to laugh despite their wounds. Against this form of sarcastic polemic even Gladstone's masterly eloquence could make no headway. But it was significant for the future that now Disraeli sounded the imperialistic note in his speeches, spoke of the reconstruction of the Colonial Empire, and described "Imperial consolidation" as one of the then great aims of the Conservative Party. With his incomparable gift of expressing a slogan-like antithesis, he proclaimed that "England would have to decide between national and international principles."

But the reproach against Gladstone implicit in such antitheses, as though he had ever been indifferent or worse to the Colonial possessions of the British Empire, was wholly unjustified. We need not attribute undue importance to Disraeli's casual reference, in a letter to Malmesbury, written in 1852, to "those wretched colonies . . . which are a millstone round our neck," but we may emphasize the fact that even then Gladstone occupied a wholly different standpoint. He had given constant attention to Colonial questions ever since those early days when he himself had been Colonial

Under-Secretary. But since then his views had undergone a fundamental change on one decisive point. Since the 'fifties he had been an advocate of the free self-government of the Colonies. Only the soil of freedom, in his opinion, could nourish that strong affection of the Colonies to the Mother Country which was the only enduring bond of Empire. As long ago as 1850, referring to the doctrines of Burke, he had protested against the notion that England should exert force and compulsion upon her Colonies. "Their natural disposition is to love and revere the name of England, and this reverence is by far the best security you can have for their continuing to be subjects of the Crown." So firmly was he convinced of the strength of this inner bond that he ventured the prophecy that "if the day of danger and difficulty should arise we may from the affection of the Colonies obtain advantage and assistance."

In one respect, however, Gladstone was at odds with the Imperialists. It was his opinion that Great Britain had quite enough to do in the Colonial Empire that was already hers, and he therefore opposed, on principle, the acquisition of new or the extension of old Colonies. And owing to this opinion he repeatedly came into conflict with the tendency prevailing in the Colonies themselves. This explains many of the difficulties of his later administrations; for often enough the expansionist tendency was victorious.

At the time when Disraeli was figuring as the defender of the British Empire against alleged inclinations to destroy it the public was made uneasy by the fact that the Government was gradually withdrawing the British troops from the Colonies. But this policy was by no means peculiar to Gladstone's Cabinet. On the contrary, it had been systematically decided upon years before by Conservative as well as Liberal Governments, and Disraeli himself, in the autumn of 1866, had written to Derby, concerning the British troops in Canada: "An army maintained in a country which does not permit us even to govern it! What an anomaly! Leave the Canadians to defend themselves!" But as matters fell out this policy was given practical effect under Gladstone's Ministry. In every single instance the recall of troops gave rise to some degree of uneasiness, which was fomented by the Conservative Press, and led to attacks in Parliament. The opponents of the policy were ready to regard this recall of troops as the beginning of a gradual but complete withdrawal from the Colonies. Gladstone met all such attacks with the categorical justification of the withdrawal of troops. His principal argument was that a colony which wishes to govern itself must bear the responsibility of defending itself. Faithful to his principle, he declined to force upon them any definite burden of defence. "What we wish," he said, "is to see the growth of the true spirit of freedom in the colonial communities which would make them not only willing but eager to share all the responsibilities of freedom and to take a part in the common burdens." That this policy was correct is admitted by all to-day.

Disraeli was far too shrewd and far too dexterous to offer any direct opposition to the withdrawal of the British troops. He asked, however, in his speech at the Crystal Palace on the 24th of June, 1872, for "a military code which should have precisely defined the means and the responsibilities by which the Colonies should be defended, and by which, if necessary, this country should call for aid from the Colonies themselves." Disraeli was afterwards Prime Minister for six years, without ever lifting a finger to establish this "code." For the moment, however, the dream of the future conjured up by his rich and impetuous imagination, increased the people's readiness to attempt its realization under another Disraeli Government.

Gladstone, in the meantime, was losing ground, not only with the people, but—which was of even greater importance for his future—with the Queen. For now begins the melancholy history of the growing estrangement between Queen Victoria and Gladstone, the more melancholy in that it was due, in the beginning, not to any political differences, but to the Queen's reluctance to sacrifice her tranquillity and her personal comfort to any sort of political or representative duties. The Prime Minister, however, as a loyal servant of the throne and a convinced monarchist, attributed the greatest importance to these duties, the more so as under the influence of what was happening in France the beginnings of a republican movement were visible in England. The Queen, whose shyness had increased during the years of her seclusion, shrank from any contact with public affairs, and if the effort was required

236

of her during the periods which she had intended to spend at Balmoral or Osborne she felt that such an exaction was a definite grievance. A Ministry which was constantly planning great reforms, and was compelled to fight a long-drawn battle with the Opposition and the Upper House, was often obliged to keep Parliament in session until well on in August, and then the Queen was unable to leave London for the country as early as she had wished. This made her almost desperate: "It is really abominable," she wrote on the 10th of August to the Lord Chancellor, "that a woman, a Queen, loaded with cares and anxieties, public and domestic, which are daily increasing, should be unable to make people understand that there are limits to her powers. What killed her beloved husband? Over-work and worry—what killed Lord Clarendon? The same. What had broken down Mr. Bright and Mr. Childers and made them retire, but the same; and the Queen, a woman, no longer young, is supposed to be proof against all and to be driven and abused till her nerves and her health will give way with all this worry and agitation and interference in her private life."

For Queen Victoria considered that she was always ailing, and the only person who was able to cope with these exaggerations with any success—General Grey—had unhappily died in March 1870. His successor as the Queen's private secretary, Colonel Sir Henry Ponsonby, was an admirable and upright character, but he had not the authority which his predecessor had acquired in long years of service. Consequently the Queen's anger and dissatisfaction, unrestrained and unassuaged, was vented upon the Prime Minister, who, with his ideas—devoted and respectful though they were— did not spare her, so that she repeatedly reproached him for not sufficiently protecting her against the demands of public life.

On one particular occasion these troubles found a characteristic expression. In the winter of 1871 the Prince of Wales was so seriously ill that for weeks the worst was anticipated. During his illness the people's affection for the royal family revealed itself in innumerable expressions of sympathy. When at the end of December the crisis was past and the patient was on the way to recovery the Government wished a public service of thanksgiving to be held in St. Paul's Cathedral, which the Queen was naturally expected to attend. At first, however, the Queen was resolutely opposed to the idea, and a very extensive correspondence, together with Gladstone's own exhaustive record of his conversation with the Queen, shows how many rocks he had to avoid, and what foresight, consideration and ingenuity he had to apply in order to make it possible to celebrate a service whose sole political purpose was to promote the affection of the English people for its ruling House. Especially revealing is the memorandum which Gladstone wrote of his audience of the 21st of December, 1871. It was not his usual custom to make such records, so that this audience must have caused him much concern. The Queen justified her objection to the solemn service of thanksgiving by declaring that "no religious act ought ever to be allied with pomp or show." What arts the Prime Minister had to employ—he, who loved best to attend Divine service in the simple parish church of Hawarden—in order to make her understand, while most carefully considering her feelings, the religious and political significance which the proposed ceremony would possess for the people! who, in view of their sympathy with the Prince of Wales in his illness, deserved that their wishes and their feelings should be respected. "Let it be considered, if you please, whether Your Majesty or those who are to appear as principal personages may not properly cast aside all thought of themselves and their own feelings in the matter; it may be most unsatisfactory to them individually, but ought we not to remember the great religious importance of such an act for the people at large; on them it will make a deep impression—it will be a signal honour done to religion in their view." Very skilfully he exploited for his purpose the Queen's anxiety to call a check to the republican movement. The study of this memorandum would be a revelation to many persons who still believe that Gladstone's relation to the Queen was sufficiently characterized by her legendary comment: "He speaks to me as if I were a public meeting!" As a matter of fact, in the end the Queen was enraptured with the ceremony, as it gave the people an opportunity of manifesting their loyalty with overwhelming enthusiasm. For the time being, at all events, she may have felt that the advice of her Prime Minister was not altogether unwise.

238

But a cause of fresh discussion was the heir to the throne himself. Gladstone's devotion to the monarchy embraced not only the Sovereign, but the whole royal family, and especially the future king. The problem of the heir to the throne was then much the same in England as in Germany. The Prince of Wales was now thirty years of age, and he found his enforced lack of employment irksome. Gladstone earnestly considered what could be done to help him. He proposed all sorts of functions for the Prince, which might gratify him and make him feel that he was not entirely superfluous. But the Queen would not hear of his proposals. All his well-considered and well-founded suggestions were rejected. To mention but one, his plan of allowing the Prince to reside several months of each year in Dublin as the Queen's vice-regent found no favour in her eyes. On the other hand, the persistence with which he continued to remind her of it, and the many excellent reasons which he adduced in support of it, had merely the effect of making the Queen dislike him. He saw and felt this—but he had done what his conscience and his sense of duty commanded.

At the close of the year 1872, a year which for Gladstone was full of difficulties and conflicts, his great rival was stricken by a heavy blow. On the 15th of December, 1872, Lady Beaconsfield died, at the age of eighty. Benjamin Disraeli had married her, a woman much older than himself, for reasons which were largely of a very worldly nature; but her unchanging love and devotion had won him so completely that he responded with equal devotion, with equal love. Gladstone was among those who regarded this marriage with admiration. It is one of the finest traits of English political life that even the keenest opposition does not exclude human understanding and human sympathy. Gladstone's letter of condolence to Disraeli is no conventional act of courtesy, but a very personal expression of sincere emotion: "You and I were, as I believe, married in the same year. It has been permitted to both of us to enjoy a priceless boon through a third of a century. Spared myself the blow which has fallen on you, I can form some conception of what it must have been and be . . . I offer only the assurance which all who know you, all who knew Lady Beaconsfield, and especially those among them who like myself enjoyed for a length of time her marked though unmerited regard, may perhaps render without impropriety the assurance that in this trying hour they feel deeply for you, and with you . . ."

Disraeli's reply was inspired by feeling as sincere: "Marriage is the greatest earthly happiness when founded on complete sympathy. That hallowed lot was mine, and for a moiety of my existence; and I know it is yours."

And now the year 1873 was to be faced. Once again Gladstone had prepared several important schemes of reform; and once again he turned to Ireland. After the problem of the Church and the agrarian problem he was anxious to solve the third of his more difficult problems: the question of University education. This task of giving Ireland a University which would be attended by young Irishmen and could yet be approved by England had been attempted by many a Ministry before Gladstone's, and many a Ministry had recoiled from its difficulties. For the problem was really insoluble so long as Ireland was governed by England and in accordance with English ideas. The Irish people was not only Catholic, as regarded the overwhelming majority, but it followed unquestioningly the spiritual guidance of the Catholic clergy. And not only did the clergy refuse a Protestant University: they would have nothing to do with any non-Catholic University. On the other hand, no English Parliament could be induced to give Ireland a purely Catholic University. The reconciliation of these diametrically opposite tendencies was peculiarly difficult at a time when the *Kulturkampf* in Prussia had intensified confessional conflicts far and wide. Only on one point was there agreement: the existing state of affairs, with the richly endowed and purely Protestant Trinity College in Dublin, and three poverty-stricken, non-confessional little colleges in the country, boycotted by the Irish as "godless," could not continue.

That Gladstone should have attacked this thorny problem, as to whose difficult and vexatious character he never had any illusions, is a sign of his courage and self-confidence. He hoped that by a third great success, in attacking the "upas tree" that overshadowed Ireland, he would again win the popular approval. Once more he gave all his personal attention to the task, which he mastered with

240

all his old thoroughness and lucidity. But for the first time his activities were tinged with something like a sense of farewell, a longing for the peace of an old age which should not be filled with unceasing labour and unappeasable conflict.

But when in February 1873 he laid his plan of University Reform before Parliament he betrayed no sign of weariness. His speech, which held the interest of the House for fully three hours, revealed him at the height of his powers. It would have been impossible to expound more lucidly and vividly a historically, theologically and politically complicated problem whose roots reach back into the fourteenth century. The retrospective portion of his speech would have done credit to the most learned legal historian, and one cannot but think highly of a Parliament which followed such a lecture with eager attention and sympathetic understanding. Again, when he came to unfold his positive proposals, he developed them so consistently and convincingly from a few great fundamental principles, and so earnestly assured his hearers that they were framed with all consideration for the feelings of any reasonable person, that the House, without distinction of party, was completely won over.

But this good impression did not survive the careful study of the printed Bill. Even Gladstone could not square the circle, and he had attempted to deal with such difficulties as were insoluble by simply circumventing them. For example, the proposed University was to have no chair of Theology, nor even a chair of Philosophy or Modern History, because these subjects could not be taught without exciting the bitterest controversies among the students of all confessions who were to attend this University on an equal footing. The worst of it was that the Catholic clergy of Ireland began to agitate against the Bill. Archbishop Manning, indeed, was in favour of it, for he clearly foresaw that the Irish Catholics could not hope within any measurable period for any solution that would be more acceptable to them. But his influence in Ireland was not great enough to overcome the opposition to the Bill. And with his failure the Bill received its death-blow.

This Gladstone was soon to realize. But he was also conscious that his political destiny was bound up with the fate of his Bill.

Not only in the sense that he must resign if it was rejected, but in a much wider sense: a defeat due to the fact that a considerable section of the Liberal Party had left him in the lurch would be "the close of his political life." So he wrote to the Queen before the decisive debate on the second reading. And when she protested, he was even franker: "He has the strongest opinion, upon political grounds and grounds other than political, against spending old age under the strain of that perpetual contention which is inseparable from his present position"; and he added a sentence which explains his later career: "And this opinion could only be neutralized by his perceiving a special call to remain: that is to say, some course of public service to be done by him better than if it were in other hands. Such a prospect he neither sees nor anticipates."

Those who had observed him in his daily activities could not fail to realize that in the depths of his soul he was always longing for time and strength to concern himself with the things that are not of this world. But it would have been quite unlike him on this account to withdraw from the fight before the decision, or to fight with less than his utmost strength.

On the other hand, at the close of the three days' debate on the second reading Disraeli characteristically summed up his objections, not so much to the Irish University Bill as to Gladstone's administrations.

"You have had four years of it. You have despoiled churches. You have threatened every corporation and endowment in the country. You have examined into everybody's affairs. You have criticized every profession and vexed every trade. No one is certain of his property and nobody knows what duty he may have to perform to-morrow."

Not one of these accusations can face the tribunal of history; indeed, those who know how infinitely greater, of recent years, has been the interference of the State, even in England, with the life of the individual, can hardly suppress a smile on reading them. But they were exactly attuned to the mood of a public which after four years of great reforms wanted nothing so much as peace and quiet, so that at the moment they were extremely effective.

Gladstone replied to this attack as from a higher plane. In the

242

gallery of the House sat a young Austrian Secretary of Legation, Ernst von Plener, who in after years was himself an eminent Parliamentarian and Minister, and leader of the German Liberals in the Austrian Parliament. Forty years later he still spoke with admiring enthusiasm of Gladstone's closing speech. "I had heard many admirable speeches from him in the course of the years," he writes in his memoirs, "but this concluding speech . . . was the greatest oratorical performance I ever heard from him, and perhaps from anyone. . . . At the end of it he worked up to a magnificent peroration: 'There is a voice which is not heard in the crackling of the fire or in the roaring of the whirlwind or the storm—the still, small voice of justice, which is heard after all have passed away. To mete out justice to Ireland . . . has been the work, I will almost say the sacred work, of this Parliament.' "

Yet Parliament, for the first but not for the last time, left him in the lurch in respect of his work for Ireland, and Ireland had to wait more than a generation for her University. His Bill was defeated by a majority of three votes. The great Liberal majority with which Gladstone had entered the House in 1868 had melted away—and with it went Gladstone's Ministry. Two days after the defeat of the Bill he tendered his resignation to the Queen.

Now it should have been Disraeli's turn to form a new Government. But he did not wish to do so. Not yet! If he had undertaken to form a Government now he must have dissolved Parliament in order to obtain a majority. He was afraid to do so. His refusal compelled Gladstone to resume office: greatly to his detriment. For his defeat had robbed him of much of that nimbus which no politician can afford to lose who draws his strength from the approval and affection of the people. The secession of a section of his party deprived him of the confidence so essential to a progressive leader. True, the Ministry was able to introduce yet another great reform, in respect of the administration of justice, thanks to the recently appointed Lord Chancellor, Lord Selborne, formerly Sir Roundell Palmer. But apart from this the resuscitated Ministry was dogged by misfortune.

An irregularity in the financial administration of the Post Office compelled three Ministers to resign. Among them was the Chancellor of the Exchequer, Lowe. Unfortunately the Cabinet insisted that Gladstone should fill this office, in which he had achieved such triumphant success, in addition to that of Prime Minister. This was much to ask of a man of sixty-four, who after a lifetime of strenuous labour was longing for peace and leisure. But his sense of duty told him that he could not refuse to comply with this request.

His compliance gave rise to a problem in constitutional law, which caused some sensation and was hotly discussed. Must the Prime Minister submit himself to re-election because he had been appointed Chancellor of the Exchequer? The Solicitor-General said: No! This was Sir George Jessel, whom Gladstone had appointed, having recognized his unusual abilities from the manner in which he had dealt with a very intricate judicial measure in Parliament. But Jessel resigned from this office a little later, in order to become one of the greatest judges of the nineteenth century. As his successor Gladstone, with characteristic magnanimity, appointed a Member whose seat was "below the gangway," William Harcourt, who had hitherto caused him much trouble by his pugnacious opposition. No one could then foresee that he would one day be Gladstone's successor as Leader of the Liberals in the Lower House. Harcourt's opinion in respect of the necessity of the Prime Minister's re-election was not entirely in agreement with Jessel's.

But the end was near. After the experiences of the last year Gladstone no longer credited his Cabinet and his followers in Parliament with the ability to accomplish great tasks. He resolved to challenge Destiny and to appeal to the electorate. On the 24th of January, 1874, he dissolved Parliament. In his election address he sought to make the nation's finances, which he had once more taken in hand, the focus of the electoral struggle, for he held out a prospect of the complete abolition of the income-tax. But the attempt was a complete failure. The Conservatives emerged from the elections with a large majority. The Reform Ministry which had inspired so many hopes six years earlier ended in grievous defeat. Was this because it had not fulfilled these hopes? One might rather say, on the contrary. It was just because the Ministry had taken its Reform programme so seriously that many of the voters deserted it. After so many exciting years they wanted peace. "One cannot go on adding to the Statute Book *ad infinitum!*" as Lord Palmerston had said to Goschen ten years earlier. John Bull had returned to Palmerston. "Flown is the spirit, but the phlegm remains." This, more than anything else, was the reason of the reversion to Conservatism.

Gladstone followed the example which Disraeli had set in 1868, and resigned without waiting for Parliament to assemble. The Queen emphatically approved of this procedure, if only because it relieved her of the necessity of concerning herself with the change of Government at a time when the visits of relatives claimed her attention. Apart from this she had not much to say to the retiring Prime Minister. He declined her offer to elevate him to the Upper House; such a distinction was unbefitting for a man whom the nation had just rejected by an unequivocal vote. On the 20th of February, 1874, he returned the Seals. His first period of office was definitely at an end.

His place was taken by the victor in the electoral campaign, Benjamin Disraeli. For the second time he became Prime Minister, but it was the first time he had possessed a Parliamentary majority which made him independent of his adversaries and enabled him to govern in accordance with his own desires. He was now nearly seventy years of age, and in the midst of his triumph he could not suppress the embittered feeling that it had come too late. But to all outward seeming he was great and powerful. The people had signified its approval, the aristocracy flocked about him with enthusiasm, and the Queen, whose hand he had kissed with the words: "I pledge my faith to the kindest of all mistresses," was becoming more and more subject to his personal charm. In such a situation Benjamin Disraeli could be even magnanimous. When in the newly-elected Parliament certain Members exercised their wit and their critical power on the defeated Gladstone, he rebuked them with vigour. "If I had been a follower of a Parliamentary chief as eminent, even if I thought he had erred, I should have been disposed rather to exhibit sympathy than to offer criticism. I should remember the great victories he had fought and won; I should remember his illustrious career: its continuous success and splendour, not his accidental or even disastrous mistakes."

So Disraeli honoured his defeated adversary and himself, who had won the victory over him.

THE LAST ENCOUNTER WITH DISRAELI

1. Resignation from the Leadership

For the second time Gladstone was defeated by Disraeli. The first time, eight years earlier, the defeat had been only a matter of a Parliamentary division, and the electors had soon shown that they disagreed with Parliament. But this time the electors themselves had delivered judgement against him. Ought not this decision to be final? Gladstone was now sixty-five. For more than half a decade the Conservatives would now be at the helm. By the earliest date at which their term of government would expire in the normal course of things he would be more than seventy years of age—if he was still alive. Was it worth while to remain in the heart of the Parliamentary conflict? Could he justify such a course to himself in his heart of hearts? To die in harness was the last thing that he desired. What political life could give of glory and success, that it had given him. But in his heart he was longing for something other than this, for what he later called "an interval between an active career and death," a pause for meditation, a return to that quiet immersion in the eternal problems of faith, a longing which had never left him; a return to his books, which had given him such joy and exaltation, and to which he had been able to devote so little time in the bygone years of exhausting labour. He too was confronted by the dilemma to which Macaulay, in the peace of his Indian garden, far from the temptations of Downing Street and Westminster, had given classic expression: "That a man before whom the two paths of literature and politics lie open, and who might hope for eminence in either, should choose politics, and quit literature, seems to me madness." And although he may not perhaps have confessed it to himself, the fact that he would have day after day to sit facing his triumphant rival did not make the thought of remaining in the House of Commons any more seductive. If only he could have been sure that his party, full of unqualified confidence, would stand close-ranked behind him! But no such assurance was possible. Even if he was not aware of the stinging criticisms which the always self-confident Harcourt—for example—was writing, he saw and heard enough to feel that there were those who were working against him in the Party.

All this confirmed him in the idea which he had already expressed to the Queen—in the spring of 1873, during the debates on the Irish University Bill—that the time had come for him to withdraw from the leadership of his party. His friends and supporters were most emphatically opposed to such a step. Catherine Gladstone could not imagine that her William should no longer stand in the foremost rank. But he did not revoke his decision, though some little time elapsed before he carried it out.

To begin with, he was no longer regular in his attendance in the House: he confined himself to appearing only on the occasion of debates in which he was especially interested. But even so his experiences were not encouraging. A Bill which proposed to set up a new ecclesiastical tribunal, in order to afford a weapon against certain Romanizing clerics of the Established Church, aroused his violent opposition, and caused him to fling himself, with all his old passion, into the thick of the Parliamentary conflict. But here he not only had the preponderant opinion of the nation, but also a great proportion of the Liberal Party against him. Sir William Harcourt came forward as the spokesman of his opponents. He missed no occasion of picking a quarrel with the Party Leader, whom he privately held responsible for the great electoral defeat. But he discovered that Gladstone, even in his then depressed condition, was still a most dangerous opponent, and still greatly his superior. His defence, though perfectly courteous, was so incisive in form that no one was in any doubt as to who was the victor in this duel. But such an incident did nothing to make Gladstone's position as Leader more agreeable.

As soon as Parliament had adjourned Gladstone went to Munich, in order to unburden himself to his old friend Döllinger. Another friend of Döllinger's was Sir Robert Morier, the British chargé d'affaires in Munich. In his private letters Morier had censured

Gladstone's foreign policy since 1870 with the greatest severity, and with all the expert's assumption of superiority over the mere politician. But now, when he came into personal contact with him, he could not help himself: he was fascinated. In a letter to his old tutor, Jowett, he confessed that in personal intercourse Gladstone exerted a quite extraordinary charm. "I have rarely enjoyed ten days of small talk and big talk more than those, and my wife, who . . . is prejudiced against him, fully coincides in this opinion."

Gladstone had a particular reason for this visit to Döllinger. The great Catholic scholar had been excommunicated by the Pope because he had obstinately impugned the dogma of infallibility formulated by the Vatican Council. Such treatment of a man whom he especially revered for his remarkable personality and his genuine piety still further increased Gladstone's abhorrence of the Vatican decree, which he regarded as a grievous blow to human liberty.

As Prime Minister he could not concern himself in any way with the deliberations of the Vatican Council, though these had agitated him profoundly. But he was fully informed of the proceedings in Rome by Lord Acton, his own friend and Döllinger's. It had especially pained him that Manning, the friend of his youth, should have played the leading part in the fight for the dogma of infallibility. Now that he had become a private citizen he was anxious to employ his newly-recovered liberty in speaking his mind on a procedure that seemed to him one of the most disastrous events in the whole history of the Christian Church. According to the fundamental conception which governed all his thoughts on ecclesiastical matters, the Anglican Church was simply a member of the great Christian "Catholic" Church, and was therefore immediately interested in the course followed by the Roman Catholic branch of this Church.

After his return to England Gladstone recorded the thoughts and the fears which were troubling him in a pamphlet on "The Vatican Decrees in their Bearing on Civil Allegiance." He felt moved by his conscience to utter a cry of warning against the aberrations of the Roman Catholic Church. As before, what troubled him most greatly was the relation between Church and State, and especially the attitude of the devout English Catholic to the State. The

Vatican Decrees, he argued, had brought into being a new absolute power, which demanded the entire subjection of the conscience. He who privately surrendered to this power, saying: "A Catholic first, then an Englishman," might, and would, under certain circumstances, find himself in serious conflict with the duties which were incumbent upon him as a subject of the Queen of England. The English Catholics, before their emancipation, had solemnly declared that they did not admit the infallibility of the Pope. "They declare on oath their belief that it is not an article of the Catholic faith, neither are they hereby required to believe that the Pope is infallible." But now their change of front was undermining the premisses of their emancipation, though Gladstone himself was resolved that he would not allow it to be questioned.

The pamphlet attracted a quite extraordinary amount of attention, both in England and abroad. Before long 140,000 copies had been sold. In Germany, then in the thick of the *Kulturkampf*, it created a great sensation. Bismarck, who a few years ago had proudly exclaimed: "We are not going to Canossa!" found in Gladstone's fears a confirmation of his policy, and sent him, on the publication of a second pamphlet, "Vaticanism," a special letter of acclamation, and had a translation of the pamphlet widely distributed in Germany. This is perhaps the only time that Bismarck unreservedly applauded anything that Gladstone did.

Naturally, there was no lack of response on the part of the English Catholics. It must have pained Gladstone greatly that his old friend Manning, now Archbishop of Westminster, and presently Cardinal, should take up his pen against him. Manning's reply to his pamphlets was incisive and personal. The militant prelate, of course, made no attempt to mitigate the conflict to which Gladstone had pointed. Privately Manning declared that Gladstone's publication of his pamphlet was the first event to cast a shadow on a friendship of forty-five years. Gladstone disputed this: their friendship had long ago been shattered. The private correspondence which arose out of this incident was closed by Gladstone with the characteristic passage: "Our differences, my dear Archbishop, are indeed profound. We refer them, I suppose, in humble silence to a higher Power. . . . You assured me once of your prayers at all and at the most solemn times. I receive that assurance with gratitude and still cherish it. As and when they move upwards, there is a meeting-point for those a chasm separates below."

Through his writings on ecclesiastical and political questions Gladstone came into conflict, not only with a friend of his youth, but also with a friend who had lately been his colleague in the Cabinet. While suffering from the shock of a private catastrophe, the Marquess of Ripon had recently gone over to Catholicism. He felt deeply wounded when he read, in Gladstone's pamphlet, a statement relating to converts: "No one can become Rome's convert without renouncing his moral and mental freedom and placing his civil loyalty and duty at the mercy of another." He wrote to Gladstone a letter of bitter reproach. But much as Gladstone regretted this personal conflict, he stood resolutely by his thesis; indeed, he begged Ripon "to offer a strong resistance to the mischief, at which I have slightly glanced." Naturally, neither of the two disputants convinced the other, but this dispute did not prevent Gladstone, when he returned to power, from conferring upon Ripon the exalted office of Viceroy of India.

Meanwhile the date of the reassembling of Parliament was approaching, and Gladstone felt that he could not further postpone his decision as to resigning the Leadership. In vain did his wife lay before him the reasons why he should not take this decision, in a moving letter in which her fond inclination to approve of all his resolves conflicted with the conviction that he would find it impossible to absent himself permanently from the field of battle: "Who could hold you when the battle-cry sounded?"

At the beginning of January 1875 he officially resigned the Leadership in a letter to Lord Granville. He wrote to the Queen also, informing her of this step, and she assured him, in her reply: "She knows that his zeal and untiring energy have always been exerted with the desire of advancing the welfare of the nation and maintaining the honour of the crown." Of what he had achieved by his exertions, however, she said not a word.

For the Liberal Party his resignation was naturally a heavy blow. It comprised many eminent Parliamentarians and Ministers of merit, but not a single man who could be mentioned in the same breath as Gladstone; not a man whose name was on all men's lips, and who had stirred the imagination of the people. Bright, who perhaps came nearest to filling the bill, was old and debilitated by illness, and quite unfitted for the daily work of the party leader. Even those who had been readiest with their criticisms of Gladstone were now overwhelmingly conscious of the great void which his retirement would create.

In the end the Party selected Lord Hartington: not least, perhaps, because he was a member of one of the greatest families of the Whig aristocracy. And in point of character and intellect he was no bad choice. No one could regard him with other than the greatest respect; but he was not in any sense the man to rouse his Party to great and daring achievements, or to sway his hearers by his eloquence. He could be trusted to avoid mistakes which Gladstone might perhaps have committed in his zeal and his faith in his own inspirations. But "whom love has never driven to excess, him it has never driven far enough."

Gladstone, having resigned, ordered his private life accordingly. He sold his valuable London house, and removed his precious collection of china and his books to Hawarden. Here he would write and study. Homer called to him again, and the theological controversies which had been excited by David Friedrich Strauss's *Old Faiths and New* gave him food for thought. An enormous correspondence had accumulated during forty busy and eventful years; with pedantic loyalty he had kept the more important letters, and all these had to be examined and duly filed. The park at Hawarden, with its ancient trees, must give him recreation and refreshment. And had he not still the right to enjoy something of that family life of which he had been so largely deprived during his years of conflict?

So Gladstone made all preparations for a peaceful and meditative old age. One thing alone he did not do. He did not resign his seat in the House of Commons. Why? Was this an inconsistency? Does it justify the reproach of his critics, that he was a victim of self-delusion, that he had never seriously intended to retire from political leadership?

We find the answer in the letter to the Queen, written on the 9th of March, 1873, in which he first mentions his idea of retiring. This idea, he said, could only be neutralized if he felt that a special task was calling him—if it was a question of doing the public a service which he could perform better than another. "Such a prospect he neither sees nor anticipates."

But he did not feel called upon to anticipate the contrary. His consciousness told him that not only was the tale of his years hidden from him, but also the problems and the involvements which the future held in store for England's politicians. He had no desire to continue indefinitely to oppose the man who was now at the political helm. But he could not banish the suspicion that this singular individual, who had already and so often surprised his friends and his enemies, might in the future follow paths which no one could foresee today, and which would be so beset with perils that it would be a duty to oppose him. Did he not introduce a Bill in the spring of 1876—and without the knowledge or approval of the Opposition—by which the Queen of England was to assume the title of Empress of India? Was this only to flatter the Queen? Or did he wish to alter the position of the Crown in the fabric of the Constitution? Ought not one to be on his guard here? Or could he with confidence leave this to Hartington?

Perhaps after all it was better that the old Leader should still retain his seat in Parliament, where he could show himself from time to time, the less often the better, in order to see that all was well.

2. The Bulgarian Atrocities

"Who could hold you when the battle-cry sounded?" Catherine Gladstone had written to her husband. Barely more than a year had elapsed when the battle-cry sounded indeed—and this time from the East.

In the spring of 1876 there was news from the Balkans: they were once more ablaze. Only some twenty years had passed since the end of the Crimean War. But the hope that Turkey would profit by the peace which the war had granted her to increase her internal stability and introduce the promised reforms had not been fulfilled. The situation of the Christian populations of the Balkans had not improved; it was worse than ever, and so, in the end, that happened which was bound to happen: the tormented peoples rebelled, first in Bosnia and Herzegovina, and then in Bulgaria.

Anxiously and distrustfully the Great Powers of Europe observed the dismal tragedy. Russia was still regarded as the special protector of the Christians of the Balkans, who in race and religion were akin to her, and Russia was suspected of wishing to boil her own pot on the Balkan fire. Her movements were suspiciously watched by the Governments of London and Vienna. Austria had obviously her own interests in the Balkans, and Disraeli had shown, by his successful *coup* of acquiring the shares of the Suez Canal, that England was extremely anxious to safeguard her route to India. But this, according to the opinion then prevailing in England, would be threatened if Russia were to seize Constantinople. It was Disraeli's hope that the Turks would be able to suppress the rebellion before the Balkans broke out into open war, which might perhaps spread throughout Europe.

Bismarck's principal anxiety was to prevent a conflict between Russia and Austria, which would have placed Germany in a very difficult position. He was therefore thankful that it had been possible, when the two leading statesmen of these countries— Gortschakoff and Andrassy—had visited Berlin in May 1876, to come to an agreement upon a course of action which found expression in the Berlin Memorandum of the 12th of May. This proposed a number of reforms which should put an end to the indefensible position in the Balkans, and invited the other members of the European concert to co-operate. France and Italy agreed; but the British Government refused. The object of its policy, in accordance with the British tradition, was to maintain the integrity and independence of Turkey, and both the tone and the content of the Note seemed incompatible with this object. Disraeli behaved as though the three Imperial Powers had injured the prestige of England by concluding an agreement without previously consulting her. However, the British Government did not suggest what steps were to be recommended or taken in the place of those outlined by Berlin. And with this the proposal for common action on the part of the European Powers fell through. A British squadron was despatched to Bezika Bay, in the neighbourhood of Constantinople, in order to deal with any possible outbreaks of xenophobia, but the Government did nothing to dispel the impression that it was intended to protect the Turks against the Russians.

In this attitude of the British Government Gladstone saw "a blunder of the first magnitude." In his fundamental conception of the situation he found himself, strangely enough, in agreement with the Queen, who in other respects was now so far from sharing his views. Greatly as she was influenced by her Prime Minister, she could not overcome her misgivings; was it right that in such a question England should divorce herself from the other Powers?

But worse was to follow. In June 1876 the Balkan correspondent of the *Daily News* told the public how the Turks had suppressed the rising in Bulgaria. It was a dreadful story. Incapable of suppressing the movement with their regular troops, they had sent "irregulars" into the rebellious districts: Bashi-bazouks and Circassians, and these had done their work by murdering, burning, torturing and raping. Whole villages were destroyed, whole communities exterminated.

Disraeli was extremely sceptical of this news, which threatened to upset his policy. He gave expression to his doubts when Mr. Forster questioned him in the name of the Liberal Opposition, in words which showed that his wonted skill and his usually unerring aim had forsaken him. He justified his scepticism as regards the reported tortures by the argument that an Oriental people like the Turks "generally terminate their connection with culprits in a more expeditious manner." This had a cynical sound, and for this reason it seemed quite out of tune with the gravity of the situation. What was even worse was the fact that he tried to dispose of the descriptions of atrocities reported by a British Consul as "coffee-house babble."

Unfortunately the reports of the Bulgarian atrocities were anything but "coffee-house babble." There might, of course, have been exaggerations, but the official confirmation which gradually came to hand proved beyond dispute that the substance of the reports was true, hideously true. And in English circles the many who, having read these reports, no longer sympathized with the traditional friendship for Turkey, came to the conclusion, just because of this contemptuous expression, that Disraeli was deliberately closing his eyes to the terrible facts.

But there was the man who could find no peace because of the news from Bulgaria. Gladstone was profoundly agitated by the thought that thousands of Christians—men, women and children— had been massacred, and that England, the champion of liberty and justice, was standing by indifferent, with folded arms—or even worse, was shielding these Turks whose hands were dripping with blood. And it affected him personally, for he was the only surviving Member of Parliament who had been a Minister in Aberdeen's Cabinet when it had allowed England to drift into the Crimean War. This war had its origin in Russia's immoderate claims as protector; but it had never been his intention that the Christians in Turkey should be left without any protection whatever, and delivered over to unrestricted oppression. He had already taken up this standpoint at the conclusion of the Crimean War. Even then he had declared in the House of Commons that it was England's duty to see that those who were "of one faith with us" were not trodden underfoot. Now he relied on the fact that "a European conscience expressed by collective guarantee" had taken the place of the "dangerous prerogative "of Russia.

When Parliament was adjourned in August 1876 Disraeli bade farewell to the House which had witnessed his struggles and his triumph and his fabulous career. As Earl of Beaconsfield he took his seat in the House of Lords. His political influence was by no means diminished thereby, and he had evidently resolved on continuing to exert it as a friend of Turkey.

All the more indefatigably did Gladstone examine the problem, whether it was not his duty and his appointed task to intercede for the maltreated and persecuted Christians of the Balkans. It was not easy for him to abandon the peace he had just regained, to re-emerge from the retirement which he "was beginning to enjoy after forty-seven years of continual struggle in English political life," and once more to "trust himself to a stormy sea," as he wrote in a letter to the Bishop of Croatia, the venerable Dr. Strossmaier.

But—"I should like," he said, "to serve my country and humanity till death. But this service can be rendered in more than one way . . . there is another far greater struggle, the struggle of Credo and Non Credo." There were the problems of the Christian faith and its relations to reason, liberty and science. "What a joy and an honour it would be for me," he wrote, "if . . . God might help me to say, were it but a few words, which might advance even the smallest of these questions. . . . That is my last hope." He must bid farewell to this dream if he were once more to fling himself into the political conflict.

So again he stood at the parting of the ways, as he had stood there forty-five years earlier, when he had to choose between the ecclesiastical and the political career, and once again he decided in favour of politics. For he felt that now that had happened of which he had spoken to the Queen in his letter of the 9th of March, 1873; now the "special call" had sounded, now he was summoned to a task which he could perform better than another—for that his successor in the Leadership of his party, Lord Hartington, was not the right man for this task was already evident, and was becoming more and more obvious. Such a problem could not be handled with cool caution, and with constant anxiety as to the attitude of the Party. It needed a man who was deeply moved by it, and who could expound it to the nation with all the fire of a great and com- passionate heart. "Good ends," he wrote to his sceptical friend Granville, "can rarely be obtained in politics without passion, and there is now, the first time for a good many years, a virtuous passion."

So he took up his pen. He was confined to his bed by rheumatism, but this could not stop him, and propped up on his pillows he wrote in three days his pamphlet on *The Bulgarian Horrors and the Question of the East,* which was published on the 5th of Sep- tember, 1876. It begins with a calm exposition of the situation in the Balkans, and how it arose, but then proceeds to a sharp criticism of the attitude of the British Government, examines into the reliability of the news of the Bulgarian atrocities, and culminates in a passionate attack upon the Turkish administration and the misery which it had brought upon the populations entrusted to it.

257

"I entreat my countrymen," he wrote, ". . . to require and to insist, that our Government . . . shall apply all its vigour to concur with the other States of Europe in obtaining the extinction of the Turkish executive power in Bulgaria." And then he uplifted his voice in an appeal that echoed through the land, and through the years: "Let the Turks now carry away their abuses in the only possible manner, namely by carrying off themselves. Their Zaptiehs and their Mudirs, their Bimbashis and their Yuzbashis, their Kaimakams and their Pashas, one and all, bag and baggage, shall I hope clear out from the province they have desolated and profaned."

This did not mean that the Turks as a nation were to be driven out of Europe, but that their rule over the unhappy people who were at their mercy should cease.

Gladstone did not make this demand in order to further any British interest. "I object," he cried, "to this constant system of appeal to our selfish leanings." He pointed to a very different lodestar, even for foreign policy: "Of all the objects of policy, in my conviction, humanity, rationally understood, and in due relation to justice, is the first and highest."

Would England hear this call? Would she be prepared to break away from a traditional friendship and a traditional distrust which was not unrelated to the most recent achievements of the British Army? The general temper of the Party was sceptical, and even the faithful Granville would have liked to erase at least the mettlesome reference to "bag and baggage."

Gladstone had not long to wait for an answer. The pamphlet sold like hot cakes; in three days 40,000 copies, and before long 200,000. At Greenwich Gladstone's constituents gathered about him in a huge meeting of demonstration and enthusiastically applauded his speech. They listened devoutly as he told them what had filled his mind as he drove through London by night: "I feel it to be an inspiring and a noble thought that in every one of these houses there were intelligent human beings, my fellow-countrymen, who when they wake would give many of their early thoughts . . . to the terrors and sufferings of Bulgaria." And with loud applause they greeted his reference to the horrors of the Neapolitan prisons: "Six and twenty years ago I endeavoured to stir up public sentiment with respect to the abuses of Government in Southern Italy, but let me render this justice to a defunct dynasty, that it would be a cruel sin and shame to compare for one moment, or in any of the most marked features of the late atrocities, that government of the Bourbon dynasty in Naples with the abominable system that has been desolating Bulgaria."

This was the beginning of an uninterrupted series of demonstrations. Wherever Gladstone showed himself, even on his private journeys, he was greeted by an enthusiastic crowd.

Lord Beaconsfield might pick holes in the style of the pamphlet, might speak derisively in his letters of "the return from Elba," or even give vent to his exasperation in such ugly phrases as "unprincipled maniac," and "never a gentleman"; yet day by day it became more evident that Gladstone had given expression to the feeling of thousands, that he had found the way to the hearts of his fellow-countrymen, that the appeal to the moral powers had made the deepest impression.

Beaconsfield, in his defence, had utterly failed to strike the right note. When in one of his speeches he spoke of Gladstone's agitation as "worse than any of those Bulgarian atrocities" he had shot one arrow that fell back on the marksman; and his ridiculous assertion that the rising of the Balkan populations was the work of "secret societies" merely shows his blindness to a national movement which Gladstone understood because he sympathized with it. Fortunately the foreign policy of England was not determined by Beaconsfield alone; he had to carry the Cabinet with him, and here he met with resolute opposition. Neither the Foreign Secretary, Lord Derby, nor the Colonial Secretary, Lord Carnarvon, nor the Secretary for India, Lord Salisbury, was able to share his persistent friendship for the Turks and his indifference to their crimes. In this matter Salisbury privately was more in sympathy with Gladstone than with his party chief, whose purely negative policy hardly went beyond the maxim that no coercion must be applied to Turkey. As to Salisbury, on the other hand, Gladstone was rightly convinced that he earnestly wished to see reforms introduced. For this reason he publicly welcomed the appointment of Lord Salisbury as the

British representative at an international conference in Constantinople that winter.

Gladstone's public declaration of confidence in Salisbury was made at a great assembly in London of the Turcophobes of all parties, at which certain other speakers, among them Freeman the historian, went altogether beyond bounds, so that the Queen indignantly declared: "She thinks the Attorney-General ought to be set at these men." But there were men like Carlyle and his faithful Ruskin, Froude, Burne-Jones, and the Dukes of Westminster and Argyll among these "culprits." For although the compact majority of London "Society" might support Beaconsfield, there were those among its more intellectually and socially distinguished members who thought more of the cause of humanity. Carlyle, whose temper had by no means grown milder with age, was so full of indignation that even in a London omnibus he fulminated so passionately against the Prime Minister and the Turks that his aristocratic companion's hair stood on end.

But the tide of popular emotion cannot always flow in the same direction. When the Constantinople conference was wrecked by the obstinacy of the Turks, and a Russian declaration of war became more and more imminent, for many people their mistrust of Russia's policy outweighed their discomfort in respect of the methods which the Turks applied in matters of internal politics. To many it seemed much more important to prevent Russia from reaching Constantinople than to liberate the Balkan Christians. Gladstone was aware of this change of feeling. But for him the question was a moral question, so that no such change of temper could induce him to alter his course. He had even the courage to call the "prestige" which was constantly involved in public discussions "that miserable and dastardly creature." What was much more serious was that the official Leader of the Liberal Party was not unaffected by this change of temper, and was by no means in complete agreement with him. Now the consequences of Gladstone's retirement from the Leadership showed themselves. He had to consider the men who had taken over the standard which he had no longer wished to bear.

The contradiction was obvious after Russia, in April 1877, had declared war on Turkey. Gladstone was afraid, as were the dissentient Ministers in the Cabinet itself, that Beaconsfield would one day enter the war on the side of the Turks. In order to prevent this he wished to move a number of resolutions in the House of Commons which would express strong disapproval of Turkey and of her support by Great Britain. But Lord Hartington and the other occupants of the Liberal front bench took exception to the resolutions. Gladstone had to admit to himself that his proposal had not found a single backer in the official circles of the Party. It was only a poor consolation if he told himself that he had found the same opposition in the previous September when he had looked, in the same circles, for approval of his pamphlet on the Bulgarian atrocities. He could not possibly let matters come to the point of a split in the Party, for Beaconsfield was already reckoning on such a disaster, all the more joyfully as it would divert attention from the dissensions in his own camp.

At last, with the help of the ever-helpful Granville, a compromise was arrived at, and Gladstone was at all events able, with the support of the Party, to introduce and explain the motives of the first of the five resolutions which he had planned. Naturally, his adversaries were fully aware of the difficulties with which he had had to contend, and they employed every expedient of Parliamentary procedure and tactics to place every possible obstacle in his way and to emphasize his isolated position. For two hours he had to fight his way, step by step, until he could speak to the point. He then spoke for some two and a half hours, to a House which was for the most part openly hostile, and when it was not hostile, at least markedly cool; but the longer he spoke the less could his hearers withstand the force of his personality, the power of his eloquence, and his great moral earnestness. When, in conclusion, he conjured up the picture of the Balkan Christians fighting for their liberty, and proclaimed his faith in England's mission as the champion of liberty, the white-haired old warrior seemed, alike to his bitter enemies and his lukewarm friends, "an inspired man."

"There were other days when England was the hope of freedom. Wherever in the world a high aspiration was entertained, or a noble blow was struck, it was to England that the eyes of the oppressed were always turned—to this favourite, this darling home of so much privilege and so much happiness, where the people that had built a noble edifice for themselves would, it was well known, be ready to do what in them lay to secure the benefit of the same inestimable boon for others. You talk to me of the established tradition and policy in regard to Turkey. I appeal to one established tradition, older, wiser, nobler far—a tradition not which disregards British interests, but which teaches you to seek for promotion of those interests in obeying the dictates of honour and of justice. . . . There is now before the world a glorious prize. A portion of those as yet unhappy people are still making an effort to retrieve what they have lost so long, but have not ceased to love and desire. . . . They seek to be diverted from an intolerable burden of woe and shame. That burden of woe and shame—the greatest that exists on God's earth—is one that we thought united Europe was about to remove . . . the removal of that load of woe and shame is a great and noble prize. It is a prize worth competing for. It is not yet too late to win it . . . but be assured that whether you mean to claim for yourselves even a single leaf in that immortal chaplet of renown, which will be the reward of true labour in that cause, or whether you turn your backs upon that cause and your own duty, I believe for one that the knell of Turkish tyranny in those provinces has sounded. So far as human eye can judge, it is about to be destroyed. The destruction may not come in the way or by the means we should choose; but come this boon from what hands it may, it will be a noble boon, and as a noble boon it will gladly be accepted by Christendom and by the world."

It is not surprising that on the morning after this speech the sixty-eight-year-old politician noted in his diary: "I am the spoiled child of sleep. This night was an exception."

Naturally, the resolution, for which the majority of the Party voted, was rejected by the House. But in the country the impression produced by Gladstone's courage, and his fidelity to his convictions, was tremendous. Of course, the "Society circles" of London, like the Queen, continued to support Beaconsfield's "spirited" policy. The Queen went so far as solemnly to write to the Duke of Argyll, a loyal supporter of Gladstone, on the 4th of

June, 1877: "I wish . . . to state *solemnly* that I know that this war might, and it is my firm conviction *would* have been prevented, had Russia not been *encouraged* in the strongest manner by the extraordinary, and, to me, *utterly* incomprehensible agitation . . . to believe that she could do what she liked without meeting with opposition." To this declaration she added an admonition "To act a patriotic part and to desist from so lamentable a course!"

And London Society eagerly accepted the statement which the Prime Minister had made in his letters and conversation—that Gladstone's true motive was unsatisfied ambition. But those who came into personal contact with the alleged demagogue received a very different impression. John Ruskin—despite his abhorrence of the Bulgarian atrocities—as a loyal follower of Carlyle, whom he revered to the point of idolatry, had a very disdainful opinion of Gladstone, whose character was so totally unlike his own. But when in January 1878 he paid a visit to Hawarden he changed his opinion completely, "I thank you very solemnly," he wrote to Mary Gladstone, "for having let me see your father, and understand him in his earnestness. It was a complete revelation to me and has taught me a marvellous quantity of most precious things, and the rashness of my own judgement (not as to the rights and wrongs of things themselves, but as to the temper in which men say and do them). How is it possible for the men who have known him so long to allow the thought of his course of conduct, now or at any other time, having been warped by ambition, to diminish the lustre and power of his name?"

One of the greatest of Gladstone's English contemporaries, whose life work and ideas belonged to a very different province— Darwin—was profoundly impressed when he made Gladstone's acquaintance. One Sunday afternoon Sir John Lubbock took Gladstone and his subsequent biographer, John Morley—and him too Gladstone now met for the first time—to the quiet Kentish village in which the great naturalist was living. Gladstone began to speak of the Bulgarian atrocities; the idea that anyone could fail to be interested in the subject had apparently never occurred to him. Darwin listened with absorbed attention. "When we broke up," writes Morley, "watching Mr. Gladstone's erect alert figure as he walked away, Darwin, shading his eyes with his hands against the evening rays, said to me in unaffected satisfaction: 'What an honour that such a great man should come to visit me!' "

It was soon plainly evident that the provinces were by no means everywhere disposed to follow the lead of the London clubs and newspapers. The personal following which Gladstone had won throughout the country began to manifest itself in a peculiar fashion, in pilgrimages to Hawarden. Enthusiastic Liberals, especially from the industrial centres of the North, went there to watch him at his favourite recreation of felling trees in the park. Here they could see him with his sons about him, and assure him of their love and devotion, and perhaps, if they were lucky, hear him deliver a short address. He was always only too ready to believe that other people must be equally moved by the things that moved him, so that it was not difficult to persuade him to speak of them. Of course, this combination of rhetoric and axe-swinging was abundantly derided and criticized, but Gladstone was as little disturbed by such criticism as the disciples who now began to flock to Hawarden.

Such appreciation and devotion had to console him for the passionate hostility which he encountered from other quarters, a hostility that increased as Russia forced her way into the Balkans, and the danger of England's intervention in the war became more immediate. The London music-halls rang once more with the pugnacious refrain which gave the name of "Jingoism" to the prevalent mood:

> We don't want to fight, but by jingo if we do
> We've got the ships, we've got the men,
> We've got the money too!

He had personal experience of the passions that were stirring the people. Excited crowds gathered in front of his house; stones were hurled through his windows, and mounted police had to clear the street. In February 1878 Mary Gladstone wrote in her diary: "Algernon West came. He told us that John Bright, hearing Papa violently abused by a lady, only said to her: 'Have you children, Madam?'—'Yes.'—'Then endeavour to show Mr. Gladstone to them, and if possible let them shake hands with him, and long before they are as old as I am they will thank you for having shown them the greatest, the purest, and the noblest of English statesmen." In the meantime Lord Beaconsfield's "spirited" foreign policy continued on its by no means equable way. The Prime Minister was confident that he could control the currents of popular feeling. The Queen, if possible, was even more passionately militant than he. But he met with opposition enough in his own Cabinet. That he did not hesitate to name his refractory colleagues to the Queen was regarded by Gladstone as a serious violation of the principles of the British Constitution. He himself, even in the most difficult situations, had always felt himself pledged to unconditional loyalty to his colleagues; the Prime Minister, in his opinion, ought to safeguard the unity of the Cabinet just as scrupulously in his dealings with the Sovereign as in Parliament itself. It would never have occurred to him—as it did to his adversary, who in this respect at least was more gifted than he—to heighten the interest of the prescribed reports to the Queen by elaborate antitheses, by stylistic touches, almost in the manner of a novel. What was more serious was that a writer who was an intimate friend of the Prime Minister's had expounded the unconstitutional doctrine that the direction of foreign policy was among the prerogatives of the Queen. This doctrine Gladstone confuted with the greatest decisiveness in a review article, which Beaconsfield did not fail to lay before the Queen, expressing his indignation as he did so. This, of course, did nothing to lessen the rift which divided her from Gladstone.

But not even the zeal with which the Queen supported her Prime Minister could overcome the opposition in the Cabinet. Finally the Foreign Secretary, Lord Derby, and the Colonial Secretary, Lord Carnarvon, resigned. Both the Queen and Beaconsfield were relieved by the departure of Derby, who had striven indefatigably for the preservation of peace, especially as Lord Salisbury was persuaded to replace him. But as a matter of fact when Salisbury entered the Cabinet Disraeli's policy of upholding the "independence and integrity of Turkey" was practically abandoned. For Salisbury was not only convinced that the separation of certain provinces of Turkey was inevitable after the Russian

265

victories: he regarded it, within certain limits, as desirable. He was not in the least inclined to plunge England into war for the sake of the integrity of Turkey. Since Bismarck also had exerted all his diplomatic genius to obtain a peaceful settlement, and had given the Russians to understand that in the event of war they could not count on German assistance, Russia refrained from exploiting to the full her military victory over Turkey, and declared herself ready to submit the peace of San Stefano (3rd of March, 1878), which had, so to speak, been wrested from her at the gates of Constantinople, to re-examination by a European Congress.

And so the Berlin Congress was held (13th of June to 15th of July, 1878), which gave Lord Beaconsfield the opportunity of exhibiting himself before the eyes of the whole world—and in an assembly of statesmen which included the greatest diplomatists of the time, and was presided over by the greatest of all—as the much-admired master of negotiation and the incarnation of British national feeling. That even Bismarck was not immune to the charm of his personality might justly fill him with pride. The mutual mistrust with which they had regarded each other from a distance was replaced by the mutual delight in which each discovered in the other a congenial character. Both masters of witty and incisive conversation, who were not dismayed by cynicism, both capable of combining elasticity with energy, they enjoyed with the satisfaction of the expert the nightly conversations which led to the success of the Congress. Lord Beaconsfield could regard it as the crowning moment of his career when the founder of the German Empire said of him: "The old Jew's the man!"

His delight in this remark would assuredly not have been lessened had he heard that Bismarck said of his English colleague that Salisbury was only a wooden lath painted to look like iron. And yet the historians are agreed that Salisbury did most of the work; that even before the Congress he had concluded with Shuvaloff, the Russian Ambassador, the agreement of the 24th of May, by which the principal points in dispute were settled beforehand.

With all this, it was no wonder that Beaconsfield was received as a conqueror when he returned to England in July, little as this ovation can have suited Bismarck, for in Russia it intensified the feeling that through his services as "broker" she had suffered a severe diplomatic defeat. With the talent for striking catchwords that distinguished him, Beaconsfield boasted that he had brought England "Peace with Honour." Not only was he greeted by the noisy jubilation of the crowd; the Queen was delighted beyond measure, and she felt that the Order of the Garter which she conferred upon him was but an incomplete expression of her gratitude.

If at this juncture Beaconsfield had gone to the country he would undoubtedly have retained or even increased his majority. But he disdained to resort to this weapon. After this success he was confident that he could now at any time triumph over his adversary.

But had he really achieved a success of which England might be proud? Had he achieved more than a personal triumph? Certainly the Russians had given way to him. But what was it that they had conceded? The main action in Berlin had been fought over the frontier which was to divide the semi-independent Bulgaria from the newly-created Eastern Rumelia, which remained part of the Turkish Empire. Lord Beaconsfield's famous special train for the departure from Berlin was ordered because on this point the Russians would not give way. It was in respect of this frontier that Bismarck had asked Lord Beaconsfield: Is this an ultimatum? and on receiving an affirmative answer, he had exerted himself to the utmost in order to bring about an understanding. But a few years later this frontier had disappeared; the artificial division of Bulgaria had lasted only seven years; the natural tendency of the nation to unite had made itself felt, and the then English Prime Minister helped to abolish the frontier which he had once laboured so strenuously to create: for he was none other than Lord Salisbury.

But there was one man who was immune from the self-delusions of the great diplomatists and the patriotic illusions of the masses, because he had greater faith in the irresistible force of a nation's ideals of liberty than in the skill of statesmen who close their minds to them. When on the 30th of July, 1878, Gladstone rose in the House of Commons to criticize the Treaty of Berlin, he must have been aware that many of his own party were looking forward to his speech in a critical and anxious mood. But once more he succeeded in making a profound impression, and not on his disciples alone. He gave acknowledgment where it was due. This he could do all the more readily, inasmuch as a great deal of what had been achieved was in far closer correspondence with his own programme than with that of his opponent. Seven million human beings were liberated entirely from Turkish rule, and four and a half million in very important respects—as far as they were concerned could one still speak of the integrity of Turkey? But against the British delegation which had done its utmost to push back the frontier of Bulgaria to the advantage of Eastern Rumelia, he brought the reproach that the cause which they had supported was not that which was in harmony with the great British tradition. England, he said, is "a country which holds itself up to be the freest of all nationalities in Europe by its traditions, by its institutions, by its principles, by its feelings. We are, therefore, entitled to expect that when the great States of Europe meet together in Congress our Plenipotentiaries shall lean toward the side of freedom and away from the side of servitude. . . . On every question . . . that became a subject of serious contest in the Congress . . . a voice has been heard from Lord Beaconsfield and Lord Salisbury, which sounded in the tones of Metternich, and not in the tones of Mr. Canning, or of Lord Palmerston, or of Lord Russell."

Such a verdict had might when it came from the lips of a man who could say, as Gladstone said: "I have sat in the Cabinet by the side of the Duke of Wellington, of Sir Robert Peel, of Lord Aberdeen . . . of Lord Palmerston, of Lord Clarendon and of Lord Russell . . . I have known the measure which they took of the rights, and duties, and powers of England, and of the limitations placed by a higher authority on all human power . . . there was not one of them who for one moment would have consented to look at such a scheme as has been contrived and accomplished in the dark by the Members of Her Majesty's present Government."

With this criticism he turned to the privy agreement which Lord Beaconsfield and Lord Salisbury had secretly concluded with the Sultan before proceeding to the Berlin Congress. By this treaty the Sultan ceded to England the island of Cyprus, of which Disraeli had said, thirty years earlier, in his novel *Tancred*, that the

English wanted it; an island which had now, as a matter of fact, been acquired only by means of an unconsidered and improvised agreement, and which did not justify a single one of the prophecies that accompanied its acquisition. In return England assumed a sort of protectorate over the Turkish possessions in Asia, with the obligation—which was really hardly possible of fulfilment—of watching over the accomplishment of the needful reforms. Both the content of this treaty and the manner in which it had been concluded excited Gladstone's most emphatic disapproval; for they exposed England, in his opinion, to the charge of having pursued a selfish and hypocritical policy, and having thereby lost the respect of other nations. He knew well enough to what an extent Europe was infected by the conceptions of *Realpolitik*, which valued nothing but material success. But he held steadfastly to what he believed to be the highest and the decisive standard.

"This setting up of our own interests, out of place, in an exaggerated form, beyond their proper sphere, and not merely the setting up of such interests, but the mode in which they have been pursued, has greatly diminished, not, as I have said, the regard for our material strength, but the estimation of our moral standard of action, and consequently our moral position in the world."

It was no wonder that Lord Beaconsfield was infuriated by this criticism. When Gladstone, in a public address, spoke of "an insane covenant," the Prime Minister replied in another public utterance that "he would not pretend to be as competent a judge of insanity as his opponent," and he proceeded to make an unmistakable reference to "a sophistical rhetorician, inebriated with the exuberance of his own verbosity." This rhetorician, he complained, was gifted with an egotistical imagination which enabled him at any moment to blacken his adversary and glorify himself in an endless series of incoherent arguments!

This unseemly and quite unusual language—unusual, for Beaconsfield rarely lost his temper—points clearly to a sense of weakness. It could hardly escape his perspicacity that the annexation of Cyprus was hardly consistent with the rôle of the unselfish champion of the "integrity and indivisibility" of Turkey. It was not long before England had to pay for this divergence from the strait way. Three years later the British Ambassador in Constantinople, Goschen, a man of such moderate views that he soon found his way from the Liberal Party to the Salisbury Ministry, wrote complaining of the difficulties of his negotiations with the Sultan:

"How often during the course of my mission did I deplore the results of that brilliant stroke of Lord Beaconsfield which secured Cyprus to us as a British possession. It prevented British Ambassadors from showing 'clean hands' to the Sultan in proof of the unselfishness of the British advice."

Perhaps the moral standpoint has, after all, a certain significance even in *Realpolitik*. To the majority of his critics, especially on the Continent, Gladstone's moral views were merely a proof that he had not the faintest comprehension of foreign politics. "To discuss the external policy of a great nation with Mr. Gladstone is pointless, because his mind simply wanders from the subject," were Herbert Bismarck's arrogant words in a letter to his eminent father (7th of March, 1885). So far as the Berlin Treaty and the disposal of the Balkans is concerned, history pronounced a different verdict when a generation later the collapse of the Turkish Empire dragged Europe into the maelstrom of the most terrible of all wars.

3. The Decision

But history takes time to arrive at its verdicts. Contemporaries rejoice in glory and outward success; so the chorus of the Press and the chatter of the clubs, the man in the street and the echoes of the outer world, all agreed in praising the great statesman who had brought home "Peace with Honour." Only a minority shared the scepticism which Gladstone had so eloquently expressed. But the imperialistic methods which so gratified England in 1878 bore fruit in the following year which she found far less agreeable. On the north-west frontier of India the pettiest causes, together with reasons of prestige, gave rise to a war with Afghanistan, which yielded no positive result worth mentioning, but in the course of which the British Minister and all his staff were murdered in a frightful massacre by the fanatical natives of Kabul. The casualties in this war were especially painful to many English people because they could not perceive that the war had any moral justification. This moral disapproval of the war was strikingly expressed by Gladstone, when in a farewell speech to his Greenwich constituents he quoted the words of the physician in *Macbeth*, in the scene where Lady Macbeth, with the guilt of blood upon her, wanders in her sleep, tormented by her conscience: "This disease is beyond my practice." And he continued: "The disease of our evil conscience is beyond the practice of all the physicians of all the countries in the world."

Still more disastrous were events in South Africa. In 1877 Lord Carnarvon, the Colonial Secretary of Disraeli's Cabinet, annexed the Transvaal Republic. The significance of this action, which was to give the English politicians occupation for a generation, was then apparent only to a very few. But when this South African policy led a few years later to a war against the Zulus, in which a body of British troops, early in 1879, was annihilated by the natives, it excited a degree of indignation which greatly diminished the popularity of the Government. The fact that in this war the only son of Napoleon III, in whom the Bonapartists saw the future Emperor of the French, was killed by the assegais of the Zulus gave the affair just that sentimental touch which most surely arouses popular feeling.

Thus it was that observers of popular feeling in both camps gradually came to realize that the triumphant mood which in the summer of 1878 had found expression in such enthusiastic applause of Lord Beaconsfield had now vanished. But even the official leaders of the Opposition could not say whether the temper of the nation had so changed that a Ministerial defeat might be anticipated at the next General Election, which would take place in 1880.

Then, in November 1879, Gladstone began his electoral campaign. To his old constituency of Greenwich, which had disappointed him so in 1874, he had bidden farewell in the spring of 1878. At that time he had not yet decided whether he would put up for another constituency. So far, no doubt, he had never considered the possibility of resuming the Leadership of the party.

But in January 1879 the Liberals of the Scottish constituency of Midlothian, near Edinburgh, which had hitherto been a stronghold of Conservatism, invited him to become their candidate. True, they had close at hand a man after their own heart, who might have been born to represent them in the House of Commons, but for the misfortune, which affected his whole career, that he was obliged, at the age of twenty-one, to enter the House of Lords. Lord Rosebery, then, whose brilliant eloquence had made him the most popular man in Scotland, could employ that eloquence only in support of the candidature of a greater man; so he directed the gaze of the Midlothian electors to the Member for Greenwich, who himself was of pure Scottish descent.

Gladstone had now no official position. He was a Member of Parliament, like hundreds of others. But that the people saw in him a leader, their leader, was evident as soon as he opened his campaign in November 1879. The journey from Liverpool to his new constituency was, as he justly wrote in his diary, "like a triumphal procession." In the railway stations at which his train stopped hundreds and thousands of people had assembled, who wanted to see him, to greet him, if possible to hear him. At the principal towns through which he passed he had to make speeches, which were wildly applauded. And in Edinburgh the incomparable Princes Street was black with human beings, eager at last to catch a glimpse of their hero, as Lord Rosebery, his host, drove him from the station to Dalmeny Castle.

So began the Midlothian campaign, which marked an epoch in English history. It was not merely the fact that it determined Lord Beaconsfield's defeat that gave it significance; but rather the fact that a man, by direct appeal to the electors, made himself not only the leader of his party, but the leader of the Ministry. This was in flat contradiction of all the aristocratic traditions which had hitherto governed English political life. His opponents were filled with indignation, which found expression in complaints of the unceasing flood of his eloquence. Only Lord Beaconsfield endeavoured to guard himself against such agitation by the simplest of means: as he proudly wrote to a friend, he "never read a word of it." "Perhaps this explains"—to quote the malicious comment of Viscount

Gladstone—"why he never mastered the case against his own policy."

Actually, Gladstone's powerful election speeches were remarkable for something very much more important than their impetuous rhetoric. As a matter of fact, the quantity of his oratorical performances is positively astonishing, and not merely astonishing in a man of seventy years; it would have been equally remarkable had he been in the prime of life. The speeches, which were published by the Liberal Party, filled two large volumes. On looking through them one is surprised by the number of problems in respect of which this elderly statesman had something definite to say. Naturally, the Balkan problem and questions of foreign politics generally were well to the fore. But to a meeting of Edinburgh shopkeepers he spoke, objectively and as an expert, of financial policy—what it ought to be, and what it was under Disraeli's Government. On another occasion he dealt with agricultural problems. And in the midst of all these political and party expositions, on a day when he had to make an after-dinner speech, and another speech at a mass meeting, he had time and energy and thought to spare for his inaugural address as Lord Rector of the University of Glasgow, to be delivered before an audience of scholars and students, the majority of whom were on the opposite side in politics, and accustomed to express their feelings without the least restraint.

"The moment he began," writes Mary Gladstone, "in his rectorial black and gold robes, the deadest silence fell on the whole assembly, and for an hour and a half they seemed spellbound. It was in his most splendid manner, and I shall never forget the solemn, earnest tone of his voice with which he ended his appeal to these youths. So noble, so strong and so high was this appeal that no one could listen without being moved, and the shout that burst from every corner of the building when he had ended can never be forgotten."

The address dealt with the progress of science and technique and their influence on the religious and moral evolution of mankind, with especial reference to the controversy between science and faith, to which he had given so much thought. To the students he recommended the four cardinal virtues of all controversies:

273

truth, charity, diligence and reverence. Although it expressed no new and surprising ideas, the address must have made a profound impression, as the confession of a man who had spent a long lifetime in earnestly wrestling with just these problems.

It was characteristic of Gladstone that he was able to deal with this subject, so remote from contemporary politics, while immersed in the problems of the day. For there is one common trait in all his speeches: he appeals, from the bottom of his heart, to the moral sense of his listeners. No matter what the subject of his speech, he never allows them to forget that above all practical standpoints are the standards of right and wrong.

How this unvarying trait affected a young and enthusiastic hearer is shown by the notes of a girl of seventeen: Laura Tennant, the daughter of Sir Charles Tennant, a Liberal Member of Parliament, and sister of Margot Tennant, now Lady Oxford. She herself, a few years later, married Gladstone's nephew, Alfred Lyttelton, but died in the first year of her marriage, to the deep sorrow not of her family alone, but of the many friends who treasured all their lives the memory of her delightful personality and her ethereal beauty; she seemed, they felt, like a being from a higher world.

"I and mother went into Edinburgh yesterday to hear Gladstone speak in the Corn Exchange. I felt as if I were in Church and tempted to kneel down and pray; he spoke for an hour and three quarters nearly. Financial speech, clear, succinct and humorous, full of energy, I longed to grip his hand and tell him it paid to be honest in life, to be true, to be your own enemy—which Dizzy is not, or rather would not be and is. After his speech, which ended at nearly five, off he went to the Grass Market and spoke to 18,000 people, labouring men, honest working Scotchmen. I am proud of them, proud of those 18,000, prouder still of Gladstone, proud of being Scotch, proud of my great-grandfather, an honest farmer, a friend of Burns, and a child of Nature. . . .

"On Friday morning we heard Gladstone deliver his Rectorial address to about 4,000. It was very fine, very full of tact, of thought, and shadow of Higher Thought. The part about Christianity could not have been better. It could not have offended Divines nor

274

have rubbed sceptics up the wrong way. Yes, it was beautiful, urging us all to work and to fill the position God has given us to fill. To toil and toil again. I met Mrs. Gladstone afterwards and said to her: Tell Mr. Gladstone from me that I thought what he said beautiful, and that he helps girls, let alone men, to be noble. She took my hand. 'Yes, yes, dear, he means to help us all.' "

And the same feelings as those here recorded by a young girl were aroused in thousands upon thousands of listeners when they heard the white-haired old man reminding them, in his incomparably musical and beautifully modulated voice, that they were responsible for the destiny of England and of the British Empire. Urgently he explained that they now had to deal with something very different from the usual conflict between Whigs and Tories, however important the questions may have been for which they had formerly contended. "What we are disputing about is a whole system of government . . . if it is liked by the people—they are the masters—it is for them to have it."—"A series of surprises, a series of theatrical expedients, calculated to excite, calculated to alarm, calculated to stir pride and passion, and calculated to divide the world, have been the daily employment and subsistence, the established diary of the present Government . . . in the opinion which I have derived from the great statesmen of the period of my youth (without any distinction of party, but if there was any distinction of party, which I have learned more from Conservative statesmen than from Liberal statesmen), the great duty of a Government, especially in foreign affairs, is to soothe and tranquillize the minds of the people, not to set up false phantoms of glory which are to delude them into calamity, not to flatter their infirmities by leading them to believe that they are better than the rest of the world, and so to encourage the baleful spirit of domination; but to proceed upon a principle that recognizes the sisterhood and equality of nations, the absolute equality of public right among them; above all, to endeavour to produce and to maintain a temper so calm and so deliberate in the public opinion of the country, that none shall be able to disturb it."

The foreign policy which was to be determined in this electoral contest was for Gladstone so central to all his thinking that—to the contrary of his usual custom—he attempted in the speech delivered at West Calder on the 17th of November, 1879, to declare its leading aspects in a few programmatic statements; for which reason it holds a special position among his public speeches. The two aspects to which he gave special prominence were as follows: The policy was designed "to foster the strength of the Empire, to preserve the blessings of peace"; not, of course, peace in the absolute pacifistic sense, since to him a war for liberty was a just and necessary war. But the preservation of peace called for co-operation with other Powers: that is, for the concert of Europe. And to this one must join a second principle: the avoidance of all special leagues or pledges which might plunge England into such complications as had but lately followed from her alliance with Turkey; rather must all agreements be made with the collective Powers. But in one decisive respect he would allow no precedence among these Powers, in order of their magnitude or strength: namely, in respect of right. "In point of right we are all equals," he said, and England must not claim "a pharisaical superiority" for herself. And as for him right and liberty were always related, so he required of England's foreign policy that it must always, on principle, allow itself to be directed by the love of liberty; for liberty was the strongest foundation of loyalty and order and the development of individual character. On this ideal of liberty were based the great achievements of British foreign policy in the past, such as the foundation of the kingdom of Belgium and the encouragement of the national unity of Italy.

In this programme historians of to-day have seen an anticipation of the principal ideals of the League of Nations. Contemporaries found it reminiscent of Palmerston: negatively, of his *civis Romanus sum* policy of 1850; positively, of his Italian policy of 1860. But more vividly than anything, of course, they saw the profound and fundamental antithesis to the ruling statesman.

This antithesis between the two personalities gave the contest, over and above its practical importance, a dramatic interest. Everybody knew that Gladstone was contending with no weak or negligible adversary, and he himself would have been the last man to ignore the quality of his opponent. No, the man against whom the inspired and indignant orator was employing the weapons of wrath and of pulverizing criticism was himself a master of the written and the spoken word, a statesman whose uncommon talents had raised him, like the hero of a fairy-tale, to the highest office in the State, had won him the favour of his Queen, and the enthusiastic devotion of a large and highly-regarded section of the population; a man before whom foreign statesmen bowed in admiration, and for whom, at his lightest utterance, newspapers innumerable fought a daily battle of words. His foreign-seeming yet intimately familiar features, with their sphinx-like smile, were present to every listener as he saw the great eyes of the orator flash with an inspired and passionate brilliance. Who would be the victor in this battle?—the acknowledged and undisputed head of the powerful Conservative Party, or the old and solitary warrior who had placed the leadership of his party in other hands, and who seemed to have in that party, in these last few years, as many critics as disciples?

"It was personality—in the person of one man—that decided the elections." This was the verdict of no party follower, but of a declared adversary of Gladstone's—Lord Balfour—delivered fifty years later, in his *Chapters of Autobiography*. Balfour, as the nephew of Lord Salisbury, had entered politics on the Conservative side; in later years he was himself the Leader of the Conservative Party and a Conservative Prime Minister. He opposed Gladstone in the electoral contest of 1880, and for many years he crossed swords with him in Parliament, where theirs were no friendly tussles. But he had much too clear a perception of genuine human greatness not to be fully aware of Gladstone's political significance. The uniquely unprejudiced character of English political life, which makes friendly intercourse possible between the most violent political enemies, had brought the two men together—young Balfour, a friend of Gladstone's daughter Mary, and the Liberal veteran; and the old man conceived an affection for this intellectually alert and highly cultivated young man. "I loved him more than any young politician," the old statesman confessed, a decade later, to Margot Tennant. When Balfour, in the evening of his life, himself an octogenarian, came to write the reminiscences of his youth, the picture of his old friend and enemy rose before him. "At the zenith of his physical powers, with all the authority of an 'Elder Statesman,' all the independence of a simple citizen, all the gifts of an accomplished agitator, he chose a cause which, as treated by him, had appealed to his particular prejudices. The atrocities on which he dwelt were, broadly speaking, only too real, the indignation which he experienced was genuine. He expressed it to audiences who knew little about the East, with immense emotional power, unqualified vehemence, and withering iteration. Furthermore, he hated the Prime Minister."

One who had heard Gladstone speak during this electoral contest, on receiving the news of his death, gave a particularly vivid description of his outward appearance:

The meeting is already in progress, when there appears "a pale-faced thin figure, with the head up and a rapt, intense gaze struggling forward to the platform, followed by a simply-clothed woman, who busies herself in warding off the hands of enthusiasts eager to touch him, or pat his back, or help him forward. That is Mrs. Gladstone, with the soft face, high-coloured like a girl's, and tremulous mouth; intent only on one thing in this life—her husband. They step up to the platform by a reporter's stool. A dozen willing hands would aid him, but it is hers which grasps his ankle to steady him lest in his eagerness he slips. He does not sit down, but exchanges a few rapid words with the chairman. She begs a seat immediately behind him. Forth he stands and begins at once: 'Mr. Chairman.' She pulls at his overcoat and one sleeve comes free. Impatiently he stops, while she tugs at the other sleeve; and the coat has scarcely gone from him ere he is flourishing in our faces the free hand: 'Mr. Chairman!' Never shall I, an unenthusiastic non-party man, forget those tones . . . it seemed to me as if someone had touched the stops of a mysterious organ, that searched us through and through."

When Gladstone began his campaign in Midlothian the date of the elections was still doubtful. In the following March Lord Beaconsfield dissolved Parliament. His electoral manifesto took the form of a letter to the Duke of Marlborough, the Lord-Lieutenant of Ireland. He endeavoured to define the point upon which the electoral contest was supposed to turn, by drawing attention to the efforts of the Irish Members to obtain Home Rule for Ireland. It was the duty of patriotic voters to defend the Union. But in vain! The electors cared nothing for this electoral slogan, but only for that which Gladstone had uttered. It was he who had given the contest a watchword, and the other Liberal leaders had to fight under his colours. It was he who emerged from the contest as the victor.

Three hundred and forty-seven Liberals, 240 Conservatives and 65 Irish Nationalists were returned to Parliament. The Liberal Party had an undisputed majority over any possible combination of non-Liberals. Gladstone's personal triumph was won in two separate constituencies. Midlothian, that had hitherto been Conservative, thanks to a long-established and highly influential aristocracy, he conquered by a gratifying majority, to the great delight of the people of Edinburgh, who could not do enough in the way of *feux de joie* and illuminations. But he had also been chosen as Liberal candidate in the great manufacturing city of Leeds, and although he had never appeared there—nor had he even officially accepted the candidature—he was elected, polling the unprecedented number of more than 24,000 votes. When he accepted the mandate for Midlothian, Leeds manifested its limitless enthusiasm by electing, without a contest, his youngest son Herbert—later to be Viscount Gladstone—who had been defeated in a London constituency.

The last duel with Disraeli had been fought, and Gladstone was the victor.

BETWEEN THE QUEEN AND PARNELL

1. Prime Minister Once More

When the dismal news of the Conservatives' electoral losses reached him, Lord Beaconsfield was staying at Hatfield House, which Lord Salisbury had placed at his chief's disposal while he himself was on holiday. He was quite unprepared for the reverse, and he found it all the more difficult to resign himself to his fate because he knew that at his advanced age this defeat must be final. No wonder that he lamented, in a letter to his trusted friend, Lady Bradford: "Alas! Alas! I cannot write a letter, I almost thought of sending you a blank sheet." But he soon pulled himself together, bearing the blow with the dignity and composure that befitted his historic position.

But almost more unhappy than the defeated statesman was the Queen, who would have been so overjoyed by his success, and who so heartily disliked his victorious adversary. In the first effusion of feeling she wrote to Lord Beaconsfield from Baden-Baden, declaring that "the grief of her having to part with the kindest and most devoted as well as one of the wisest Ministers the Queen has ever had is not to be told."

Privately, she evidently credited the victor in the electoral contest with the reverse of these flattering attributes. "Of course I shall not take any notice of Mr. Gladstone, who has done so much harm," she wrote a week later to Beaconsfield. "Do not be indulgent, but make them (the Liberals) feel what they have brought on themselves."

Anything but a Gladstone Cabinet!—was the Queen's resolve. Undoubtedly it was her privilege to choose the Minister who should undertake the formation of the Liberal Cabinet. The only question was, whether the man she chose could perform such a task. Indisputably Gladstone was not the legitimate Leader of the Liberal

Party. He himself had declared, in his first electoral address in Midlothian: "I hope the verdict of the country will give to Lord Granville and Lord Hartington the responsible charge of its affairs." Thus the Queen was only exercising her legitimate privilege if she sent for Granville or Hartington. But it was, of course, less in harmony with the spirit of the Constitution and tradition that she should discuss the question with the retiring Prime Minister. His advice was that she should send for Lord Hartington; advice whose propriety was certainly not enhanced by the fact that he described Lord Hartington as "in his heart a Conservative." When Disraeli added that he was "very straightforward in his conduct," the Queen soon had an opportunity of convincing herself of the truth of this description; for at his first audience Hartington told her flatly that although neither he nor Granville had discussed the matter with Gladstone, they were both convinced that without him the formation of a Liberal Cabinet would be impossible, and that he would not accept any post but that of Prime Minister. Only the wilfully blind would have disputed the obvious fact that the electors had voted for Gladstone, and for him only; he had really received an overwhelming vote of confidence: the great majority of the successful candidates had been elected in his name, and nothing would content electors and Members but that he should take the helm. Hartington was much too honest and too perspicacious not to recognize this, but one can hardly blame the Queen if she could not at once adapt herself to this new democratic method of leaving the choice of the Prime Minister to the people, so that all she had to do was to give her formal approval. In vain did Hartington argue that Gladstone had fought against the Government only, and had always been perfectly loyal to the sovereign. She had become far too accustomed to identifying herself with her—that is, Disraeli's—Government. Hartington, therefore, with a heavy heart, was obliged, in obedience to the Queen's insistent orders to consult first Granville and then to ask Gladstone whether he would enter the Cabinet under Granville or himself.

It was as he had foretold. Of the Queen's permission to tell Gladstone all that she had said to him he tactfully made very little use. But even without this aggravation, it was a great blow to Gladstone when he heard that the Queen, whom he had served so often to the utmost of his ability, should now decline to send for him. True, Mrs. Gladstone tried to console him with the thoroughly feminine explanation: "All that is only Dizzy." But this, of course, was only a poor consolation. Naturally his answer was "No," however carefully he tried to disguise it in terms of becoming loyalty. He was ready to support a Granville or Hartington Ministry as a private Member; but as for entering it as Minister—no! Definitely, no!

With this refusal Hartington had to return to Windsor. He took Lord Granville with him, as the person most nearly concerned. His invariably pleasant and tactful manner would doubtless make it easier for the Queen to submit to the inevitable. She did at last submit to it, when both statesmen had urged upon her the irrefutable reasons why after this election only Gladstone could become Prime Minister. But, she told them, "I should rely greatly on their controlling him and assisting me."

So the Queen's attempt to get rid of Mr. Gladstone by the means recommended by Beaconsfield had failed, and on the 23rd of April, 1880, he again stood before her in order to receive her command to proceed with the formation of a Cabinet. She received him, as he recorded in the exhaustive memorandum written before he left Windsor, "with perfect courtesy." Her own notes of the occasion read more like a record of a reprimand with which she opened the period of enforced collaboration. But Gladstone was evidently determined to overlook such unpleasantness. "Altogether," he concluded, "I was well satisfied" . . . And: "I kissed Her Majesty's hand."

With this obeisance Gladstone became the Queen's Prime Minister for the second time. For, as he cautiously explained to the Queen, he had no doubt whatever of his ability to form a Cabinet. Of course, the two friends who had withdrawn in his favour must receive portfolios. Lord Granville again went to the Foreign Office, with whose work he was familiar; and he certainly possessed many valuable qualifications for the post. But he was sixty-five years of age, and not everyone had Gladstone's astonishing faculty of retaining his powers of work undiminished in spite of increasing age. The longer the Cabinet survived, the less able did he find himself to cope with the burden of work, especially as he had in the end to confront an opponent of Bismarck's calibre. Hartington could take over the important administrative work of the India Office. Forster, who had had such a disputatious time of it at the Board of Education, now accepted a no less thorny office, becoming Chief Secretary for Ireland. A number of aristocratic Whigs, whom Gladstone always regarded as indispensable, were invested with offices of varied importance. All these appointments were simple enough.

The formation of a Cabinet became a problem only when it came to finding places for the younger and especially the more Radical party leaders. Whether Sir William Harcourt, the brilliant Parliamentary debater, who became Home Secretary, was to be reckoned among the Whigs or the Radicals was doubtful, even to those who knew him best. John Bright, who to please Gladstone accepted a seat in the Cabinet as Chancellor of the Duchy of Lancaster, was still regarded as the embodiment of the Radical ideal. But no one expected him to be particularly active, and there were other men there who in the last few years had fought the Radical battles and had zealously supported Gladstone during the electoral contest. They demanded their share in the Government, not only because of their own efficiency, but because they could not under any circumstances allow the Cabinet to fall under the influence of the Whigs. The contrast between the two tendencies in the last Parliament had manifested itself repeatedly; on one occasion so visibly that the Radical leader, Joseph Chamberlain, had described Lord Hartington as the "former leader" of the Liberal Party. A very blunt and self-confident gentleman was this Joseph Chamberlain. Conscious of the undisputed success which he had achieved as a municipal reformer and indefatigable Party organizer, he was accustomed to express his views with absolute frankness and recklessness. Beside him was the man whom the Radicals regarded as their second leader, Sir Charles Dilke, whose exceptionally sound and comprehensive erudition and great Parliamentary ability no one could dispute. But Dilke had drawn upon himself the wrath of all well-disposed persons, for he had dared, at least theoretically, to advocate the Republican constitution. How could such a man be called to the Cabinet?

Further, Gladstone clung with conservative tenacity to certain administrative principles. A man might enter the Cabinet only by way of some subordinate post in the Government—an under-Secretaryship or the like. This had been Peel's principle, and in Peel Gladstone still revered with unshakable loyalty the master from whom he had learned most of what he knew. Neither Chamberlain nor Dilke had ever held such a post.

Gladstone believed that it would suffice if he made one of the two an Under-Secretary. He turned to Sir Charles Dilke, but to his no small astonishment Dilke made some very unusual stipulations. Chamberlain and Dilke had made an agreement that they would enter the Ministry together or not at all, and then only if one of them were given a seat in the Cabinet. Gladstone had to give way, and Chamberlain entered the Cabinet as President of the Board of Trade. He was "radiant"—so Gladstone's secretary reported—when he left the Prime Minister's room after his appointment. Dilke had to content himself with an Under-Secretaryship in the Foreign Office.

But this was by no means the end of the trouble which the two Radicals caused the Prime Minister. He had to make their appointment seem acceptable to the Queen, and this was extremely difficult. He had to cite precedents from the last thirty years—after all, there were plenty of them—and before she would give way had to assure her that Dilke himself now regretted his Republican divagations as youthful follies. Until he did so she declared that Dilke must not be "brought into contact" with her. She was not inaccessible to Lord Granville's argument, that it was "much safer to have the advanced Radicals in office than out." But she insisted that Dilke must declare in writing that he had renounced his Republicanism, and she carefully kept a copy of his declaration.

If the Queen had privately consoled herself with the thought that the Prime Minister, who was now seventy-one years of age, would soon retire from practical politics, he soon gave her an unmistakable proof that he himself had the fullest confidence in his undiminished capacity for work. In addition to the Premiership he took for himself the office of Chancellor of the Exchequer, one of the most strenuous as well as one of the most important of Ministerial posts. He wished to avoid thereby the trouble which the mistakes of another Chancellor had given him in his first Ministry. That the labour involved would be too much for a man of his years apparently never occurred to him. He felt perfectly at home in matters of financial administration; for example, he still knew exactly how the profits of a malt-house had been reckoned forty-five years earlier; and with the help of the brilliant staff of permanent officials, at whose head was Algernon West, his former private secretary, he introduced, with the best results, a reform of the duty on beer.

When Gladstone surveyed the Cabinet which he had taken such pains to assemble, he could tell himself that it comprised a number of men of great political and administrative talents. But was this an unmixed advantage? Lord Granville consoled the Queen's confidential secretary, General Ponsonby, with an amusing simile from the gastronomic sphere with which he was so familiar: "The Government is like bread sauce—made of two substantial elements. The few peppercorns are very obvious, and perhaps give a little flavour, but do not affect the character of the food." But a serious observer could hardly have failed to realize that with such a number of strong personalities, who were accustomed to take up a very definite position in respect of disputed questions, the Cabinet would only too often be in danger of a split. To lead such a Government, despite the authority which he exercised, was no enviable task for the Prime Minister. Disraeli, a master in the art of managing people, had won the highest praise from the experts for the way in which he dealt with his Cabinet. But even he, at critical moments, had to suffer the loss of such eminent colleagues as Lord Derby and Lord Carnarvon.

Neither in the knowledge nor in the management of men could Gladstone be compared with Disraeli. Chamberlain, long after he had gone his own way, excused this weakness by stating that Gladstone, by virtue of his extraordinary abilities, was so far above all his colleagues that he had no proper standard by which to estimate them. While Disraeli was able to win the friendship of his Ministers, Gladstone was generally divided from them by a certain gulf, greatly as they revered him. Only Granville, with whom he had worked for so many years, took the liberty of calling him simply "Gladstone." For the others he was always "Mr. Gladstone." In view of his advanced age it was inevitable that the question of a successor should occur to more than one of his paladins. Further, a progressive Ministry finds it much more difficult, because it is progressive, to agree upon the matter of tempo than one whose political tendency is to remain static.

If the Prime Minister cast his eyes on the opponents who faced him in the House of Commons he had nothing to fear from the front bench of the Opposition. There was no one there who was even remotely a match for him. The Leader of the Opposition was Sir Stafford Northcote, a blameless gentleman of long political experience, but not a man to inspire courage in his followers or anxiety in his adversaries; moreover, he had for a long time been Gladstone's private secretary, and never regarded him without a certain trepidation.

But below the gangway which divides the official from the more irregular opposition, sat a few men who were longing to cross swords with him, and who were resolved to cause the Government every conceivable kind of trouble, even if at times they had to throw a principle overboard. There, above all, was the younger son of the Duke of Marlborough, Lord Randolph Churchill, a Parliamentary debater of the first rank, full of youthful pugnacity, not over-burdened with principles, and without the smallest respect for the old gentleman whose fate it was to lead the Opposition. Beside him sat young Arthur Balfour, who had hitherto made but little impression in Parliament, but was known as a writer on philosophical subjects, versatile, and extremely gifted.

But much more important than these appeared another group "below the gangway": the "Third Party," the Irish Nationalists. At their head was a man who had attracted a very great deal of attention in the previous Parliament, and had also given great offence. He was now to reveal himself as one of the greatest of party leaders: Charles Stewart Parnell.

The Members returned to Westminster by the Irish constituencies had for decades been demanding Home Rule: that is, the dissolution of the Union established by Pitt, which for them was embodied in Dublin Castle, the seat of the English Lord-Lieutenant, and the creation of a Parliament in Dublin, which would be subordinate to the Imperial Parliament, but would be competent in Irish affairs.

Owing to the limited franchise and the great influence of the purely English landlords, the number of Home Rule members was not excessive, and there was little cohesion in their ranks. More than one of them allowed himself to be won for the Government by a lucrative office. In the House of Commons they were ineffective. At their head, in the 'seventies, was a very honest and greatly respected lawyer—Isaac Butt—who regularly introduced a motion that Home Rule should be granted to Ireland, but patiently acquiesced in the fact that it was as regularly rejected by an overwhelming majority; for both the English parties were at that time Unionist. Hardly a single Member regarded the question of repealing the Union as worthy of examination.

Conditions in Ireland were lamentable. Since the fall in the price of grain the Irish farmers, who were nearly all tenants, had been in sore straits, and the general distress led to agrarian troubles and acts of violence. The Government was accustomed to respond with Coercion Acts, by which they gave the authorities in Ireland powers far in excess of what would have been possible in England. Apart from a few critics, political circles in England regarded this as an undesirable but inevitable necessity.

The whole situation was transformed when Parnell made himself the Leader of the Irish Party. He had been elected by an Irish constituency in 1875, when he was still under thirty. Strangely enough, by his origin, his religion and his economic position he was completely divorced from the mass of the Irish people, which consisted of small tenant farmers, Catholics of Celtic descent, and more or less uneducated. Parnell was a Protestant; he came of a family of English origin, and was the son of an American mother. He was a large landowner, who leased his land, and a Cambridge man, though he had left the University without taking a degree. All this was more appropriate to an English Liberal or Conservative than to an Irish Home Ruler. But it was perhaps these very points of difference that assured him of the leadership of the Irish at Westminster.

Parnell had hardly entered the House of Commons when he resolved to show England that Ireland's desires and necessities could not be disposed of by merely ignoring them. He had soon discovered that the extraordinarily liberal standing orders of the House offered a Member innumerable possibilities of making himself most unpleasantly conspicuous if he were resolved to reckon on the hostility of *both* the English parties. He was not the inventor of the method of obstruction—for this credit is due to the Conservative Party—but he developed it into an art of which he became a master and he contrived to persuade the whole of his party to adopt it. He had already shown what he could do in this way in the recent Conservative Parliament. The election of 1880 had increased the number of Home Rule Members, and, what was even more important, the Home Rule faction elected him as its leader. By so doing it placed in his hands a power of which Government, Parliament and nation were soon to become conscious.

Before the Irish difficulty revealed itself in all its magnitude the new Prime Minister had to deal with another kind of difficulty, the result of his own vehemence. In one of his election speeches he had spoken of Austria in a manner which was not compatible with the position of a Prime Minister, or of a Member who might at any time become one. The painful consequence was that after his appointment as Premier he was obliged to write a letter of apology to the Austrian Ambassador in London. This was hardly calculated to add to his reputation with the diplomatists of Europe, and least of all with the most eminent of them. Bismarck was already fond of referring to him as "Professor Gladstone." That a popular agitation, and one which was based mainly upon moral arguments, should alter and remould the foreign policy of a great empire was completely opposed to his own conception of the methods of foreign policy.

But the peculiarity of the situation was that the Governments of Great Britain and Germany, in their anxiety to safeguard the peace of Europe, were admonishing each other to preserve it. In

288

the last year of the Beaconsfield Government Bismarck approached the Prime Minister through the German Ambassador, Count Münster, with the suggestion of a sort of alliance; but this led to no practical result. Naturally it would never have occurred to Bismarck to make a similar appeal to Gladstone. He regarded Gladstone's abhorrence of the Turks as equivalent to a leaning toward Russia. Further, in German diplomatic circles the English Liberals were regarded as such unconditional pacifists that it would be quite out of the question to rely on them. Count Münster was therefore greatly astonished when Lord Granville, in the course of one of their first conversations, spoke most firmly of the necessity of taking measures against Turkey, and protested emphatically against the erroneous opinion of foreigners that the new Ministers were "peace at any price" men. Münster reported this conversation verbatim to Berlin, apparently in order to give Bismarck the opportunity of correcting his prejudice. At the same time the British Ambassador in Berlin, Lord Odo Russell, who had a great admiration for Bismarck, and was highly esteemed by the Chancellor, wrote home endeavouring to dispel English prejudice against Bismarck. His reports on the German Chancellor's affection for England were not, indeed, taken seriously by all circles in London. Sir Charles Dilke remarked, commenting on such a letter of Russell's, that Bismarck seemed to have been making fun of Russell.

Bismarck soon had occasion to see that even "Professor Gladstone" could act energetically enough in certain cases. Included in the legacy of unsettled affairs which the Liberals had taken over from the Beaconsfield and Salisbury Governments was the implementing of the Treaty of Berlin, with which no real progress had been made during the two years which had elapsed since its conclusion. Neither Greece nor Montenegro had as yet received its new frontiers. The Porte was procrastinating with a skill born of centuries of practice, and the European Ambassadors in Constantinople could get no further. The first thing that Gladstone did, since he considered that Sir Henry Layard was not sufficiently energetic, was to replace him by Goschen. He could not bring Goschen into the Cabinet, because in a matter of domestic politics—Franchise

Reform—he had taken up a position in flat opposition to his party. Now Gladstone had found for him a task of great importance, for which he believed him to be excellently well qualified.

More than anything, Gladstone wished the just claims of Montenegro to be satisfied. For this little nation, which had defended itself with the greatest valour against the Turkish oppressors, he cherished an almost romantic affection. First of all he endeavoured to persuade the Concert of the Great Powers to act in unison, in order by their common pressure to induce the Porte to give way. In September, at the instigation of England, there was a naval demonstration off Dulcigno, though this was unfavourably viewed by the other Powers. Bismarck privately informed his family physician, Dr. Cohen, that Dulcigno was madness, Gladstone was a crazy professor, and his enthusiasm for the Bulgarians was sheer nonsense. The Queen seemed to be of almost the same opinion. She overwhelmed the Prime Minister with letters and telegrams, in which she insisted that Disraeli's Turkish policy must not be abandoned, and flatly declared that she would not give her consent to a war with our old ally, Turkey. Gladstone, however, knew what was at stake. "If Turkey befools Europe at Dulcigno," he wrote to a colleague, "we may as well shut up altogether." And this time he had luck. The Sultan suddenly gave in before the "concert" had broken up.

Gladstone had followed these developments with the greatest anxiety. He had remained in London with Granville in October, so that he could resort to serious measures in case of need. Day after day went by, without the longed-for news of the Sultan's surrender. "One morning"—so his private Secretary, Arthur Godly, later Lord Kilbracken, relates—"he was sitting at his writing-table in Downing Street, busily engaged on his daily work. Then the door opened very quietly, and Lord Granville came on tiptoe, with a paper in his hand. I saw him at once, but Mr. Gladstone, intent on his work, was unconscious of his presence. Lord Granville then, brandishing the paper (which was a deciphered telegram) above his head, proceeded to execute a *pas de joie*, still silent and on tiptoe, round the room; he danced it very gracefully, with wavings of his hands, and at last met Mr. Gladstone's astonished gaze. Thereupon he stopped and read out the telegram; the Turk had surrendered. Instantaneously Mr. Gladstone exclaimed, with indescribable fervour: 'Thank God! Then I can go down by the 2.45!' "

In Berlin, it seems, no one was overjoyed at the news of England's success. Bismarck, in conversation with Hohenlohe at Friedrichsruh, vehemently censured Gladstone's policy, complaining that it was simply promoting Russian interests in the East, and neglecting the English. Lord Odo Russell, who also visited Bismarck at Friedrichsruh, summed up his impression of a long conversation with the Chancellor: "The impression . . . is that he is rather jealous of Her Majesty's Government having been put forward by all the Powers to take the lead in Eastern affairs." He urged his Government to beware of this mood, lest Bismarck should break up the Concert.

The warning was heeded in London, and at the beginning of 1881 Goschen, who was on holiday abroad, returned by way of Berlin; in order to invite Bismarck himself to take the lead in the further discussions with Turkey in respect of the Greek frontier. Bismarck accepted the invitation. Goschen, whose own ancestry was German, enjoyed some long and intimate conversations with Bismarck, who exerted all his incomparable personal charm—a sign that Goschen's attention had pleased him, and that the British negotiator was personally agreeable to him. He dictated in Goschen's presence a note which laid down the lines on which the question was to be dealt with. Russell was delighted with this result; he hoped that the imminent settlement of the Greek question by the common efforts of England and Germany would dispel the suspicion of Bismarck which prevailed in London. However, there were many difficulties and differences of opinion to be overcome before Turkey at last gave way in this matter also (in May 1881), and agreed to cede Thessaly to Greece.

But while Gladstone's Government was able to record the most gratifying success in the domain of foreign policy, it had to cope with increasing difficulties at home.

At the outset there arose out of a trifling cause a conflict which inflamed men's passions to the utmost, but after a few years the matter was allowed to drop, and no serious attempt was made to revive it.

At the opening of every new Parliament the Members have to take a prescribed form of oath. Among the newly-elected Members was the Radical, Charles Bradlaugh, a man who with iron determination had worked his way up from the humblest beginnings. Bradlaugh's creed consisted of a number of very positive convictions, any one of which was calculated to enrage the middle-class society of the period. He was not only an atheist, but he loudly proclaimed the fact. He had written a pamphlet attacking the House of Lords, and he was an advocate of artificial birth-control. Nevertheless, having been lawfully elected, he could, of course, have taken his seat in Parliament without more ado, if he himself had not provoked a conflict. He informed the Speaker that his convictions forbade him to take an oath; he wished instead to make an affirmation of the same content. After the House had decided that he had no right to make an affirmation, he stated that he was prepared to take the oath. But in the meantime a few Opposition Members had discovered that this was a splendid opportunity for heckling the Government. They were the members of the little group that had gathered round Lord Randolph Churchill, and which people were beginning to call the "Fourth Party." They protested loudly and solemnly against the notion of allowing an atheist to take the oath; they exploited with demagogic artfulness the prejudices which Bradlaugh had provoked, and seizing the initiative, they did everything to make the understanding which the Government and the official heads of the Opposition were ready to come to impossible. They won a brilliant tactical victory. Gladstone had to look on while the leadership of the House which was elected in his name slipped out of his hands. In vain did he, who had once been the passionate champion of a narrow clericalism, and whose piety and sincere belief in God were known to all, now advocate tolerance and religious liberty; in vain did he point to the indisputable right of Bradlaugh's constituents to be represented in Parliament; the majority chose to express their abhorrence of Bradlaugh's blasphemous views by putting the matter to the vote. The struggle continued for years. Bradlaugh was forcibly expelled from the House. The House ordered his arrest and released him after one day's imprisonment. He offered himself for election again and again, and was always returned to Parliament. He took the matter to the law-courts, with varying success. In the end he lost his case, but Lord Coleridge uttered the memorable words: "Persecution is a very easy form of virtue. . . . It is easy to turn on someone who differs from you in opinion, and in the guise of zeal for God's honour to attack a man whose life perhaps may be much more pleasing to God than your own."

This may not have sounded very pleasantly in the ears of those who had provoked the persecution of Bradlaugh, but they could console themselves with the thought that they had done wonders as party politicians; they had repeatedly succeeded in getting a majority against Gladstone, and for five years they had excluded Bradlaugh from the Lower House. That all this excitement was artificial was shown by the General Election of 1885. Bradlaugh, as a matter of course, was again elected. The Speaker, determined to put an end to the tiresome scandal, simply refused to accept the protest against allowing Bradlaugh to take the oath. Bradlaugh then sat in the House of Commons until his death, and won universal esteem. Three days before his death the House unanimously expunged from the records the resolution which had once excluded him; an expression of remorse which Bradlaugh, now, at the end of his strenuous life, wrestling with death, was in no condition to understand. So complete was the conviction of the indefensible nature of the pretext on which the House had fought so passionately a few years earlier.

This whole conflict, which casts such a singular light on the intellectual make-up of a Liberal British Parliament in the last quarter of the nineteenth century, is of importance here only because for Gladstone it was the occasion of what was perhaps his most magnificent speech. For several years the miserable squabble had been giving rise to ugly scenes and insoluble conflicts, when in 1883 Gladstone attempted to settle it by legislation which would give every Member the right, if he had scruples as to taking a religious oath, to make a simple affirmation of loyalty. On the 26th of April, 1883, he spoke in support of this measure in a speech whose nobility of thought was expressed in language of equal nobility, and which was inspired by a spirit of intellectual liberty that was all the more remarkable because it was the utterance of a man whose opinions were infinitely remote from those of the man for whom he was demanding toleration. The finest passage in his speech was that in which he dealt with the argument that everyone was, as a matter of fact, admitted to the House, without distinction of religious creed, under the sole condition that he must confess to some sort of belief in God.

"Where will you draw the limit?" he cried. "You draw it at the point where the abstract denial of God is severed from abstract admission of the Deity. My proposition is, that your line is worthless. There is much on your side of the line which is just as objectionable as the Atheism on the other side. If you call on us to draw these distinctions, let them be rational distinctions. I do not say let them be Christian distinctions; but let them be rational distinctions. I can understand the rational distinction, that you should frame the Oath in such a way that its terms should recognize, not merely the acknowledgment of the existence of the Deity, but the providence of the Deity and man's responsibility to the Deity, and in such a way as to indicate the knowledge in a man's own mind that he must answer to the Deity for what he does, and is able to do. But is that your present rule? No, Sir. You know well that from ancient times there have been sects and schools that have admitted in the abstract, just as freely as the Christian admits, the existence of a Deity, but who have held that, though Deity exists, yet of practical relations between Him and man there can be none.

"Many Members of this House will recollect, perhaps, the noble and majestic lines—for such they are—of the Latin poet. Divinity exists—as these, I must say, magnificent words set forth—in remote, inaccessible recesses of which we know nothing; but with us it has no dealing, with us it has no relation.

> "Omnis enim per se divum natura necesse est
> Immortale aevo summa cum pace fruatur
> Semota a nostris rebus sejuntaque longe.
> Nam privata dolore omni, privata periclis,

Ipsa suis pollens opibus, nihil indiga nostri,
Nec bene promeritis capitur, nec tangitur ira."[1]

The impression produced by this speech has been recorded by
two who were present at its delivery; men who were not only
experienced Parliamentarians, but scholars and historians who were
accustomed to surveying periods and peoples: John Morley and
James Bryce. Decades later they still recalled that impression.
"There were perhaps not twenty men in the House of Commons
who could follow the sense of the lines so as to appreciate their
bearing on his argument. But these sonorous hexameters—hexameters that seemed to have lived on for nineteen centuries to find
their application from the lips of an orator to-day—the sense of
remoteness in the strange language and the far-off heathen origin,
the deep and moving note in the speaker's voice, thrilled the
imagination of the audience and held it spellbound, lifting for a
moment the whole subject of debate into a region far above party
conflicts. Spoken by anyone else, the passage culminating in these
Lucretian lines might have produced little effect. It was the voice
and manner, above all the voice, with its marvellous modulation,
that made the speech majestic."

Certainly in those days no such speech could have been delivered
in any other Parliament in the world, and even in the English House
of Commons, where classical learning was still cherished, it would
not have been possible at a later period. Only a man who in his
far-away youth had received the great tradition of those statesmen
of the eighteenth century who were rooted in classical antiquity,
and who was honoured for his life-work and his idealism, could
still venture, in the year 1883, to recite in the Latin tongue the
pregnant verses of an ancient didactic poem.

This magnificent speech, admired alike by friend and enemy,
could not at the time prevent party spirit and prejudice from
triumphing. But not a word of contradiction was spoken when

[1] For the very nature of Divinity must of necessity enjoy immortal life
in the profoundest peace, far removed and separated from our troubles;
for without any pain, without danger, itself mighty by its own resources,
needing us not at all, it is neither propitiated by services nor touched by
wrath.

Gladstone, a few years later, on the day after Bradlaugh's funeral, summed up, in a hostile Parliament, the outcome of all these disputes:

"A distinguished man and admirable member of this House, was laid yesterday in his mother earth. He was the subject of a long controversy in this House—a controversy the beginning of which we recollect, and the ending of which we recollect. We remember with what zeal it was prosecuted; we remember how summarily it was dropped; we remember also what reparation has been done within the last few days to the distinguished man who was the immediate object of that controversy. But does anyone who hears me believe that that controversy, so prosecuted and so abandoned, was beneficial to the Christian religion?"

2. Ireland Again

"A danger, in its ultimate results scarcely less disastrous than pestilence and famine . . . distracts that country. A portion of its population is attempting to sever the constitutional tie which unites it to Great Britain."

In these words Lord Beaconsfield, in his electoral manifesto of the 8th of March, 1880, referred to the increasing unrest in Ireland. But what had he done to conjure it in the six years of his Government? Nothing had been done to alleviate the economic misery of the Irish tenant since Gladstone's Land Act of 1870. In order to deal with the unrest he had passed a Coercion Act which expired on the 1st of June, 1880. But he had done nothing to prolong its operation after this date, although by reason of his great majority, and the docility of the House of Lords, he was perfectly well able to do so, and the views expressed in his manifesto seemed to make such action obligatory.

Thus when Gladstone and his Secretary for Ireland, Forster, took office, they were confronted at once with a great responsibility, of which they were perfectly conscious. The economic condition of Ireland had greatly deteriorated in the last few years, and they now had to reckon with Parnell, the Leader of an absolutely compact Party, resolved to go to any lengths.

The situation of the Irish tenants was dependent on two economic factors, the result of the harvest, and the price of agricultural produce, especially of potatoes. Since 1878 there had been a decline in both. One bad harvest had followed another, and the prices of potatoes—and of grain—had fallen as a result of overseas competition. The situation of the tenants could be read, as on a barometer, in the number of evictions. Where things went badly with them they fell into arrears with their rent and the number of evictions showed a rapid increase. Now this increase had become constant. In 1878 there were two and a half times as many evictions as in 1877; in 1879 almost three times as many. And the numbers for 1880—when more than 2,000 families were evicted—were far in excess of any previous figures.

The Irish tenant, as a rule, was not only poor; he was the victim of a most inequitable land law. It was a law which a ruling class had forced upon a people subdued by violence. The English had seized the soil far and wide and leased it to the Irish. All the labour of cultivating the soil fell upon the tenants, while the landlord was concerned only to draw the rents, which he spent, as a rule, in England; many Irish landowners never even setting foot on their property. Apart from Ulster, where the farmers were mostly Protestant Scottish and English immigrants, who in the course of time had obtained more equitable conditions of tenancy, the tenant did not even profit by the improvements which he might make in the property. When the lease expired they passed to the landlord, who paid no compensation for them. What was even worse was that when harvests were good and prices high the rents were put up, while it depended on the good will and the good sense of the landlord whether they were lowered again when harvests were bad and prices low. Perhaps the increases of rent were not quite so frequent and so much the rule as the tenants asserted. But this did not alter the situation. For divided as they were by religion and history and national ideals, landlord and tenant confronted each other as enemies, each always ready to believe the worst of the other. That the rent was prohibitive in the case of many small tenants was obvious in view of the increasing number of evictions.

The Irish had long been given to responding to economic oppression by agrarian crimes. Isolated houses were burned to the ground; stores of produce were destroyed, and cattle driven off or maimed. The victims of such attacks were most frequently farmers who had dared to take over a farm from which an insolvent tenant had been evicted. As the number of evictions increased, so did the number of agrarian crimes. From 1878 to 1880 the numbers rose from 301 to 2,585!

The Irish politicians exploited the discontent and despair of the Irish peasants for their own ends. In 1879 Michael Davitt, with the help of Parnell, founded the Land League. Davitt was one of the most remarkable figures of the Irish movement. As a child he had been turned adrift, with his father, by eviction; and as the result of an accident in a factory, in which he was earning a scanty living at the age of eleven, he lost his left arm. Nevertheless, he had worked his way up, and with a passion that was sufficiently explained by his sufferings, but also with an integrity that was acknowledged even by his opponents, he had flung himself into the campaign for the betterment of the Irish peasantry. English justice had struck him a heavy blow: in 1870 he had been sentenced to no less than fifteen years' penal servitude; and he owed it to a humane impulse of the Conservative Home Secretary, Cross, that he was liberated in 1877 on ticket-of-leave.

The Land League announced that its aim was to protect tenants against unjust rentals. The advocates of legislative methods found themselves cheek by jowl with the more radical elements, who were influenced by the irresponsible American Irish, who gave the League abundant pecuniary support. It was an excellent instrument of agitation, and Parnell soon contrived to obtain control of it. Backed by the League and the Irish Party in Parliament, he was able to make any Government unpleasantly aware of his existence.

He was resolved to make the most of this fact. The peculiar symbolism of the English Parliament imparts a decisive political significance to the part of the House in which the members of a Party take their seats. Hitherto the Irish had always sat on the same side as the Liberals, but beneath the gangway, which signified their independence of the Liberal front bench. Now, however, Parnell's followers took their seats below the gangway on the side of the Opposition, although this made them neighbours of the Conservatives. This demonstrated Parnell's maxim, that the Irish must always be in opposition; no matter which party was in power. Only those Irish members who declined to accept Parnell as their leader continued to sit beside the Liberals.

When Parliament assembled the Government had to come to two decisions. Should they attempt to govern Ireland without coercion? Both Gladstone and Forster answered this question in the affirmative. They were aware, however, that something must be done to alleviate the lot of the Irish tenants. Gladstone had already proved, by his Land Act of 1870, that his reforming zeal did not stop at St. George's Channel. Forster, who had accepted his onerous office with the depressing feeling that his task was one that exceeded human powers, was keenly sensible of the miseries of the people in his charge, and was anxious to mitigate them as far as this was possible. Both believed that a policy of agrarian reform offered the only possibility of breaking the vicious circle of agrarian crimes and coercion.

They wished first of all to improve the position of the evicted tenants. There had been more than a thousand evictions in the first six months of 1880. The Government introduced a Compensation for Disturbance Bill, which, under certain by no means excessively generous conditions, would indemnify the victims of eviction for their losses. It was a fairly inoffensive measure, far milder than the Acts which succeeded it. But it was enough to excite the greatest indignation among the Irish landlords. They formed a class which had hitherto been pampered by the Administration and the Legislature, and had yet to learn the wisdom of the legend of the Sybilline Books. The political danger lay in this, that many of the leading aristocratic families were among those financially interested; indeed, the Ministry's first loss was due to this fact, as Lord Lansdowne, the head of an old and powerful Whig family, which had great possessions in Ireland, resigned his office. On the other hand, Lord Hartington, who was in the same position, was able to consider the general interest before the particular, and gave the Bill his emphatic support. Lord Randolph Churchill, to whom every occasion was welcome which would enable him to attack the Government, condemned the Bill in unbridled language as the first move in the social war, the incitement of the masses against the possessing classes. Such phrases showed how great was the opposition which Gladstone would have to overcome if he wished to introduce any serious reforms, and how much the champions of the landowning interest had yet to learn before they could understand his warning, that only such reforms would give the State the clear conscience which it must needs possess before it could defend the rights of property.

This time, of course, the great majority of Liberal Members were loyal to their leader; so that he could at least pass the Bill through the House of Commons, although Parnell found a pretext for declining to vote. He was already applying his disastrous tactics of treating reforms not from the practical point of view, but from the standpoint of the agitator.

But Parnell's mistake was as nothing to that of the House of Lords, in which the representatives of the landowning interest formed a compact and short-sighted phalanx. The Lords rejected the Bill by an overwhelming majority. The people—so Lord Acton wrote to Mary Gladstone—would be justified in declaring that an assembly which allowed itself to be guided by base and selfish motives when it was a question of preventing ruin and starvation was not only a wrong to the poor but was also a disgrace to the community. Lord Beaconsfield, who in his electoral manifesto had so significantly hinted at the storm which was threatening in Ireland, had here an opportunity of conjuring this storm and of demonstrating his far-sightedness. He did the very opposite. He encouraged the Lords to resist the Bill; and so he had the satisfaction of once more helping to defeat Gladstone, who had defeated him so signally at the polls. But Ireland and Great Britain had to pay the price of this triumph; for the rejection of the Bill, which Gladstone regarded as "one of the most deplorable among the legislative performances of that House," was, as Parnell's biographer has said, "the signal for extreme agitation in Ireland." An Irish leader, Dillon, declared that Ireland should be grateful to the

Lords, for they had shown it "that no good thing could come out of London."

Parnell sounded the same note. He turned the agitation against the Government, although it was not in any degree responsible for the rejection of the Bill. So much the better, however, for the purposes of the agitation.

But now Parnell's agitation had created a new and peculiarly dangerous weapon: the boycott. The name, like the thing itself, was a product of the Irish conflict. In a speech delivered at Ennis on the 19th of September, 1880, Parnell incited the Irish peasantry to make war upon all who dared to oppose the Land League— that is, those peasants who had the courage to take over a holding from which another had been evicted.

"What are you to do to a tenant who bids for a farm from which his neighbour has been evicted?" he asked the crowd.—"Kill him! Shoot him!" came the answer.—"No," replied Parnell, in his quietest manner, "I wish to point out a more Christian and a more charitable way . . . when a man takes a farm from which another had been evicted, you must show him in the roadside when you meet him, you must show him in the streets of the town, you must show him at the shop counter, you must show him in the fair and in the market-place, and even in the house of worship, by leaving him severely alone, by putting him in a moral Coventry, by isolating him from his kind as if he was a leper of old—you must show him your detestation of the crime he has committed, and you may depend upon it that there will be no man so full of avarice, so lost to shame, as to dare the public's opinion of all right-thinking men and to transgress your unwritten code of law."

A few days later Captain Boycott, the land-agent of an English peer, learned exactly what this new method meant. As he did not submit to the dictation of the Land League, all his workers left him there and then. No one would tend his cattle or plough his fields. No shopkeeper would sell him anything; no postman dared to bring him a letter or telegram. This "boycott" aroused the greatest excitement, and made itself felt even at a distance. Protestants from Ulster hurried off to help the victim; and troops had to be sent to protect him. The whole apparatus of Government became feverishly active. But not all the help in the world could save the bold captain from his fate: he had to vacate the field and leave it to the victorious Irish farmers.

The effect of this and similar cases soon made itself felt. The Land League, and the masses of peasants flocking to join it, became more conscious of their power: but the landlords were anxious and intimidated. Naturally, they appealed for help to the Lord-Lieutenant in Dublin, to the Government in London, and even to the Queen, whose sympathies were well known. The Queen forwarded their appeal, in an even more emphatic form, to the Premier. She reproachfully pointed to the fact that a state of affairs prevailed in Ireland which had not its like in any civilized country. "The Government must be firm and clear itself from grave suspicion on this subject," she said. It must take immediate measures against the "monstrous" Land League; "they should not be delayed or the Government will be held responsible for loss of life." Lord Beaconsfield, with whom at this time she was carrying on a brisk correspondence, did not fail to pour oil upon the flames, assuring her with scornful self-complacency: "As for Liberal administration in Ireland, it has taken the form of anarchy."

But for the responsible statesmen the problem was by no means as simple as it was for the exasperated Queen. Was it possible to deal with the Land League by the ordinary judicial and administrative methods? And if not, was the Government to ask Parliament once more to give it exceptional powers and coercive legislation, when only a few months earlier it had declared that it would deal with Ireland by the ordinary methods of the law? It had not renounced Coercion in any arbitrary spirit, but in consequence of a profound aversion to such methods, in which it was supported by public opinion, Conservative as well as Liberal. There are two institutions of his public law of which the Englishman is proud, because they were won by prolonged and bitter struggles, and embody the safeguards of personal liberty: Habeas Corpus and trial by jury. The Habeas Corpus Act of 1679, the result of the struggle between King and Parliament, safeguards in a unique and inimitable manner the right of every prisoner to judicial examination of the reasons for his arrest, and therefore safeguards the liberty of the person against the arbitrary administration of the law. But the principle that no one may be sentenced in respect of a crime save by the unanimous verdict of twelve of his fellow-countrymen is older than Parliament itself. Any exceptional law—or Coercion Act, in the English terminology—involves at least the temporary suspension of these two safeguards, or at all events of one of them. The Englishman is therefore loth to resort to such methods so long as any other expedient is possible.

Gladstone shared this aversion with all his heart. In October 1880—that is, when his anxieties in respect of Dulcigno left him no rest by day or night—Forster having proposed that Habeas Corpus should be suspended in Ireland, he resisted the proposal, with the argument that they must first endeavour to fight the agitation of the Land League with the existing methods of the law. He succeeded in convincing the Queen of the necessity of this course. Accordingly, charges in connection with the Land League agitation were brought against Parnell and a dozen of his subordinates. But the jury system, that worked so well in England, was useless in Ireland, at a time of extreme political excitement, in a political case. At the conclusion of a trial which lasted for twenty days the jury declared that "we are unanimous that we cannot agree" on a unanimous verdict—which practically amounted to a verdict in favour of the accused. Ireland received the news of this decision with an outburst of jubilation; *feux de joie* were lit all over the country—and the American contribution to the funds of the Land League were doubled.

Even before this verdict was returned the Cabinet had resolved to introduce a Coercion Bill. For months the battle for the Bill raged to and fro in Parliament. Forster and the Lord-Lieutenant —Lord Cowper—became every day more and more convinced, not only that the normal administrative and judicial methods would be insufficient, but also that the emergency power to commit suspected persons without judicial sentence would suffice to quell the disorder. This, however, was opposed by the Radical Cabinet Ministers: not only by Joseph Chamberlain, the leader of the young Radicals, but also by the veteran John Bright. Gladstone too had serious doubts as to the propriety of such a measure.

303

But the Queen pressed him harder than ever. When, in the middle of November, in the course of the prescribed report on the Cabinet meeting, he informed her that the whole time had been taken up with the discussion of the Irish question, she complained that this "does not give me as much information as I could wish . . . I trust you will write me fuller details to-morrow." Apparently she wished to know *which* Ministers had opposed Coercion. She had already, in letters to Lord Granville, endeavoured to play off the moderate against the Radical Ministers. Disraeli, in cases of conflict in the Cabinet, had not scrupled to name those of his colleagues who had opposed him. But Gladstone could not be persuaded to do this; in his opinion it would have been a serious offence against the solidarity of the Cabinet, and the obligation of mutual loyalty among the Ministers, and also an infringement of an important Constitutional principle. He therefore sent the Queen a very full report, containing a most lucid exposition of the problems discussed, and the various arguments for and against the solutions proposed—but he named no names. This discretion on his part did not prevent the Queen from writing to Lord Hartington and Forster and requesting them to pay no attention to Bright and Chamberlain. "The Government," she wrote on Christmas Eve, "has two very Radical and very dangerous Members, and the Queen thinks *one* especially dangerous." Undoubtedly she had in mind the Right Honourable Joseph Chamberlain. Only five years later she was to speak of him in very different terms.

In this report Gladstone dealt also with the crucial question: whether the suspension of the Habeas Corpus Act would strike at the root of the mischief. Everything depended on whether the "conspiracy against property" was confined to comparatively small groups, which could be checkmated by commitment, as Forster asserted, or whether so large a proportion of the nation was involved that such a measure would be inadequate.

One thing, however, he emphasized. Legislation must on no account be restricted to measures of repression. Such measures must go hand in hand with legislative reforms for the improvement of the economic situation of the tenants. Here again the Queen dissented. She wanted to accelerate the repressive measures and retard the reforms. Over and over again she returned to the attack: "The Queen wishes to repeat her decided opinion that *no* measure of *any* kind should be brought forward *till* those for Coercion . . . have been passed."

But Gladstone remained firm. When finally the Cabinet gave way before Forster's urging, and even Bright and Chamberlain shrank from the responsibility of refusing the Irish Administration the instrument which they declared to be indispensable, it was resolved at the same time that a Land Law should be introduced which would satisfy the most urgent of the tenants' demands. Forster too held this to be indispensable; and even the Ulster tenants were prepared to go over to the League if these demands were not satisfied.

In the last days of the year 1880 the decision was taken. When at the close of this year Gladstone looked back on the first stage of his Governmental achievements, he could hardly avoid the realization that he was confronted with tasks and with obstacles which were almost too much for a man over seventy years of age, who had nearly fifty years of Parliamentary life behind him—and who, six years earlier, had already felt that the time had come when he must retire into private life. True, he had so far been spared any great reverses; for he did not take the Parliamentary defeats in the Bradlaugh affair for more than they were worth. But of success there was not much more to record than the clearing up of the Montenegro question, while the Boer problem appeared to be decidedly more critical now than when he took office. And the same must be said of the Irish question. Even though it had not yet presented itself in all its terrible gravity, it was depressing enough for him to reflect that in consenting to a new Coercion Act he had been forced to derogate from a principle of his political philosophy. And in addition to all other difficulties there was the difficulty of his personal relations with the Queen. Wherever he turned she opposed him, whether Turkey, or the Transvaal, or Ireland was in question. She was trying to excite conflicts in the Cabinet. If he accepted new colleagues from the sphere of rising Parliamentary talents, she took exception to their "very extreme opinions"; even in the case of Leonard Courtney, a man whose great intellectual independence was equalled only by his encyclo-paedic knowledge, and who for years had written the leaders for *The Times*. Or in that of George Trevelyan, the nephew of the great historian Macaulay, to whom he had dedicated one of the most vital of English biographies, and who had just enriched the historical literature of England by a masterly study of the early career of Charles Fox. Each was to prove himself, in a long career, a good patriot and a loyal servant of the Crown, and a man of thoroughly moderate opinions. But at that time the Queen regarded them as on the further side of the line beyond which she was unwilling to go when it came .to appointing Ministers. To Gladstone himself she was always courteous, but he was perfectly sensible of the reserve with which she met him, and of the fact that she "never"—as she wrote to Lord Beaconsfield—"wrote except on formal *official* matters to the Prime Minister." He did not, perhaps, know just how often and how vivaciously she was writing to his predecessor and his enemy, but he could trace the influence of that enemy, feel that he was working against him. How would it be when the practical difficulties were greater still, as it seemed that they would be?

And another thing he could not conceal from himself—that he was beginning, sometimes, to feel the burden of his years. His splendid constitution, which had enabled him to make such fabulous efforts, was showing the first signs of failure. One evening in August 1880 he came home shaking with fever. He grew rapidly worse, so that his faithful physician, Dr. Clark, turned an anxious countenance on his distracted wife and daughter. On the 2nd of August, which was Bank Holiday, thousands of people flocked to Downing Street, anxious to inquire as to the condition of their beloved leader. But after a few days his natural vitality got the better of the illness, and when he returned to Westminster, after a short sea voyage, he astonished the House by his energy and his mental alertness. "It has been an eventful, wonderful year, and with all the rocks ahead and gathering clouds the prevailing feeling is thankfulness," Mary Gladstone—then in her thirty-fourth year—wrote in her diary on New Year's Eve, 1880. She shared with her mother the task of looking after the well-being of her father, whom she loved and worshipped, and she also undertook secretarial work for him. She sat beside her mother in the Ladies' Gallery of the House when he was speaking, and helped him to entertain the intellectual celebrities who found their way to Downing Street. Her chief adviser, in matters of conscience, was Gladstone's great friend and admirer, Lord Acton. In the storm of criticism that so often raged about them she asked the great historian what would be the verdict of posterity on her father. It was precisely in the critical days of December 1880 that Lord Acton answered this question in a letter—a letter as long as an essay, and as full of thought as a profound biographical study. From the standpoint of a man whose business it was to survey the nations and the ages, he pointed to his friend's position in English history. He placed him on a level with Chatham, Fox, Pitt, Canning and Peel, and he declared that Gladstone united the highest qualities of those five statesmen without their weaknesses. As an orator he placed him on a level with the greatest orators of the past. But what Lord Acton especially praised in him was: "the vigorous and perpetual progress of his mind. Later ages will know what in this critical autumn of a famous year is only guessed, that even now at seventy, in his second Ministry, after half a century of public life, his thoughts are clearing, moving, changing, on the two highest of all political questions."

And this was the reason why Queen Victoria and Gladstone could no longer come to a closer understanding—why they must grow even farther apart as his unresting intellect ranged farther afield from its first beginnings.

The first days of the year 1881 showed at once that this was to be a year of storm and stress for England, and especially for the Prime Minister. After he had with the greatest trouble obtained the Queen's assent to the passage in the speech from the Throne which referred to the evacuation of Kandahar, the section dealing with the legislation in respect of Ireland caused the greatest sensation in Parliament. The Irish began their policy of obstruction even during the debate on the Address, so that the House was in session for no less than twenty-two hours.

But this was only a foretaste of what was to come in the debate on Forster's "Protection of Person and Property Bill" for Ireland. Forster introduced the Bill on the 24th of January: on the following day the Prime Minister moved that the Bill should have precedence over all other business before the House. The Bill and the motion fanned the Irish opposition to white heat. It was true that Forster's Bill was a very extreme measure. It empowered the Lord-Lieutenant, and therefore, in actual fact, the Secretary for Ireland, to arrest every Irishman who was suspected on sufficient grounds of revolutionary practices and to keep him in custody until the end of September 1882. Only sheer desperation can have inspired the Secretary to propose such a measure. For he was expressing his actual feelings when he declared: "If I had thought that this duty would devolve upon the Irish Secretary I would never have held office; if I could have foreseen that this would have been the result of twenty years of Parliamentary life, I would have left Parliament rather than have undertaken it."

Forster was a Liberal and a Quaker, full of compassion for human suffering, and prepared to act in obedience to the dictates of humanity. But he regarded the Land League and its terrors with such horror that he felt himself obliged to sacrifice his feelings to the supreme duty of defending the State.

The Irish Members, naturally, cared not a straw for Forster's feelings. They saw in him the enemy against whom every weapon is justified. Parnell and his henchmen inspired the Irish with a boundless hatred of the Secretary. They endeavoured to obstruct the progress of his Bill by every expedient that an inventive mind could devise. Parnell had at his beck and call a group of the most dangerous Parliamentary fighters. Tim Healy's vicious tricks of fence, Sexton's masterly rhetoric, Biggar's bluff intrepidity were exploited by Parnell with supreme ruthlessness; the more enraged the House became, the more fiercely it opposed this contempt of its highest traditions, the cooler and more incisive was Parnell. When the veteran democrat, Bright, who had fought a hundred battles for justice and liberty, heedless of the applause or disfavour of the mob, and who had opposed the Coercion Bill as long as he could in the Cabinet—when Bright explained to the House why he now supported it, and indignantly reproached the Irish for their insolent contempt of Parliamentary traditions, they attacked him no less intemperately and bitterly than they had attacked the Irish Secretary, much to the detriment of the Irish cause, as they would realize in years to come.

The Queen might well write to the Prime Minister: "Surely something must be done to put down those shameless Home Rulers." The standing orders of the House afforded little opportunity of doing this something, and they could not be reinforced without the co-operation of the Conservatives. In the first fight against the Land League, of course, they were on the side of the Government, and Lord Randolph Churchill's attempt once more to put the spirit of opposition before everything found no support even among his friends of the Fourth Party, and, indeed, came near to disrupting it. The feeble Northcote could not make up his mind to agree to a tightening up of the standing orders. But here the Queen intervened, and working through Lord Beaconsfield, managed to stiffen his morale.

The crisis came finally on the 2nd of February, after a session which had lasted, without intermission, for forty-one hours. After previous agreement with Gladstone the Speaker himself took the Chair at 9 a.m. and declared to the exhausted assembly, in a short and incisive address, that the question whether the Bill was to be introduced had been sufficiently debated, and that the House would now divide. It was done so quickly that the Irish had no time for deliberation. Before they had recovered from their surprise the House had voted. When the Radical Labouchere, at the beginning of the next session, asked the Speaker on what provision of the standing orders he had based his action, the latter drew himself up in the Chair, and solemnly wrapping his official robes about him, he replied in words that have made the name of Speaker Brand for ever memorable: "I have acted on my own responsibility and from a sense of duty to the House." The delighted and enthusiastic applause of the House, which was repeatedly renewed, showed the Irish that this time they had gone too far; and the whole country regarded Brand's action with delighted approval.

But the very next day showed that the war was still to be waged with undiminished violence. On the order of the day were the

Prime Minister's proposals for tightening up the standing orders. But before he could expound his reasons for these proposals, the Irish asked if it were true that Michael Davitt, who had been released from prison on ticket-of-leave, had been imprisoned again. Sir William Harcourt, the Home Secretary, not only replied in the affirmative, but embittered the Irish by his incisive tone and his refusal to give the House any justificatory details. An Irish Member, Dillon, interrupted him, refused to obey the Speaker, and was expelled from the House. Hardly had Gladstone begun to speak when Parnell sprang up and moved "that the right honourable Member be not longer heard." He too was expelled. So it went on, until at last all the thirty-five or thirty-six Irish Members had been excluded from the House. Only now could the proposals be moved and debated, and at last, at three o'clock in the morning, accepted. Gladstone, in his official letter to the Queen, calls this "the most extraordinary night known in Parliament certainly for fifty years, and probably for a much longer time." And "he cannot conclude without expressing his strong sense of the immense public service which has been rendered by the Speaker on this occasion," for "his firmness in mind, his suavity in manner, his unvaried patience, his incomparable temper under a thousand provocations."

But thanks were due also to his own endurance and his undismayed courage, on which even the reports of the police on intended attempts upon his life made no impression. Lord Lansdowne, who had left the Ministry in the previous year, precisely on account of the Irish question, and who was also becoming more and more critical in his attitude to Gladstone, could not withhold his admiration when he heard one of his speeches in the House of Commons: "He was ceaselessly interrupted by the Irish savages, but it was like a lion surrounded by cur dogs—every time that one came near enough he got a pat that sent him off limping."

Gladstone had once more shown that in case of need he could attack an insubordinate adversary with the utmost vehemence and endurance, even though he was seventy-two years of age, and had at the same time to deal with an infinite number of other difficult tasks, for at the very time when these Parliamentary storms were claiming his attention he had to prepare his Budget, keep a watch over the problems of Africa, and elaborate the Irish Land Bill with its hundred highly intricate clauses; for Gladstone had resolved, not only that he would bring it in immediately following the Protection Bill, but that he himself would pilot it through Parliament. Yet with all these efforts and all this excitement he still retained the mental freedom and alertness which delighted even the most exacting observers whom he met on a social footing. Benjamin Jowett, the great scholar and pedagogue, met him one evening at Tennyson's. He was fascinated. "The Prime Minister was marvellous. He had been working all day, and was the most brimful of conversation of anybody in the company. . . . After dinner Tennyson read us 'The old order changeth.' . . . It was pleasant to see the entire absorption and devout inclination of the head with which Gladstone listened to him."

Gladstone's Land Law of 1881 is to-day generally recognized as one of the great reforms which definitely, in the course of a generation, lifted the Irish peasant to a higher level of well-being and personal liberty. In principle it was a bold and extremely important step, for it no longer left the rent to be fixed by the only seemingly free agreement between landlord and tenant, but opened the way to its official determination. Any tenant could appeal to the Court, which would fix the "fair" rent—to be binding on both parties for a term of fifteen years—at a figure which was consistent with the situation of the two parties and the productive-ness of the soil. This meant, in practice, the reduction of the unreasonably high rents to a practicable figure, and the protection of the tenant against arbitrary increases of rent in times of increasing harvests and rising prices—which, as a matter of fact, did not occur. In practice, the rents were reduced by the Courts, on an average, by some 20 per cent. The Act also gave the tenant the right to sell his lease, and thus to indemnify himself for improve-ments effected in the soil.

The agitation of the Irish cultivators had summed up their demands in an incisive formula: The three F's—fair rent, fixity of tenure, and free sale. All these demands were granted by Gladstone's Land Law.

But these fundamental notions could be expressed in a practicable and legally unassailable form—owing to the intricate problems of the Irish law and the peculiar technical methods of English jurisprudence—only in a Bill which comprised a great number of carefully elaborated clauses, which offered both Oppositions abundant opportunities of attacking it and of moving amendments, since every single provision seemed to the Conservatives an intolerable encroachment on the rights of the landlord, while the Irish declared that it was tame to excess and inadequate. Both the landlords and the Irish fought the Bill obstinately at every stage. Owing to their opposition, to pilot the Bill through innumerable sessions was a quite peculiarly difficult task, the brunt of which rested on the shoulders of the Prime Minister. He himself introduced and explained the Bill in a great speech, distinguished as much by the speaker's bold conception of reform as by his supreme mastery of every detail.

But he had to make a painful announcement. The Duke of Argyll, who had supported him with such enthusiasm in the conflicts arising from his Balkan policy, had resigned from the Cabinet because he could not support the Land Act. What he could not tell the House was that the Queen, on hearing of Argyll's resignation, had on the same day written to him stating that "the Queen fears that this (i.e. the Land Bill) is not to be so moderate as she was at first led to hope. Can Mr. Gladstone not modify some of the clauses?"

This difficulty too had to be overcome. During the many months of debate on the details of the Bill the Prime Minister himself had to make countless speeches, parrying attacks, making concessions, and answering questions. He himself, of course, added to the difficulties of his task. Gladstone could never resist the temptation of replying to the questions of the Opposition with a circumstantial thoroughness which was intended to clear up all doubt and misunderstanding, but which often brought his colleagues on the Treasury bench to the verge of despair; especially when the Opposition—and above all, the members of the Fourth Party—detected and exploited this weakness; with a cleverly simulated thirst for information following up each answer with a new question, which elicited yet another answer.

All too seldom did he show that he was not lacking in humour, and that he was able, by a witty retort, to silence this kind of opposition. Once three of the four members of the Fourth Party had spoken in rotation, and in their zeal to outdo each other they had said a good many things that could not be reconciled with one another. Then Gladstone rose to his feet and quoted a verse from the prophet Joel. "That which the palmerworm hath left hath the locust eaten, and that which the locust hath left hath the cankerworm eaten, and that which the cankerworm hath left hath the caterpillar eaten." This time the laugh was on his side, and even the partisans of the Fourth Party were temporarily suppressed.

Not until the end of July had the Bill passed through all its stages in the Lower House. It was accepted by a great majority; but Parnell and his followers took no part in the division. He had compelled his faction to adopt this attitude—though many of its members realized what blessings the Bill might confer upon the Irish peasants—by threatening to resign the chairmanship. A bad omen, this: once more agitation had got the better of practical needs.

And now the Bill had to pass through the Upper House. Would the Lords offer the same opposition as they had offered to the incomparably more anodyne Bill of the previous year?

In the meantime there had been great changes in the House of Lords. On the 19th of April, 1881, Lord Beaconsfield had died. Benjamin Disraeli's extraordinary and almost fabulous career had reached its close, amidst the universal mourning of the whole nation. All were conscious of the loss which the public life of the country had suffered in the death of this great and unique figure; and none more so than the Queen, who called him, in her diary, "one of my best, most devoted and kindest of friends, as well as wisest of counsellors. His loss is irreparable to me and the country. To lose such a pillar of strength at such a moment is dreadful!"

To Gladstone the death of his all but life-long adversary brought a peculiarly difficult task. It is one of the admirable customs of the English Parliament that when one of its protagonists has died the Party leaders on either side sheath their swords and seek, in emulation, to estimate his enduring significance. It is for the Prime

313

Minister to suggest that the dead man shall be publicly honoured; and so it was Gladstone's task to invite the House of Commons to erect a monument to Lord Beaconsfield, in a speech which had to present his qualities and his achievements in the best possible light.

Barely had great orator found it so difficult to speak. True, he was innocent of the weakness—so general outside England—of seeing, in the political opponent, a personal enemy. For many a man whom he had encountered for decade after decade in the heat of political conflict he cherished as a personal friend: as, for example, Arthur Balfour, for whom he felt almost a fatherly affection. Of Lord Salisbury he himself had said that he could not be angry with him, however violently he attacked him. Lord Salisbury's mother had been kind to him when he was still quite a young man, and he could remember Salisbury as a little fellow in a red frock, romping about on an ottoman!

But Disraeli—that was another matter. In him he saw not only a political enemy, but the representative of a false moral principle.

He was not blind, of course, to the man's quite extraordinary capabilities. No great fighter would wish to underestimate his chiefest adversary. On the day when he received the news of Disraeli's death he wrote in his diary: "It is a telling, touching event. There is no more extraordinary man surviving him in England, perhaps none in Europe." He had the greatest admiration for Disraeli's political courage; he used to say that he had known only three men who really possessed such courage: Sir Robert Peel, Lord John Russell and Disraeli; Palmerston he expressly excluded, for "Palmerston had the appearance and reputation of courage without the reality." He especially appreciated Disraeli's courage in standing up for the rights of his former co-religionists. "His perfect loyalty to his wife, and his perfect loyalty to his own race" were, in his opinion, Disraeli's most admirable characteristics. The Jewish question might be the only subject in respect of which Disraeli held strongly liberal views. "Then," said Gladstone, "he was much more than rational, he was fanatical. He said once that Providence would deal good or ill fortune to nations according as they dealt ill or well with the Jews."

314

Gladstone still remembered, in his old age, how Disraeli spoke in the House of Commons, with unfaltering courage, in favour of the abolition of all legal restrictions affecting the Jews: "How manfully he sticks to it, though he knows that every word he says is gall and wormwood to every man who sits around him and behind him!"

Great as was Gladstone's lifelong affection for Peel, once his teacher, he unreservedly recognized the infallible confidence and the persuasive power with which Disraeli headed the attack against him on the occasion of his conversion to Free Trade. This he regarded as absolutely the zenith of Disraeli's Parliamentary activity. But he had an equal admiration for the marvellous adroitness which Disraeli had revealed in the fight for Franchise Reform in 1867, and by which he had wrested the palms of victory from Gladstone himself.

It was true that he saw, in just this adroitness, a certain Mephistophelian quality. To him it seemed possible only on the basis of an absolute lack of principle. He was convinced that it was actually all one to Disraeli how the franchise was distributed, whether England adopted Free Trade or Protection, and on what class the incidence of taxation rested. All his life Gladstone retained the opinion of Disraeli which he had expressed, in 1850, in a letter to his wife. After expressing his unbounded admiration of a brilliant speech of Disraeli's he said: "Never, last night or at any other time, would I go to him for conviction, but for the delight of the ear and the fancy."

But in Gladstone's eyes the lack of principle and conviction were, in a politician, a serious moral defect. He saw in this defect the evil spirit which had demoralized the political life of England. Of a moral nature, too, was his abhorrence of the spirit of jingoism which Disraeli had reared in the hearts of the British nation, and which was in flat contradiction to the spirit of international understanding, the spirit to which Gladstone had often done homage, as in the *Alabama* affair, at the expense of his own popularity.

It therefore cost Gladstone a severe inner conflict before he could compose the speech in appreciation of his dead enemy with which he addressed the House. To his daughter Mary, who suggested that such appreciation was incompatible with his own moral judgement, he replied: "Parliament and the nation had backed him up: they were responsible for him; a statue should be given to a man according to the place he occupied in the public estimation, History must eventually judge as to the result. If all the wits in the world were gathered into one man, and that man occupied the whole of his lifetime in the judgement of a moral action, he would be incompetent to do it."

Lord Acton, however, who on principle weighed the past and the present on a moral balance, was not of this way of thinking. He saw in Gladstone's eulogy of Beaconsfield the *one* great offence against principle for which he never forgave his friend.

There was no unanimity even in Gladstone's Ministry; neither Bright nor Chamberlain nor Dilke was in favour of the memorial. The result was a letter of reprimand from the Queen's private secretary to Gladstone, who thereupon had to find justification for his dissenting colleagues. Gladstone's speech, at all events, found favour in her eyes.

With Disraeli's death the position which Gladstone held in the popular estimation was naturally modified. Now, without dispute, he was the greatest Parliamentarian in the United Kingdom. He had become, for the English people, "the Grand Old Man." He had no longer any rival of his own calibre. The Conservative Party was unable to place at its head a man who enjoyed even approximately the same regard as their dead leader. Indeed, they could not at first agree upon any unanimous leadership. They had to content themselves with making Lord Salisbury the leader of their party in the House of Lords, while Northcote, whose insufficiency could now hardly be disputed, became the leader of the Conservatives in the House of Commons. The provisional character of this arrangement inspired Lord Randolph Churchill with the audacious hope that he himself might contrive to become the successor of Beaconsfield. An article on "Elijah's Mantle," which excited a great deal of comment, revealed this plainly enough to anyone who could read between the lines. An audacious but idle hope! In a few years' time he was to learn to his discomfiture that his fascinating qualities as Parliamentary and public speaker were far from enabling him to match himself with a man of Lord Salisbury's superior intellect and great political experience, and that his flashy but intrinsically meaningless watchword of "Tory Democracy" was bound to betray its inner contradictions directly he tried to realize it in practice.

Lord Salisbury's first experience as leader of the majority in the Upper House was not very encouraging. He had to define his attitude toward the Irish Land Bill. He himself regarded it as an infringement of all Conservative principles, but he was to learn, to his disappointment, that those who were immediately affected —the Conservative Irish landlords—could not summon up the courage to oppose it. He therefore contented himself with a few amendments, and the Bill found its way back to the Lower House. But now the Queen intervened. She had already admitted that "to do justice to the tenant is right, but not if it is done at the expense of the innocent landlord." Now she urged the Prime Minister to leave the amendments untouched. "The Queen sincerely trusts that Mr. Gladstone will . . . not oppose as many of them as he possibly can."

In vain did the Prime Minister, in a detailed reply, explain to the Queen that the majority of the Irish Members, even the Irish Conservatives, had voted for the Bill: "and only by the Bill Your Majesty's Government can hope to beat the Land League." The Queen urged both Gladstone and Lord Salisbury to come to an understanding. But it was Gladstone alone that she blamed; "Mr. Gladstone," she complained, "has no feeling but for the House of Commons, and the Upper House and Opposition generally distrust him very much." So, when a compromise had already been arrived at, she wrote to Lord Granville a letter in which she did not hesitate to speak of "that high-handed dictator style of Mr. Gladstone." Her confidence in Granville's well-known tact must have been unlimited.

However, the true difficulties in the way of the Bill did not come from the quarter from which the Queen had expected them, but from the precisely opposite direction. Parnell made an attempt to "sabotage" the Land Bill: he advised the peasants not to appeal to the new Courts before decisions had been arrived at in definite cases selected by the Land League. This meant, for one thing, that the blessings of the Land Act would not at once be felt by the Irish peasants, and also that the Land League was persisting in its claim to be the actual dictator in Ireland. However this policy might appear to smack of demagogy, Parnell's motives were really of a more politic nature. His great anxiety was lest the revolutionaries, conspiring in secret, might estrange him from the peasants—and the American paymasters. For this reason he was afraid to let it seem as though he was welcoming a gift from English hands.

To the Government, however, this policy naturally appeared as a malicious frustration of a great and beneficent reform, especially as Parnell allowed himself to be extolled on the occasion of huge Irish demonstrations as the "uncrowned King of Ireland." Forster's reports on the state of affairs in Ireland were becoming more and more apprehensive, and Parnell's speeches more and more domineering. Forster, before long, requested that Parnell also should be arrested under the Coercion Act, and Gladstone was every day more inclined to the view that in the end it would be impossible to avoid arresting him. But before he would allow himself to take his last and perhaps disastrous step he resolved to give the Irish leader yet one more public warning.

The opportunity which he took of giving this warning was a visit to Leeds, on which he thanked his loyal supporters in that city for returning first himself and then his son Herbert to Parliament, with enormous majorities, and this without any co-operation on his part.

Gladstone's visit to Leeds in October 1881 was a triumph of absolutely unprecedented magnitude, in which a great industrial city honoured its chosen hero with enthusiastic vehemence. If Randolph Churchill and his friends believed that they had shaken the Prime Minister's popularity by their policy of pinpricks they must have been sadly disappointed. Day after day Gladstone was rapturously fêted; day after day he had to speak; for a man of seventy-two an almost superhuman effort.

The leading journalist of Leeds, Sir Wemyss Reid, gives in his reminiscences a vivid description of these days, which shows us the "Grand Old Man" at close quarters. One day he had first to speak on Free Trade and Protection in the Chamber of Commerce; then at a banquet at which hundreds were present; and lastly at a mass meeting of thousands.

"I observed," says Sir Wemyss, "that after having gazed with admiration upon the brilliant scene he leant forward, and covering his face with both hands, remained for some time in that attitude." The explanation was furnished by Mrs. Gladstone, who here, as usual, was always at his side. "He was praying. Do you know what he told me last night? 'If I were twenty years younger I myself would go to Ireland as Irish Secretary.' The mass meeting followed. The hall was so large, the crowd so enormous, the murmur of voices so loud that the speakers' words were hopelessly drowned. But then Gladstone spoke. First, for some minutes, there were songs of greeting; and then repeated outbursts of applause. Now at last he lifted his hand. The gesture was followed by the breathless silence of thousands. And now his voice was heard: clear, distinct, and musical, so that every word was audible in the farthest corner of the vast hall. For an hour and a half he spoke, while the thousands hung upon his lips with delight and admiration."

When at last, after the close of the meeting, Reid saw him in the committee-room, he had all the appearance of an old man utterly exhausted by the tremendous effort; wrapped in a long cloak, deathly pale, with closed eyes, he lay in an armchair while his wife gave him a few sips of tea, when he gradually recovered somewhat. But so great was his vitality that on the following evening he was once more the soul of the company gathered about him at the dinner-table.

A matter-of-fact German, entirely disinterested in the conflicts of English politics, who judged all the acts of the orator with the utter scepticism of the Bismarckian era, was present on this occasion. Max Eyth, who afterwards founded the German Agricultural Society, the "wandering engineer" who had "followed the plough and worked at the bench," was then employed in Fowlers' world-famous manufactory of agricultural machinery. He was persuaded by his employer, a prominent Liberal, to listen for once to an example of Liberal oratory. Even his scepticism was banished when he heard "the old gentleman with the intellectual, rather tired face" speak so persuasively and suggestively, and in comparing the German and the English conceptions of style he wrote: "There is perhaps more in the spoken word than those believe who do not understand how to use it—at least, when it is supported by principles and by a life like those of this old man."

The political world had looked forward to the manifestation in Leeds with tense anticipation, and none was more anxious than the Queen. When she heard of the intended banquet she sent her Prime Minister a telegraphic warning: "Let me express a hope that you will be very cautious . . . the times are serious." But she read the report of his speech with the greatest satisfaction. For Gladstone had spoken in the most urgent and serious tone of Ireland, of its troubles and difficulties and dangers, and had given Parnell a plain and solemn warning. "He desires to arrest the operation of the Land Act; to stand as Moses stood between the living and the dead; to stand then not as Moses stood, to arrest, but to spread the plague. If it shall appear that there is still to be fought a final conflict in Ireland between law on the one side and their lawlessness upon the other ... then I say without hesitation, the resources of civilization against its enemies are not yet exhausted."

Everyone in that assembly, everyone in England and Ireland knew at once what was meant by these words: Parnell would shortly be arrested if he did not mend his ways.

But that Parnell had no intention of doing. His reply to the Prime Minister was couched in such inflammatory and insulting language that it seemed as though he wished to compel the authorities to arrest him. When after this meeting a friend asked him who was to take his place if he were imprisoned, he gave an answer that every Irishman understood: "Captain Moonlight will take my place." This was the name by which threats of violent retaliation upon recalcitrant landowners or farmers were commonly signed.

On Wednesday the 12th of October, 1881, a Cabinet meeting was suddenly called. For five hours the question was debated, whether Parnell should be arrested. When Forster at last got his way he hurried off to the post-office and telegraphed the pre-arranged cue to his representative in Dublin. Next morning Parnell was arrested in his hotel.

320

While the police were waiting outside the door of his room to take him away, Parnell hastily scribbled the following lines:

"My own Queenie,
     I have just been arrested by two fine-looking detectives, and write these words to wifie to tell her that she must be a brave little woman and not fret after her husband. The only thing that makes me worried and unhappy is that it may hurt you and our child. I can never have any other wife but you, and if anything happens to you I must die childless. Be good and brave, dear little wifie,
Your own Husband."

The woman to whom these lines were addressed was Katherine O'Shea, the wife of Captain O'Shea, M.P. For more than a year she had been Parnell's mistress. Whenever Parnell suddenly disappeared—when his friends and his enemies lost sight of him for a time—he was usually staying at the country house at Eltham, where Mrs. O'Shea was living, separated from her husband, thanks to the generosity of an elderly aunt. In January 1881 O'Shea once tracked Parnell to Eltham, and challenged him to a duel. But the duel was never fought, and the valiant Captain cooled down, although Parnell and his Kitty had continued to live together. The child which she carried beneath her heart was Parnell's. But O'Shea, before long, was acting as Parnell's confidential agent.

Parnell's imprisonment was greeted in England with delight. When Gladstone communicated the fact of his arrest in the Guildhall, at the traditional Lord Mayor's banquet, the illustrious company cheered as though England had won a new Battle of Trafalgar. The Queen telegraphed her approval to Gladstone. But the Irish response was a revolutionary movement of unprecedented violence. The Land League issued a manifesto requiring the tenants to pay no more rent. Parnell signed it against his convictions: he could not fail to realize that it would bring misery upon countless farmers, without helping the cause. As a matter of fact, the state of Ireland at this time beggared description. Murder, incendiarism,

321

violence, cattle-driving and maiming were becoming common-places. Parnell had prophesied truly: Captain Moonlight had taken command.

All this time Parnell, in Kilmainham gaol, was suffering acutely. He was, of course, treated with all possible consideration, but he was not the man to suffer patiently the martyrdom of several months' loss of liberty. His longing for Katherine O'Shea, his anxiety in respect of her and their child, which was born during his imprisonment, aggravated his impatience and his eagerness to find a way out of the impasse.

And the Government also was endeavouring to do the same. Both offensives had really petered out. Parnell's discomfiture in prison could not console the Cabinet for the fiasco of Forster's policy of Coercion. The longer it continued, the less could the Radical members of the Ministry, like Bright, and especially Chamberlain, give it their approval. Then came the news that Parnell was prepared to negotiate. But the man who brought this news was none other than Captain O'Shea.

In April 1882 Parnell had been granted leave to attend the funeral of a nephew in Paris, and had hurried to Eltham, where Katherine O'Shea was able to show him his newly-born child—which died during his visit. Captain O'Shea was there too, and together with Parnell he agreed on the terms of a letter which he —ostensibly of his own accord—was to send to Gladstone. This was the first step towards an understanding. In the Cabinet Chamberlain courageously offered to conduct the negotiations himself, even though he ran the risk of being disavowed if they failed.

He met Parnell and O'Shea, and suggested the lines of an under-standing. Parnell was ready to use his influence with the Irish people in order to ensure that there should be an end of the campaign of violence and the refusal of rent, provided the Government passed an Act which would so deal with the arrears of rent that the tenant could remain on his farm without undue sacrifice.

When Chamberlain reported this offer to the Cabinet the great majority of the Ministers voted for the release of Parnell and his fellow-prisoners—two other Members of Parliament. At the same time, they were unwilling—and Gladstone most of all—to make any sort of agreement or promise. At a later period Gladstone always vehemently denied that he had ever entered into any sort of agreement with Parnell. And here he revealed one of his peculiarities. In itself, the conclusion of an agreement, in which the mutual concessions of the parties could be objectively stated, was quite unobjectionable. The imprisonment of a political opponent who is menacing the peace of the nation can never be an aim in itself, but only a means of safeguarding that peace. If any agreement was needed for that purpose there was no reason for either party to feel ashamed of it. But to a man with Gladstone's conception of the position and the dignity of a Minister of the Crown a "treaty" with a prisoner of State was simply inadmissible. Also he feared, and this not without reason, that Parnell's position in Ireland, upon which so much now depended, would be jeopardized if he let it be known that he had entered into an agreement with him. It is possible, too, that he was thinking of the Queen, for Granville, as ambassador from the Cabinet, had only with the greatest difficulty induced her to consent to Parnell's release.

Her sympathies were unmistakably on the side of Forster, the only member of the Cabinet to disapprove of the new turn of policy, and who, in consequence of his defeat, had tendered his resignation.

Parnell, in the meantime, his leave having expired, had returned to Kilmainham gaol, and thither Captain O'Shea repaired, as plenipotentiary from the Cabinet. Neither he nor Parnell appears to have been at all scandalized by this singular arrangement. O'Shea was at the time the confidant of Chamberlain, and Chamberlain was reckoning on succeeding to Forster. Since it was his policy that had triumphed over Forster's this expectation was not altogether unjustified, especially as his administrative talents were proven and undisputed.

But Gladstone had ordained otherwise. He had appointed as Lord-Lieutenant, in the place of Lord Cowper, retired, Lord Spencer, an intimate friend, and the head of one of the great Whig families which for him were of such importance. But unlike his predecessor, Spencer was to have a seat in the Cabinet, so that he could represent in person the policy which he had to execute in Dublin. This modified the position of the Irish Secretary, who would no longer be in the Cabinet. Gladstone conferred this post on a younger disciple, a family connection, who by reason of his ideas for agrarian reform in Ireland appeared to be peculiarly suited for the position. This was the younger brother of Lord Hartington, Lord Frederick Cavendish, who had married a niece of Mrs. Gladstone's, Lucy Lyttelton; a man generally liked and respected, of whom Gladstone himself said in later years that his mind was "in political action of a truly angelic purity." In the Liberal Party it was assumed that this was the first step in a distinguished career. But Fate ordained otherwise.

For Chamberlain this was a serious disappointment. If he explained it to himself by saying that Gladstone's feelings towards him were not exactly benevolent, he was probably not far wrong. The Liberal Leader had not the gift which had so distinguished Disraeli, of gathering younger men about him even if they came from quite a dissimilar environment. For a man so strongly rooted in tradition as Gladstone the Radical screwmaker from Birmingham, whose opinions on all questions were so ruthlessly and bluntly expressed, and whose unusual self-confidence was so crudely manifested, was always a somewhat alien phenomenon. Probably Gladstone would have agreed with the judgement which a good judge of men, Lord Esher, committed to paper twenty years later: "Chamberlain's faults all come from his upbringing. Clever as he is, he has never learnt the self-restraint which everybody learns at a great public school or at a university." Add to this that Gladstone was always having difficulties with the Queen on Chamberlain's account. Could he persuade her, who had already demurred to his conferring a subordinate office on Leonard Courtney, to agree to the appointment of the far more notorious and far more dreaded Chamberlain to what was, perhaps, at the moment, the most important of all posts?

That quite apart from this the new direction of Irish policy was fraught with difficulties became evident to Gladstone when Forster, with the readily granted permission of the Queen, gave the usual justification of his resignation in the House of Commons. He had filled a conspicuous position in the political life of the nation far too long for this resignation to be regarded merely as one of those resignations which inevitably, from time to time, occur in any Cabinet. Everyone felt the significance of the step, and the enemies of the Government welcomed it as justifying even more violent assaults on its passionately attacked leader. If anything was calculated to lash the passions of the House to a higher pitch, it was Parnell's appearance at the very moment when Forster had begun to speak. The tempestuous delight with which the Irish welcomed the return of their leader after several months' imprisonment accentuated more than anything else could have done his triumph over the man who had sent him to prison, and who was now a fallen star.

Fallen, but by no means innocuous! Henceforth Gladstone had an enemy who knew where to strike him.

In spite of Forster's bitterness, the Queen's resentment, and the resistance of the Conservative Opposition, the way was now clear for a policy of agreement and pacification in Ireland, and it was as the representative and supporter of this policy that Lord Frederick Cavendish hurried across to Dublin on the day after Forster's speech in the Lower House. And then all hopes were shattered by a frightful tragedy.

On Saturday the 6th of May, 1882, London Society was enjoying the amenities of the season. In the houses of political, diplomatic and society hostesses the usual evening receptions were being held, at which all the anybodies who were somebodies were accustomed to meet one another. In the clubs of Pall Mall and Carlton House Terrace politicians and journalists were indulging in an hour of leisure after a busy and exciting week, or strolling from one club to another, enjoying the beauty of the spring evening. And then a disturbing rumour—vague at first and intangible—began to pass from mouth to mouth. Someone, it was said, had been murdered over in Ireland. Then a journalist, coming from the office of his paper, brought the news of an attack on the Irish Secretary. There was an excited gathering about the doors of the Reform Club. Further news increased the general excitement. At last the truth, the terrible truth was known: The Secretary of State for Ireland,

325

Lord Frederick Cavendish, and the Under-Secretary, Burke, had been murdered in Phoenix Park, Dublin.

On the afternoon of the day on which the new Lord-Lieutenant, Lord Spencer, had made his solemn entry into Dublin, a consultation had been held in Dublin Castle. Lord Frederick and Burke, about seven o'clock, set off to walk home together through Phoenix Park. Here a murderous gang of Irish conspirators was lying in ambush for the detested Burke, who on this occasion, unhappily, was not, as usual, guarded by detectives. Lord Cavendish, apparently, was unrecognized by the murderers, and was attacked merely as the chance companion of the chosen victim. With knives whose blades had served as surgical instruments the murderers fell upon the two unarmed men and killed them within sight of Viceregal Lodge, where the Lord-Lieutenant heard the cries of the victims.

Sir William Harcourt, to whom, as Home Secretary, the official account was despatched, received the news late that evening, at the Austrian Embassy, where he was dining; Gladstone and his wife being among the guests, though they had already left when the telegram arrived. Harcourt had not the heart to convey the dreadful news in person to the Prime Minister; he preferred to leave that duty to Mr. Gladstone's private secretary, Edward Hamilton. He found the Gladstones, just before midnight, on their return home. It was a terrible blow to both. Gladstone staggered, as though about to collapse. "Lord Frederick was like a son to him," writes Granville. Both hastened at once to the unhappy widow of the murdered man—their niece, Lucy—in order to comfort her in the first hours of her grief. "Lucy," wrote Gladstone to the Queen, "received the awful blow in a manner which only her noble character as a woman and a Christian could have rendered possible." In this bitterest hour of her life she tried to console the old man. "Uncle William, you did right to send him to Ireland," she said to the deeply afflicted Gladstone. And when Mary Gladstone spoke to her next morning, before starting for church, Lucy cried to her: " 'Pray that what Uncle William says may come true' (the saving of Ireland through the sacrifice of Freddy's innocent blood)."

Parnell had spent Saturday night with Katherine O'Shea. On Sunday morning he accompanied her to London, where he was to consult with members of his party. At a suburban railway station he bought a Sunday newspaper. He had hardly glanced at it when he cried out in horror. The crime which cost Lord Frederick his life had struck a deadly blow at him and his policy. For it was clear to him at once that all England would hold him responsible for this murder.

Could he have read the letter which the Queen that very morning was writing to Lord Granville he would have found his fears confirmed. "She must hold those responsible," she wrote, "who recommended the release of not only the three Members of Parliament, but of many other suspects, as responsible for the lives of her subjects." This action had been "an encouragement to crime," as Forster had prophesied it would be.

Parnell, who naturally knew the Irish Party better, saw that this was the work of the desperadoes supported by Irish-American money, to suppress whom was one of the purposes of his policy. The correctness of his opinion was manifest when the criminals were at last detected and brought before the Court. The murderers belonged to a group who called themselves the "Invincibles"; they obeyed, as their leader, a mysterious "Number One," and their aim was to excite open revolution by acts of terrorism. They had repeatedly plotted to murder Forster, who had escaped from them as by a miracle only a few days before his resignation. The head of the gang, one Carey, who had hitherto been known in Dublin for a pious sort of man in a comfortable position, ratted with the fear of death before him. In order to save himself from the scaffold he turned "Queen's evidence." But he did not escape his fate. While attempting to place the ocean between himself and the site of his crime he was executed by an emissary of the Nationalists' vengeance.

In the first moment of despair Parnell wished to retire altogether from political life. "How can I carry on a public agitation," he cried, "if I am stabbed in the back in this way?" He sent Gladstone a letter in which he offered to resign his seat if Gladstone considered that this would be desirable in the interest of the Irish cause. Gladstone, however, dissuaded him from such a course, for at that moment, with things as they were, he saw in him a counterpoise to the forces of revolution. In this he was perfectly correct. Violent though he seemed, Parnell was privately opposed to revolution. His first action after his release was ruthlessly to suppress the Women's Land League instituted by his own sister, as this feminine radicalism was peculiarly obnoxious to him. To Michael Davitt, who once asked him in jest what Parnell would do to him when he was the ruler of Ireland, he replied, only half in jest: "The first thing I should do would be to lock you up."

Chamberlain and Dilke also advised Parnell to remain at his post. He therefore abandoned the idea of retiring, and in conjunction with the other Irish leaders he issued a manifesto which condemned the murder in the strongest possible terms. But he was compelled to realize that the Government would now be forced to revert to the policy of Coercion.

Before Gladstone announced the return to Coercion he had the painful duty of making a speech in commemoration of the victims of the crime. The whole House was moved as he cried, hardly able to control his emotions:

"One of the very noblest hearts of England has ceased to beat, and has ceased at the very moment when it was just devoted to the service of Ireland, full of love for that country, full of hope for her future, full of capacity to render her service."

In connection with this speech an incident may be mentioned which is characteristic of Gladstone; as regards both the fearlessness with which he did what he held to be his duty, and the evil interpretations which were placed on his actions by his enemies. On the evening of this day a Conservative Member of Parliament indignantly informed a circle of acquaintances that he had walked behind Gladstone on his way home from the House, and had seen him lurking behind the Duke of York's Column talking to an abandoned woman. Gladstone, who was told of this statement by a faithful admirer, contented himself with replying that "the presence of X—— was not unperceived on the occasion . . . but the conversation was not of the nature he imagined and possibly desired." As Gladstone's more intimate friends were well aware, he had done what he could, ever since his undergraduate days, to "save fallen women," and in co-operation with Mrs. Gladstone and various clerical friends, such as Bishop Wilberforce, he had zealously continued with this work, often in contempt of all worldly prudence. He did not shrink from personal conversations in the public street, although on one occasion, in 1854, this practice had led to an attempt at blackmail, with which he dealt by immediately denouncing the criminal. In his diary he himself confesses that his behaviour was not in accordance with human prudence; but he regarded such work as a duty laid upon him, and welcomed "the charge which doubtless has been sent to teach me wisdom and which I therefore welcome."

The new Coercion Bill for Ireland, which was now more than ever necessary, though it differed, often for the better, from Forster's Act, was piloted through Parliament by Harcourt and applied by Lord Spencer with indefatigable energy and undaunted courage. He was vigorously supported by the new Irish Secretary, Sir George Trevelyan, who expended in fighting the unrest in Ireland the energy which would otherwise, perhaps, have been devoted to his historical work on the American Revolution.

The Government, however, proceeded with the reforms upon which it had resolved before the Phoenix Park murders, and it passed legislation settling the question of arrears of rent on the lines which had been indicated in the negotiations with Parnell. The Queen, once more, was disapproving. She thought the settlement an untimely concession to "evil-doers," and she conjured Granville to rid Gladstone of Chamberlain, whom she described as "his evil genius." She even informed the Foreign Secretary that "the want of cordiality and readiness to act with us on the part of the great Powers is the result of the want of confidence which they have in us—and in Mr. Gladstone," which was due in particular to his Irish policy. As Granville could not be shaken in his loyalty to the Prime Minister, the Queen urged the Prince of Wales to use his influence in this direction with Lord Hartington. "The mischief Mr. Gladstone does is *incalculable*," she wrote to him, and she accused Gladstone's followers of being entirely devoid of patriotism. "Patriotism is nowhere in their ranks."

But the Bill which so distracted the Queen had a curious fate, which might really have taught her that the Irish problems were

329

not so simple as they appeared to her. After the House of Commons had accepted the Bill Lord Salisbury opposed it in the House of Lords, in a vehement speech, as an infringement of the Eighth Commandment, and carried some amendments which to some extent affected the very nucleus of the Bill. But Gladstone, despite the pressure which the Queen brought to bear upon him, did not give way, and he saw to it that the amendments were rejected by the Lower House.

Now the House of Lords was again confronted with the question, whether it should insist upon its own point of view and provoke a conflict, or perhaps even a General Election. Salisbury was resolved on this course, but once again his followers left him in the lurch. Above all, the Irish peers, who were materially interested in the Bill, preferred the payments, modest as they were, of which it gave them some hope, to fruitless distraints upon their tenants. So great was Salisbury's disappointment that he could not refrain from expressing it in his concluding speech. This was a fresh defeat, and Lord Granville, the Leader of the Liberals in the Upper House, was able to report to the Queen that one peer had observed, during Salisbury's speech: "How differently Lord Beaconsfield would have dealt with it!"

In the meantime events had occurred in a very different arena which completely altered the political situation, and at first conferred a fresh popularity on the English Government; on the 1st of July, 1882, a British fleet had bombarded Alexandria, and a little later British troops were landed in Egypt.

3. Africa

Heavy as were the storms which Gladstone had to weather in the domain of domestic politics, the foreign horizon was no whit more cheerful. It was the destiny of his second Ministry that hardly a year passed without the threat of trouble abroad, so that the most peace-loving of all statesmen was constantly confronted with the question: "Peace or War?" And further, as he steered the ship of State it was constantly seized by powerful currents which had their origin in Windsor or Westminster.

Already, in 1880 and 1881, South Africa had given him a difficult problem to solve. The annexationist Boer policy of Lord Beaconsfield could not be liquidated as quickly as had been expected after the result of the electoral contest, very largely because of the persistent opposition of the Queen. The result was a Boer rising under the leadership of Paul Kruger, and this led to an almost open conflict between the Queen on the one side (who demanded, first and foremost, that her authority should be re-established), and on the other side the majority of the Cabinet, who wished to negotiate. The most determined supporter of this policy of negotiation was Chamberlain; the same man who twenty years later was foremost in advocating the policy of subjecting the Boers. The policy of negotiation prevailed in London, but in Africa, on the 27th of February, 1881, the British troops were taken by surprise at Majuba and were defeated by the Boers, their general being killed.

From a military point of view the battle of Majuba was of no great importance. The strength of the British force was only a few hundreds, and the killed numbered about ninety. But it was a defeat! Troops of the regular Army had been beaten by rebellious farmers! All the patriotic feelings of the English were aroused. The natural reaction of the people was: "Revenge for Majuba!" For a patriotic Government only one course appeared possible: the despatch of a considerable army, in order to compel the Boers to surrender at discretion.

Gladstone resolved upon the very opposite course. The disaster of Majuba Hill did not induce him to abandon the policy upon which he had previously determined. There had been needless bloodshed in Africa; but that did not seem to him a sufficient reason for replacing the policy of negotiation, which had previously seemed the correct policy, by one which must lead to fresh bloodshed. In his opinion the true courage consisted, not in wiping out military defeats by military victories, but in holding to the policy already accepted as the right one, even at the risk of being condemned as a weakling by public opinion.

In his resolution to make peace Gladstone might have appealed to the authority of a man who in other respects was almost his antithesis. Bismarck, during Goschen's visit, had touched upon the

Transvaal problem, and had uttered a warning against fighting against "the white man" in South Africa. "He thought it more important for us even to stop the war as soon as we could, rather than to think of our military honour there. I quote this, as Bismarck is generally brutal in subordinating everything to military considerations."

The end of it all was that the annexation of the Transvaal was quashed, under certain conditions which were to safeguard British suzerainty. Few actions of Gladstone's earned him bitterer reproaches than this. The word "Majuba" became a symbol for a policy of disastrous weakness. Certainly the Government cannot be acquitted of the reproach that it made the solution of the problem more difficult by its own lack of directness. But the resolution to continue negotiations in spite of Majuba does not deserve this criticism. Gladstone himself, when accused of weakness, doubtless found consolation in the thought that he had saved the countless human lives which a policy of revenge would have sacrificed. The moral courage which he manifested in concluding peace won him many admirers. Burne-Jones greeted the conclusion of peace with enthusiasm: "Now it feels such a nice world to live in all suddenly, and now one can abandon oneself to fresh hopes and be happy. It is a new start in history, and who knows what bright things may not follow from it."

But the average contemporary was far from sharing the idealistic views of a Burne-Jones. Many could see only the military defeat and the political surrender, and of those who lived to witness the many complications that ended in the Boer War, many saw the beginning of all the trouble in what they called Gladstone's retreat after Majuba.

Though the consequences of the conflict with the Boers lay far in the future, the results of an Egyptian involvement were becoming very rapidly and overwhelmingly insistent. The Egyptian question, of course, was closely connected with the problems of the Great Powers of Europe. For the Egyptian question was part of the problem which continued, ever and again, down to the day of the Serajevo murder, to threaten the peace of Europe—the problem ot the liquidation of the Turkish Empire. But for England the special difficulty of this problem dated from the construction of the Suez Canal, which to the British Empire, as Bismarck expressed it in his incomparably plastic idiom, was as vitally important "as the nerve in the neck that connects the spinal cord with the brain." Therefore, he considered, "Egypt is as necessary to England as her daily bread."

This importance was still further increased and emphasized by the acquisition of the Suez Canal shares, which Disraeli so adroitly effected in 1876, representing it to the Queen and the nation as an incomparable triumph. But brilliant though this operation was, it was equally pregnant with consequences that in 1876 lay far beyond the horizon even of Disraeli's imaginative vision. The financial policy of the Khedive Ismail had resulted in a monstrous load of debt, and the poverty-stricken country could no longer bear the burden of the frequently usurious interest on the foreign loans. The French and the English, as the principal creditors, were obliged to take over the administration of the Egyptian finances. Anglo-French control was the next step (1876); then Ismail was deposed; and his deposition was followed by disorders inspired by a mixture of economic and nationalistic motives.

The leader of this movement of revolt was an Egyptian colonel, Arabi Bey, who very soon succeeded in making himself the controlling power, so that he was able, in September 1881, to compel the young Khedive Tewfik to dismiss his Prime Minister and appoint him as Minister for War, while promoting him to the rank of Pasha.

Whether the English could have come to an understanding with this rebellious Nationalist party, as the English Radicals desired, is today as much a matter for dispute as it was then. The French refused to negotiate under any circumstances. They supported the Khedive unconditionally, and persuaded the English Government to join them. The most earnest desire of the British Government—as it was that of Gladstone and Granville—was to co-operate with France: on the one hand, so that England alone should not bear all the responsibility; and on the other hand, in order to prevent France from indulging in a solo performance of her own.

333

Englishmen saw behind France the mighty figure of Bismarck. It was known that he favoured the overseas activities of France, as he considered that they were calculated to divert her thoughts from the lost provinces of Alsace and Lorraine. The two statesmen who at this time possessed the greatest influence in France were ready to fall in with this idea: they were, the Prime Minister, Jules Ferry, and the President of the Chamber, Léon Gambetta, the soul of the national defence in the Franco-German War. Jules Ferry was in a special sense the champion of Colonial expansion, and for this reason was ready to co-operate with Bismarck, so long as the latter left him a free hand in this respect. Gambetta's object was to make France more self-reliant, more self-confident, and also to make her independent of Bismarck's policy. He saw that new constellations of power were in process of formation in Europe which offered France new possibilities of recovery from the devastating defeat of 1870.

A few months after Arabi's revolt the Ferry Ministry was overthrown, and Gambetta, for the first and last time, replacing Ferry, stood at the head of the French Government. France and Europe expected great things of him. He himself took over the Foreign Office and endeavoured to promote friendship with England along two different paths: by the conclusion of a liberal commercial treaty, and by common action in Egypt. Here, of course, his ideas were not those of England. Gladstone was on principle averse to a policy of annexation; it was in conflict with the ideals which he had proclaimed in his Midlothian campaign: "with the humanitarian efforts of which London is so enamoured," and which seemed to Bismarck so out of place in those responsible for the foreign policy of a great State. Gambetta had no such humanitarian notions.

As against the Arabi movement four attitudes were conceivable.

France and England could regard it as a national movement which would be capable of development, and with which they could co-operate in restoring order and reforming the national finances. But to this policy Gambetta opposed a most positive refusal.

The second possibility was the recall of the Sultan as the legitimate ruler of Egypt. But with this policy also Gambetta refused to co-operate.

334

The third possibility was that of common intervention on the part of England and France. This was the goal for which Gambetta was actually making. The British Government was anxious to avoid such intervention, but if the worst came to the worst it was prepared to adopt this course.

The fourth possibility was the intervention of England only. To Gambetta, naturally, such a solution was abhorrent; and the British Government itself was not anxious to act alone. Yet this was the solution that finally emerged as the result of all the political confusion, all the negotiations and conferences and outrages.

At first Gambetta's policy was victorious. He proposed a common declaration. Granville, anxious to maintain good relations with France, was persuaded to agree to this proposal. The resulting Note (9th of January, 1882) expressed itself in forcible terms in favour of retaining the Khedive. But this course was predestined to failure, because the two Powers had different notions of the means to be employed. France had armed intervention in mind; England proposed to rely on moral persuasion. It is one of the paradoxes of history that a few months later each Power had arrived at the point which it had sought to avoid: England had landed an army in Egypt, and France, with no footing in the country, was impotently protesting. It is not surprising that neither Power was content with the arrangement.

Among the causes that led to this paradoxical solution was an event which no one had foreseen. Gambetta and his Ministry, from which so much had been hoped, fell on the 20th of January, 1882, defeated in matters of purely domestic policy, having been little more than two months in power. Before the great patriot had recovered from his fall he was overtaken, in his forty-fifth year, by sudden death, in circumstances that were long obscured by mysterious rumours.

What would have been the destiny of France and of Europe had he been allotted the span of life on which the average man, and even the average politician can reckon, is one of the unanswered questions of history.

His successor, Freycinet, was not the man to pursue the French policy in the same resolute spirit. It is true that in May he agreed to an Anglo-French naval demonstration off Alexandria, but this failed in its purpose, as neither Power was willing to land troops. The consequences was that Arabi became more powerful and the Khedive more impotent, and the state of the country more intolerable. In June there were riots in Alexandria in which some fifty Europeans were killed. Naturally, the Europeans fled from the country in their thousands. Arabi, however, began to fortify Alexandria, evidently against the fleets of the Western Powers.

In London this development was followed with great anxiety, and opinions were sharply divided. The attempt to bring about a common action of the European Powers got no farther than the futile Constantinople Conference, at which Turkish diplomacy, greatly to its own detriment, displayed all its old genius for postponing everything and allowing nothing to be accomplished. In the English Cabinet there were heated arguments as to what was now to be done. In these the representatives of the old and the new Radicalism were completely at loggerheads. Old John Bright was opposed to any kind of intervention. Chamberlain, however, as Granville recorded with astonishment, revealed himself as "almost the greatest Jingo." Of the other Ministers, the majority held armed intervention to be unavoidable. In France, however, caution got the better of impulsiveness. Freycinet was afraid lest public opinion might leave him in the lurch if he involved the country in an adventure outside Europe which apparently would lead to war. On the 3rd of July the London Cabinet—of course, with the enthusiastic approval of the Queen—resolved to give Admiral Seymour orders to threaten Arabi with bombardment unless work on the fortifications was discontinued. The French admiral was invited to co-operate. But the French fleet, instead of co-operating, weighed anchor and made off, leaving to the British all the responsibility, all the glory, and—Egypt.

The bombardment of Alexandria cost Gladstone the colleague to whom in respect of fundamentals he felt most closely akin: John Bright, now in the seventies, was unwilling to accept any sort of responsibility for military action. He could not foresee whither it would lead, and he did not know in what still greater injustice it might not involve the Government.

In vain did Gladstone expostulate: "I address you as one whom I suppose not to believe all use whatever of military force to be unlawful; as one who detests war in general and believes most wars to have been sad errors (in which I greatly agree with you)." In this case the use of force had been justified, because it was a blow at the rule of violence, and had led to a lasting and a peaceful solution of the Egyptian question. "I feel that in being party to this work I have been a labourer in the cause of peace." So far was he from foreseeing how much blood would have to be shed before the Egyptian question was settled.

In England, the overwhelming majority approved of Gladstone's action. The House of Commons supported his policy—apart from a very few hostile votes—once he had explained that England "would look to the co-operation of the Powers," but that in case of necessity "the work would be undertaken by the single power of England."

The French Chamber, which dealt with the matter on the following day, offered the completest contrast to the unanimity of the English Parliament. For the French their dread of the mysterious schemes of Bismarck, who might take advantage of an entanglement in North Africa, outweighed the chagrin of losing their foothold in Egypt and their alliance with England. In vain did Gambetta, with all his eloquence, in the last speech which he was ever to make in the Chamber, speak once more in favour of an active policy. The Chamber paid more attention to the warning of that great overthrower of Ministries, Clemenceau:

"Europe is swarming with soldiers. The whole world is waiting. The Powers are keeping themselves free for the future. Let us preserve the liberty of France!"

The Freycinet Ministry was forced to resign on the 29th of July, 1882. Henceforth the French contented themselves, since they could not prevent England from intervening, with making her task in Egypt as difficult as possible. That in doing so they often found themselves working for the same ends as Bismarck shows how completely they had diverged from the policy which Gambetta had in view. The unsolved Anglo-French problem was a source of difficulties to England until France had suffered the diplomatic defeat of Fashoda, and until the treaty of 1904, in which British supremacy in Egypt was balanced against French supremacy in Morocco, and from which emerged the Entente of the two Powers. There was thus a direct connection between the 11th of July, 1882, when the British warships bombarded Alexandria, and the 4th of August, 1914, when England entered the World War at the side of France.

From the bombardment of Alexandria all that was to follow evolved with the logic of facts, which so often master the statesmen who imagine that they can control them. With the first shell that was fired by a British warship against the Egyptian port England had definitely and irrevocably undertaken the task of restoring order in Egypt by force of arms. A few weeks later Sir Garnet Wolseley, with a British army, had landed on Egyptian soil. On the 13th of September, at Tel-el-Kebir, he gained a decisive victory over Arabi. From that day onwards England was the actual ruler of Egypt. The actual but not the legitimate ruler! Must she take this second step also?

A few days before the battle of Tel-el-Kebir Lord Granville was approached by the Tempter, in the guise of no less a person than the eldest son of the German Chancellor, Count Herbert Bismarck. Herbert, then a young Councillor of Legation, in his thirty-third year, was often employed by his father in diplomatic activities and inquiries to which he wished to give a private rather than an official character. By such employment he could gradually school him in the part which he intended him one day to play as his successor. Possibly, too, the Chancellor hoped that such activities would help his son to forget the pain which he himself had inflicted upon him by forbidding his marriage with Elizabeth Carolath.

Herbert Bismarck paid many visits to England, where he was received by the leading politicians with the greatest friendliness, and with all the interest attaching to the son of the greatest and most influential of living statesmen. No one was more friendly than Lord Granville, who entertained him with the lavish hospitality of the English *grand seigneur*. This did not prevent Herbert from sending to Berlin the most critical accounts of his conversations with Lord Granville. After reading a letter describing a conversation which he had had with Granville in January 1881, at the time of the "common Note," the Chancellor informed his ambassadors "that England is at the present time being governed with a lack of foresight that hardly has its equal in all the long history of that country; she is entirely subject to the French leading-strings, and relies only on the friendship of France." But although the bombardment of Alexandria had shown him that this view was not wholly correct, it suited his schemes well enough. Count Hugo Lerchenfeld, who was just then at Varzin, speaks of the Chancellor's exasperation on receiving a telegram from the German Consul in Cairo, to the effect that he had associated himself— without referring the matter to the Wilhelmstrasse—with the protest of the other consuls against the bombardment of Alexandria. "It was clear," writes Count Lerchenfeld, "that the Prince wanted England to establish herself in Egypt, and the bombardment was just the way to do it." At all events, Bismarck did not hesitate to draw his conclusions from the altered situation. In September he sent Herbert to London with precise instructions: he was to assure the Foreign Secretary that he set much greater store on the friend-ship of England than on Germany's immediate interests in Egypt, which were not very extensive. When Granville explained that England had no thought of annexing Egypt, Herbert assured him most emphatically that the British annexation of the country would not be incompatible with German interests; that "his father would not oppose even annexation." It is not astonishing that the British Minister was completely under the impression that Bismarck had advised England "to take Egypt," though it was hardly diplomatic of him to confide this, in a weak moment, to the House of Lords.

This attitude of Bismarck's, which meant that no trouble need be anticipated from the other Great Powers, was naturally of great assistance to the British Government. Nevertheless, it continued to be absolutely opposed to annexation. Gladstone would not diverge from his original line of action. Could one question whether "Egypt is to be hereafter . . . for the Egyptian people? . . . I say for the Egyptian people, just as Bulgaria for the Bulgarian people,"

339

he wrote to Harcourt, who at Balmoral had been beset by the Queen with demands that could hardly be distinguished from demands for annexation. Was Gladstone afraid that Bismarck might exploit the establishment of the English in Egypt for other ends, especially in the Balkans, and that his sympathies might be withdrawn from England as suddenly as they had now been offered? And as a matter of fact—though it is difficult to say which was cause and which effect—when France, two years later, while Jules Ferry was in power, after the failure of a conference on the problems of Egyptian finance, looked to Germany for support, her advances were readily though cautiously welcomed by Bismarck. "France can attain a powerful and perhaps predominating position if, as against the naval supremacy of England, she seeks to direct the naval policy of the Powers with navies of the second rank," he informed the French Ambassador in Berlin. And one day in October 1884 Herbert Bismarck was sitting opposite the French Premier, Jules Ferry, on the Quai d'Orsay in Paris, discussing the prospects of common Franco-German steps in Egypt. On this occasion he astounded Ferry by declaring that Germany considered that it was "desirable," in her interests, "to uphold Mr. Gladstone." Ferry had every reason to be surprised, for he knew, of course, what was common gossip in all the Chancelleries and newspaper-offices of Europe, that the Chancellor accompanied his every mention of Gladstone with ironical and satirical comments, and that he could find nothing more scathing to say of his political opponents at home than to accuse them of wishing to form "a Gladstone Ministry." Perhaps, too, he had heard that the Chancellor's most intimate collaborator, the sharp-tongued Lothar Bucher, who hated the Liberal statesman with all the bitterness of a converted revolutionist, was fond of declaring that Gladstone was really "Freudenstein" ("Joy-stone").[1] We can therefore imagine the delight with which Herbert, in his letter to his father, described the effect of his remark: "Herr Ferry greeted this remark with a positive sigh of relief, as though an incubus had suddenly been lifted off his chest; a quick look of deep satisfaction passed over his features, he interrupted me with the greatest vivacity,

[1] *Freudenstein* has a Jewish sound in German ears.

adopting a much lighter tone, and said: 'Certainly, this is of the greatest importance to all concerned: I am delighted to hear you say this, for Mr. Gladstone is the only English Minister who takes the English promise to evacuate Egypt seriously, and the only one whose word we need take seriously.'

" 'I am very glad,' I remarked, 'that we have touched on this subject, for I know that you have heard from many sources that the German policy is concerned only to overthrow Gladstone. This is quite false; the Chancellor even considers that, apart from England herself, all the rest of the Powers, in their own interest, must wish more than anything to keep Mr. Gladstone in office.' M. Ferry laughed heartily at this observation. . . ."

If Gladstone had by any chance seen this report he would probably have had some difficulty in understanding just what there was to laugh at, and he certainly would have regarded it as a great but well-merited compliment that the leading statesmen of a foreign nation should privately confess that one could rely upon his word.

Queen Victoria, presumably, was of a different opinion. In her eyes pacification of the country by the sacrifice of blood and gold gave England a right to permanent advantages. "To have sacrificed so many precious lives and to have spent so much money . . . without reaping any benefit from it at all!" she protested; and she vigorously opposed the reduction of the army of occupation, and still more vigorously the announcement that the troops would be evacuated within a measurable space of time. Soon, indeed, there were happenings that made any withdrawal impossible for years to come; and which must now be recorded at some length.

But the Egyptian Sphinx had still an enigma in store for Gladstone; one of which neither he nor his colleagues could yet know anything as they sat round the table in Downing Street in July 1882, and formed the fateful resolution to turn the guns of the British warships on Alexandria. London had as yet received no reliable news of the curious religious movement inspired by the Mahdi, which for a year or so had been spreading in Central Africa, and was soon to gather up the savage tribes of the southern Sudan. The góspel of the Mahdi was a gospel of war, a war of annihilation against all who were deaf to his proclamation of the Kingdom of God.

His irresistible progress was explained, of course, by political and national causes. For sixty years the Sudan had been ruled by Egypt; that is, it had been ruthlessly and cruelly exploited. Slave-hunters devastated whole villages and chased the terrified negroes into the trackless forests. "There is not even a dog howling for his lost master": so Sir Samuel Baker had described this country in 1870. Though the rule of the Mahdi was the rule of brute force, the nations preferred it to the tyranny of the Pashas of Cairo.

A few months after the battle of Tel-el-Kebir it was realized both in Cairo and London that the Egyptian Government of the Sudan was on the point of collapse. The question was, whether to abandon the Sudan or whether to make an energetic attempt to drive out the Mahdi. The Egyptian Government in Cairo was absolutely opposed to surrendering the Sudan. The British Government, however, took the view that this was a matter which did not concern it. "It has not been included within the sphere of our operations, and we are by no means disposed to admit . . . that it is within the sphere of our responsibility." It must leave the responsibility of the steps proposed by the Egyptian Government to that Government. This was a logical standpoint, and one that could be supported for many practical reasons. But in the light of ensuing events it was seen to be indisputably erroneous, for it could not be permanently adhered to. In the end the British Government was obliged to accept the extended responsibility which it had endeavoured to avoid.

For the Egyptians' attempt to cope with the Mahdi ended in an absolute catastrophe. The Egyptian Army, under Hicks Pasha, fell into an ambush and was cut down to the last man. The consequence was that the tribes of the Sudan, which had so far held back, went over to the Mahdi.

Sir Evelyn Baring, whom Gladstone had sent to Cairo as British representative, saw that the Egyptian Government was quite incapable of coming to any sort of decision. He explained to Granville that for good or ill the British Government must decide what was to be done, and that really the only possible decision was to give up the whole of the Sudan, including the city of Khartoum, which, lying on the Nile and garrisoned by Egyptian troops, was the key position of Egyptian power in the Sudan.

With this Gladstone's Cabinet was confronted with an extraordinarily difficult and serious decision; quite apart from the fact that the Egyptian Government preferred to resign rather than agree to the withdrawal. A retreat is always unpopular, and for an Opposition nothing is easier than to accuse a Government of cowardice.

The Queen acquiesced, though with regret, in the abandonment of the Sudan by Egypt. Lord Granville had to explain what sacrifices England would have to make in order to conquer the Sudan, the Egyptians being evidently incapable of doing so: an army 20,000 strong would have to be sent out, volunteers asked for, the reserves called out, and millions paid by the British taxpayer, to be raised for a purpose in which it was difficult to see that England was in any way interested.

To decide, in London, on the evacuation of the Sudan was easy enough: it was not so easy to effect the evacuation. A number of Egyptian garrisons were scattered about the Sudan, and these must be rescued from the hordes of the Mahdi. But in view of the incapacity of the Egyptian administration, the responsibility for rescuing them fell on the British Government.

The English Press took up the matter. W. T. Stead, who had followed John Morley as editor of the *Pall Mall Gazette*, and who, in this position, was able to influence public opinion, suddenly informed the British public that there was only one panacea: General Gordon must be sent to the Sudan.

General Gordon, or "Chinese Gordon," as he was popularly called, was a most unusual character. Brave and self-effacing, a brilliant soldier, eccentric and pious, a believer in the literal truth of the Bible, and filled with a mystical belief in his own mission, he had placed his sword, and his magical influence over his subordinates, at the service of many foreign rulers. In China he had helped the Manchus to suppress the Taiping rebellion. He had served under the Khedive as Governor-General of the Sudan: in Cape Colony he had been in command of the Colonial troops; in

India he had for a short time been private secretary to the Viceroy, Lord Ripon; on his own account, armed only with his Bible and his walking-stick, he had investigated the Holy Places of Palestine; and now he was on the point of proceeding to the Congo in the service of King Leopold II of Belgium. Chance—or Destiny—brought him once more to England. Landing at Southampton, he was met by Stead, who promptly interviewed him. Gordon had no objection to saying what he thought about the Sudan. The *Pall Mall Gazette* of the following day contained an interesting interview, skilfully edited by Stead, and also a leading article which contained the categorical demand: Gordon must be sent to the Sudan.

Gladstone was then at Hawarden. He was prevented by illness from attending the Cabinet meetings in Downing Street. Granville wrote to him that Gordon engaged himself, through his personal influence over the tribes concerned, to arrange for the unimpeded withdrawal of the garrison of Khartoum; under these circumstances "might it not be advisable to put a little pressure on Baring?" Twice already Baring had protested against the despatch of Gordon.

Gladstone agreed, and Granville made a third appeal to Baring, who now agreed to the employment of Gordon, on the express condition that he must pledge himself to effect the withdrawal as quickly as possible, and must place himself under the orders of the British representative in Egypt—that is, of Baring himself.

Even before Baring's reply had reached him, Gladstone had laid down the conditions under which he would agree to Gordon's despatch: "If he reports what should be done, he should not be the judge who should do it, nor ought he to commit us on that point by advice officially given." In a word: he must not take the responsibility upon himself.

Unfortunately the commission which Gordon actually received was very different from that which Gladstone had cautiously advised. In the Prime Minister's absence the matter was settled by a committee of four Ministers. These were: Lord Hartington, Secretary for War, Lord Granville, Foreign Secretary, Lord Northbrook, a relative of Baring's, the First Lord of the Admiralty, and Sir Charles Dilke. They were four men of calm judgement and ripe experience. But in this case they acted with an undue haste that is difficult to understand, and for which a heavy price was paid.

General Wolseley, the victor of Tel-el-Kebir, and an admirer of Gordon's, who warmly recommended his despatch to the Sudan, explained to him, after consultation with the Ministers: "Government are determined to evacuate the Sudan, for they will not guarantee the future Government. Will you go and do it?" On Gordon's assent, Wolseley took him into the room where the Ministers were waiting—"Did Wolseley tell you our orders?" they asked.—Gordon replied: "Yes, you will not guarantee the future Government of the Sudan, and you wish me to go up and evacuate now."—"Yes," replied the Ministers; and with that the conversation was ended.

This is Gordon's own description.

That same evening Gordon left for Egypt. The Ministers themselves saw him into the train at Victoria. "Lord Granville bought the necessary tickets; the Duke of Cambridge opened the railway-carriage door. . . . Lord Wolseley . . . carrying a leather bag, in which were two hundred pounds in gold, collected from friends at the last moment, for the contingencies of the journey. The train started. As it did so, Gordon leant out, and addressed a last whispered question to Lord Wolseley. Yes, it had been done, Lord Wolseley had seen to it himself; next morning, every member of the Cabinet would receive a copy of Dr. Samuel Clark's Scripture Promises."

So Lytton Strachey describes Gordon's departure.

On the following day Granville asked Hartington: "We were proud of ourselves yesterday—are you sure we did not commit a gigantic folly?" Had he asked Lord Salisbury, he would have received an unequivocal answer. When Lord Salisbury, in his library at Hatfield, read in the newspaper of Gordon's appointment he threw the sheet down with the words: "They must have gone absolutely crazy!"

And Gordon's appointment was, in fact, a grievous blunder; for despite his brilliant capacities and his noble qualities he was absolutely unsuited for the task which now confronted him. It called for a man who with iron self-discipline would subject his will to that of another, who would allow nothing to turn him aside from the given directions, who would soberly take advantage of every opportunity of performing a difficult but by no means glorious task, and who would know how to be silent when speech was dangerous. And of all this Gordon was the exact antithesis. He was eccentric, full of illusions, vacillating in his opinions and resolutions, but always absolutely convinced of the correctness of his standpoint at the moment, believing that he was a better judge of things not only than the Government in London, but also than the Consul-General in Cairo. Further, he had an insuperable inclination to publish all his desires and opinions in the Press, and he considered that he was absolved of any obligation of obedience if his requirements were not fulfilled. He himself made this confession in his diary:

"I own to having been very insubordinate to Her Majesty's Government and its officials, but it is my nature and I cannot help it. . . . I know if I was chief I would never employ myself, for I am incorrigible."

It had been fortunate indeed if only one of all those who were involved in this disastrous expedition had understood Gordon as well as he understood himself in this moment of enlightenment. A man who is accustomed to ask the Prophet Isaiah for advice when he is in difficulty is not inclined to obey anyone's orders, as Sir Evelyn Baring wrote to Lord Granville on the 21st of January; but when this letter reached London Gordon was already in Cairo.

As a matter of fact, within a very short time Gordon had transformed the task which had been set him into a task of an absolutely different nature, and none of his superiors had protested with sufficient energy against this transformation. He presently surprised the Ministers by a proposal which he, they might have thought, would have been the very last man to make. During his former Governorship of the Sudan he had come into conflict with Zobeir, the greatest and most powerful of the slave-dealers. Zobeir's son had been captured and shot as a rebel by Gordon's lieutenant. Now he met Zobeir in Cairo, and after some conversation with him he was seized by the notion that this man, who knew how to deal with the Sudanese, and had great influence with them, ought to accompany him to Khartoum as his chief collaborator. A "mystic feeling" told him that they would accomplish great things together. Baring protested, but Gordon had hardly reached Khartoum when he proposed that Zobeir should be appointed his successor as Governor-General of the Sudan, and that high distinctions should be conferred upon him. This time Baring agreed.

But for the Ministers the problem was not so simple. Quite apart from the question whether Gordon's present confidence in Zobeir was or was not justified, the fact remained that Zobeir, to use Gordon's own words, was "the king of slave-hunters." The Englishman considered that the campaign against slavery was one of his country's chiefest titles to glory, and the Anti-Slavery Society would be up in arms if a British Government were to make such man the ruler of the Sudan. Forster, the old Quaker, who, comprehensibly enough, was not too well disposed toward his sometime colleagues, was prepared to lead an immediate attack against them in Parliament, and neither the Liberal nor the Conservative Party could well disregard the popular excitement which Gordon himself had foolishly aroused by an interview published in *The Times*.

Only one of them thought otherwise: Gladstone. He wished to do what the men on the spot thought necessary. But Gladstone was ill and could not take part in the Cabinet meetings. A colleague sought him out on his bed of sickness and expounded, in a two hours' conversation, the reasons why Zobeir should not be appointed: the chief of these being the fact that the appointment could not be defended in Parliament. "All those in the Cabinet who are in the House of Commons," he said, "were positive that no Government, Liberal or Conservative, would send Zobeir." —"Gladstone considered it very likely that they could not bring Parliament to swallow Zobeir, but believed that he himself could." Never, perhaps, had Gladstone given such frank expression to his sense of superiority.

Would Zobeir's appointment really have changed the course of Destiny? Who can say? But those of Gordon's biographers who attributed the negative decision of the Cabinet to Gladstone's personal prejudice, in order to draw the usual comparison between the man of action, untroubled by theory, and the unpractical doctrinaire, were writing without troubling to ascertain the facts.

But now what was to be done? Gordon was in Khartoum, and he did not appear to be making any attempt to retreat northwards. He considered that since he had been deprived of Zobeir he must now be left to do what he thought best. He spoke of "smashing the Mahdi." He overwhelmed Baring with telegrams, and often enough those despatched in the evening contradicted the telegrams of the morning.

But the withdrawal was becoming less and less a matter within his power to decide. The tribes of the region surrounding Khartoum rose in support of the Mahdi, and before long Gordon was completely surrounded. Only his few small steamers were able, by way of the Nile, to maintain a connection with the outer world.

Immediately the Government was asked—first by the Queen, but then also by Baring—to relieve Gordon by a military expedition. In Parliament the Conservative Opposition took up the cry, and here it found itself supported not only by the Irish, who were glad of the opportunity of making things difficult for the Government which had passed the Coercion Act, but also—and this made a much deeper impression—by Forster. Undoubtedly Forster was seriously troubled about Gordon's fate, but his lasting resentment in respect of his dismissal gave his attacks a quality which was peculiarly painful to his old colleagues. He wounded Gladstone deeply by a description which, because it was given by a sometime friend, was cited against him times without number, and which was particularly damaging to him: "He can persuade most people of most things, and above all, he can persuade himself of almost anything." It should not have surprised Forster that a man as calm and moderate as Hartington should have refuted this "bitter, personal and apparently well prepared and long meditated attack upon Gladstone's sincerity."

But what was it actually that prevented the Government from immediately fitting out an expedition to relieve Gordon? To some extent the delay was explained on technical grounds: the heat and low water on the Nile were reasons why no expedition could be sent in the summer, and the question which of the theoretically possible routes should be followed by the relieving force was the subject of long and heated discussion by the Government's military advisers. It did not seem that delay was dangerous, for Gordon, according to his own reports, was provisioned for months to come, and the storming of the fortified city by the hordes of the Mahdi was regarded as impossible from the military point of view. But these technical considerations did not suffice to explain the hesitation of the Government. There was a more essential consideration: Gladstone objected to allowing Gordon to prescribe his policy for him. What he had written to Granville on the 16th of January—that Gordon must not under any circumstances assume the responsibility himself—was still decisive for him. He had the impression that Gordon wanted to force the Government to pursue his policy of "smashing the Mahdi," and for that purpose to do exactly what it had refused to do at the outset—namely, to employ military force in the Sudan. He believed that Gordon was detained in Khartoum, not so much because he was surrounded by the Mahdi's followers as because he chose to remain there. An eyewitness has described how Gladstone, who was staying in the country, first read in a newspaper Gordon's telegram to Baring, in which he spoke of the crushing of the Mahdi, and the "indelible disgrace" which would rest upon those who left the Egyptian garrisons of the Sudan in the lurch: "He took up the paper, his eye instantly fell on the telegram, and he read it through. As he read, his face hardened and whitened, the eyes burned as I have seen them once or twice in the House of Commons when he was angered—burned with a deep fire, as if they would have consumed the sheet on which Gordon's message was printed, or as if Gordon's words had burnt into his soul, which was looking out in wrath and flame. He said not a word. For perhaps two or three minutes he sat still, his face all the while like the face you may read of in Milton—like none other I ever saw. Then he rose, still without a word, and was seen no more that morning."

It assuredly is not easy to deal with a general who from a distance of many hundred miles threatens his Government with "indelible disgrace" if it does not do what he considers proper. Gordon must not take upon himself the responsibility to which Gladstone was always referring, and which was his; for the despatch of an army to Egypt would have more repercussions, in many directions, than Gordon could realize in Khartoum. One could not send English troops to the Sudan, and from the standpoint of England's general foreign policy there were serious objections, as would very soon be evident, to transferring Indian troops from India to Egypt.

But however many arguments there were against the despatch of a relief expedition, even statesmen are subject to the law of Mephistopheles: "The first time we are free, the second we are slaves." And indeed, from the day when Gladstone consented to Gordon's appointment, he had lost the power of free decision. From the moment when Gordon's life was seriously endangered he could not do otherwise than employ the resources of the Empire to rescue him. No nation will suffer its hero to be left in the lurch, and the notion that it is the lot and the duty of a soldier to risk his life, even in a forlorn hope, will always be as remote from its considerations as the question whether one should sacrifice the lives of hundreds, perhaps thousands of soldiers in order to save one.

At the beginning of June Gladstone wrote to the Queen that "Ministers have been and are very seriously engaged in examining the various routes and methods by which in case of need aid could be supplied." Up to the middle of July the Cabinet had not yet decided whether an expedition was to be despatched. Then the Secretary for War, Lord Hartington, forced a decision by a memorandum in which he renounced all responsibility for the military policy in Egypt unless the question was definitely decided at once: was Gordon to be rescued or abandoned?

Early in August the Cabinet asked Parliament to vote the necessary credits for the expedition. At the end of August General Wolseley, whose plan of campaign had been adopted after lengthy discussion at the War Office, sailed for Egypt as commander of the expedition. Not until October did he leave Cairo for the Sudan. The leaders of the expedition proceeded with great caution, making systematic preparations for all eventualities. Then for long weeks the column made its way through the desert, and the boats were hauled up the cataracts of the Nile.

Meanwhile General Gordon was waiting in Khartoum. He was short of ammunition; the supplies of food were running low; the Mahdi's hordes were pressing closer; the discipline of his own inferior troops was loosening. Day after day he climbed up to the roof of Government House, turning his telescope toward the north, whence his rescuers must be approaching. Day after day he suffered the same disappointment; nothing was stirring, there was nothing to be seen. Day after day he reckoned anew, always with more depressing results, how long he could still hold out. At last, at the end of December, the expedition reached Metemmeh, where the first skirmish with the Mahdi's troops occurred. On the 24th of January they met Gordon's steamer from Khartoum. But it was the 28th before the van of the expedition, on two steamers, came within sight of Khartoum. Then they heard a voice crying from the bank: "Khartoum has fallen, Gordon is dead." The officers could see the Government House through their field-glasses; it was a blackened ruin.

Two days earlier, on the 26th of January, 1885, Gordon's tragic destiny was accomplished.

The news that Khartoum had fallen naturally caused an outburst of emotion in England: of grief for the fallen hero, of indignation with the Government which had failed to save him. The Queen herself was the first to express both emotions. She sent to Gladstone, Granville and Hartington telegrams in which she said: "To think that all this might have been prevented and many precious lives saved by earlier action is too frightful." These telegrams were not in cipher, as was usually the case with the Queen's telegrams to her Ministers, they were despatched in ordinary script, so that before long their contents were generally known; and we may conclude, from a note in her diary, that this was what she had intended. When Gladstone's private secretary, Edward Hamilton, commented to Sir Henry Ponsonby, private secretary to the Queen, on this unusual procedure, the Queen gave a most ungracious answer, which almost aggravated the affront, and Ponsonby had to justify himself when she reproached him with attempting "to calm Mr. Gladstone." The Prime Minister himself wrote her a long letter of justification, which was a dignified reply to her message. "It is probable," he said, "that abundent wrath and indignation will on this occasion be poured out upon them (the Ministers responsible), nor will they complain if so it should be ... Perhaps among the most difficult (of reproaches to answer) would be the reproach of those who might argue ... that the most prudent course would have been ... to assume no responsibility for the lands beyond the desert." In short, that England should have confined herself to protecting Egypt proper, which had never been seriously threatened by the Mahdi's rebellion. As for Ponsonby's letter to Hamilton, he requested Hamilton to reply to it, with the dry comment that "Her Majesty is the best judge of what to say and how to say it."

But one thing was perfectly clear to the aged Prime Minister: that it was he who would have to bear the burden of reproach for this national catastrophe. He foresaw, as its necessary consequence, the fall of his Government; but that, as he wrote in his diary, was "one of the least points." He foresaw, also, that his posthumous reputation would suffer in consequence of the Gordon tragedy. Five years later he wrote to his sometime colleagues:

"In the Gordon case we all, and I rather prominently, must continue to suffer in silence. Gordon was a hero, and a hero of heroes; but we ought to have known that a hero of heroes is not the proper person to give effect at a distant point, and in most difficult circumstances, to the view of ordinary men. ... My own opinion is that it is harder to justify our doing so much to rescue him than our not doing more. Had the party reached Khartoum in time, he would not have come away (as I suppose), and the dilemma would have arisen in another form."

But the Ministry did not fall, as was generally expected. Lord Rosebery was its saviour. He had resigned from the Ministry some time before this, because Gladstone had not given him the post which he believed he had a right to claim. But now that the menacing storm-clouds were massing round the head of his old friend and leader, he wrote to him as follows:

"The question is now less one of policy than of patriotism. We have to face a crisis such as rarely occurs in a nation's history, which the nation should therefore face with a united front. The Government at such a juncture has a right to appeal to the public spirit and place under requisition the energies of everybody."

Gladstone gladly accepted his offer of help, and so the Government was able to open the Parliamentary session reinforced by a widely beloved and generally popular Minister. Laura Tennant wrote to the new Minister: "The step you have taken is, to my mind, one of the noblest things I have lived to see."

Rosebery's good example put courage into the ranks of the Liberal Members, and the Conservative vote of censure was defeated. But the Government majority was very small—only 14 votes. The Cabinet considered whether it should resign. After a long debate Gladstone had his way. He was opposed to the evacuation of a position which had not been stormed by the enemy; so the Cabinet remained in office—to the Queen's great disappointment.

In the debate on the Conservative vote of censure the Government had declared that it intended to make war upon the Mahdi. The Radicals, led by Morley, demanded the evacuation of the Sudan. Each side was able to quote Gordon's opinions in support of its views. Parnell, with his Irish followers, voted with the Conservatives, and also for Morley's amendment; although the policy demanded in the vote of censure was the exact opposite of that recommended in the amendment; so completely, for him, did tactical considerations outweigh practical.

The Queen, of course, emphatically advocated the military occupation of the Sudan, and the despatch of a punitive expedition against the Mahdi; and when General Wolseley asked for the appointment of Governor-General of the Sudan she could not understand why the Cabinet did not at once comply with his wishes. In vain did Gladstone send her a list of ten reasons why the appointment should not be made. In her eagerness to impose her will upon her Ministers the Queen even went to the length of sending Lady Wolesley "in strict confidence" a letter full of vehement reproaches against the Government, in which she gave the General's wife the almost incredible advice that Wolseley "should even threaten to resign if he does not get strong support and liberty of action."

But now it became apparent that the Sudan question could be considered only within the frame of international policy as a whole, and that a Sudanese expedition was a luxury in which the British Empire could not lightly indulge in view of the critical state of affairs abroad. The Empire was suddenly reminded of the fact that it had to provide for the defence of more important regions.

The fresh complications occurred at the point where, six years earlier, the foreign policy of Disraeli had suffered a fatal defeat.

At the beginning of April 1885 it was learned in London that a Russian force, under General Kamaroff, had driven the Afghans out of the Penjdeh valley. This valley belonged to the disputed Turkoman frontier region to the north of Herat. But Afghanistan was now recognized as a British sphere of interest. In 1884 Great Britain and Russia had agreed to delimit the frontier by means of a common commission. Since December 1884 the British Commissioner had been waiting in vain, on the spot, for his Russian colleague, who kept on inventing fresh protests for delaying his arrival. Under these circumstances the military operation of the Russians appeared to be a deliberate provocation, and the peril of an Asiatic war which would infallibly involve Europe presented itself to the startled imagination.

But now the aged Gladstone showed that in case of need he could act both swiftly and energetically, and that those were sorely mistaken who had imagined, and had sought to persuade others, that his foreign policy would be influenced by a sentimental tenderness for Russia. On the 27th of April he asked Parliament for a credit to cover the expenditure that would be necessary in the event of complications in Central Asia. At this time his situation was anything but comfortable; the recollection of his Sudanese policy was damaging to his reputation, and the request for a war-loan of several millions, coming from him, of all people, must have seemed astonishing for the moment. But his personality, even more than his gifts of oratory, triumphed over every obstacle. He spoke very seriously, very solemnly at moments, as the guardian of England's honour, warning the House very plainly of the possible consequences if that honour were violated; and his speech made such a profound impression on the House that all Party differences receded into the background, and the House unanimously voted the required credits. One thing, he declared, he would say with fullest conviction: England would do all that diplomacy could do to avoid a breach; but if that breach should occur she would abide with tranquil mind the verdict of civilized humanity, for she would have done her utmost to prevent bloodshed.

Peace was preserved, and the Russian provocation withdrawn. War was prevented simply by Gladstone's timely energy, and by his speech, which was read with eager attention by the outside world. The Russians acquiesced in an arbitration treaty, and the peril of war was averted. At the same time, England had obtained the conditions on which she was obliged to insist. In view of this result, what either side might have contributed towards the final agreement was of altogether secondary importance. Only the fundamental hostility of the Continental diplomatists could represent this as a fresh defeat of Gladstone's feeble policy, and pretend that the Russians had now opened up the road to Herat.

This diversion of British policy to Asia had the necessary consequence, that the punitive expedition to Khartoum was abandoned; greatly to the Queen's regret.

She had begun a correspondence with General Wolseley of such a nature that she had to ask him "to *destroy* this letter as it is very *confidential.*" But the General, ready though he was to indulge in scathing criticism of the Government, and more especially of Gladstone, could not conceal his belief that "as soon as we have settled this false prophet and set up a native government at Khartoum, I am sure the sooner we sever our connection with the Sudan the better." In such critical times it would never do to leave a considerable proportion of the British Army tied up in the African desert.

It was only with the greatest reluctance that the Queen at last gave in; not without writing from Darmstadt a letter to Lord Granville, in which she criticized Mr. Gladstone with a severity most unusual in the intercourse of a constitutional sovereign and his or her ministers.

4. Bismarck

When the Russians held up the delimitation of the Afghan frontier to which they had agreed by delaying the despatch of their commissioner, Lord Granville suspected that Bismarck was at the back of this move; that if he had not actually suggested it to the Russians, he had encouraged it by his silent approval. In the Cabinet meeting after the Gordon debates Granville had advised resignation, for he believed that Bismarck would continue to make mischief as long as there was a Liberal Government at Westminster. As the conflict with Russia grew sharper, all sorts of news came to hand that confirmed the suspicion that Berlin was not sorry to see it. Prince Bülow, in his reminiscences, tells us that Herbert Bismarck, in a company which included foreign diplomatists, exclaimed, in a lively tone: "If England and Russia fall foul of each other, I can only say: a pity if a single blow misses its mark!" But Bülow was doubtless right in thinking that Herbert's eminent father did not share his son's irresponsible opinion. It is true, however, that even in Berlin there were many who deplored the fact that the Chancellor had not made more use of his tremendous authority in the direction of preserving peace by friendly advice to St. Petersburg. The Crown Prince and his wife especially—as Bismarck's confidant Bucher told Busch—appear to have complained that he had not done so, while the Quartermaster-General, Count Waldersee, the leader of the militarist party, thought that one should rather do "the contrary"—that is, encourage the Russians in their unyielding mood. When the crisis was already passing the Chancellor took advantage of an article in *The Times* in order to submit to the old Kaiser, who had not envisaged the danger of war without anxiety, a complete exposition of his policy. In this he emphasized the fact that it was not in Germany's interest "to hinder Russia if she preferred to seek the occupation which she needed for her army in Asia rather than in Europe." But the culminating point of his exposition is found in the following passage: "For the German policy, therefore, there is a very strong temptation to promote hostile rather than friendly relations between Russia and England. We have, however, conscientiously resisted this temptation, and have done nothing to further the likelihood of war; but in practising this abstention, on general Christian principles, we still owe it to the German nation to avoid doing anything that might lead to diminishing Russia's hostility to England only to bring it upon ourselves."

For this reason the German Government had most rigidly refrained from advising St. Petersburg, even in a friendly manner, to keep the peace. His principles, however, had not prevented the German Chancellor, by agreement with the Russian Government, on the basis of the secret "Three Emperors' Agreement" of 18th of June, 1881, and 24th of March, 1884, from persuading the Porte that in the event of war it must close the Dardanelles to British warships, while the German Ambassador in Constantinople had actually urged the military authorities to strengthen the defences of the Straits. Bismarck had even seen to it that France was invited to take part in the diplomatic representations to the Porte.

This was the last offshoot of the policy of Franco-German co-operation against England. This policy had reached its climax in the first months of 1885; Bismarck having resolved to exploit in the interests of a German colonial policy the antagonism between France and England which had been aroused by the Egyptian question.

Originally the notion of creating a German colonial empire had by no means met with universal approval in German political circles. Not many, perhaps, went so far as the Crown Princess, who in a letter to her mother described it as "stupid." But many doubted whether the acquisition of German colonies in Africa or Polynesia was worth the risk of conflict with England. Such doubts were expressed, for example, by the Ambassador, Count Münster, in a letter to Rudolf von Bennigsen, the leader of the National Liberals. Even Bismarck, in 1881, had expressed himself in the strongest terms as opposed to any colonial policy, and several years later, when it appeared that the results of this policy were not particularly encouraging, he even exclaimed, in the Reichstag: "I am no colonizer!" His temporary conversion to a colonial policy was not wholly unrelated to the requirements of domestic politics. With his unerring intuition of the German psychology

357

he had realized that it offered him an excellent means of unseating his opponents, who since the Reichstag elections of 1884 had been exerting a Parliamentary influence which he found exceedingly inconvenient, and whom he suspected of intriguing against him with the Crown Prince and Princess. The external situation was exceptionally favourable, so long as Jules Ferry was responsible for the French policy.

Bismarck was all the more exasperated when Lord Granville, in the heat of conflict with his Conservative opponents, was guilty of a diplomatic indiscretion which was of a kind which might have seriously disturbed the Franco-German understanding. In the Gordon debate a Conservative peer, the Duke of Richmond, had cited, by way of retort, certain disapproving comments of Bismarck's on the Government's Egyptian policy. Granville had countered with the observation that even to please a Bismarck the British Government could not renounce its privilege of forming its own decisions. It felt the less bound to consider his views inasmuch as it had paid no more attention than its predecessor to Bismarck's advice to "take Egypt."

Although this remark was addressed to the Opposition rather than to Bismarck, it none the less found a joint in the Chancellor's armour, and he reacted vehemently. On the 2nd of March, 1885— that is, while the wound of Khartoum was still smarting, and the conflict over the Afghan frontier was daily becoming more acute— he attacked the British Government and its diplomatic methods in the Reichstag with a violence unprecedented as between the Governments of countries that wish to live in mutual peace. Before the whole world the English Foreign Secretary was "told off" as a bungler by the acknowledged master of international policy.

Simultaneously with this Parliamentary scolding, the Chancellor gave the word to the *Norddeutsche Allgemeine Zeitung* to open a journalistic campaign against the British Government. On the very day when Bismarck delivered his speech in the Reichstag this journal began a series of articles filled with attacks upon the Blue Books published by the British Government, and complaints of the attitude of the British Foreign Office in respect of the German proposals. One special cause of reproach was the fact that the

358

Foreign Office had paid no attention to the Chancellor's Note of the 5th of May, 1884, which had reminded it that those responsible for German policy would have to seek an approach to France if the British Government refused to enter into an agreement.

As a matter of fact, the British Government had never defined its attitude in respect of this Note. But the reason for this was very simple and very pertinent. The Note of the 5th of May, 1884, had never been presented in London. Bismarck had already made the same reproach on the 24th of January, 1885, to the British Ambassador. This Ambassador was no longer the Odo Russell (Lord Ampthill) in whom he had such confidence: for he, to the detriment of Anglo-German relations, had died in August 1884. Gladstone had wished to send to Berlin the most able of British diplomatists, Sir Robert Morier, but Bismarck had described him as undesirable, for he was known to be a friend of the Crown Prince and Princess; so Sir Edward Malet was sent in his place, whom Bismarck had known since his Frankfort days, but who never succeeded in achieving a position like that of his predecessor.

When Malet's report of his conversation with Bismarck was received in London, the whole Foreign Office was turned upside down in the effort to find the supposedly unanswered Note of the 5th of May, 1884. It was not to be found, and Granville asked the German Ambassador to call on him. Concerning his conversation with the latter, he wrote to Gladstone on the 9th of February, 1885, to the effect that Munster was quite beside himself with dismay. He went home to examine his files, and he found, not only the famous Note, but also a telegram to the effect that it was not to be presented. "He begged me to keep this secret."

Granville restricted himself to publishing Malet's report of his conversation with Bismarck in a Parliamentary Blue Book, together with his written reply to the Ambassador on the 7th of February, 1885, in which he formally assured the latter that he had never received the Note of the 5th of May, 1884. The *Norddeutsche Allgemeine Zeitung*, however, repeated the reproach that this important Note had been disregarded, paying no attention to Granville's explanation, although it sharply criticized the rest of his reply.

It looked, therefore, very much as though Bismarck were trying to cause a breach. Lord Salisbury, on the day of the Reichstag speech, wrote to a friend that he could not be sufficiently grateful to the fourteen gentlemen who—by the vote of censure—"stood between us and such a legacy." The Press, on either side of the Channel, was full of excited comments. The Paris correspondent of *The Times*—probably de Blowitz, whom Bismarck hated sufficiently without this—was already drawing ominous comparisons between the Chancellor's conduct now and his behaviour towards the French Ambassador Benedetti in respect of the Belgian question. As a matter of fact, Bismarck was by no means desirous of a breach. He had no sooner discharged his resentment in the Reichstag than he sent his son Herbert to London in order to negotiate with the Government.

Herbert Bismarck, who stayed with Lord Rosebery in London, had conversations with Granville, Gladstone, Dilke, Chamberlain and other members of the Cabinet. Dilke, whom he described in his report to his father as "the most businesslike of the English Ministers," was not, it seems, favourably impressed; for he notes in his diary that the object of Herbert's visit was "to induce us to dismiss Lord Granville and Lord Derby." Herbert's report of his interview with Granville was such that one is compelled to doubt whether the conversation between a young man of thirty-six and a Minister of seventy really took such a form. It is true, however, that not long afterwards his German friends—including Waldersee—were saying of Herbert Bismarck that "he had accustomed himself to behaving as though he had been his father, and was blunt and rude."

That Herbert thought he could adopt an attitude that would have befitted only his father is obvious from the contemptuous comments on nearly all the British Ministers contained in this report. He spoke of Joseph Chamberlain's "stupifying lack of political judgement" and "a surprising ignorance of the present and possible constellations of power in Europe." The German Empire has learned to its cost how incorrect was this arrogant judgement. But he reserved his greatest contempt for Gladstone's total inability to understand the nature of the foreign policy of a great country. The joke is on young Bismarck here, for the old man thus stigmatized was the same Gladstone who lifted the car of State on to the rails again. He realized that in view of the British difficulties in Egypt, the Sudan, and Afghanistan, the favour of Prince Bismarck was worth a mass. The wishes and misgivings of the Colonies, which were far more averse to German penetration than the Government at Westminster, must give way to the German desire for colonial expansion.

So when Lord Rosebery brought Herbert Bismarck into touch with Gladstone and John Bright at his hospitable table, and Herbert, who, as Gladstone wrote to Granville, behaved himself in a perfectly modest amd amiable manner, began to speak of the German colonial policy, the Prime Minister gave him some notion both of his intentions and of his difficulties. He was able to remind Herbert that he had already, in the previous winter, publicly welcomed the colonizing efforts of Germany. And he took the first opportunity of making in Parliament a fair and friendly explanation of these efforts, which were welcomed by England. Prince Bismarck cited Gladstone's words with approval in his next speech in the Reichstag, and on the strength of them he was able to reproach Windthorst, the Leader of the Centre, with the fact that Gladstone had a better understanding than he of Germany's colonial policy. Thus an atmosphere was created that was favourable to understanding, and it was possible before long, thanks to Gladstone's vigorous initiative, to overcome the difficulties and conclude an agreement in respect of the disputed boundaries.

The German Chancellor might well be content with this rapid progress. For a fortnight after this friendly explanation of Gladstone's in the House of Commons one of the chief pillars of the anti-English policy collapsed.

On the 30th of March, 1885, Jules Ferry, after more than two years of government, was overthrown in an extraordinarily stormy and exciting session of the Chamber. "You are no longer a Ministry! You are defendants!" Clemenceau had exclaimed—Clemenceau the "Tiger," the implacable leader of the Radicals, in a passionate speech. The implied meaning of this accusation was: Co-operation with Bismarck is a betrayal of *la revanche*. The elemental emotions of the French people had called check to a policy such as a political leader can venture upon only as long as fortune favours him. The French Prime Minister, who in October 1884 had begged Bismarck not to overthrow Gladstone, had now actually fallen before him, though his fall preceded Gladstone's only by three months. But while Gladstone twice regained power and formed a Government, the 30th of March, 1885, was the end of Jules Ferry's career.

5. Franchise Reform and Defeat

While all the cares and anxieties of foreign policy were besieging the Prime Minister, he had to cope with tasks in the domain of domestic politics that made the greatest demands on his energies and his diplomacy. Apart from the Irish question, eternally unsettled, he was busy with the franchise reform to which he had set his hand at the beginning of 1884. The problems of the franchise are among those questions which are most violently disputed as long as they remain problems, but which arouse hardly any interest once they are solved. Half a century later Gladstone's franchise reform is sufficiently described if we say that it merely completed Disraeli's reform of 1867, by extending the wider franchise which these had conferred upon the urban voters to the country, so that in future even the agricultural labourer would be able to vote. It increased the number of electors by more than 50 per cent, from three to five millions. The principle of the Bill for which George Trevelyan had been preparing the way for the last ten years was so obviously just that even the Opposition could not offer any direct resistance to it, so that it was accepted in the Lower House by an unusually large majority.

Only two details are of real historical interest: the Opposition of the House of Lords, and the extension of franchise reform to Ireland.

The opposition of the Upper House, in view of the impossibility of open resistance, took the form of demanding that it should be combined with legislation effecting the redistribution of the constituencies. Now, Gladstone had already promised that such a Bill should be introduced before the dissolution of Parliament. Practically, then, the two parties had little to quarrel about. But Lord Salisbury insisted that the two Bills ought to be passed at the same time, to which Gladstone and the Lower House were unwilling to agree, as they did not wish to imperil the franchise reform. This dispute acquired real importance because of the Queen's vigorous intervention. She pressed the Prime Minister to give way, and even urged him to dissolve Parliament and proceed to a General Election; but this would have meant playing the Conservatives' game for them. Gladstone had to refuse to adopt such a policy of retreat; not only because it was against his own conviction, but also because it would have brought him into flat opposition to his own party, especially its Radical section. The Radicals, under Chamberlain's resolute leadership, made the opposition of the Lords the cornerstone of a violent agitation against the Upper House. Chamberlain himself, in his extremely effective campaigning speeches, adopted a very decided tone, and threatened the Lords, without undue circumlocution, that the people would restrict their power if they stood in the way of electoral reform. This, however, roused the Queen again, as she considered that Chamberlain's attitude was incompatible with the obligations of a Minister of the Crown. For in her eyes the Upper House, being, as she said, an independent Chamber, "free from the terror which forces so many Commoners to vote against their consciences," was an incomparably valuable and inviolable component of the British Constitution, whose defence was obligatory upon all Ministers without exception.

Once more, of course, it was the Prime Minister who had in the first place to bear the brunt of her wrath. With the most meticulous attention the Queen kept watch upon every speech of Chamberlain's, and the moment she found anything obnoxious she wrote a severe letter to Gladstone, complaining of this "most dangerous" Minister, "one to whom she fears Mr. Gladstone is inclined to listen to far more than to those who hold moderate opinions." Gladstone did all that he could to appease his extreme colleague. He could not fail to realize that the criticisms which the Queen directed against Chamberlain were intended for him also; indeed, she reproached him vehemently for a harmless speech which his own son made. But Chamberlain was by no means disposed to allow anyone to stop his mouth; moreover, he very well knew that popular opinion was on his side. The more impatient the Queen became, the more he felt that he was the champion of the old English liberty of speech against an obsolete tyranny. The Queen could of course dismiss him, he said to Dilke, but then he would be able to start a national attack on the Lords. As usually happens in such cases, he too discharged some of his resentment upon the man who stood between him and the Queen, and it took all Gladstone's patience and dexterity to avoid a breach that might have imperilled the whole of his reforms.

The actual conflict between the old and the young Liberal turned upon the question of a compromise which Chamberlain was unwilling to make. Gladstone, however, was in favour of an understanding with the Lords, not only because the Queen was doing her utmost to persuade him to take this course, but because he himself considered it necessary, in order to avoid a constitutional conflict, with all its incalculable consequences. For the old politician, whom the Queen had accustomed herself to regard as an extreme Radical, and almost as a revolutionary, was really as firmly rooted in tradition as any Conservative. The Queen herself must have realized this, to her astonishment, when Gladstone laid before her a memorandum in which he considered the question, as was his manner, from every side, and presented it in its constitutional context. The Queen had to admit that she was "greatly struck by the fairness and impartiality" of his exposition. This, however, did not prevent her, a few months later, when she was writing to the Duke of Argyll, from describing Gladstone's well-considered speeches as "stupid, rash and undignified," while she had nothing to say against Salisbury's uncompliant tone.

When at last it was possible, thanks to her resolute insistence, and the skilful touch of her private secretary, General Ponsonby, to institute personal negotiations between the two Party Leaders, she was surprised to hear that "the conciliatory tone" of which Mr. Gladstone had spoken was "entirely corroborated by Lord Salisbury with respect to Mr. Gladstone." At the conclusion of the long protracted but finally successful negotiations the Queen's letters and telegrams to the Prime Minister assumed an amiable and almost cordial tone which had long been absent from them, and which was very soon to disappear again.

Gladstone had in some degree ensured the final success of the negotiations by entrusting them to one of his two refractory Radicals, Sir Charles Dilke. This had the effect of appeasing the Radical wing. Actually, in the end it was the Whigs who objected most strongly to the compromise; and with justification, for in the long run they had to pay the cost. Under the new arrangement the majority of constituencies returned only one member, whereas most of them used to return two. Hitherto the Liberals of both wings had, by agreement, each produced a candidate. They could do so no longer, and as a rule it was the left wing that controlled the Party machine and selected the candidate.

In actual fact, from the time of the franchise reform of 1884 the Whigs were no longer an independent political force; while the Irish Home Rulers became a powerful party.

For the new Bill reduced the franchise qualification in the rural constituencies of Ireland to the level of that required in the English constituencies. This reduction had been opposed in the debate in the Bill by Plunket (not a member of the Irish Party), in a speech which made a deep and lasting impression. Referring to the much lower cultural level of the Irish peasant, he foretold that the extension of the suffrage would enormously increase the power of the disloyal Home Rulers, and the end of it would be that Ireland would break away from the United Kingdom. Events have shown that his prophecy was largely justified. Yet the counterargument with which Gladstone demolished Plunket's speech was irrefutable. If it really came to a conflict with Ireland, England would have placed in her enemies' hands the most forcible evidence against her—that she had refused to grant to Ireland the privilege which she herself enjoyed. The large majority that voted for the extension of the Irish franchise included Lord Randolph Churchill and his friends—the first sign of a party tactics which in the following year was to be applied with extraordinary success.

So, after all, the year 1884 ended with a great political victory for Gladstone. But the labour and anxiety of these agitated weeks seem to have overtaxed the nerves and the health of the septuagenarian. Morley thought him greatly aged at the close of the year. When the strain of the session was over Gladstone found that he could no longer count on what had been his indispensable restorative in all his battles—the undisturbed sleep at night, which had never before evaded him. By the New Year it began to look as though he had reached the limit which Nature has set to the working capacity of even the most active of mortals. There were whispers that he was about to retire, and at once the most difficult of problems presented itself. Who was to be his successor, who was to raise the colours when they fell from the failing hand of the aged leader? Would it be Lord Hartington, who had already carried them once in a time of emergency?

Granville was so aged that he was out of the running. But if Hartington were to form a Government would Chamberlain and Dilke serve under him?

Gladstone himself, at this time, was undoubtedly seriously considering whether now the time had not come for his final retirement into private life. It is probable that the thought had always been lurking at the back of his mind, that there should be, between the end of his public activities and the close of his life, a period of quiet meditation, of return to his beloved books; a time of absorption in the eternal problems of religion, and of inward preparation for "that undiscovered country from whose bourne no traveller returns." His impaired health might well be a warning that this time had come. Could he not say, precisely now, after the introduction of the franchise reform which assured the progress of democracy in England, that his life-work was completed? When his faithful friend, Lord Acton, conjured him even now to continue his work, Gladstone replied to him with a letter that had almost the character of a political testament. In it he castigated the demagogy of the Right, which concealed itself behind the label of Tory Democracy, for it was "not ennobled by love and appreciation of liberty." The new Liberalism, he believed, was thus ennobled; yet he could not deny that he watched it with misgiving. "Its pet idea is what they call construction—that is to say, taking into the hands of the State the business of the individual man."

But he had faith that the "economic, pacific, law-regarding elements, the sense of justice which abides tenaciously in the masses, will never knowingly join hands with the Fiend of Jingoism."

Had he Chamberlain in mind as he penned this last sentence—Chamberlain, who in many Cabinet debates had unfolded views that even Granville had declared were Jingoistic? If so, this was a marvellous prescience of the strange evolution of this most Radical of Radicals. But the remark concerning the constructive aims of the new Liberalism certainly refers to Chamberlain. For once more he was rousing public opinion by a series of inflammatory speeches, and the tone of each succeeding speech, especially when he touched upon social problems, was more drastic than that of its predecessors. He spoke in the style of Rousseau of the primitive and innate and equal rights of all to the good things of this world. He asked—and the question seemed to shake the foundations of the existing order—what "ransom" the possessing classes were willing to pay for the security which they enjoyed. He called upon his friends to ensure that this England, which had hitherto been called the Paradise of the rich, should not become the Purgatory of the poor. Naturally enough, not only did the Queen take fright again, but all the moderate members of the Cabinet were infuriated by this kind of plain speaking. Gladstone had to admonish his irrepressible colleague most seriously, while endeavouring to coat the bitter pill by marked appreciation of his phenomenal energy. It is impossible to say whither this difference might have led had not the Gordon catastrophe intervened.

When Gladstone wrote the letter of which we have spoken to Acton his health had improved, and it appeared almost that his illness had left him stronger than before. It seems to have been one of the peculiarities of his astonishing physical constitution that his restless desire to be up and doing were increased after every passing indisposition. It needed only a new and critical problem to rouse them again to full activity.

And such a problem was not lacking. The Cabinet meetings of the next month, though urgent problems of foreign policy were causing anxiety, were devoted more and more to consideration of that eternal problem of domestic politics: Ireland.

The actual cause of this absorption in the Irish problem was the expiration of the Crimes Act which followed the murders in Phoenix Park. By its means the Lord-Lieutenant, Lord Spencer, had governed Ireland with a courage only equalled by his shrewdness and understanding. Beside him, as Secretary of State, was Campbell-Bannermann, Trevelyan having sacrificed his health to this thankless office. Both regarded a renewal of the Crimes Act—though perhaps with a few mitigations—as indispensable. For a long while now there had been Irish outrages and attempted assassinations in England, and dynamite explosions in public buildings had caused great uneasiness. The Queen had to be constantly guarded by the police, for Harcourt, as Home Secretary, feared that attempts might be made upon her life, and Gladstone, who much against his will enjoyed the same protection, complained that he was ashamed to think of what he was costing the English taxpayer.

But the Radical members of the Cabinet had no faith in the protective efficacy of Coercion, which ran counter to their political creed. They were meditating other methods of exorcising the Irish peril.

Chamberlain had once more got into touch with Parnell, who, as everyone foresaw, was certain to return to Parliament with increased power at the next General Election. The go-between was once more none other than Captain O'Shea, who was acting, with undiminished pride, as the confidential henchman of his wife's lover. The result of these negotiations was a proposal whose protagonist in the Cabinet—armed with a manuscript written by Katherine O'Shea—was Chamberlain, while it was supported by no less a person than Cardinal Manning, the spiritual head of the Catholics of Great Britain.

This proposal was for the introduction of local self-government in Ireland, with elected corporations. This was to culminate in a Central Board, to be elected by County Boards. This Board was to take over a great many branches of the administration for which Dublin Castle had hitherto been responsible; such as education, poor relief, public health, and public works, while the judiciary and the police would still be under the administration of the Lord-

368

Lieutenant. This Central Board would not have been a Parliament. Chamberlain made it absolutely clear that he was not in favour of a separate Irish Parliament. But it would none the less have been a representative assembly elected by the Irish people, and it would doubtless have been subject to the ruling influence of Parnell.

The advisability of creating such a Central Board was hotly debated at several Cabinet meetings. Lord Spencer was emphatically opposed to it, and his fellow peers, with the exception of Granville and Hartington, followed his lead. But Gladstone was definitely in favour of the Board; declaring it (in conversation with Granville) to be "the only hopeful means of securing crown and state from an ignominious surrender in the next parliament after a mischievous and painful struggle."

But once more he could not induce the Cabinet to support him. When on the 9th of May the majority rejected the proposal he felt that an opportunity had been lost which would never recur. "Ah, they will rue the day," he said of the peers who had rejected the policy. "Within six years, if it please God to spare their lives, they will be repenting in sackcloth and ashes!" These were prophetic words. He foresaw all the strife and misery and heartbreak that were yet to emerge from the Pandora's box of Ireland, which, perhaps, it was still possible to close. But even he could not foresee what a part he himself was to play in the tragedy.

While attempts to arrive at a solution were still being made by the Cabinet—though Ministers of both ways of thinking were resigning—and Harcourt was busily negotiating in all directions, there fell a sudden and unexpected blow which brought Gladstone's second Ministry to an untimely end. On the 8th of June, 1885, the House of Commons was debating on the Budget introduced by the Chancellor of the Exchequer, Childers. The Leader of the Conservative Opposition, Sir Michael Hicks-Beach, moved an amendment in respect of two essential proposals of the Budget. Gladstone opposed the amendment in a vigorous speech, that betrayed no signs of exhaustion, and all supposed that the Government would secure at least a small majority. But it was defeated, at a late hour of the night, by 264 votes against 252: thanks to a tactical coalition of the Conservatives with the Parnellites, which Churchill had long striven to bring about, and in consequence of the absence of some 70 Liberals.

When the surprising result of the division was announced Lord Randolph Churchill leapt upon a bench, and waving his handkerchief, cheered like a schoolboy who has at long last overthrown a stronger adversary. The Irish, in triumph, shouted "Coercion!" Only Parnell contented himself with a significant smile. The white-haired Prime Minister, however, quietly continued his letter to the Queen, which he wrote, punctually and methodically, with his own hand, at the close of every session.

On the following day the Cabinet resolved upon resignation. The Queen, who was staying at Balmoral, remonstrated. To her the crisis was not only unexpected, but inopportune. She did not believe that the Conservatives were prepared to take over the Government—and she had no wish to return to Windsor in the heat of the summer. "The Queen," she wrote to Gladstone, "is a lady—nearer seventy than sixty—whose health and strength have been most severely taxed during the forty-eight years of her arduous reign and . . . she is quite unable to rush about as a younger person and a man could do." Moreover, she did not care to be in Windsor during the confusion of Ascot Week. It was not without difficulty that she came to realize that the Prime Minister—who himself was nearer eighty than seventy—could not leave London at the very moment when he was dissolving his Government and travel to the Highlands in order to make his report. As it was, he explained in writing the reasons which, in his opinion, were forcing him to resign.

A few days later Lord Salisbury was Prime Minister, Lord Randolph Churchill had a seat in the new Cabinet, and—most visible sign of his personal triumph—Sir Stafford Northcote, whom he had pursued with such rancour, yielding to pressure, quitted the Lower House. As Lord Iddlesleigh he was transferred to the political reserve of the House of Lords.

There he would have found his late chief again—if things had gone as Queen Victoria desired. When it became clear that Gladstone's resignation was irrevocable the Queen offered him an earldom. Her observations during the few days that preceded the offer exclude the possibility of regarding it as a mark of special esteem. We may much rather suspect that she wished to facilitate the task of his successor, by translating the old man, whose Parliamentary and rhetorical gifts made him so dangerous, to a place where he could exert little influence and therefore do little damage. But she nevertheless contrived to couch her offer in gracious and well-chosen words of unwonted warmth. "It must," said Gladstone to Granville, "have cost her much to write, and it is really a pearl of great price." In his reply he vied with the Queen in the warmth of his language, assuring her that her letter would be "a precious possession to him and to his children after him." But he declined the honour. "Any service that he can render," he wrote to her,"if small, will, however, be greater in the House of Commons than in the House of Lords. . . . When the circumstances of the State cease, as he hopes they may ere long, to impose on him any special duty, he will greatly covet that interval between an active career and death which the profession of politics has always appeared to him especially to require."

It is to be presumed that the Queen was not overjoyed to receive this letter. So she had not done yet with this exasperating old man!

Then came the traditional bestowal of honours on the recommendation of the retiring Premier—there were some artists among the recipients—and then the farewell audience with the Queen, which passed off without any disturbing incident. And then Mr. Gladstone was once more a private citizen.

IN ALLIANCE WITH PARNELL

1. Interval

On the morning after the defeat of the 8th of June Mary Gladstone, still agitated by the news, wrote to a friend:

"I *cannot* take it in—that this is the End of his political life, nor can I believe it—and the worst of it is, I don't wish it not to be, and yet I know I shall mind horribly if it is. . . . Lord Acton can't bear it, because it makes Parnell King, which he thinks the very worst thing in the world. Papa is just what you would imagine—quite calm and as if being released from a very heavy burden. . . ."

The sense of liberation with which Gladstone laid down his high office—achieved with such difficulty, so long and vigorously defended—was not explained merely by the consideration with which most of his colleagues welcomed the fall of the Ministry— that they were excepted from the apparently irreconcilable differences of opinion which divided the Cabinet in respect of the Irish question. He felt the urgent need of a pause, of an interval of physical refreshment after his superhuman exertions—an interval of calm meditation upon the experiences of the past few years, and of consideration as to his own attitude in the future.

Physical relaxation the physicians declared to be absolutely necessary. When Gladstone had retired from the turmoil and urgency of the last days of his Government to the quietude of his beloved Hawarden the inevitable reaction set in. An especially menacing symptom was the complete exhaustion of the nerves of the larynx. The greatest living orator of the British Empire seemed in danger of losing that marvellous voice whose tones had been a delight and an inspiration to millions of his fellow-countrymen. Dr. Semon, the great throat specialist, who had left his German home to achieve a successful career in England, prescribed absolute silence. The patient must be "silent as a Trappist"; then all might yet be well.

It was important, then, that he should be released at once from all political activity. In earlier years wealthy friends of his had vied with one another in inviting him to join them on an autumn voyage. By these voyages his health had always benefited greatly. Now again a friend of his, Lord Brassey, placed his yacht, the *Sunbeam*, at his disposal for a voyage to Norway, and Gladstone thoroughly enjoyed the fresh sea breezes, the new impressions, the respectful enthusiasm of the Norwegians, and the excursions ashore, on which he astonished his younger companions by his inexhaustible endurance and his imperturbable good humour. At the beginning of September he returned to England completely recovered and refreshed, and in full possession of his voice, to find himself confronted at once with the necessity of making the most difficult decisions. The weeks following his return were described by Mary Gladstone in her diary as the time of "the crisis as to the Leadership of the Liberal Party."

Once more he was faced with the problem which he thought he had solved a decade earlier, only to go back on his resolve. Should he continue his political activity, or should he retire from the Leadership of the Liberal Party? This time, undoubtedly, the decision must be final. If he now resigned the Leadership of the Party, this would mean that he would withdraw once and for all into the background, and perhaps that he would soon disappear altogether. But if he retained the Leadership, this might mean that he would once more have to form a Government; for in a few months' time a General Election would be held, with a greatly increased electorate, and it was by no means impossible that it would mean another victory for the Party.

But after the experiences of the last five difficult years he felt little desire to form another Government, nor again to be Queen Victoria's Prime Minister. That the Queen would not welcome his return he knew very well. And he realized as clearly that she could make things very difficult for him. She was growing more militant with increasing age, and no mentality could have been more antithetical to his own. "Horse-Guards all over," was his comment on a particularly warlike letter written by the Queen in February 1884; and even the gentle Granville had observed, sarcastically, that "the Queen should ask the Empress Eugénie whether she now thinks she was right in urging her husband to undertake the Mexican war as well as the Franco-German war."

Even worse than the material differences of opinion, in respect of which Gladstone may have admitted subsequently, now and again, that the Queen was in the right, were her constant attempts to control him in respect of the details of government—as, for example, in questions of personnel. When in August 1881 she protested, through Ponsonby, against Leonard Courtney's appointment as Under-Secretary for the Colonies, although, in point of constitutional law, her sanction was not required in the case of such appointments, the indignant Prime Minister circulated Ponsonby's letter among the leading members of the Cabinet, with the following comment: "I think this intolerable. It is by courtesy only that these appointments are made known to her Majesty."

She criticized not only the speeches of his colleagues, but also his own, in severe and acrimonious tones, yet it sometimes came out that she had not even read the speech of which she complained; but she did not think fit to apologize when her mistake had been pointed out to her. "No schoolmaster could govern a school on such principles; there had been no expression of regret," Gladstone complained in his diary. If she thought she had discovered him at fault she rebuked him in unsparing terms, which would have been more fittingly employed to a youthful gentleman in waiting rather than to a venerable statesman whose deeds were recorded on many a page of English history.

In August 1883 Donald Currie, one of the wealthiest of British shipowners, invited Gladstone for a voyage on his splendid yacht, the *Pembroke Castle*, as one of a distinguished company which included Tennyson and old friends like Algernon West and Laura Tennant. The yacht made a longer voyage than was originally intended, and one day she dropped anchor off Copenhagen. The King of Denmark, who was a blood relation or a connection by marriage of most of the European sovereigns, happened at the time to be entertaining a few crowned heads, among them the

374

Tsar and Tsarina, and the King and Queen of Greece. Since even crowned heads are subject to the weakness of wanting to see what the celebrities are like of whom they read every day in the newspapers, the whole illustrious company presently came on board, and the King of Denmark honoured Gladstone, Tennyson and the rest with an invitation to the castle, where they spent a very enjoyable day in the midst of the whole royal family of Denmark.

But the Prime Minister had forgotten Her Majesty, and overlooked the fact that he should have had the Queen's permission to leave England and English waters. She, however, rebuked him for this formal misdemeanour in a letter full of indignation and resentment, and she further complained to Granville of his chief's "escapade." "The Prime Minister," she said, "is not a person who can go about where he likes with impunity," and "is not gifted with prudence in speech."

Naturally in the conversations between Gladstone and his royal visitors and hosts all political subjects were carefully avoided on either side. But it is possible that the Queen was not above resenting the fact that such honours as are commonly paid only to crowned heads should be vouchsafed to the Prime Minister whom she so disliked.

She rebuked him, and "he bore it with a smile." But the continual annoyance which he suffered while in office brought him sometimes to the verge of desperation. Walking one day with Rosebery, in January 1883—that is, before the worst dissensions in respect of the Gordon relief expedition—he suddenly exclaimed: "The Queen alone is enough to kill a man"; and when Rosebery laughed he continued: "This is no laughing matter, though it may sound so"; and he enumerated half a dozen instances in which the Queen had added to his difficulties. At this time he knew nothing of many of the letters by which she was seeking to aggravate the dissensions between his colleagues, to say nothing of her curious correspondence with Wolseley and his wife.

And while he felt little inclination to serve another term as the Queen's Prime Minister, he had also to confess that he had not always been successful as the head of his Cabinet. He had often been defeated in respect of important questions; had frequently

375

made concessions which he afterwards repented; and all too often his authority had been insufficient to effect a compromise between contradictory views, and the Cabinet had broken up without achieving any practical result, so that it gave observers the impression that it lacked a hand at the helm. The preconceived opinion of many persons that the G.O.M. would rule his Cabinet like a despot had proved to be only too far removed from the truth. Lord Acton once said, very truly, that Gladstone's authority was greatest over the mass of the electorate, less in Parliament, and least of all in his Cabinet. In Parliament he was lacking in those petty yet indispensable arts which make a political instrument of human vanity; instead of shaking hands with his disciples, right and left, thanking this Member for a speech just delivered, and encouraging that Member to make another, he hurried straight through the corridors to seek with all possible speed a spot where he could write his letter to the Queen without being disturbed.

How much more adroit had Disraeli's behaviour been! At the end of the session he still remained perhaps for an hour in his place, and every one of his supporters who so desired could exchange a few words with him. But in Gladstone's case it was all the Liberal Whip could do to induce him to sacrifice a few minutes now and again, in order to have some conversation with at least the more important of his followers. Those who sat at his table were amazed by the richness and variety of his conversation and his interests —but how few could partake of this pleasure!

Even the members of his Cabinet often had reason to complain that he did not admit them sufficiently to his confidence and that he took no personal interest in them. Even a man in Lord Rosebery's position, whose brilliant personality was assuredly not unappreciated by Gladstone, had to confess after a visit that the Prime Minister had not spoken a word about his own affairs, although he had previously discussed them in his letters. In the Cabinet his tendency to hedge about his point of view by so many parentheses that no one could be quite sure which side he was really taking often did him a certain amount of harm. The material differences between the Ministers were considerable, and men like Chamberlain and Dilke on the one side, and Hartington on the other, were not disposed to diminish them. While Dilke and Chamberlain were only too quick to find a formula to express a very definite point of view, Hartington was only too slow to arrive at a definite opinion—often enough after the Cabinet had risen, and then he held to it with inflexible determination. The two former were indispensable by reason of their influence on the masses, and especially on the urban and rural working classes, and the latter because of his extraordinary reputation with the aristocracy and the upper middle class, who greatly preferred, as their leader, the eldest son of the great and renowned house of Cavendish rather than the screwmaker from Birmingham.

The seed of discord which had threatened the party had sprung up into dangerous weeds now that the Diadochi were quarrelling in public. The discord was more obvious than ever in the electoral contest, for Chamberlain had announced his own "unauthorized programme," which comprised sweeping social and political demands, and which was publicly opposed by Hartington and the moderate Liberals. Could the aged Gladstone trust himself to control this unruly team with the energy at his command in the seventy-seventh year of his life? But if he dropped the reins, who could pick them up? With all his weaknesses and limitations, was there anyone else who could compare with him in personality, authority, popularity, experience and wisdom? Would not his beloved Party, the Party whose greatness was his achievement, and which had uplifted him to greatness, fall asunder? So Harcourt believed, among others. His labours in the Cabinet, in co-operation with Gladstone, had transformed him from a fault-finding critic into a devoted personal disciple. Gladstone, he declared, was "the only universal amalgam" of the Party. When in May 1885 the dissensions within the Cabinet were threatening at any moment to disrupt it, Harcourt described the state of the party by a simile: "The Liberal Party is like a first-rate man-of-war just going into a general action, the ship sound, the crew eager to fight and win, and the Captain looked up to with enthusiasm. Only the gentlemen in the gunroom insist on blowing out their own and others' brains just before going into action, and so the ship is captured."

The material differences of opinion and other difficulties would not be less in future: that was certain. They were even bound to become greater, since the Irish question, so largely responsible for intestine dissension, was become more and more urgent. Although in other respects the most divergent views were held of the outcome of the General Election at the end of the year, upon one point all were unanimous: Parnell would return to the House more powerful than ever. The great majority of the one hundred Irish seats would be captured by men who would be under Parnell's command, and he would use his power relentlessly in order to impose his will upon Parliament. His specific intentions were shrouded in the secrecy and silence to which he was so addicted, and which impressed his subordinates as greatly as it irritated them, while it kept the political augurs busy.

In one case, of course, even the expected reinforcement of Parnell's party would be unavailing: namely, if the two great English parties were to combine for the purpose of defence. But it was just this that was becoming more impossible with every day of Conservative government.

Gladstone was aware that the Parliamentary ambush to which he owed the fall of his Government was the result of a conspiracy between the Conservatives and Parnell. The Irish knew that the majority of the Cabinet was in favour of renewing Coercion; and the Conservatives gave them an assurance that if they were returned to power they would govern Ireland without coercive legislation. This had been the avowed policy of Churchill, who behaved as though the overthrow of the Liberals on the 8th of June had been his personal victory, and who was rewarded by a seat in the Cabinet. But Gladstone was able to conclude, from many indications, that the Conservatives were ready to satisfy Parnell's requirements, not only in the matter of Coercion, but also in respect of a much more important and comprehensive question, namely, Home Rule.

The most significant indication to this effect was that Salisbury had appointed as Lord-Lieutenant of Ireland—with a seat in the Cabinet into the bargain—Lord Carnarvon, who was definitely in favour of Home Rule. Lord Carnarvon was in many respects a representative of one of the finest types of the English aristocracy.

A man of independent convictions, he had twice—in 1867 and 1878—resigned from his office as Minister rather than co-operate in a policy of which he could not approve. Highly cultivated, a classical scholar, capable of improvising an oration in Latin, he occupied his leisure with the translation of Homer. Benevolent and warm-hearted, he was keenly sensible of the misery prevailing in Ireland, and he considered how it could be alleviated. Among the possible remedies he did not exclude a separate Irish Parliament. It was known that he was greatly interested in the views of Sir Charles Gavan Duffy, one of those Catholic Irishmen who were persecuted at home as revolutionaries, and who had achieved a distinguished career overseas as a Colonial administrator. Sir Charles, with the approval of the Irish, had publicly advocated a Conservative Home Rule policy. Carnarvon had accepted the position of Lord-Lieutenant under the express condition that he would not apply Coercion. "I object," he said, "to founding our policy on the renewal of a Coercion Bill. My colleagues will in conjunction with me consider the whole future policy of the government of Ireland." The Government must approach the Irish problem absolutely without prejudice; which meant that a conversion to Home Rule was at all events conceivable.

Of what was done and said in the councils of the Party while the Conservative Cabinet was being formed, Gladstone had no knowledge. But it was plain to him that what Lord Carnarvon had said was the Government's official declaration, and that the Government was opposed to Coercion and in favour of conciliation. He saw that the Irish people, who had constantly threatened Spencer, gave Carnarvon a joyful and friendly welcome, and he could guess who and what was at the back of this. But what he did not know was that Parnell, who had fled from any personal contact with the Liberal Government, had met Lord Carnarvon, in all secrecy on the 1st of August, in an unoccupied dwelling-house in the West End. There, undisturbed, they had discussed Irish policy, and the result of that discussion was something like an alliance between the Conservative viceroy and the Irish party leader. The fact of this meeting was a secret known to only three persons apart from Carnarvon and Parnell; the go-betweens on either side who had brought about the meeting, and—the Prime Minister, Lord Salisbury. Not only had he given his approval beforehand of the secret meeting, but Carnarvon afterwards gave him an exact account of the conversation. So well was the secret kept that it was first divulged forty years later, in Lord Carnarvon's biography. Salisbury not only concealed the whole matter from his own Cabinet, but after Parnell himself had published the fact of the interview, he obstinately refused to allow Carnarvon to state that he had known anything of it. He thought it best to conceal his part in the matter even from the Queen.

While Gladstone, of course, had no exact knowledge of this interview, he was none the less able to draw his conclusions when Salisbury, in October, spoke in an electoral address of the extension of the English institution of self-government to Ireland, and of the advantages which a central authority possessed over merely local authorities. This speech did not, of course, pledge the Conservative Party leader to anything, but it helped to arouse in the Irish the hope that he would show understanding for their aims if they were victorious in the elections. Even before this, in a debate on one of the worst of the Irish assassinations (at Maamtrasna), not only Lord Randolph Churchill, but also Sir Michael Hicks-Beach, the Chancellor of the Exchequer and Leader of the House, had made speeches which seemed to suggest that the Government was moving away from Lord Spencer and approaching Parnell, so that even the Queen protested against this playing with fire.

Any doubts as to what was happening behind the scenes were dispelled by Parnell's electoral manifesto of the 21st of November. He requested the Irish voters everywhere to vote against the Liberal candidates. So he revenged himself for Kilmainham; and so, above all, he prepared the way for the policy toward which he had long been making: the policy of attaining a position in Parliament which would enable him to play the rival parties against each other.

Even in the ranks of the Irish politicians this surprising change of front was not universally welcomed. Tim Healy, who already regarded Parnell with considerable mistrust, saw in Gladstone the only man who could solve the Irish problem. To the Radical Labouchere, who in these uncertain times was able to indulge his arachnoid talents to the full, he wrote that Gladstone was the only one who had shown no bitterness, and had kept the controversy *in den regionen, wo die reinen Formen wohnen.*

After all these happenings the idea of a common front of Conservatives and Liberals, which should reject the Irish demands, was naturally abandoned—if it had ever been seriously entertained. To Gladstone it was clear that this manœuvre of the Conservatives had so altered the situation that a return even to the conditions obtaining before his overthrow was impossible. The Irish problem must be solved! But the man who dared to grasp the torch which should lead his followers out of the wilderness would quite possibly ignite a powder-barrel.

When Gladstone asked himself whether he was called upon to take this mission upon himself, his psychological situation was like that of Bismarck in 1877, which the Chancellor described by one of his memorable similes—by the image of a sportsman, wearily plodding homewards in the twilight after roaming the woods all day. You could not make him turn back by telling him that there was a covey of partridges close at hand, but you could if you informed him that there were wild boars in the next thicket.

He was, of course, confronted with an immediate and enormous difficulty. Could he pledge his Party to accomplish a task which had hitherto been excluded from its programme? Even though the great majority of Liberals had privately regarded all the Irish Coercion Acts with varying degrees of abhorrence, it was extremely doubtful whether they were disposed toward a positive fulfilment of the Irish demands.

He could be quite assured of Lord Hartington's opposition. During the electoral campaign he had expressed, in continual polemics against Parnell, his absolute opposition to Home Rule, and even Gladstone's most urgent admonitions had not persuaded him to express himself with greater reserve. But was greater willingness to be expected from the opposite wing—from Chamberlain and Dilke? In the spring they had been advocating, not Home Rule instead, but a policy of extreme conciliation. But now?

In the meantime Parnell had put an affront upon them of whose seriousness he seemed to be wholly unaware. Hitherto he had kept in touch with them through O'Shea, but now, thanks to his *rapprochement* with the Conservatives, he thought that he had no further need of them. The more Chamberlain pressed him— through O'Shea—to declare himself plainly, the more evasive and ungracious he became, and in July—in the very week when the interview with Carnarvon was arranged—Chamberlain came to the conclusion that Parnell did not wish to speak out.

And further, the Irish Press, apparently at Parnell's dictation, by violent personal attacks on Chamberlain and Dilke, made it impossible for them to pay an intended visit to Ireland. Chamberlain was not the man to hesitate when his plans were thwarted. He told O'Shea, in a few blunt words, that he washed his hands of the affair. In the place of a probable friend Parnell had now an open adversary, of whose power he had no just conception.

In October Gladstone invited Chamberlain to Hawarden for a friendly explanation. He had expected to find in him a great measure of agreement in respect of Ireland. But for Chamberlain a great many other questions were of more importance than the Irish, and his agreement with Gladstone's views was more apparent than real. Neither of the men spoke his whole mind. When Parnell's electoral manifesto appeared Chamberlain wrote to Labouchere that Parnell was against them. He had foreseen as much. Parnell had tricked his associates and deceived many of his own friends. "I really think," said Chamberlain, "he will force us all, Radicals and Liberals, to reject all arrangement with him." And a little later he declared: "I am convinced from personal observation that the workman will not stand much more in the way of Irish conciliation or concessions to Parnell."

When Chamberlain wrote these letters he knew that his comrade in arms, Dilke, would be placed *hors de combat*, at least for a long time to come. In July 1885 Dilke was accused by another Member of guilty relations with his wife, and he had to look forward to appearing as co-respondent in the Divorce Court. The case, which was first heard in February 1886, was the political ruin of Dilke, in whom his friends had seen the future Radical Prime Minister. It was the parallel and prelude to a tragedy which was to have. even more far-reaching consequences: the Parnell-O'Shea tragedy.

In this year of preparation Mr. Gladstone had been in correspondence with Mrs. O'Shea, in order to gain authentic information of Parnell's plans and intentions. After the Phoenix Park murders Parnell had felt the need of negotiating with Gladstone directly. But as he shrank from visiting him openly, and as Gladstone would not hear of secret interviews in the style of Lord Carnarvon's, Katherine O'Shea acted as Parnell's envoy. Their few personal interviews were restricted to the year 1882. But in 1885 she often received letters for Parnell, some of them written by Gladstone himself, some by his chief Whip, Lord Richard Grosvenor. What Gladstone wanted to know was whether an understanding with Parnell was possible. By the end of July he had to abandon the attempt as fruitless. The secret interview with Carnarvon was about to take place.

Five years later, when the catastrophe overtook Parnell, Gladstone was often accused of hypocrisy, because he had known of Parnell's adulterous relation with Katherine O'Shea and had none the less employed her as go-between. But it is very doubtful whether he was really aware of the nature of their relation. It was not his way to listen to the gossip of lobby and corridor, and Herbert Gladstone, who knew his father well, denied that he knew anything of the matter. He had certainly reason to take it for granted that Mrs. O'Shea's part in these negotiations was not in any way disagreeable to her husband. For O'Shea himself had suggested t Herbert Gladstone, with whom he was on friendly terms, that his wife would be a suitable go-between. And there was more: in 1885, when O'Shea was hard put to it to find a constituency, Mrs. O'Shea made use of her relations with Gladstone and Grosvenor to obtain for her husband a Liberal candidature in Liverpool.

The conclusions which Gladstone drew from the involved situation were that he was not in a position to retire, but that he could not yet lay down any definite Irish policy. On the 5th of October he wrote to Granville: "I remain at present in the leadership of the Party, first with a view to the election, and secondly with a view to being, by a bare possibility, of use afterwards in the Irish question if it should take a favourable turn." On the 17th of

383

September he issued his address to his electors in Midlothian, which spoke of a solution of the Irish question, but in phrases so general that no one could say how far he was prepared to go. He observed the same caution in his election speeches, which he delivered with all the fire of youth, and which aroused his faithful Scots to their wonted enthusiasm.

Then came the elections, and the results were truly remarkable. Gladstone himself was victorious in Midlothian, winning by a two-thirds majority, a fairly conclusive proof that his popularity had not suffered under the ill-success of his Government. On the whole, the Tories were successful in the English boroughs, and especially in London. But in the rural constituencies, where the new electors, and especially the agricultural labourers, registered their votes, the Liberals won victory after victory; 331 Liberals were returned as against 251 Conservatives. They were therefore justified in regarding the result of the election as a national vote of confidence.

But—and this "but" was an important qualification—Parnell was returned with 86 followers. Ireland had elected 85 Parnellites, 18 Conservatives, and not a single Liberal. Parnell, if he allowed his faction to go over to the Conservatives, would make a Liberal Government impossible. If numbers only counted, he could boast that he had achieved his aim: in the new Parliament his was the deciding voice. It seemed that Lord Acton's prophecy was fulfilled: Parnell was king.

2. *Home Rule*

It was the 8th of June, 1886; the time, between one and two o'clock in the morning. The Speaker of the House of Commons announced, while the Members listened in tense and breathless silence, the result of the division on Gladstone's Home Rule Bill. The Noes had it: 343 against 313! The victors—Conservatives and Liberal Unionists—leapt from their seats, climbed upon the benches, waved their hats, and cheered in a turmoil of enthusiasm that continued for some minutes, and the cheers were repeated again and again. For the first time in his life the Premier—now in his seventy-eighth year—seemed to collapse under the weight of a task that exceeded even his powers. In vain the Irish members tried to encourage him by a stormy ovation. Then they turned with passionate hatred on the man who had killed the Bill, and their shouts of "Judas! Traitor!" followed Chamberlain until he had left the House.

. . . . .

6th of December, 1921. Downing Street; the time, three o'clock in the morning. Seven English Ministers and five Irish delegates were signing the "Articles of the Agreement for a Treaty between Great Britain and Ireland," which created an "Irish Free State" with its own Parliament and its own Government under the English Crown. The English Ministers who were the first to affix their signatures were the Liberal Prime Minister, David Lloyd George, who had first entered Parliament as a supporter of Gladstone, Joseph Chamberlain's son Austen, and Winston Churchill, the son of Lord Randolph Churchill, who had once whetted the passions of the opponents of Home Rule with his "Ulster will fight and Ulster will be right!" But the Irishmen who affixed their signatures to the document, writing their names in the Irish form, which was barely intelligible to the English, were not constitutional Parliamentarians of the stamp of Parnell and McCarthy—the Irish had sent the Parliamentary party packing—but blood-bespattered revolutionaries who had shot from behind the hedges at English soldiers and policemen; like that Michael O'Coileain, whom the English called Michael Collins, and who only a few months later was himself shot dead on the highway, slain by the bullets of his own irreconcilable countrymen.

. . . . .

These two dates enclose the tragedy of the conflict between England and Ireland, a thirty-five years' campaign which brought endless misery to countless men and women, exposed the British Empire to the peril of a civil war before the outbreak of the World War, caused a revolution during the World War, and gave rise to years of guerilla warfare and murder and incendiarism after the World War. The solution emerging from all this strife differs in

385

one essential point from that proposed by Gladstone: Protestant Ulster is separated from the Irish Free State; but it has dissolved the tie which bound Great Britain and Ireland far more radically than Gladstone ever intended, or than Ireland's then representatives desired.

. . . . .

It is in the light of this historic experience that we should regard the self-appointed task to which Gladstone devoted himself in his seventy-eighth year, and to which he sacrificed not only the last years of his active life, but also the unity of his Party.

When the result of the elections of November and December 1885 was known, all three party leaders were confronted with decisions of the greatest consequence.

Lord Salisbury could strike the balance of his flirtation with the Irish. Their help, in the election, had given him some twenty contested constituencies: that is, it had sufficed to deprive the Liberal majority of their superiority over all conceivable combinations. But it was not enough to enable him to continue in office. His Government would have been completely dependent upon Parnell. This, for the proud Lord Salisbury and his party, would have been intolerable. There would have been one way out—if the right wing of the Liberals had broken away from their party and had formed a coalition with the Conservatives. This was the Queen's desire; it was a solution which she passionately recommended. She conjured Salisbury in the most pathetic manner not to leave her in the lurch, especially in view of the problems of foreign policy—she was greatly engrossed by the insurrection of the Bulgars under the leadership of Alexander of Battenberg. She called for a strong coalition of all moderate parties, and appealed for help to Goschen in particular; he must see that the Government did not fall "into the reckless hands of Mr. Gladstone, who can persuade himself that everything he takes up is right, even though it be calling black, white, and wrong, right." Goschen would gladly enough have obeyed this summons, but that he had to confess that the Conservatives had not "any practicable alternative policy for solving the Irish problem." But Lord Hartington, without whom Goschen's accession was valueless, was far too loyal to consider changing his party.

Through General Ponsonby the Queen conveyed the same idea to Sir William Harcourt, whom she regarded with special favour; but for him the thought of splitting the Liberal Party was the most intolerable of all notions, so that Ponsonby had to return with a flat refusal.

For the time being, then, this solution was impracticable, and Salisbury, without undue hesitation, abandoned his policy of coquetting with the Irish. As he himself confessed to Carnarvon years later, he had—unlike the latter—not the slightest inclination to satisfy the nationalistic desires of Ireland. And now, it seemed to him, it was time to make this difference, hitherto concealed, perfectly clear. He laid Carnarvon's policy before the Cabinet, and the Cabinet rejected it unanimously, only the Viceroy himself voting for it. Carnarvon wished to resign immediately, but at the request of his colleagues he agreed to preserve appearances by postponing his resignation. But the news leaked out, and an indiscretion on the part of a journalist led to his resignation in January. The Queen, however, told Lord Salisbury that Carnarvon had let the reins slip and had governed Ireland badly.

With this a chapter of Conservative party politics was definitely closed. No one doubted that the second step—the adoption by the Conservatives of the policy of Coercion—would soon follow.

Parnell, of course, was not slow to perceive that as far as the Conservatives were concerned he had played his part, and that it would no longer pay him to support them. The question was whether it would now be possible to come to an understanding with Gladstone.

On the 29th of December, 1885, the Queen wrote to Goschen: "I am convinced that Gladstone has persuaded himself again that it is his mission to do great things for Ireland." In her deeply-rooted aversion for Gladstone the Queen read into his mind more than had yet taken shape there. For the truth was that he had not yet persuaded himself of his mission; he was still wrestling with his destiny, hoping that he might be spared this hardest task of all.

The weeks that followed the elections he spent at Hawarden,

constantly pondering over the Irish question, often conferring and corresponding with the leading members of his party: with Hartington, Granville and Spencer. The old system of ruling Ireland by the methods and in accordance with the desires of the English landowners was, as Salisbury had quite rightly emphasized, gone for ever. A new system must replace it. If the Government did not wish to return to the brutal expedients of beleaguerment and coercion, it must decide upon a system which would meet with the approval of the Irish themselves. After the result of the elections no one could repeat and no one could believe the old fable, that the Irish population were not in agreement with Parnell. But Gladstone saw more than this. He saw that Parnell did not by any means represent the most dangerous variant of Irish policy. "There is a Parnell party," he wrote to Hartington, "and a separation or civil war party, and the question which is to have the upper hand will have to be decided in a limited time." And so—he seems to have concluded—one must help Parnell in order to avoid civil war.

The first decades of the twentieth century have shown how correctly he judged the situation. But the result of his consultations was not altogether satisfactory. One thing, however, did give him great satisfaction: Lord Spencer, who really knew what it meant to wage war against the insurgent Irish people, and who in the spring of that year had still been an advocate of the policy of the strong hand, had now come round to his way of thinking. From Granville, whose personal devotion to his old friend outweighed all other motives, no difficulties were to be anticipated. But Hartington, who confessed, in confidence, that he found it difficult to follow Gladstone in conversation, persisted in an attitude of flat negation, and he proclaimed as much in public.

But while Gladstone, on principle, carefully avoided binding himself by any public utterance, his son Herbert surprised the world by a sensational announcement.

Herbert Gladstone, even during the electoral contest, had frankly confessed that he was in favour of Home Rule. It goes without saying that he was constantly discussing this question of the day with his father, and that he did his best to urge Mr. Gladstone to follow his example. On the other hand, he was in regular correspondence with Labouchere, who seems, in this crisis, to have played, more and more definitely, the part which Germanic mythology has attributed to the squirrel that whisked in and out of the boughs of the world-tree Ygdrasil. Busybodies and newsmongers came to him from every political camp, and he with visible satisfaction reported to Peter what he had heard from Paul. Once Lord Randolph Churchill sought him out, declaring that he had nothing to do in the India Office, and threatening, for Gladstone's benefit, that he would mobilize 90,000 Ulstermen to fight Home Rule. On another occasion Healy confided to him that Parnell was half-crazy, was hiding himself, and was led by his underlings, who were all for an understanding with Gladstone, the only man with a heart and a head for this task. Then again Chamberlain wrote to him that he by no means shared Gladstone's longing to return to office. And Labouchere delightedly regaled each confidant with what he had learned from the rest.

Labouchere now put Herbert Gladstone on his guard; there were those who were intriguing against his father. On the one hand the Whigs—for example, Lord Hartington, and Lord Robert Grosvenor, the late Liberal Whip—and on the other hand Chamberlain and Dilke, were endeavouring to shoulder the Irish question into the background, and so to eliminate Gladstone as regarded the future. On receiving this warning at Hawarden Herbert Gladstone hastened to London, where he was told by Liberal journalists that "without any information the Liberal Press throughout the country was perplexed and confused." It ought to be given a hint as quickly as possible, to prevent it from adopting an anti-Home Rule attitude.

Without previously consulting his father, Herbert Gladstone, on the 16th of December, gave certain "information" to the head of a large news agency. On the following morning the newspapers published an exhaustive account of Gladstone's ideas on the Irish question, citing as their source his son and confidential collaborator. The newspapers said a great deal more than Herbert Gladstone had intended, but he had committed the blunder of neglecting to stipulate that the articles should be submitted to him before publication.

The result was not at all what Herbert Gladstone had expected.

389

Protests rained upon him from every side. "Fat all in the fire," he himself wrote in his diary. Gladstone had to despatch reassuring letters and telegrams in all directions. He declared publicly that he was in no way responsible for the interview; that it was not an accurate representation of his views, but a "speculation" on them. But in vain! Everyone believed that the "Hawarden kite," though flown by the son, was the work of the father.

Then Gladstone made a last attempt to save Ireland from becoming the apple of party discord. Not far from Hawarden was the seat of his friend the Duke of Westminster, and Arthur Balfour, the nephew and political collaborator of Lord Salisbury, was visiting the Duke. One day Gladstone suddenly made his appearance there, and drew Balfour into confidential conversation. This interview was presently followed up by a letter. In this Gladstone laid great emphasis on the fact that it would be a public misfortune "if this great subject should fall into the lines of party conflict." He hoped that the *present* Government would deal with the matter. If it did so he was prepared to support it. "You are at liberty," he said, "if you think desirable, to mention this to Lord Salisbury." This meant, of course, that Balfour was invited to mention it.

This was the last opportunity of closing Pandora's box. It was allowed to pass. Salisbury laid Gladstone's proposal before the Cabinet. Lord Carnarvon was not present, and the rest of the Ministers voted unanimously against it. Gladstone had to be content with the courteous response that the Government did not wish to make any announcements before the speech from the Throne. This was plain speaking enough. He knew that the die was cast. The Rubicon *must* be crossed, and it was his destiny to be the first to venture on the crossing; for at the last elections the people had expressed their trust in him as their appointed leader.

Now events moved quickly: the opening of Parliament, the debate on the Address, and the unavailing attempts of the Government to provoke Gladstone into declaring his plans for Ireland. He explained that he preferred to retain his freedom of action, and as an "old Parliamentary hand" (the words were remembered as a sort of nickname) he advised the new Members to do the same.

On the 26th of January the Government announced that they intended to introduce new coercive legislation. Now was the time for action—the time to overthrow the Government. Gladstone informed Harcourt of his decision. "What?" cried Harcourt, incredulous: "Are you prepared to go forward without either Hartington or Chamberlain?" A few hours later the thing was done. A Liberal amendment to the Address—it demanded the agrarian policy for which Chamberlain had coined the slogan "Three acres and a cow"—was accepted by 331 votes against 252. The majority included 74 of the Irish, but 18 Liberals voted with the minority. Among them was not only Goschen, but also Lord Hartington and Sir Henry James, who had been Attorney-General in the last Liberal Ministry, and who, by so voting, threw away his chance of the Woolsack; 76 Liberals refrained from voting, among them John Bright. The rift in the Party was apparent.

On the following day Salisbury resigned. With a sigh Queen Victoria had to dismiss him and send for Gladstone, since even Goschen, to whom she appealed again, could suggest no other solution. Before January was out Gladstone was engaged in forming his third Cabinet.

It was a depressing task, for now he was to see who would forsake him and who follow.

On the right wing of the Party, Lord Hartington, Lord Derby, Lord Northbrook, Lord Selborne (hitherto Lord Chancellor), Sir Henry James, and of course Goschen, refused office, while Lords Granville, Spencer, Kimberley and Rosebery came aboard the Government craft. The refusal of Hartington, the representative of the great house of Cavendish, spelt the end of the supremacy of the Whig aristocracy in the Liberal Party, the close of a period which had endured for two hundred years. For a man so rooted in tradition as Gladstone this was an especially grievous loss.

The loss of the Whigs gave added importance to another question: How far could he persuade the left wing to collaborate with him? That old John Bright had refused to do so was not surprising; but his absence was soon felt. Of decisive importance—since Dilke was no longer available, owing to his personal catastrophe—was Chamberlain's attitude. Gladstone was bound to do his very utmost to gain him for the Cabinet. But either he misjudged the real significance of Chamberlain, or he had misgivings in respect of the man and his policy which caused him to approach him with a certain reluctance. The office which he proposed was the Admiralty, which was not likely to tempt him greatly. When he declined it, the Prime Minister asked him: "Then what office would you prefer?" "The Colonial Office," said Chamberlain. "Oh! A Secretary of State!" replied Gladstone; and the refusal so indicated must have mortified Chamberlain deeply, because of the implied motive: for it sounded as though he were not considered good enough for one of the higher and more authoritative offices. Finally they both agreed on the Local Government Board, which at all events was not a particularly showy post. Chamberlain made no secret of his objections to Gladstone's Irish plans, and he agreed to join the Cabinet only when the Prime Minister assured him that in doing so he was not pledging himself to any particular scheme; the Cabinet would first of all have to "examine" whether it could "comply with the desire widely prevalent in Ireland for the establishment of a Legislative Body to sit in Dublin calculated to support and consolidate the unity of the Empire on the combined basis of Imperial authority and mutual attachment." This was the formula which Gladstone proposed to all whom he invited to join his Cabinet.

Although the negotiations with Chamberlain ended in a positive result, they were none the less disastrous; they showed Chamberlain that his leader neither liked him nor had any great confidence in him, and that being what he was, he found it difficult to hide his feelings. And then Gladstone made one appointment which of course was not intended to mortify Chamberlain, but which none the less was a grievous blow to his ambition: he appointed John Morley Irish Secretary and Cabinet Minister.

Morley and Chamberlain had for many years been close friends and political allies, despite the profound psychological and intellectual differences between them. Morley was a scholar, a political theorist, a historian, a literary artist; Chamberlain a practical man of action. But in spite of the fundamental dissimilarity of their standpoints, they had arrived at the same conclusions in respect of practical politics, and for many years they had journeyed on as comrades. Morley was one of the small group of Radical leaders who from time took counsel together. Their political friendship had already been subjected to a strain during these weeks of Cabinet-building, for Morley had expressed himself, publicly and emphatically, in favour of Home Rule. And now, when the delighted Morley went up to Chamberlain in order to tell him of Gladstone's magnificent offer, his old friend turned very pale. "My going to Ireland," wrote Morley in his reminiscences, "was the sudden arrival of a long apprehended peril to a cherished private intimacy, and of mischief to the commonwealth." But it was something more than this. One whom he had hitherto regarded as a younger comrade—Morley had sat only three years in Parliament—was suddenly raised to a position of greater importance than his own, and which he himself had striven for years to obtain. This was too much for him. The sensitive Morley was deeply hurt when at the first Cabinet meeting which he attended Chamberlain barely passed the time of day. But the Prime Minister had to suffer the consequences of this ill-humour.

One thing gave Gladstone great satisfaction: the willingness with which Harcourt, who had hitherto shown little liking for Home Rule, not only joined the Cabinet as Chancellor of the Exchequer, but also applied his remarkable talents to furthering his policy: the performance of the Conservatives during the previous year having convinced him that a new Irish policy was inevitable.

Lord Herschell made an eminent Lord Chancellor. But when it came to appointing a Foreign Secretary, Gladstone was confronted with a difficulty of a personal nature. Lord Granville, since the painful conflict with Bismarck, was regarded, not only by many of his own party, but above all by the Queen, as a failure. Personally he was more intimate with Gladstone than any of his colleagues, and in the last few months especially he had given signal proof of his loyalty. Nevertheless, the Prime Minister resolved to sacrifice him to the Queen's protest, in so far as he appointed him to the Colonial instead of to the Foreign Office. This was a great blow to Granville, who felt that he was ill repaid for his loyalty, and it was some days before he could reconcile himself to his fate. When he finally decided to accept the Colonial Office Mrs. Gladstone was so delighted to see their old friend return to them that she fell on his neck and kissed him. In respect of the appointment of a Foreign Secretary the Queen exerted her full authority in Lord Rosebery's favour. His winning personality pleased her, and she had confidence that he would pursue a more active and vigorous foreign policy on the lines laid down by Lord Salisbury. Further, his appointment would be well received in Berlin—he was a friend of Herbert Bismarck's, though he was soon to learn to distrust him—and in the previous spring he had carried through successful negotiations with the German Chancellor. Here too Gladstone did as the Queen desired, and this appointment met with widespread approval in the country.

On the whole, the Cabinet which Gladstone had got together greatly exceeded the expectations of the sceptics. Apart from the omissions with which he had had to reckon beforehand, it testified to the wealth of talent still at his disposal.

On the day of his appointment as Prime Minister Gladstone's daughter Mary, who had been his zealous helper, was married to the Reverend Harry Drew, the curate of Hawarden. The Londoners took advantage of this wedding to give an impressive demonstration of their affection. Enormous crowds lined the way from Carlton House Terrace to Westminster, in order to cheer the Prime Minister and his family. The Prince of Wales, the Princess of Wales and their son, the late King George V, testified to their esteem for the aged servant of the Crown by signing the marriage register as witnesses, and below their names two future Prime Ministers, Lord Rosebery and Arthur Balfour, affixed their signatures.

From the scene of the wedding Gladstone went to Osborne to wait on the Queen. Knowing what her feelings were, he cannot have had a pleasant journey. "He looked very pale as he entered, then there was a moment's pause, and he sighed deeply," she wrote in her diary. On the whole the audience passed off better than either had anticipated. Gladstone was evidently anxious to fall in with her personal wishes as far as possible. "He struck me," she wrote, "as being less Radical himself than he used to be, and as intensely in earnest, almost fanatically so, in his belief that he is almost sacrificing himself for Ireland." How completely must Gladstone have been possessed by his mission if even the Queen was not immune to this impression!

Only two months later Gladstone laid before the House of Commons the draft of his Home Rule Bill. Possibly it would have been wiser to let the new Cabinet and the new Parliament occupy themselves with other questions first, in order to find their feet and get their bearings; perhaps with one of the social problems in which Chamberlain was so greatly interested, and which would have afforded him an opportunity of showing what he could do as a legislator. But Gladstone was an old man, who could not know how many years would yet be granted him, and who therefore hastened to accomplish the one task on which his heart was set. "An old man in a hurry": the malicious term of derision coined by Churchill some years later already had some truth in it. And from the very first the Queen was persistently urging him to divulge his plans. Gladstone therefore hurried on the "examination" to which he had pledged the Cabinet at the time of its formation, and, as was to be expected, he proceeded, as quickly as possible, to frame a positive answer to the question, and a draft Bill, which the Prime Minister himself elaborated with Morley's help. It was also Morley's task to negotiate with Parnell and to make sure that the Irish would accept the Bill. He found in the Irish leader a very capable negotiator, who had a keen eye for essentials and knew when to sacrifice the non-essential, but he had no real constructive talent, and his outlook was restricted. Once the Prime Minister himself took part in the conference. The impression which he received on this first encounter with the Irishman was summed up in the words: "Very clever!"

But the more concrete the plans became, the more refractory was Chamberlain. He tendered his resignation, and Gladstone accepted it—as Chamberlain himself considered, and other members who were present at that decisive Cabinet meeting—without exerting himself unduly to persuade the resigning Minister to remain. He had evidently convinced himself that any lasting agreement with Chamberlain in respect of the Irish question was impossible, and he therefore preferred even a negative decision to prolonged vacillation. Perhaps the old man would have taken more pains to avoid or at least to postpone the breach if he had liked the younger man better. And he quite certainly underestimated the strength which Chamberlain was presently to reveal in battling against him.

On the 8th of April, 1886, when Gladstone went down to the House to make Home Rule a living issue, he never for a moment failed to realize that he was approaching the most critical point of his political career, and that he must be prepared for the most difficult battle of that career, in which he would have to face every kind of opposition from every conceivable quarter. But he knew that the spirit in which he now, in his old age, accepted battle, had found a rousing echo in the hearts of countless Englishmen. It was raining cats and dogs as he went down Whitehall from Downing Street to the House, but the whole street was black with people, who cheered him so loudly that the Members in the House were aware of his coming long before he appeared.

In the House itself not only was every seat occupied, but for the first time since the Commons had sat in St. Stephen's Palace there were chairs on the floor of the House for those who had been unable to find a place. Not only had Members been fighting for places ever since the early morning, but many had installed themselves on the green-upholstered benches the night before, in order to be sure of obtaining a seat. Side by side with the old Parliamentarians who had already seen Gladstone the victor in many a wordy battle—and in whose midst the white head of John Bright was conspicuous—there were newly-elected Members who had never yet heard the greatest of living Parliamentarians. The galleries were crowded with the diplomatic representatives of foreign Powers who wished to give their sovereigns their personal impressions of this historic session.

When Gladstone rose to speak he was greeted by the applause not of his party alone, but above all of the Irish, whose cause was now for the first time to be represented by a great English statesman. For three and a half hours he spoke, this man of seventy-eight, and not for a moment did the concentrated attention of a single listener in the House relax. Friend and foe were equally swept off their feet by this marvellous display of physical and intellectual energy, which seemed to defy all the laws to which human power is subject. Forty years later one of the most passionately militant of Irishmen, William O'Brien, lamented that no art and no technique could convey to later generations the overwhelming impression produced by that speech and that speaker. What are the mere words of the speech, as the shorthand-writer recorded them, without those things that were the soul of his greatness as a speaker? "The shorthand note is powerless . . . to bequeath to after times any adequate notion of the untranslatable things which were after all the soul of his greatness as an orator—the massive figure set foursquare to all the world's contumely in a great cause—the immense leonine head framed in its silvery mane—the great kindled eye whose expression changed in the course of a single speech from majesty to scorn and from scorn to fun, and back again to heaven-kissing sublimity—above all the incomparable melody of a voice which had the power of transmuting common words into a no less grand but a more tender Gregorian chant." Such a lament reminds us of Goethe's complaint of the song that looks to us "dismal in letters black on white." For who has the imagination that will show him the living man behind the printed words? Those who read the verbatim report fifty years after they were spoken will find a masterpiece of construction and logically ordered presentation; no passionate effusion to appeal to the emotions, but a revelation of the whole task and all the difficulties of that task, which seeks by means of reason to compel the listener to accept the speaker's conclusions. Life is breathed into the long history of Ireland and her relations with England, and that history is compared with the experiences of other states and peoples. The futility of the policy of violence is revealed, and the claim of every people to its right in its native soil is admitted. The fundamental features of the complicated measure which is to solve a multifarious problem of legislation and administration are lucidly described and justified; provision is made for possible improvements, and assurance is given that all such possibilities will be readily examined. Polemic is reduced to a minimum; the speaker's own mistakes are not glossed over; but the personality and the achievements of Lord Spencer are singled out for the warmest praise. Spencer, declared the speaker, "represented the

397

flower of the British aristocracy . . . which to high birth and influence of station unites a love of liberty and of the people as genuine as that which breathes within any cottage in the land." All the measures proposed arise from one great fundamental conception, and the peroration culminates in an impassioned appeal to Parliament to co-operate in this work of justice and conciliation.

When Gladstone, after the stupendous effort of the day, sat down to dinner in the peace of his own home, the widow of the murdered Secretary of State for Ireland, Lucy Cavendish, sat beside him again for the first time since the murders in Phoenix Park.

But the great impression produced by Gladstone's speech did not, of course, prevent his adversaries from offering the most violent opposition to his Bill. The nucleus of the Bill was the establishment of a separate Irish Parliament of two chambers, with a separate Government dependent upon it, both being competent only in Irish—as opposed to Imperial—affairs, and subject to the British Crown and the Parliament at Westminster. Irish peers and members of Parliament would no longer sit in the two British Houses of Parliament. There would be no separate fiscal system, no Irish fleet or army, and minorities—especially the Protestants—would be assured of protection. The great problem, of course, was whether such a degree of Irish independence was compatible with the unity of the Empire, and whether the Protestant minority could be protected against oppression by the Catholic majority.

Not only did the Conservatives—including Lord Randolph Churchill—unanimously deny that these things were possible, but a great proportion of the Liberals were of the same opinion. Chamberlain's violent attack made less impression on Parliament and the country than Hartington's moderately worded but actually most decided rejection of the proposals. With one stride the man who had never yet achieved anything more than a *succès d'estime* took his place in the front rank of Parliamentary speakers. He did not bewilder people by original terms of speech; what he said was just what the typical average Englishman was inclined to say, but it was for this very reason that it made so great an impression, especially as it came from the lips of a man of undisputed honour and integrity, and one of the highest social position. The Queen hastened to assure him of her gratitude and admiration; in him she saw the proof that patriotism and loyalty come before party. It says much for Hartington's firmness of character that in his reply he did not fail to stress the fact that even now party differences made any lasting coalition of Conservatives and moderate Liberals impossible. Now, of course, the Queen saw Chamberlain in quite a new light; in the past she had regarded him with apprehension and disapproval, but now that he was at odds with his former colleagues she did her best to make his position less difficult.

To Gladstone himself the Queen wrote, about a month after the Bill had been laid before the House: "The Queen can see *only* danger to the Empire in the course he is pursuing. The Queen writes this with pain as she always *wished to be able* to *give* her Prime Minister her *full support.*"

This was at the close of an exchange of letters which were highly characteristic of the two correspondents. Gladstone repeatedly referred in almost pathetic tones to the responsibility which was weighing him down: "He is deeply sensible of the considerate and gracious manner in which Your Majesty treats a question necessarily painful. It deepens the sorrow with which he finds himself, under the influence of motives which Your Majesty would never wish him to disobey, prosecuting a policy which Your Majesty has not approved. It would be great presumption on his part to mistake the mere strength of his own conviction for certain proof of being right; and he is well aware that, if he is wrong in this capital matter, all the labours and efforts of a long life cannot save his memory from disgrace. This can neither repair the mischief, nor console the sufferers."

The Queen was not appeased by such a tone. She repeated and emphasized her protest, and she criticized the manner in which Gladstone was conducting his campaign. He saw plainly enough that she was longing for the moment when the rejection of Home Rule would rid her of him.

Both in Parliament and in the country, all ranks were arming themselves for the decision. Gladstone believed that he would find more support among the electors than in the House. As a matter of fact, the greater proportion of the Liberal organizations were behind him. But Birmingham, which had always stood in the forefront of the Liberal Party, was faithful to Chamberlain when, with the courage that was all his own, he confronted his electors, and, while recognizing the principle of Home Rule, repudiated the form of Home Rule which had been proposed. It is characteristic of the Liberal electors that even those who repudiated Home Rule refused—as Goschen disconsolately informed the Queen—to co-operate with the Conservatives. A great meeting in the Covent Garden Opera House, at which Hartington and Goschen appeared in conjunction with Salisbury, aroused but the faintest echoes throughout the country.

The matter would be decided on the second reading of the Bill. The nearer it approached, the more obvious it became that Chamberlain would hold the casting-vote. The Whigs, who followed Hartington and Goschen, were not strong enough to give the Opposition the majority. But if the Radicals who followed Chamberlain were to join them Gladstone's defeat was assured. For weeks on end attempts were made to find a basis of agreement. A Land Bill which Gladstone had intended as an addendum to Home Rule in the landowner's interest was dropped on account of Chamberlain's opposition. Even in respect of the question whether the Irish Members were to remain at Westminster—as Chamberlain advocated—Gladstone was inclined to be compliant. On the 27th of May he called a meeting of the Liberal Members who accepted the principle of his Bill. Of 333 Liberals 220 attended. At this meeting he suggested a way out of their difficulty: if the second reading were accepted on principle he would allow an interval to elapse before taking the Bill through its final stage. The proposal met with approval, and it seemed as though a considerable proportion of the doubters were prepared to adopt this expedient and save the Ministry from defeat by voting for the second reading. But this hope was soon dispelled when the skilful tactics of the Opposition elicited from Gladstone the explanation that the "reconstruction" which he had led them to expect was not to be extended to the Bill as a whole, but only to the question of retaining the Irish Members at Westminster.

Now Chamberlain in his turn gathered his supporters about him. The question which he submitted to them was, whether at the second reading they should refrain from voting, or whether they should vote against the Bill. They decided to vote against it. The casting-vote lay with a Member who was not present, but who had written to Chamberlain: John Bright.

For the last time in Gladstone's career the man intervened who had been his comrade in arms in the fight for the poor man's franchise, and to whom he had been attached by mutual personal respect and by a common faith in the moral forces of political life. For Bright there were insuperable obstacles in the way of his voting for Home Rule; he regarded it, as he wrote to Gladstone, as "a measure which is offensive to the whole Protestant population of Ireland."

His point of view was influenced by his own painful experiences of the Irish Members; they had violently and unjustly assailed him in respect of a difference of opinion, and he regarded them as "rebels." His personal affection for Gladstone had prevented him from publicly opposing the Bill, but when Chamberlain urgently besought him to attend one of his meetings, he wrote a letter in which, as a matter of fact, he expressed the wish that a sufficient number of adversaries would refrain from voting to prevent the rejection of the Bill, but that for his own part he intended to vote against it. His example, not his advice, was efficacious, after Trevelyan, in persuasive language, had interpreted the letter in this sense. And with this the destiny of the Bill was decided.

The days of Parliamentary debate could no longer influence that destiny. Neither Parnell's nor Gladstone's concluding speeches had any perceptible effect on the voting. Parnell, to the astonishment of his bitterest enemies, rose to a truly statesmanlike height, and spoke with well-considered and impressive moderation, like a man who was conscious that in a little while the responsibility for the destiny of a whole nation might rest upon his shoulders: spoke as an enthusiastic Irish patriot, but also as the champion of a stable political order. At the close of his speech he made a sensational revelation: that on the eve of the last election Conservative leaders had held out hopes of an Irish legislative body in Dublin. Sir

Michael Hicks-Beach, the official leader of the Opposition, contrived to counter this revelation by a flat denial, but on the following day Lord Carnarvon, in the House of Lords, confessed to having entered into secret negotiations with Parnell.

Gladstone's concluding speech was a masterpiece of Parliamentary dialectic and persuasive eloquence. He opened fire upon the most dangerous of his opponents, Joseph Chamberlain, who had boasted that a dissolution of Parliament had no terrors for him. "I do not wonder at it," retorted the old man, in a tone of supreme irony. "He has trimmed his vessel, and he has touched his rudder in such a masterly way that in whichever direction the winds of heaven may blow they must fill his sails. Supposing that at an election public opinion should be very strong in favour of the Bill, my right honourable friend would then be perfectly prepared to meet that public opinion, and tell it: 'I declared strongly that I adopted the principle of the Bill.' On the other hand, if public opinion were very averse to the Bill he again is in complete armour, because he says, 'yes, I voted against the Bill.'" And so on, in the same style, until, as he expressed it, amidst the hilarity of the whole House, he had "nearly boxed the compass," and had shown that Chamberlain was prepared for every eventuality.

But at the close of his speech he spoke in moving tones of "Ireland . . . at your bar, expectant, hopeful, almost suppliant." With unsparing courage he confessed the blunders committed by England in her treatment of the sister isle, the darkest blot on the pages of her otherwise so glorious history. And he concluded with an appeal to the House: "Think, I beseech you; think well, think wisely, think, not for the moment, but for the years that are to come, before you reject the Bill."

．　　　．　　　．　　　．　　　．

But even this moving conjuration could not avert the rejection of the Bill, and a few days later the country was again in the turmoil of the electoral contest. The Liberal Party was disrupted; 93 Liberal Members had voted against Home Rule. Now the Liberal opponents of Home Rule formed a separate "Liberal Unionist" Party. They numbered in their ranks men like Hartington and Chamberlain,

Goschen and Bright; that is, men who were held together only by this one question. With tactical shrewdness the Conservatives withdrew their candidates where the Liberals were Liberal Unionists.

This disruption of his party was a grievous blow to Gladstone, the more so as it meant the end of many a lifelong friendship. That John Bright should have publicly opposed Gladstone was a tragedy to both. When two years later the old Quaker lay on his last bed of sickness, he bade his son send Gladstone his last message: that he could not forget the unchanging friendship which he had received from him, and the many services which he had rendered his country. The letter which Gladstone wrote in reply to this message terminated the relations of the two champions of British democracy on a note of reconciliation that was worthy of them both. Less worthy was the attitude of the Duke of Westminster, who in the days of the Balkan problem had been one of Gladstone's most zealous comrades in arms. In that period of enthusiasm he had Gladstone's portrait painted by Millais. Now he sold the portrait, that he might no longer behold those once beloved but now detested features. Charles Tennant bought it, the father of Laura and Margot Tennant, afterwards presenting it to the National Gallery.

The electoral contest was fought with a passion that led both sides to commit many blunders. It was a blunder that Gladstone, in one of his addresses, should speak of the battle which he must fight "with the masses against the classes." It was a still worse blunder that Lord Salisbury should declare that the Irish were incapable of self-government, comparing them with the Hottentots. His recipe for Ireland was "twenty years of resolute government"— that is, government by Coercion Act, and this recipe was almost literally applied.

The upshot of the elections was a heavy defeat for Gladstone. Only 191 of his supporters were elected, against 315 Conservatives and 78 Liberal Unionists. Parnell's party again numbered 86. In his own constituency Gladstone was re-elected without opposition, and in the neighbouring constituency of Edinburgh Goschen, who had opposed him with especial vehemence, lost his seat.

Election results do not constitute a final vote on a policy of such scope and novelty as Gladstone's Home Rule policy. But they afford an adequate standard for judging the tactical skill with which this policy is furthered. It was a serious error to present a policy so novel and so revolutionary to the electors in so abrupt a fashion, after so little preparation. It is true that in the six months that preceded the election there had been much talk about Irish politics, but it had not been sufficiently definite to prepare the electors for such a change of policy. After Gladstone had privately convinced himself of the necessity of such a change he believed that the electors would perceive that necessity as quickly as he had done: and this, of course, was a serious error. To ask them, now, to have confidence in Parnell and his followers, when for years they had regarded them as the enemies of England, who did not shrink even from crime, was requiring too much of them. Especially was it asking too much of the Liberals, for only six months earlier Parnell had attacked them in his electoral manifesto. His over-estimation of pure tactics and his under-valuation of psychological and material factors had done serious injury to himself and to his cause.

It goes without saying that Gladstone resigned after this defeat, and was again replaced by Lord Salisbury, to the great satisfaction of the Queen. But the great question now was whether he should abandon the fight. He was now seventy-seven years of age. The new Parliament, in which his party had shrunk to a minority, would in all human probability last for five or even six years. It was not likely that he would live to see the end of it, and it was still less probable that he would be called upon to continue his work. The simplest and most commonplace considerations must have determined the old man to lay aside the bow of Odysseus, and seek, far from the scene of strife, the rest which he had so richly deserved by more than fifty years of battle for his country and his convictions.

But such simple and commonplace considerations did not enter the mind of the vanquished leader. He saw before him the vision of Ireland as he had described her in the peroration of his last great speech: expectant, hopeful, almost suppliant. He felt himself pledged by the words in which he had pleaded the cause of Ireland before the world. He would not and could not betray the policy in whose support he had involved his loyal followers—and indeed the great majority had proved their loyalty. And he could still see no one who was capable of bending the bow of Odysseus. But he could feel his own strength reviving under the burden of the new task, and—perhaps temerariously, but heroically none the less—he took it upon himself to open up the path to liberty for this Ireland that stood waiting at the bar of the House.

3. The Great Forgery

After the turmoil and the conflict of the last few years Gladstone sought repose in the same place, and in the same company, as after his defeat in 1874; on the Tegern See, with Lord Acton and Dr. Döllinger. He found refreshment in conversation that had nothing to do with politics—talks on religion, the Church, and Homer; in the reading of French comedies, and in the agility of an old man of eighty-seven who rivalled him as a hill-climber. Returning home, he read his Homer—perhaps for the thirtieth time—with all the old delight, always discovering new beauties, and he wrote some new essays on the poet. Tennyson's latest poem, too, he made the subject of a discussion in which he opposed to the disgruntled pessimism of the poet his own unshakable faith in the blessings of progress; and a few months later he was deep in an essay on Mrs. Ward's free-thinking novel *Robert Elsmere*, in which he once more fought "the battle of faith." When this year of his greatest disappointment drew to its close he wrote, on his birthday, in his diary, that he was "quite off the line of an old man's direct preparation for passing the River of Death." But in the next sentence he made his confession: "I cannot abandon a cause which is so evidently that of my fellow-men, and in which a particular part seems to be assigned to me."

In the political world the year 1886 ended with a first-class sensation. Lord Randolph Churchill, on the formation of Salisbury's new Cabinet, was invested not only with the office of Chancellor of the Exchequer, but also with the Leadership of the House of Commons. The services which the erstwhile leader of the "Fourth Party" had rendered the Conservative cause were thus richly rewarded. The manner in which he acquitted himself as Leader of the House had earned general applause. All the greater was the amazement of the public when *The Times* two days before Christmas announced that Lord Randolph Churchill had resigned. This singular man, who as long as he was fighting his way up had somewhat unscrupulously considered the sensational rather than the practical effect of his actions, had contended with the greatest tenacity, in his capacity of Chancellor of the Exchequer, for a programme of retrenchment, and when he found that he could not disregard the protests of the Admiralty and the War Office, he not only tendered his resignation, but informed the newspapers of the fact—to the great annoyance of the Queen—before the sovereign was apprised of it. Churchill had apparently believed that by this *coup de main* he could get his way; he knew that the Conservative masses relied on him and preferred him to any other public speaker; and he knew also that in the Commons he was the strongest debater on the Treasury bench. He thought it was out of the question that Salisbury, whose party had no majority in the Lower House, could continue to govern without him. But how greatly he had under-estimated the power and the skill and the attitude of the Premier! Salisbury had no thought of surrendering. After a few days of uncertainty he was once more firmly seated and had his party well in hand, and the office which Churchill had abandoned was filled by a first-class expert. This was Goschen, the first Liberal Unionist to find his way into the Conservative Cabinet, and this with the approval of Hartington, who had himself declined to enter it. Churchill was utterly defeated. "I forgot Goschen!" he is said to have exclaimed. He had actually ruined his own political career before he had completed his thirty-eighth year. He never again filled a Ministerial office.

A few days after Churchill's political suicide the public learned of the death of the man whom Churchill had fought as long as he had led the Conservatives in the Lower House. Lord Iddlesleigh—formerly Sir Stafford Northcote—had been appointed Foreign Secretary in Salisbury's Cabinet. The Prime Minister wished to profit by the shuffling of posts occasioned by Churchill's resigna-tion by taking the Foreign Secretaryship for himself; it was a post for which he had a liking, and he was well aware of his mastery of foreign policy. In the excitement of reconstruction Lord Iddlesleigh suffered an apoplectic stroke, which led to his sudden death at Lord Salisbury's door, for he was just about to call on the Prime Minister in order to consult him. A generation earlier this adversary of Gladstone's had served him as private secretary, and Gladstone, making an obituary speech in the House of Commons, spoke of him with sympathy and appreciation.

Churchill's resignation had remarkable repercussions on the other side. "Randolph has given me a merry Christmas," Harcourt wrote to Morley. For a moment it looked as though the healing of the Liberal rift was possible. Chamberlain, who was a personal friend of Churchill's, and had found many points of political contact with him, saw his fall as the triumph of the unteachable Tories, whom he still regarded as the enemy. In a speech which he delivered on the day of Randolph's resignation he seized the occasion to hold out an olive-branch to his sometime friends. He suggested a "round table" conference, with a view to reaching an agreement. He even wrote a conciliatory Christmas letter to John Morley, who had previously been so close a friend, and who had wounded him most deeply, when on the day after the division of the 8th of June he had quoted in the Eighty Club:

> Look! in this place ran Cassius' dagger through;
> See what a rent the envious Casca made;
> Through this the well-beloved Brutus stabbed!

The "round table" conference was held, and Mark Antony and Casca took part in it. But the attempt to reach an understanding failed, though Harcourt, in particular, had done his utmost to bring it about. The only result was that Trevelyan, who with Chamberlain had represented the Unionists, returned to the Liberal Party.

So the Liberal Unionist Party was and remained a fact. It never attained to any great numerical strength, and it gradually lost its significance as an independent party. But it had a very significant influence on subsequent developments, inasmuch as it gradually shepherded into the Conservative ranks certain social and economic circles, and also many political thinkers, who by their tradition and intellectual attitude properly belonged to the Liberal camp.

Gladstone, for example, to his great sorrow, saw his own nephew, Alfred Lyttelton, go over to the Unionists; he afterwards became a member of Balfour's Cabinet.

From 1886 onwards Gladstone lost more and more of his followers in the leading social and business circles, and the notion which the members of these circles entertained of him became more and more unfavourable. The change was especially apparent in the domain of foreign policy. The two men who were mainly responsible for the Boer War—Joseph Chamberlain and Alfred Milner—were originally members of the Liberal Party, from which they seceded as Liberal Unionists. Perhaps the principal historical significance of the Liberal Unionist Party consists in this, that it lifted Chamberlain to a position in which he was able to give a new direction to British policy.

"Chamberlain's character is remarkable," wrote Gladstone to Lord Acton in January 1887, "as are in high degree his talents. It is one of my common sayings that to me characters of the political class are the most mysterious of all I meet." The old man did not live to see the full revelation of the Chamberlain mystery. But as early as 1886, after the great defeat at the polls, he had warned Bryce against him. It doesn't, of course, concern me—he said in effect—but those of you who are still in public life in twenty years' time will see what mischief Chamberlain can do.

·　　·　　·　　·　　·

In the meantime, Irish policy had relapsed into the disastrous vicious circle of suppression and rebellion. On the side of the Irish a new tendency was perceptible when the Government rejected an agrarian measure demanded by Parnell. They devised the so-called "Plan of Campaign," which amounted to this: that the tenants of a landowner would offer to pay him in common the rents which they considered fair, and if he refused they would pay him nothing at all, but hand the rents over to a campaign fund. This was incontestably an illegal procedure, and it led to an extreme aggravation of the conflict, and the victimization of many tenants, who were evicted and economically liquidated. Parnell had no share in this "Plan of Campaign," which sprang from the fertile brain of William

O'Brien. He foresaw that it would lead to a new period of Coercion, and his anticipation was correct.

On the Government side, in March 1887, there came to the fore a new protagonist who from that time onwards played an increasingly important part. Sir Michael Hicks-Beach, the Irish Secretary, had been compelled to resign by serious ophthalmic trouble, and in his place Lord Salisbury proposed to the Queen "his clever and agreeable nephew," young Balfour. This was a bold step; not only because it awakened the suspicion of nepotism, but before all because Balfour was known to the public only as a clever and witty young man, but by no means a strong personality; a man who had as yet nowhere proved his mettle. The Irish rejoiced beforehand; they were already looking forward to disposing of "Clara," as they derisively called him. But how completely were they deceived? The supposedly effeminate weakling proved himself to be not only a first-class debater, whom not all the Parliamentary arts of Healy and Sexton could disconcert, but also a ruthlessly thorough administrator, who, coldly smiling, employed with relentless severity all the means of enforcing authority at his disposal.

In order to govern in this fashion a Crimes Bill was needed, and Balfour did not hesitate to introduce a measure which cast the majority of previous coercion laws into the shade; above all, inasmuch as it was not to be a temporary but a permanent measure. Hitherto every Government, in concession to the ideal of the same law for all parts of the kingdom, had agreed that this ideal must only be temporarily disregarded. But Balfour wished to make an end of this. His Crimes Bill had no term set to it; and it was left to the Viceroy to say where it should be applied, and for how long. Gladstone vehemently attacked the Bill. He described it as the confirmation of his prophecy, that the only alternative to his Home Rule policy was the policy of Coercion. But the Government finally succeeded in passing the Bill, only a few of its worst provisions being eliminated.

And now began a period of what Salisbury had called "resolute government," a policy which his nephew actually put into practice. It cannot be denied that this policy achieved a certain degree of success, inasmuch as it eventually succeeded in suppressing the opposition, but it did so only at the cost of arousing an ever-increasing aversion in the population of Great Britain. For although many Englishmen had rejected Gladstone's Home Rule as a dangerous experiment, it was still less to their taste that methods should be employed on the other side of St. George's Channel which no English or Scottish provincial town would have put up with for a week. They were especially exasperated by the fact that Balfour's political opponents were treated as common criminals; this was a violation of the British sense of fair play. English Members of Parliament went to Ireland, saw the executive at work, and returned with horrified and indignant accounts of what they had seen. A Member of Parliament who belonged to the moderate wing of the Liberals, and who subsequently left that party because it was too radical for him, published, nearly fifty years later, the journal which he had kept at the time, with the comment that he could take back nothing that he had written, although Balfour, thanks to his great achievements in later years, now appeared to him in a different light. His sketches give a picture of a despotism whose government was disgraced by misery and injustice.

An affair which caused the greatest sensation in England was an incident at Mitchelstown, where the police fired on the assembled crowd; one man was shot dead and two were mortally wounded. The coroner's jury, after an inquest of seventeen days, returned a verdict of wilful murder against the chief police officer and five of his men. Balfour, however, declared in the House of Commons, at a time when he could not possibly have received any conclusive official communication, that "the police were in no way to blame, and that no responsibility rested upon anyone except upon those who convened the meeting." Labouchere, who had been an eye-witness of the affair, flatly contradicted him. Gladstone was so enraged by the incident and its treatment by the Government that he cried, at a Party meeting, "Remember Mitchelstown!" and for years "Remember Mitchelstown!" was a watchword.

But even more than by the excesses of the Government in Ireland, the public opinion of Great Britain was engrossed by other happenings, which developed, from a journalistic polemic, with

410

dramatic intensity, into an absorbing and sensational political drama. On the morning when the division was to be taken on the second reading of Balfour's Coercion Bill an article appeared in *The Times* which, like several previous articles, dealt with the subject of "Parnellism and Crime." This great newspaper, which enjoyed unequalled authority throughout the English-speaking world, was doing its utmost to ensure that the defeat which Home Rule had suffered at the hands of the electors in 1886 should be final, by proving to British readers that the Parnellites were the instigators and abettors of the worst of crimes. The series of articles, of which the first appeared early in March 1887, was published in pamphlet form in order to bring it before the largest possible public. Several articles had already appeared when, on the 18th of April, 1887, *The Times* laid before its readers an especially effective document. The article, entitled "Parnell and the Phoenix Park Murders," declared that Parnell, who immediately after the murders had publicly and solemnly condemned the crime, had expressed himself in the contrary sense to the "inner circle" of the Irish. In proof of this *The Times* referred to a letter of Parnell's in its possession, and of whose authenticity it had convinced itself after the most careful and meticulous examination. This letter of the 15th of May, 1882—that is, nine days after the day of the murders—stated that the writer regretted "the accident of Lord Frederick Cavendish's death," but added: "I cannot refuse to admit that Burke got no more than his deserts."

This letter was reproduced in facsimile which contained the signature "Charles S. Parnell."

The significance of this revelation was obvious, and *The Times* did not fail to stress it in a leading article: Gladstone's allies were the intimate associates and constant abettors of the worst criminals.

The excitement in Parliament was indescribable. All expected that Parnell would rise at the opening of the session and make a statement in respect of the letter. The reporters were all agog to give his declaration to the public. But hour after hour passed, and Parnell said nothing, and with every hour the number of those increased who believed in the truth of the accusation. At last, when it was getting on for one o'clock in the morning, and most of the newspapers had already gone to press, Parnell rose and declared that the letter published by *The Times* was "an audacious fabrication." He had never written or dictated such a letter, nor seen it until it appeared in *The Times*.

If an English politician had made this statement public opinion would have been very largely reassured; for even his bitterest political opponent would have taken it for granted that he was an English gentleman, who would not utter a deliberate lie. But to make this assumption in the case of an Irishman—and the leader of the Irish into the bargain—was another matter altogether. The distrust and hatred of the Irish had risen to their climax since the murders in Phoenix Park and the various dynamite outrages which had been perpetrated in London in prominent public buildings, and even in Underground and other railway stations. It was true that none of these outrages could be traced back to Parnell, but this—the man in the street was convinced—was merely a proof of his diabolical cleverness: one could well impute them to a man who for years had consciously wounded English susceptibilities, and had unscrupulously changed his allegiance, and whose whole manner was so puzzling and mysterious. This explained much of the opposition upon which Gladstone had come to grief. When an English gentleman is libelled he indicts his slanderer before a jury, and the Court sees to it that the truth is revealed. If Parnell wanted people to believe him he should sue *The Times* for damages in a libel suit! So thought, so spoke the famous fellow who boards the bus with an umbrella under his arm, whose opinion—according to Palmerston—is what really governs England.

But Parnell did not go to law. He could not look to a London jury for an impartial verdict, and he felt that the verdict of Irish jurors would make no impression on the English. Instead of resorting to the Law Courts he requested the House of Commons to appoint a select committee to examine the charges brought against him. The Liberals supported this request, but the Government refused it, and so, for the time being, nothing was done. This naturally strengthened the suspicions of his opponents, suspicions which were zealously fostered by the Unionists. Lord Salisbury described him as a man "tainted with the strong presumption of conniving at assassination." Gladstone might speak never so persuasively of the "union of hearts" which was to replace the "paper union"; but so long as the average Englishman harboured this suspicion he could not hope to advance his cause.

It was more than a year before any progress was made in the matter, and then it was due to *The Times* itself. More and more convinced, as time went on, of the triumph of its cause, it continued to publish articles on "Parnellism and Crime." But while Parnell and his followers lay low, a man whom *The Times* had surely overlooked took proceedings against the journal. This was the former Irish M.P., Frank Hugh O'Donnell, a somewhat fantastic personality, so little liked by Parnell that at the time of the 1885 elections he had not even included him in the list of party candidates. O'Donnell complained that he had been libelled in a *Times* article, and sued the journal for damages, which he moderately estimated at £50,000. The suit was completely futile, and *The Times* could have won its case without making any special effort. On the contrary, however, it held this to be a splendid opportunity to deal the death-blow to the Irish leader, and so to Gladstone's Home Rule policy.

The Times was represented by the Attorney-General, Sir Richard Webster; for in those days the law officers of the Crown—the Attorney-General and Solicitor-General—were still allowed to appear for private clients. Although Webster appeared in Court not as Attorney-General, but as an ordinary counsel, the impression produced was, naturally enough, that the Government was identifying itself with *The Times* in this lawsuit.

Webster, in the conduct of the case, did not confine himself to defending his client against O'Donnell's lame attack; he waged a vigorous counter-offensive, and not against the plaintiff, but against Parnell. Day after day, for three days, he read a large number of additional letters of Parnell's which were in the possession of *The Times*, and which inculpated the writer both as a man and a politician.

This case is not a creditable page in the history of the English law. It was a violation of the principle which in general is most scrupulously respected—that a party to a lawsuit may not incriminate anyone who is not himself a party to the case and is not represented. But here the principle was disregarded, and this by the law officer of the Crown who should have been the first to defend the great traditions of English justice.

Parnell replied to this new attack in the House of Commons, with the unequivocal declaration that none of the letters were written by him, that they were one and all forgeries. Once more he demanded the appointment of a select committee of the House to examine the accusations brought against him. Again the Government refused. But matters had gone so far that it could not content itself with a merely passive attitude. Now, it believed, was its opportunity to strike the death-blow not at Parnell alone, but at the whole Irish movement. It therefore offered a commission of three judges, but they were to examine not only the accusations brought against Parnell, but the whole conduct of the Irish Land League in the past. They allowed Parnell only the choice between unqualified acceptance and flat refusal. Any limitation or modification of this programme was excluded beforehand.

Parnell quite correctly replied that the Government ought not to leave it to him to decide whether an investigation should be made, for if the charges brought against him were substantiated he was a base and infamous criminal, and it would be the plain duty of the Government to proceed against a Member of Parliament who was guilty of such crimes. But in his anxiety to obtain some form of investigation he was willing to overlook any constitutional objections. Gladstone too felt that no obstacles should be placed in the way of this investigation, for the people must not be allowed to believe that Parnell dreaded the ordeal. But together with Harcourt he severely condemned the Government's procedure, as contrary to all English traditions.

The special Commission proceeded on the lines of an English court of justice. The interested parties could therefore be represented by counsel. And the most eminent counsel in the country appeared before the Commission. For *The Times* the Attorney-General appeared again, Sir Richard Webster, who had so successfully begun the fight; beside him stood, among others, Sir Henry James, the legal light of the Liberal Unionists, a sign that this party took a very special interest in the subject of the inquiry. As a matter of fact, they had insisted far more urgently than the Conservatives on the appointment of the Commission.

Parnell was represented by another Member of Parliament; not a member of his own party—indeed he deliberately passed over Healy, who never forgave him for it—but a follower of Gladstone, who had been Attorney-General in the last Liberal Ministry: Sir Charles Russell. Russell was regarded as the greatest criminal lawyer of his time; a master of forensic eloquence and cross-examination. *The Times* had been paying him a retaining fee in order to make sure of his services when required; but Russell terminated this arrangement when that journal's attacks upon Parnell became the political sensation of the day; for he himself was an Irishman and a Catholic, and a convinced advocate of Home Rule. As his junior he chose a younger colleague who had first entered Parliament in 1886, but who was recognized by his friends as combining an unusually acute intellect with great eloquence and imperturbable coolness: Henry Herbert Asquith, the future Prime Minister. His distinguished career began with his appearance before the Parnell Commission, while Russell's here touched its zenith.

Of all the questions which the Commission had to investigate Parnell was interested only in the one which concerned him personally: the question whether the letters in the possession of *The Times* were genuine. He was not only a great egoist, but also a great realist. If the letters were shown to be forgeries, it was his conviction that no one would trouble about all the rest of the affair, however his enemies might strive to make it seem important.

If for this reason Parnell was eager to come to the question of the letters as soon as possible, his enemies were anxious to do just the reverse. They had the upper hand to begin with, and the Commission dragged on for weeks through the endless web of agrarian unrest, seditious speeches, and inflammatory newspaper articles which in actual fact no longer interested anyone. The benches allotted to members of the public were more sparsely occupied with every session. Only once was the interest in the case revived, when Captain O'Shea entered the witness-box. There were sufficient rumours about his wife's relation to Parnell to justify the most various expectations as to his evidence. Further, it was known that he had been employed as negotiator between Chamberlain and Parnell, and that since the two had been at odds he had sided with the Englishman. He was no longer in Parliament; before the division on the Home Rule Bill he had resigned the seat with which an Irish constituency had provided him at Parnell's dictatorial behest.

But the examination of O'Shea was a disappointment. His evidence consisted materially of old stories, most of them long familiar, of his negotiations with Liberal Ministers. Counsel on either side treated him with the greatest consideration, and did not press him too hard. But he, apparently, was glad of the opportunity to express his conviction that the disputed letters were genuine. In his appearance "he had very much changed in the direction of what was then known as 'the shabby genteel.' " The days when he could play with the idea that he might one day be Irish Secretary were manifestly past.

      .   .   .   .   .

At last, after months of drudgery, the Commission came to the thing that really mattered, to the alleged letters of Parnell. How had *The Times* got hold of them? Everyone had assumed that before it published them this great and world-famous newspaper had observed every imaginable precaution to confirm the authenticity of the letters—quite apart from the fact that at the time of their publication it had expressly stated that all such precautions had been taken. But actually, it appeared, it had acted with the most astounding irresponsibility. This emerged more especially from Asquith's cross-examination of the manager of the newspaper, Macdonald. He had to confess that he had bought the letters, at the price of many thousands of pounds, from a young political agent, who for his part had received them from an old Irish journalist, Pigott, who had given a rather mysterious account of the manner in which they came into his hands. But the manager had done nothing worth speaking of to verify his story.

A few days later Pigott himself appeared in the witness-box; an elderly, bald-headed man with a flowing white beard, amiably smiling, a single eye-glass screwed into one eye. He replied to

Webster's questions in the most obliging manner, quietly and definitely; all seemed fair and above-board.

But the questioning of the witness was followed by cross-examination; and the cross-examination was in Russell's hands. The Irish knew all about their worthy compatriot, Pigott. They knew that in a long but inglorious career as a journalist he had always, with complete objectivity, placed his pen at the disposal of anyone who had pressed a few guineas into his ever-open hand. Parnell had received the most important information from a very distinguished source: from the Archbishop of Dublin, Dr. Walsh, to whom Pigott had addressed a few of his ingenious begging and blackmailing letters; for the Catholic clergy were then in the Parnellite camp, and were supporting his agitation. It was not astonishing that Russell, armed with all this material, should have brought Pigott to book. But the art with which he compelled the poor wretch to confess that one after another of his fables was a lie, and to drop the mask of the man of honour, revealing himself in his true colours—an unprincipled rogue, a forger and a perjurer—not only excited the admiration of the expert, but made an indelible impression on the many thousands who with breathless interest followed the cross-examination day after day in the newspapers. At the end of the second day a poor, broken, trembling old sinner stumbled out of the witness-box.

The examination of Pigott was to have been continued, after a two days' interval, on the following Monday. But when the session was opened Pigott was not present. In his place was a written confession, which he had made before Henry Labouchere in the presence of an impartial witness. It admitted what everyone had taken for granted since his collapse in the witness-box; Pigott himself had forged the letters.

And then, the inevitable sequel. The Attorney-General, on behalf of *The Times*, withdrew the charges against Parnell. A warrant was issued for Pigott's arrest. In the meantime he had naturally fled the country, but a few days later he was traced to Madrid. As the police were on the point of arresting him he saved himself by a revolver-bullet from further examination and prosecution.

The political effect of this revelation of forgery was tremendous. Public opinion now took the part of the unjustly accused man as passionately as it would have turned against him had he actually written the letters. Thousands who would have imputed any crime to the Irish leader now changed their opinion of the man who had been fought with such poisoned weapons. They seriously asked themselves whether the demands of the nation whose spokesman he was might not perhaps be justified; and whether they had not perhaps been wrong to desert the "Grand Old Man" who had committed himself to his policy. The Liberals who had remained faithful to Gladstone felt their confidence renewed, and conceived fresh hopes of the success of their cause. The bye-elections registered victory after victory.

When Parnell rose to speak in the House of Commons for the first time since the exposure of the forgeries, he was given such an ovation as few politicians have experienced. Not the Irish alone, but the Liberal Members to a man, the white-haired Gladstone at their head, rose from their seats and cheered the man who had emerged so brilliantly justified from a painful ordeal and the persecution of his enemies. A Conservative leader who was pitted against Parnell, not only in Parliament, but also in the Courts, afterwards wrote a description of the scene:

"It was an incident which might have disturbed the balance of mind of a smaller man. I saw Mr. Parnell erect among the whole standing crowd. He took no notice whatever . . . when they had resumed their places he proceeded to make a perfectly calm and quiet speech, in which he made not the smallest reference, direct or indirect, to the incident, extraordinary as it was, which had just happened. I thought, as I looked at him that night, that man was a born leader of men—calm, self-confident and powerful."

The great demonstration in the House of Commons was followed by innumerable demonstrations throughout the country, which manifested and confirmed the political alliance between Parnell and the followers of the Grand Old Man. Liberal clubs competed to secure Parnell as a speaker, and at a meeting of the Eighty Club, which rallied the active Liberals, Lord Spencer, who as Viceroy of Ireland had been bitterly attacked by Parnell and his followers, offered his hand to Parnell, a symbolic action which was greeted with enthusiasm by the supporters of Home Rule. Edinburgh, which was regarded as the headquarters of the Gladstonian movement, conferred the freedom of the city upon Parnell. In short, a wave of enthusiasm, submerging all former hostilities and national enmities, seemed to be bearing Home Rule onwards to success, and Gladstone's indefatigable preaching of the "union of hearts" seemed at last to be falling upon a receptive soil. The most visible outward sign of Parnell's newly-won position was the fact that at the close of the year 1889 Gladstone invited him to Hawarden, in order to discuss the future draft of a Home Rule Bill. That the man whom Gladstone had once denounced as an enemy of civilization, and had cast into prison, could now be a guest at Gladstone's family seat, which by all English Liberals was regarded with a sort of reverence, showed more plainly than anything else could have done how the times, and his position, had changed.

Mary Gladstone wrote of this visit: "Much excitement in the atmosphere. He spent the whole evening closeted in the Temple of Peace. Was next him at dinner. . . . We talked over the Commission. He never shows emotion, has a cool, indifferent manner, in sharp contrast to the deep, piercing gaze of his eyes, which look bang through, not at, yours. He looks more ill than any other I ever saw off a death-bed, refined and gentlemanlike in looks, voice and ways, speaks with perfect calmness on burning points and quite frankly." The political gossips related that Mary Gladstone had suddenly began to speak of the theatre, and had asked Parnell whom he considered to be the greatest living actor: to which he was said to have replied: "Your father!" Gladstone himself told Morley that Parnell was one of the best hands at negotiation he had ever met. Of the history of Ireland and England, which was always in Gladstone's mind, Parnell had, of course, barely the faintest notion.

In Parliament Gladstone returned to the attack in the debate on the report of the Parnell Commission. After sitting for several months, during which time hardly anyone paid any attention to it, the Commission had finally concluded its arduous labours, and the three judges summed up their findings in a report of several hundred

419

pages. Seldom has a Parliamentary publication been expected with tenser anticipation. When the hour of its release approached Members of Parliament and journalists gathered in hundreds before the door of the publishers' office in order to obtain a copy at the earliest possible moment. Only Parnell had contented himself with asking the secretary of the Commission to give him, in confidence, the gist of the findings; upon which he coolly commented: "Well, really, between ourselves, I think it is just about what I should have said myself."

The Report acquitted him personally of all the charges brought against him. That it also declared that a whole series of indictments brought against the Irish Party were proven made no impression on the majority of the public. It was just as Parnell had foretold: the sensation attaching to the forged letter on the Phoenix Park murders had completely exhausted the public interest in the rest of the controversy.

As a matter of course, the letter was made the subject of a great debate in the House of Commons. To the colourless motion of the Government, which confined itself to a conventional expression of thanks to the three judges, Gladstone proposed an amendment, which severely censured the calumnies uttered against Members of the House. He justified the amendment in a two hours' speech, whose eloquence even a Conservative opponent described as "a stream of molten gold"; a speech delivered with an intonation and gesticulation which were "a positive miracle in a man of his great age." The speech was not only a backward survey, from the loftiest standpoint, of a decade of Irish strife and Irish reforms; it was also a passionate protest against the envenoming of the political conflict by personal defamation. It culminated, at the conclusion, in a stirring admonition to each of his Conservative opponents, not to vote on party principles, but "as individuals, man by man . . . to place himself in the position of the victim of this frightful out-rage; to give such a judgement as would bear the scrutiny of the heart and of the conscience of every man when he betook himself to his chamber and was still."

The close ranks of the Conservatives sat still and speechless as this old man of eighty-one, who could look back upon six decades of political conflict, leant far over the table of the House, appealing in his most persuasive tones to their conscience as English gentlemen. Though the voting in the division that followed some days later may have followed the usual party lines, uninfluenced by this appeal, no one who heard it could forget it, and it was echoed a hundredfold by the nation.

Only one man broke away from the Conservatives. Lord Randolph Churchill had regarded the Commission, from the outset, as unconstitutional and politically a blunder, and had submitted his ideas on the subject in writing to the Government. He now rose to deliver a passionate speech, in which he made the most immoderate attack upon the Government. The malady of which he died some years later had him already in its grip, so that he lost all self-control, striking blow after blow until he flung the words in the Government's face: "What is your result? A man—a thing—a reptile—a monster—Pigott, the bloody, depraved, loathsome Pigott! Pigott! Pigott!" he hissed, with breaking voice, while his party friends drew away from him as once the Roman senators, at Cicero's "Quo usque tandem," had withdrawn from the conspirator Catiline.

From this day onwards Randolph Churchill, as far as this party was concerned, no longer existed. The political campaign which had been begun in order to sweep Parnell out of the way and so make an end of Gladstone's Irish policy ended actually in the political annihilation of the man who a few years earlier had been the idol of the Conservative masses, and who with boyish impetuosity had led the chorus that rejoiced in Gladstone's overthrow.

And yet the day was not far distant when the man now hailed as victor and triumphator, and regarded as the peer and ally of Gladstone, was to be brought to the very ground.

THE BREACH WITH PARNELL
AND THE LAST MINISTRY

1. O'Shea v. O'Shea and Parnell

On the 5th of February, 1890, John Morley was dining with Parnell's legal adviser, the brilliant and much-esteemed solicitor, George Lewis. He afterwards gave Harcourt an account of their conversation:

"George Lewis . . . told me the state of things as to P. By the time you get this all the world will know that *The Times* has settled for £5,000. I told Lewis that in my judgement he had done an extremely wise thing, and was very lucky. . . . He told me much else, which cannot well be written down. I can only say that when the time comes, Walter will have his five thousand pounds' worth of revenge. It will be a horrid exposure, and must, I think, lead to the disappearance of our friend."

What was the "horrid exposure" of which Gladstone's chief collaborators were writing so anxiously? Harcourt understood the allusion well enough. During his turn as Home Secretary the police had acquainted him sufficiently with Parnell's visits to Mrs. O'Shea at Eltham. But hitherto Captain O'Shea had apparently made no protest against the rôle of betrayed husband, although there was no reason to assume that he knew less of the affair than other people. After all, in the last two years Katherine O'Shea had given birth to two daughters, who were undoubtedly Parnell's children; as Sir Edward Clarke, who had appeared for O'Shea in the Divorce Court, declared years later. Nevertheless, O'Shea had acted as Parnell's liaison officer up to the year 1886. In the election of 1885 he had allowed his wife and Parnell to obtain a Liberal candidature for him, and when he was defeated Parnell had used all his authority to get him elected in an Irish constituency, to the great indignation of many of his party—for example, Biggar, who angrily opposed the candidature—as they did not regard O'Shea as an Irish Nationalist; in which they were justified. Biggar, at the time, sent Parnell a telegram which proved to be prophetic: "The O'Sheas will be your ruin."

That since then the relations between Parnell and O'Shea had altered considerably for the worse was obvious when O'Shea was examined before the Parnell Commission. But even then there was nothing to suggest that he had any intention of taking proceedings in respect of Parnell's relations with his wife. He had returned to Spain, where, by a singular chance, he was the last English-speaking person to see Pigott alive. In a Madrid café he was struck by the appearance of a man who seemed to answer to the description of the forger; and on the following day he learned that Pigott had shot himself.

Between O'Shea's examination before the Commission—October 1888—and the institution of proceedings for the divorce of his wife fifteen months had elapsed. On Christmas Eve, 1889, Parnell was served with papers as the co-respondent in O'Shea *v.* O'Shea and Parnell.

What had happened in the meantime, that O'Shea should suddenly take exception to a relation which had already continued for nearly a decade? The biography of Parnell that Katherine O'Shea published twenty-four years later does little to elucidate the matter. Various indications lead us to conclude that it was written with the collaboration and under the influence of the O'Shea family, and in many passages it betrays a tendency to present O'Shea's attitude in as favourable a light as possible. His own declaration, that he had only just learned that Parnell's relation to his wife was a guilty one, was received by those who knew the parties with the greatest scepticism. Many assumed that O'Shea had been persuaded to take proceedings by those who had been hardest hit by Pigott's forgeries. Chamberlain, in particular, was often regarded as the wire-puller behind the scenes, but this assumption was convincingly contradicted by his biographer. The probability is that the death of the wealthy aunt who had supported the O'Sheas during the last few years, and who had appointed her niece Katherine O'Shea her sole heiress, had provided the motive for his proceedings. Another motive, perhaps equally strong, was thwarted ambition and envy; the countless ovations which Parnell had received, and especially his visit to Hawarden, drove the defeated rival to strike the death-blow. But that Parnell's political enemies helped him to do so—for the cost of proceedings in the Divorce Court must have exceeded his own means—is also highly probable.

Parnell, being cited as co-respondent, was confronted with a critical problem. Which was he to put first—his political task or his private desires? If only his personal wishes had been concerned, he could have rejoiced at the dissolution of the O'Sheas' marriage, for this would enable him to marry the woman he loved, which he had long passionately wished to do. In that case, of course, he must do nothing to prevent the divorce, but must allow the proceedings to take their course as quickly and inconspicuously as possible. But if his political task was to come first he must appear in Court and oppose the divorce. Adultery, of course, could not be disputed, but Parnell and Katherine O'Shea could justly claim that O'Shea had connived at it for years, and had even profited by it. This would mean that O'Shea's petition would be rejected, and the impression produced on the public would be less damaging to Parnell than to the petitioner.

It was Parnell's doom that he could not decide for either course, but wavered to and fro. First he decided to contest the case, so that when the matter came into court his adversary would be able to wash his dirty linen in public to his heart's content. And then, when the case came up for hearing, he decided to put in no defence, and thereby deprived himself of the opportunity of denying false assertions and confuting false witnesses.

As the date of the hearing approached he displayed the greatest confidence—at least, to all outward appearance. In talk with a Liberal friend, who, after the wretched experience of the Dilke case, was intensely apprehensive of the outcome, he appeared certain of victory. A few days before the hearing he spent an evening in political consultation and personal conversation with John Morley. Before they parted Morley very cautiously asked him whether certain imminent legal proceedings would lead to his temporary disappearance from political life? He smiled broadly. Disappear? "No chance of it! Nothing in the least leading to disappearance . . . will come out of the legal proceedings. The other side don't know what a broken-kneed horse they are riding!"

He assured his Irish followers also that he would come out of the affair with flying colours. They were therefore thunderstruck when two or three days before the case he casually informed one of them that he did not propose to defend it. "For God's sake!" cried the startled Irishman, and he was not in the least consoled when Parnell coolly assured him that the whole thing would be "a nine days' wonder."

The case was heard in the middle of November, and it could hardly have been more disastrous for Parnell. O'Shea's counsel, Sir Edward Clarke, a Conservative Member of Parliament and a famous pleader, contrived to exploit the situation in such a way that he not only won a complete victory for his client, but inflicted a crushing moral defeat on Parnell. In the light of the evidence, which the judge accepted without demur, Parnell appeared as the unscrupulous and treacherous destroyer of the conjugal happiness of a friend. For example, one of the servants declared that on the husband's arrival Parnell had fled from his wife's boudoir by way of the fire-escape; the story was probably a lie, but for months to come the fire-escape was a godsend to the music-hall artists.

Naturally the newspapers gave the widest publicity to the case, and of course the public devoured the spicy reports. Naturally, too, the Conservative Press, in heavy leading articles, damned the man who, although he had not connived at political assassination, was yet an adulterer and the betrayer of his friend. And Stead, who had an infallible feeling for the opinions of the typical Englishman, sounded the whole register of indignation in order to fan the flames. The respectable Englishman thought as his Queen did, who wrote in her diary: "Parnell is shown up not only as a man of very bad character, but as a liar, and devoid of all sense of honour or of any sort of principle." And she added, surely not without satisfaction: "Now Gladstone is put into great difficulties by it."

Among the Liberal Party leaders the greatest consternation prevailed. Gladstone, who had been soothed and reassured by

425

Morley's report, wrote immediately after the exposure: "It is after all a thunderclap about Parnell. Will he ask for the Chiltern Hundreds? He cannot continue to lead. What could he mean by his language to you?" Campbell-Bannerman, who was not easily perturbed, declared: "Whether they are right or wrong, my belief is the Scotch will not tolerate P. in his position of quasi-partnership with the Liberal leaders." And Harcourt, who thought much more of the Liberal Party than of Home Rule, repeated with a sigh the words with which Bolingbroke had once lamented the untimely death of Queen Anne: "How does Fortune banter us!"

To make bad worse, not only was the opening of Parliament at hand, but also the yearly meeting of the Liberal Party. Three days after the end of the O'Shea divorce case it assembled at Sheffield. Harcourt and Morley, who represented Gladstone, were at once besieged on every side: Parnell must resign! The Nonconformists in particular, who in many districts constituted the backbone of the Party, and for whom morality played a decisive part even in contemporary politics, declared that they could not reconcile it with their conscience to remain the allies of an adulterer. Only with the greatest difficulty, and by urgently imploring the Nonconformists to have consideration for their venerable leader, did the two friends contrive to avert a public expression of this feeling. But they gave their leader a vivid account of the situation, and he, at Hawarden, was daily receiving letters from his supporters, begging him to make it clear that he had broken with Parnell.

Gladstone disliked nothing so much as the rôle of a moral arbiter. "I do not constitute myself as a judge," he wrote to Harcourt, "in any respect or degree of the merits of the case. . . . What, because a man is what is called a leader of a party, does that constitute him a censor and a judge of faith and morals?" What concerned him was merely the political problem. In view of the attitude which the electorate had adopted, if he could judge of this from all the opinions which were reaching him, could one expect to convert the people to Home Rule as long as Parnell was the head of the Irish Party? In a few years there must be a General Election; and for Gladstone all depended on the then attitude of the electors. For then he would be in his eighty-third or eighty-fourth year; then he would have reached the appointed limit of the most indestructible vitality.

There was little time for negotiation; on Tuesday the 25th of November Parliament would assemble; on this date the Irish Party must meet together and elect their chairman. The best thing that Gladstone could do, then, was to go to London with all speed in order to confer with his colleagues. But then he would have missed Divine service on Sunday at Hawarden, and this he could not make up his mind to do. So it was that the decisive conference could not be held until Monday afternoon. Harcourt, Morley and Granville took part in it.

Morley was deeply dejected. He was not only the most convinced of Home Rulers; he had been most intimate with Parnell, and had put the greatest trust in him. He still hoped for a friendly understanding with him. Parnell's secretary, often the only person acquainted with his whereabouts, served as the confidential channel for messages to him; and on the previous evening he had told Morley that it was his impression that Parnell was ready to surrender. The Liberal leaders were unanimously agreed that he must resign in the interest of their common cause. It was settled that Gladstone should write to Morley a letter to be forwarded to Parnell, in which he recalled the fact that after the Phoenix Park murders Parnell had offered to resign, and expressed the opinion that his resignation was now necessary, despite the splendid service which he had rendered to his country. For Parnell to remain at the head of the Irish Party "would render my retention of the leadership of the Liberal Party, based as it has been mainly upon the prosecution of the Irish cause, almost a nullity."

This letter, when the conference was over, was entrusted to an Irish Member of Parliament, Justin McCarthy, the Vice-Chairman of the Irish Party, who promised to give it to Parnell before the party meeting at which the Chairman was to be elected.

The following day began with unfavourable omens. Parnell's secretary informed Morley by telegram that he could not get into touch with his chief. All attempts to reach him failed. There was no doubt that he was in hiding, in order to foil any attempt on the part of the Liberals to communicate with him before the Party meeting. The only hope was McCarthy; and he did manage to catch Parnell in the House of Commons itself, before he could enter the committee-room. But Parnell took the letter, read it throughout without a word, put it into his pocket, and went into the room. Without breathing a syllable of the letter he had just received, he allowed himself to be re-elected Chairman. But McCarthy could not bring himself to tell his colleagues what Parnell was keeping from them.

In the meantime the House had assembled for the debate on the Address. What happened then was without precedent. The Address was accepted without debate. The Members were thinking of something other than the Address. With lightning swiftness the news of Parnell's re-election as Chairman had spread through the House. No one had believed it possible. While Chamberlain beamed with satisfaction over his adversary's fatal blunder, the Liberals were absolutely beside themselves. "Our men were mad, frantic, cursing, crying—the whole place in an uproar—a horrible scene which I could not stand," wrote Harcourt's son, the general confidant of the Liberal bodyguard. In the meantime Parnell sat sullenly in the smoking-room, "and behaved as though he were no longer interested in the matter."

This was the decisive hour in Parnell's life, and in the history of Ireland. In this hour Home Rule was buried for a generation, Gladstone's further activity was robbed of its meaning, and the first step was taken on that path of blood and tears that led to the Easter Rising of 1916 in Dublin, the death of Sir Roger Casement on the scaffold, and the civil war. For in this hour Parnell failed to stand the test which Goethe has called "the bitterest of all this life's ordeals": it was not in the man to conquer self. He sacrificed his mission and his people to the burning ambition that possessed him wholly, that prevented him from seeing things as they were, and induced him to shatter the alliance which was indispensable to the unity of his party and to Ireland's destiny.

Before the proceedings in the Divorce Court he had "entertained the idea of leaving England with Mrs. O'Shea, and taking the two girls, born in 1883 and 1884, who were unquestionably his daughters." To the demand that he should defend the case he obstinately opposed the argument that all that he cared about was the divorce, so that he could marry Mrs. O'Shea. Now—in the hour of decision —it was plain that all this, whether consciously or unconsciously, was a delusion. In actual fact it was the post of leader to which he clung, so obstinately that he was not willing to relinquish it even for a time. "Resign, marry, return!" Cecil Rhodes advised him by telegram: Rhodes, who had shown his interest in Home Rule by an extraordinarily generous subvention. But in vain.

Parnell's obstinacy forced Gladstone to assume the offensive. For the sake of peace and quiet in the evening of his life—already so far advanced—it would have been better had he followed the course at which he hinted in his letter to Morley—better if he himself had withdrawn from political life if Parnell refused to resign. And assuredly, as late developments were to show, it would have been better for the future of the Liberal Party, which, apart from a brief interval in 1892–1895, had to go a-wandering in the wilderness because of its alliance with Home Rule. But Gladstone was at all times a fighter whom no difficulties could intimidate; as much of a fighter now in his old age as he had been in his youth. And he was conscious that his resignation under these circumstances must have meant the end of Home Rule—and he was possessed by the belief that it was his mission, a mission with which he had been charged, to satisfy the national desire of the Irish people by a free understanding with the British people. A more sober thinker might perhaps have thought otherwise, but he was no sober thinker, and if he had been he could not have achieved what he did achieve.

Gladstone replied to Parnell's deliberate disregard of his letter by giving it to the Press. Many Irish Members learned for the first time from the newspapers what Gladstone had written and how Parnell had kept them in the dark. In the political world the publication of the letter was a first-class sensation. It meant the rupture of the alliance which since 1886 had been the central fact of English politics.

Parnell put up a passionate and reckless resistance. In vain did the Irish Members, who had only now come to realize the full gravity of the situation, make every imaginable attempt to get free of his leadership, for good or for ill. Parnell did not hesitate to take the chair in the party meetings in which his attitude was discussed, and as chairman he conducted the meetings in accordance with his own ideas. "He treated us," said one of his opponents, "as though we had committed adultery with his wife!" In his desperate mood he tried to divert the wrath of the Irish upon Gladstone. He issued a "manifesto" in which he not only accused the Liberal leader of wishing to betray the Irish, but also published the substance of his confidential negotiations with him. The result was, of course, that he fell out of the ranks of reputable politicians, and that those followers of Gladstone who had been but reluctant supporters of Home Rule thought as Harcourt did: "The blackguardism of the man," he wrote, "will be patent to all the world. . . . Poor Morley is much cast down. To me I confess it is a relief to have done with such a rascal. I feel some satisfaction in remembering that I have never shaken hands with him."

The end of the famous struggle in Committee-room No. 15 was the disruption of the Irish Party. When it was clear beyond a doubt that Parnell would under no circumstances give way, Justin McCarthy left the room, and the greater number of the Irish Members followed him. Henceforth there were Parnellites and Anti-Parnellites, who fought each other so passionately that Gladstone wrote: "Mr. Gladstone can find no parallel in history to the present Irish dementia, except the furious quarrel among the Chosen People in Jerusalem while Titus was thundering at the gates." Never again did the Irish submit to the will of one man. With the fall of Parnell the unity of the Irish movement was destroyed for ever.

Parnell was to live only a few months longer. They were months full of ugly and fratricidal conflict, of venomous accusations against Gladstone and his followers—excepting only Morley, whom Parnell had always trusted—of exhausting agitation and humiliating defeat. He had just time to marry Katherine O'Shea. Then one day he returned to her from a visit to Ireland, ill, exhausted, annihilated. His illness lasted only a few days: on the 6th of October, 1891, Charles Stewart Parnell drew his last breath. He was only forty-six years of age.

The aged Gladstone followed this tragedy of self-destruction

430

with a sympathy in which his sorrow for the untimely end of an unusual man was far greater than his disappointment in respect of the ingratitude which he had suffered. Even in the days of Parnell's most violent attacks upon him he refrained from any bitter comment. "Poor fellow!" he said, when he heard of some fresh desperate step of the uncrowned King of Ireland. At the close of his own life he had a long conversation with Parnell's biographer, Barry O'Brien, in which he described the dead man as "the most remarkable man I ever met. I do not say the ablest man; I say the most remarkable and the most interesting." And he concluded with the words: "What a tragedy! I cannot tell you how much I think about him, and what an interest I take in everything concerning him. A marvellous man, a terrible fall!"

The tragedy of that fall was its inevitability. Soon after Parnell's death Gladstone asked Morley: "You have no regret of the course we took?"—"None, none! It was inevitable. I have never doubted. That does not prevent bitter lamentations that inevitable it was."

But to Queen Victoria her grandson Wilhelm, who had now been seated for two years on the throne of the German Emperors, wrote as follows: "The sudden fall of Parnell and the exposure of the plans of Gladstone are such a piece of good fortune, as seldom falls to a statesman, and right glad I am for Lord Salisbury and you." What German interest the German Emperor could have thought to be involved is not conceivable.

2. *The Last Ministry*

Gladstone, when he formed his fourth and last Ministry, was eighty-three years of age: eight years older than Palmerston was when he became Prime Minister for the last time. The General Election was held in the summer of 1892, and Gladstone had had great expectations of it. He had hoped for a three-figure majority, which would have enabled him to pursue an independent policy, dependent on the Liberal Party alone. This expectation was grievously disappointed. Certainly the Liberals managed to win fifty-seven seats from the Conservatives and twenty-three from the Liberal Unionists, in itself a very considerable success, and a proof of the progress which Gladstone's policy had made in a few years. No observer of this election could doubt that his success would have been complete but for the catastrophe of 1890 and the fratricidal strife of the Irish. But as things were the victorious progress had been interrupted at a decisive moment, and Gladstone's majority was only forty even if all the Irish voted with him. This was a result which could not satisfy Gladstone's requirements, nor was it agreeable to the pride of the Englishman. An especially bitter drop in the cup of this aged campaigner was the result of the election in his own constituency of Midlothian, a name connected with his own in the proudest triumph of his life. It returned him indeed, but only by a majority of 700, whereas he had hitherto been accustomed to majorities of 4,000 to 5,000.

The disappointment must have been doubly grievous for a man of Gladstone's age. J. J. Jusserand, the French diplomatist, whom Morley had introduced to Gladstone, has given us the following glimpse of the days preceding the poll. One day in June 1892 Jusserand was lunching alone with Gladstone. In order that he might speak more freely his host had dismissed the servants, "going with light step to the sideboard and carving the joint with a perfectly steady hand. When he spoke to his wife he called her 'darling' as tenderly as though he had not been married a year; she watched him admiringly. He spoke on every conceivable subject. From Egypt and the colonial problem to the history of Corfu and the influence of Dante in France and England; but especially of the great question of the elections, of whose outcome he was perfectly confident."—" 'Tell me of a Conservative,' he said to me, 'who can count on a majority!' "

But after the elections Morley wrote to Harcourt: "I must tell you, *strictly* between ourselves, that the physical decline, in consequence of the reaction from the lofty hopes of a three-figure majority and all the rest of it, rather alarms me. More definitive, alas, is the danger in which he finds himself in the region of sight—now seriously threatened. A tragedy indeed. Only let us take care that the last scenes of Act V shall not be unworthy and ignoble."

But was the fifth act to be played to the end? Once more Gladstone was faced with the fateful question of his old age: should he continue the fight, or should he resign? Was there any sense in continuing to fight for Home Rule when the chances were so slender; he would ask rather, was there any chance at all? If there was any chance, that, for his inflexible militancy, was all that mattered. He had given the Irish hopes that he would fight for their cause; he must not disappoint this hope, especially since they had even deserted their leader on his account. "I am as fast bound to Ireland," he wrote to Lord Ripon, "as Odysseus to the mast of his vessel."

His resolution, then, was already taken. Directly Parliament assembled Asquith moved the decisive vote of no confidence, justifying the motion in a speech which was a brilliant example of his unusual faculty of saying a very great deal in a few words, and saying it in a striking manner. The division, in which almost as many Members took part as in the historic division on the first Home Rule Bill of the 8th of June, 1886, gave a majority of forty against the Salisbury Government, which at once resigned. And on the 15th of August, 1892, Gladstone stood for the fourth time before Queen Victoria, in order to receive her mandate to proceed with the formation of a Cabinet.

On the journey to Osborne he was accompanied by Sir Algernon West, his private secretary in those far distant days of his first Ministry. Since then West had entered the Treasury Department, and had been promoted to the very important post of Chairman of the Board of Inland Revenue. Now, though no more than sixty years of age, and greatly esteemed by his colleagues, he had just retired. But his newly-won freedom he unselfishly placed at the disposal of his former chief, who had since become his friend. Without accepting any office or official title, he acted as confidant and liaison officer between the eighty-three-year-old Premier and the Ministers in their often difficult transactions, and by his conciliatory personality and his comprehensive knowledge of men and things he made up for the inevitable restrictions placed upon the old man's daily intercourse with his colleages. This was a task for which all the Ministers had reason to be cordially grateful to him; and he, of course, in this way enjoyed many a glimpse behind the scenes, and in his diary, published thirty years later, he describes

433

many human and all too human traits and incidents. Algernon West, though he held no official position, acted as the chief of the Prime Minister's secretariat, and relieved him of some part of the endless spadework of his office, especially by dealing with the uninterrupted flood of letters. He also introduced a technical innovation by which Gladstone had never yet profited: he found him a secretary who could write shorthand. He had, indeed, to take advantage of a serious affection of the eyes before he could induce Gladstone to accept such a revolutionary innovation. Hitherto—though the notion seems almost inconceivable to a later generation—the Prime Minister had written most of his letters with his own hand. But the letters to the Queen had, as before, to be written by Gladstone himself. This, inexorable etiquette required of him. Nevertheless, his task was lightened by arranging that Harcourt should take over the duty of reporting on the day's proceedings in the House of Commons.

The Queen had expressly emphasized her wish that West should accompany the future Premier; but when he reached Osborne she not only ignored him, but deliberately slighted him by inviting his host, Sir Henry Ponsonby, to dinner, but not himself. This little touch was calculated to strengthen the impression which Gladstone himself received during his official audience. When it was over he told West that he imagined that the conversation between Marie Antoinette and her executioner must have been rather like this audience. At this first conversation he forgot the prescribed ceremony of kissing the Queen's hand; but on the occasion of his second conversation he repaired his fault. The Queen, however, could not refrain from remarking, with pedagogical severity: "This ought to have taken place yesterday morning." The same mistake was made by Sir Henry Campbell-Bannerman, when on the 5th of December, 1905, he received the mandate of King Edward VII to form the first Liberal Cabinet after long years of Unionist government; but when the King's attention was afterwards drawn to the omission he smilingly decided that the ceremony should be taken as having been observed.

In her diary the Queen described the Prime Minister whom the nation had once more forced upon her as greatly aged: "I thought

434

him greatly altered and changed, not only much aged and walking rather bent with a stick, but altogether; his face shrunk and deadly pale, with a weird look in his eyes, a feeble expression about the mouth, and the voice altered." It was as though she could not do enough in the way of recording the symptoms that seemed to promise her a proximate relief from this incubus; she did not, of course, consider that in her presence Gladstone lost something of his usual composure, the more so as her obvious hostility conflicted with the reverence which he, as a matter of conviction, felt incumbent upon him. In order that the outside world should be in no doubt as to her feelings, she allowed it to be announced, in violation of all tradition, that she had accepted Lord Salisbury's resignation "with regret." In the throng of hostile personalities who surrounded him at Court he might find some consolation in the personal veneration which he received from the Prince of Wales; and the Princess of Wales was even so courageous as to confess her sympathy for Home Rule.

The Queen had informed him beforehand that there was *one* man whom she would not have in the Ministry, and this was Henry Labouchere, the Radical Member of Parliament, and the editor of the weekly periodical *Truth*. It was precisely this combination that excited her aversion, for not only was *Truth* addicted to the bold and ruthless criticism of all manner of institutions and events, but it also published all sorts of spicy social gossip.

This prohibition, for several reasons, placed Gladstone in an extremely difficult position. Labouchere, the idol of the House of Commons smoking-room, where, consuming innumerable cigarettes, he exercised his wit on friend and foe, might be a dangerous opponent, by no means to be despised in view of the small Government majority. In such a matter Gladstone, to all outward appearance, must take the whole responsibility upon himself, as it was not consistent with his conception of the position of the Crown that any sort of political transaction should be influenced by the wishes of the sovereign. And lastly: he had never read *Truth*, had really never had the leisure to read it; now, for the first time, he must study its pages. "I do not like," he said, "to leave any of our hard workers out or treat them badly." But he had to give way,

435

and the manner in which he acquitted himself of this prickly task was such that even the Queen had to express some sort of appreciation. He could, of course, do nothing to prevent Labouchere from harassing him with the full force of his resentment; or even airing his grievances to foreign diplomatists—as he did, if Eckardstein is to be believed. One could overlook the fact that he coined the most biting epigrams on Gladstone, such as the malicious comment: "I do not mind Mr. Gladstone always having an ace up his sleeve, but I do object to his always saying that Providence put it there." What mattered very much more was that Labouchere, in his anger, got rid of his considerable share in the *Daily News*, and the necessity of finding the money to buy him out weakened the paper for a long time to come.

The Labouchere affair was disagreeable, but it could not prevent the formation of a Liberal Government. But there really was some danger that it might be prevented by the attitude which Lord Rosebery adopted. Since 1886, when he had first gone to the Foreign Office, there had been a great change in his private life. In November 1890—that is, at the very time of the Parnell catastrophe—he had lost his dearly beloved wife, Hannah Rothschild. It was years before he recovered from this blow. It was true that he had returned to political life in May 1892, but the extreme nervous irritability from which he was still suffering made him shrink from accepting office. When Gladstone again offered him the post of Foreign Secretary he declined it, on the ground that his shattered health and his insomnia unfitted him for so difficult and arduous an office. But this, of course, was not his only reason; he was equally troubled by the doubt whether, in the new Cabinet, he would be able to pursue what he believed to be the correct foreign policy. For a few days it seemed as though the formation of a Cabinet might prove to be impossible on account of this one obstacle. In the end he had a long and disturbing interview with Gladstone. When Rosebery told him that he would not be able to understand how seriously his nervous system was undermined by the shock which he had suffered in 1890, the old man interrupted him, declaring with great emphasis that he understood it perfectly, for there had been years when he too had felt an abhorrence for a life of political conflict. Nevertheless, Rosebery persisted in his decision, and Gladstone dismissed him with the solemn words: "May God Almighty in His infinite mercy and kindness lead you to the right decision!" The Prince of Wales also urged Rosebery to accept the Foreign Office, and at last he relieved the tension by his telegram: "So be it!"

That Gladstone had other troubles at this time is shown by an admission which he made to Rosebery a little later: You have no idea, he complained, of what I have been through in the last few weeks. Do not repeat what I tell you to a human soul: by *one* man I have been brutally treated! Who this man was Rosebery, of course, does not say.

In view of all the difficulties encountered, the completed work is all the more deserving of recognition. Granville had passed away in 1891: a heavy blow to Gladstone, but one which he bore with the unconscious economy of emotional expenditure peculiar to the man of action. Lord Acton, who had counted on a seat in this Cabinet, had to content himself with a Court appointment in which he won appreciation from the Queen. But for almost every post Gladstone was able to find an excellent candidate: Harcourt for the Exchequer; Ireland, of course, was again confided to Morley; Herschell returned to the Woolsack. Of the old guard Spencer, Campbell-Bannerman, Ripon and Trevelyan again gathered round their old ruler. What was even more important, he was able to include younger men, and in Asquith, especially, he recognized the man who had a great future before him, and although he had never yet held any office Gladstone made him, at the age of thirty-nine, Home Secretary with a seat in the Cabinet. This was very different treatment from that which Chamberlain had received in 1880 and 1885! But at all events Gladstone never had cause to regret his generosity to Asquith. He proved to be one of the most reliable supports of the Ministry, capable of braving all the storms of Parliament.

But imposing as the Ministry may have appeared to the outward view, there was one thing which it did not possess: internal harmony. It included too many difficult temperaments. Harcourt, a witty and hot-tempered man, felt it his duty, as Chancellor of the

Exchequer and deputy leader of the House of Commons, to lecture his colleagues on their own business, and this he did with a lack of consideration which gradually exasperated them all. Rosebery complained that he was being passed over: and John Morley, for all his fine qualities of character and his great ability, suffered from an almost old-maidish susceptibility, which inspired the humorous Campbell-Bannerman to refer to him, in private conversation, by the nickname "Priscilla." Still, he enjoyed in the fullest measure the confidence of the aged leader, who described him in his diary as his greatest support.

But Gladstone's colleagues, naturally enough, found that intercourse with a Prime Minister of eighty-four, who was hard of hearing, and was often unable to read (he was suffering from cataract), was by no means plain sailing, and the faithful Algernon West had his hands full; here diverting an attack, there intercepting an expostulating letter, and now arranging for a personal interview with Gladstone—often with surprisingly favourable results on either side. For however exasperated this or that Minister may have felt at times, they all had a real affection for the indefatigable old man, with his unquenchable fire, his noble idealism, his intellectual superiority, and his unfailing loyalty. But all naturally told themselves that sooner or later would come the moment of his retirement. Who would then take his place? Harcourt? Lord Rosebery? Spencer? It was not surprising that the "Papabili" should eye one another with a certain jealousy.

From the very outset there was no lack of material differences in the Cabinet. Rosebery soon saw that his premonition had been correct; he came into violent conflict, not only with Harcourt, but also with Gladstone, over the question whether the British Empire should take over the great African province of Uganda, which the East African Company declared that it was no longer able to administer. Harcourt asserted, supporting his assertion by a wealth of argument, that it would be an intolerable political and financial burden; Rosebery obstinately defended the thesis that evacuation would be unthinkable, and threatened to resign. In the end, with the help of the indefatigable Algernon West, a provisional agreement was arrived at, and the Cabinet was off the rocks again. But such divergent conceptions of foreign policy were at the bottom of the differences from which the Liberal Party was to suffer for yet another decade.

However, the most important problem before the Cabinet was, of course, Home Rule. Here the Prime Minister encountered difficulties with the Cabinet and with the Queen.

In October he ventured to submit to the Queen an exhaustive memorandum, expressing the fundamental ideas of his Irish policy. "At the present juncture," he wrote, "the views of Your Majesty's actual advisers . . . are hardly at all represented, and as Mr. Gladstone believes, are imperfectly known in the powerful circles with which Your Majesty has ordinarily political intercourse." The Queen took objection to this observation, which she sharply contradicted; indeed, she even disputed his right to appeal to the majority of the people, since the people knew nothing of his ideas. Naturally, it was easy for Gladstone to refute this objection; naturally, also, it was quite impossible for the two to agree.

In the Cabinet the worst difficulties came from Harcourt, who was regarded only as a lukewarm supporter of the cause. For this reason Gladstone contrived to avoid appointing him to the Cabinet Committee which had to prepare the draft of the Bill. It consisted of Morley, Spencer, and Campbell-Bannerman as men with experience of Irish administration, the Lord Chancellor (Herschell) as a jurist and a master of political compromise, and James Bryce, who had recently won fame by his great work on "The American Commonwealth," as an authority on constitutional problems. In this Committee Gladstone set to work on the Bill, discussing eagerly, objectively and patiently each clause in turn, and carefully considering all objections, for he knew that here he was surrounded only by willing and helpful friends.

Before their work was completed Gladstone, in obedience to his doctor's orders, was compelled to take a holiday in Biarritz, which had once before restored his shattered health and cured his insomnia. And once again, on his return, he surprised his intimates by the elasticity and vigour with which he resumed his labours. He led the difficult Cabinet debates on the Bill, and he succeeded in getting it ready for the opening of Parliament at the beginning of February

1893. Yet one more passage of arms with the Queen—she protested that the Bill should be entitled a Bill "for the *better* government of Ireland"—and he was ready to lay it before the House.

The speech in which he did so was an astonishing performance for a man of eighty-three. The thought of it had so excited him that he had slept very badly the night before. Nevertheless, he was able to speak for two and a half hours. His voice indeed failed him a little at times, but at the beginning of the speech, and at the end, he was at the top of his form. The speech, of course, had not the sensational and exciting character of the speech in which he had introduced the first Home Rule Bill of 1886. The fundamental ideas of the Bill were unchanged; he had discussed and explained them a hundred times; the innovations, though some of them were of material importance, did not affect the main conception. Even his opponents could but recognize the great intellectual labour and the idealistic impulse which had enabled the old man to surmount a thousand obstacles, and which, even now, gave his speech its special resonance.

Then followed the long Parliamentary battle for the Bill. The Unionists fought it with the greatest energy, using all the means that procedure allowed, and confiding on the Upper House, on whose decision they could rely. Their tactical leader was Balfour, who never failed to devise some new form of obstruction; their most dangerous champion was Chamberlain, who again and again measured swords with his old leader. It was a spectacle to hold men breathless; here the white-haired old leader, fiery, pathetic, voluble, lavish of new and felicitous expressions, and inspired by his faith in his mission; there the erect and resolute man with the sleek black head and the piercing glance behind the glittering monocle, downright, laconic and aggressive in his speech, which fanned the anger of the Irish to a white heat, and provoked them to loud interruptions, that enabled him to display his mastery of repartee. Speaker Peel, as an impartial observer, declared that at that time Chamberlain was "the best speaker in the House with one exception, and the best debater without exception." But Chamberlain himself confided to his son that "Gladstone is the only man I am afraid to have follow me." From time to time there was a flash of passionate eloquence from Randolph Churchill, but already the shadow of the deadly illness rested upon him that was sure to lay him *hors de combat* and soon after to bring him to the grave.

The Prime Minister was supported, not only by Morley, but also in a special degree by Asquith, after whose speech the old warriors rejoiced that there was after all someone to take their place. But he himself bore the chief burden; he carried every clause in his head, and he could give exhaustive reasons for every one. If he was compelled to beat a retreat he had the knack of veiling his retirement in a blaze of rhetorical fireworks that left his friends in the best of spirits and filled his opponents with amazement and admiration.

Incidentally, a bimetallist interpellation compelled him to make a long speech in which he dealt with the question of currency with a mastery that excited the admiration of all who, at home or abroad, had concerned themselves with this most difficult and controversial problem of political economy. That he was only too willing to lecture his opponents at inordinate length, sometimes even delaying the progress of the debate, could not astonish those who had watched him for decade after decade; such failings do not become less conspicuous in old age.

But however sharp the conflict, however passionate the scenes between Chamberlain and the Irish, the protagonists were not forgetful of what they owed to the great traditions of the House of Commons. When Gladstone had attained his eighty-fourth birthday Balfour rose to his feet, saying: "Perhaps the right honourable gentleman will allow me on my own part and on that of my friends to offer him our most sincere congratulations." And when Joseph Chamberlain's son Austen delivered his maiden speech, Gladstone described it as a speech which "must have been dear and refreshing to a father's heart." Bowing low at this, Chamberlain was more moved in the sight of the House than ever before or after. Randolph Churchill, in private conversation, could not refrain from expressing his admiration of the incomparable vitality of the old man. "That is the man you have deserted! How could you do it?" he asked a Liberal Unionist.

Eighty-two long sessions were occupied by the various stages of the debate, and the Prime Minister played an active part in all of them, at least until the dinner interval. He had to reply not only to his opponents in the House, but also to the Queen, who sent him critical and disapproving letters and messages. At length all was done, and on the 1st of September, 1893, the House of Commons voted for the third reading of the Bill by 347 votes against 304. The majority had held firm to the last.

This was an achievement, but unfortunately all were aware that the final fate of the Bill was not yet decided. For now the Bill had to go to the Upper House, and there it would certainly be rejected.

It was rejected, by a majority which showed that not a ripple of the movement which involved such a great proportion of the electorate had yet reached the region of the Lords. The peers turned up in their hundreds, including even the "backwoodsmen" who had never before in all their lives taken part in a division of the Upper House. The "Noes" were 419. The little handful of Government supporters were completely swamped; they numbered no more than 41. But among the "Noes" was many a peer who owed his rank of hereditary legislator to Gladstone. Nothing could have revealed more visibly the great loss which English Liberalism had suffered by Gladstone's conversion to Home Rule. Since then the Liberals in the House of Lords have been only an inconsiderable minority.

What was to be done now? Go on governing as though nothing had happened? Or dissolve Parliament and proceed to a General Election? The one course was as unsatisfactory as the other. A fresh election after so short an interval was advisable only if the country was exasperated by the attitude of the Lords. But of such exasperation no symptoms were perceptible. The endless debates on Home Rule had rather diminished than increased the popular interest in the subject. The average Englishman had little inclination to sacrifice interests that concerned him more intimately to the Irish. The Lords, it was said, must fill the cup of popular discontent by further rejections of popular measures passed by the Commons. For the time being, the Cabinet continued its labours, and even piloted a few useful and progressive Bills through the Lower House. But the unusual burden of work accomplished in the year 1893 had exhausted Parliament, and all were waiting for some decisive change.

A few months more, and the impulse came from a problem which cropped up with extreme suddenness. Public opinion, in England, is always moved, at intervals, to periodical panic by the notion that the navy has grown too weak to protect England against the assault of two hostile Powers. Such a panic broke out in 1893; for various reasons, not the least of which was an unfortunate collision between two battleships. The Press took the movement in hand, the Conservative Opposition introduced an appropriate Bill, and the Sea-Lords caused the First Lord of the Admiralty, Lord Spencer, to demand a great increase in the naval estimates. The Queen intervened with an epistle in which she declared that the reinforcement of the Navy was essential in view of the Franco-Russian alliance.

Once more, the Queen's opinion was undoubtedly in tune with the temper of the nation, and most of the Ministers were willing to sanction the estimates. Accordingly, Spencer's demands were supported by the majority of the Cabinet. The Chancellor of the Exchequer, Harcourt, offered some resistance at first, but at the end of the year he surrendered. There was only one Minister who did not surrender—and that was the aged Premier.

Gladstone was conscious that it was he who had built up the finances of the British Empire on the basis of bourgeois thrift, and that these finances, for nearly fifty years, had been one of the sources of England's strength. Now he saw them imperilled by the demands of the Admiralty, and worse still, it seemed to him that the peace of Europe would be endangered if England entered upon an armaments race, in which the other Powers would take part—and he was, of course, thinking principally of France and Russia. He foresaw the victory of "accursed" militarism, the transformation of Europe into an armed camp, bristling with weapons, and the bankruptcy of all the States involved. To this point of view he held with all the strength of a deep-rooted conviction and the obstinacy of old age. He was not prepared, at the end of a long life, to burn what he had adored, and when he looked at many of his dissentient colleagues he reflected that they were still at school when he was already a responsible Minister and debating this same question with Palmerston.

The rift could not be bridged; sincerely as this or that Minister

443

tried to bridge it who all his life had been wont at decisive moments to prove his loyalty to Gladstone. Spencer himself, who had given such effective support in the fight for Home Rule, was greatly troubled by the difference that had arisen between them. But neither friendly representations nor political polemics made any impression on the Prime Minister. He could not give in; and yet, at the same time, he was becoming more and more subject to the weakness and the pains of old age; his sight was threatened by cataract, and he was growing deafer. "The gates of the senses are closing," he complained. Reading was becoming more difficult; even his daily reading of the Bible. Was it worth while to make a concession against which his conscience revolted merely in order to remain in office a little longer? Already, in a Cabinet meeting at the beginning of January, he had spoken of his resignation, and it was only with difficulty that he was persuaded to postpone it until his return from Biarritz.

The majority of the Ministers were now agreed that Gladstone's resignation had become inevitable, and Gladstone himself felt that it was time to inform his wife of the state of affairs. This painful task fell to the lot of John Morley, who after dinner at Downing Street, while Gladstone and a friend sat down to a game of backgammon, suddenly found himself confronted with the necessity of telling her the unvarnished truth. "The poor lady," he wrote, "was not in the least prepared for the actual stroke. Had gone through so many crises, and they had all come out right in the end. . . . Would not the Cabinet change, when they knew the pride with which his loss would surround them? . . . What a curious scene! My breaking to her that the pride and glory of her life was at last to face eclipse, that the curtain was falling on a grand drama of fame, power, acclamation; the rattle of the dice on the backgammon board, the laughter and the chuckling of the two long-lived players, sounding a strange running refrain."

Twice the faithful Algernon West hastened to Biarritz in order to make a last attempt to bring about an understanding. Above all he was anxious to postpone the inevitable retirement to a moment and an occasion worthy of the great career that was now ending; and another sometime private secretary, Arthur Godley, seconded

444

his efforts. But Gladstone remained inexorable. No Prime Minister would have given in here, he cried: or at most, Palmerston!

In the meantime he had a plan which shows that his spirit was unbroken to the last. When the Upper House rejected a few Liberal Bills he held that the moment had come to utter the war-cry: "Down with the Lords!" But none of the Ministers agreed; they were better acquainted with the temper of the country.

So, inevitably, the end had come. After his return from Biarritz on the 23rd of February, he declared, at a Cabinet meeting, in his most businesslike tone, that now the moment had arrived to end his co-operation with the members of the Cabinet. On the 1st of March, 1894, he held his last Cabinet meeting. At the conclusion of the meeting Lord Kimberley rose, as the eldest of the Ministers, to speak a word of farewell. It was more than he could do. His voice failed him after the first few sentences, and when he went up to West in the ante-room the tears were running down his cheeks. It cost even the self-controlled and sarcastic Harcourt the greatest effort to continue his speech to the end. Meanwhile the aged Premier sat motionless, pale as marble and as rigid. His features were expressionless. And then, in a few sentences, he spoke his parting word. Once more the familiar voice was heard; speaking very quietly, but with perfect articulation; "then, hardly above a breath, but with every accent heard, he said: 'God bless you all!' "

His resignation was still a Cabinet secret. When that same evening he spoke in the House of Commons only a very few were aware that it was for the last time. In a fiery speech he declared war upon the Lords. So far had the statesman evolved who had always, with justice, regarded himself as the guardian of the constitutional tradition, and who only ten years earlier had confessed to John Ruskin his firm belief in the aristocratic principle. After the last words of this final speech he left the House of which he had been a Member for sixty-two years; never again to enter it. Next morning the Members learned from the newspapers that the Prime Minister, in view of the increasing infirmities of age, had tendered his resignation; and they one and all felt that Parliament had lost the greatest

445

Member who had been known for many decades, perhaps for centuries.

One thing remained for Gladstone to do: to take his farewell of the Queen. He had already advised her of his intention in an audience, and had elicited from her only a cool regret in respect of the *reason* of his resignation; the fact itself she accepted with complete equanimity. On the 3rd of March, 1894, he stood for the last time before Queen Victoria, in order to hand her his written resignation. "The conversation may be called neither here nor there. Its only material feature was negative. There was not one syllable on the past: except a repetition . . . of the thanks . . . in the matter of the Duke of Coburg. There was the question of eyes and ears, of German versus English oculists. . . . Some reference to my wife, with whom she has had an interview, and had ended it affectionately, and various *nothings.* . . ." These are Gladstone's own notes. "The Empress Frederick was outside in the corridor. She bade me a most kind and warm farewell, which I had done nothing to deserve."

The Empress Frederick may have been thinking of the farewell of another statesman of which she had been a witness just four years earlier. It was in March too when Bismarck had begged her to intervene with her son, who was now seeking to turn him out of office no less eagerly than he had once praised him as the statesman beyond compare. Since then the old man in the Sachsenwald had pursued the young Emperor who had cast him off with his loud resentment and his bitter tongue. Such disturbing behaviour was not to be anticipated from the old master of Hawarden. Never had his unshakable loyalty permitted him to say a single word against his Queen in public. The pages in which he gave utterance to the pain and the disappointment inflicted by such treatment at the close of a connection of more than fifty-two years were safely locked away. On the 1st of September, 1841, he had sworn fealty, as Privy Councillor, to this same Queen, then a shy and inexperienced young woman. He tormented himself by asking why the Queen had accorded him so little sympathy, and he recalled an incident of travel, sixty years before, comparing himself to a mule that inspires his rider with aversion, no matter how honestly he does his duty.

446

This woeful confession, he writes, "will never pass the door of my lips on its passage to the ear of any human being." He even instructed the members of his family to publish nothing, after his death, that concerned his relations with the Queen during the last few years. For thirty years they did as he desired, until hostile attacks forced them to take the defensive.

What hurt Gladstone most, at this final audience, was that the Queen did not give him the slightest opportunity of discussing the question of his successor, although he had previously been given a hint that he should do so. But she had evidently made up her mind to exclude him henceforth from exerting the least influence. Gladstone knew his Cabinet better than anyone else; he knew what difficulties would threaten his successor, whoever he might be. He himself wished to recommend Lord Spencer, who, he believed, had the needful experience and authority, and whose appointment would have obviated the otherwise inevitable conflict between Harcourt and Lord Rosebery. As far as his services to the Party went, and his standing in the Cabinet, Harcourt, the accomplished Parliamentarian, had undoubtedly the first claim. But as a colleague he was unbearable, and had exasperated even those who, like Morley, were actually most intimate with him. Rosebery had the better prospects, the more so as the Queen had a liking for him.

It was Rosebery who became Gladstone's successor: but not for long. On the 21st of June, 1895, he was overthrown by a chance division, though this actually put an end to a situation which had become untenable. A time of intestine strife and fruitless opposition followed, until a decade later a new period of Liberal government began.

3. Epilogue

With the announcement of Gladstone's final retirement into private life the English people felt that a chapter of their history was closed. The last of those statesmen was leaving the stage who had fought the battle of Reform in 1832; the last who already had a political reputation when Queen Victoria ascended the throne; the only one who had preceded Bismarck, and who, as a responsible Minister, had lived through and survived the whole Bismarckian period, an age that had given the world a different countenance. It was a long-drawn period, in which England also, quite apart from the fundamental transformation of the technical aspects of everyday life, had seen many profound transformations, especially in the distribution of political power, and of these changes Gladstone's dynamic collaboration was not the least effective agent. But one important factor had remained unchanged: Parliament, as the centre and the symbol of the State, in which the political power shifted, from time to time, from one to the other of its two parties; both of which, despite all modifications of detail, were equally rooted in the property-owning bourgeoisie, and had always hitherto shown themselves capable of assimilating and continuing all new movements. Still political England differed from the Continental States in the absence of a separate Labour Party. And those who pondered over the causes of this phenomenon found one of the most important in the fact that the great majority of working-men, in England, Scotland and Wales, beheld their political ideal in Mr. Gladstone, who for decades had set his face against every injustice, and had taken up arms against all oppression; who believed in the moral community of the human race, and who, at critical moments, had given practical expression to his confidence in the British working class. To be sure, he was no Socialist, but an outspoken individualist, yet this did not alienate him from the British working-man, and if he stretched the concept of Socialism to cover far more than it should have done, often condemning some harmless piece of State intervention as "Socialistic," they consoled themselves with the thought that younger colleagues would lend a hand and get their own way. The uniform veneration which innumerable workers and many of the middle classes felt for the Grand Old Man stood in the way of their political disintegration.

That with him by far the most interesting figure had disappeared from political life both friend and foe were agreed, and the more they tried to regard him objectively, uninfluenced by the passions which he had provoked as a militant politician, the more conscious they were of his loss. Not only his old friends, but even those who had hitherto been his political opponents, sought the old man in

448

order to express their veneration, and to conclude the long fight in peace and friendship.

After his farewell Gladstone had retired to Dollis Hill, the property of Lord Aberdeen, who had placed it at his disposal for a period of rest. Here among the visitors was none other than Joseph Chamberlain. No one, perhaps, had wounded the old man more grievously in the political conflict, and the fact that they had once been allies had added to the pain of the wounds. Now, however, he felt an urging to forget the eight years of battle and once more to grasp his old leader's hand. The visit passed off to the mutual satisfaction of both. "Mr. Gladstone was well and cheerful. He was most cordial and thanked us for our visit and seemed really pleased to see us. I told him that we missed him very much in the House of Commons. 'You are very kind,' he said, and then with apparent feeling, 'You have often been very kind to me.' Yet this is the man with whom the Gladstonians suppose I am at daggers drawn."

They spoke of old times, and Gladstone, in his talk, drew upon the inexhaustible treasury of his memories. On his way home Chamberlain summed up his impression in the words: "The old man is incomparable!"

That Balfour also went to see him goes without saying; no political feuds could destroy the friendly regard which they cherished for each other. In 1896 Balfour and his sister cycled to Hawarden. Gladstone was shocked. The First Lord of the Treasury does not run about the country on a bicycle! "He is, and always was," wrote Balfour, in a letter in which he gave an amusing description of this visit, "in everything except essentials, a tremendous old Tory, and is particularly sensitive in the matter of dignities." Then followed hours of lively and versatile conversation; neither the old man nor the comparatively young one was ever at a loss for a subject. Gladstone spoke of three men whose personal acquaintance he had never made, a fact that he still regretted; a curious trio—Sir Walter Scott, Lord Melbourne, and Dr. Arnold.

After a few days of pleasant companionship the First Lord of the Treasury once more bestrode his bicycle. Mr. Gladstone, interested and amused, went out to see his visitors ride off, "and not content with this, he ran (these eyes beheld him) across the lawn," to reach a point where a bend in the drive brought the riders close to him again. "He really does know," wrote Balfour, "how to grow old with cheerfulness and dignity."

Even now Gladstone could not be idle. A few weeks after his resignation a translation of some of the Odes of Horace appeared from his pen. Theological essays and a new volume of his *Gleanings* followed, and in 1896 he edited a two-volume collection of the writings of Bishop Butler (1692–1750), whom he regarded as the greatest "teacher of the laws of ethical co-operation between God and man," followed by a large volume of his own theological writings. But he had greater plans in view. He had told Mrs. Humphry Ward in 1890, in the course of a discussion of her novel, *Robert Elsmere*, that he still had two objects in life: one was to carry Home Rule, the other was to prove the close connection between the Hebraic and the Olympian revelations. In the first task he had failed; but he persisted in the second up to the year before his death. Not until 1897 did he confess to her: "I have begun seriously to ask myself whether I shall ever be able to face the 'Olympian Religion.'" Further, in 1894 he had had to undergo an operation for cataract in the right eye. It was successful, but henceforth he had to do all he could to spare his eyes; and since he could not bear to be idle he accustomed himself for a time to write with his eyes shut. He was all the more delighted when a progressive improvement gradually made it possible for him to read and write at least half as much as of old. In 1897 he fervently thanked God because he found it possible "to get through in a given time about half the amount of work which would have been practicable under the old conditions. . . . My power to read . . . for a considerable number of hours daily, thank God, continues. This is a great mercy." In the course of a few weeks' holiday he was still able to read twenty books, among which, he adds, there were several novels. But he also read the two-volume biography of Cardinal Manning as soon as it appeared, and was quite shocked by the glimpse into the excessively worldly mode of thought of the man with whom he had once been so intimate. He continued his diary until the end of his eighty-seventh year; then old age compelled him to relinquish a habit of seventy years' standing. On the 29th of December, 1896, he confided his thoughts and feelings to its pages for the last time. "As to politics," he wrote, "I think the basis of my mind is laid principally in finance and philanthropy. The prospects of the first are darker than I have ever known them." In this lament he gives expression to the fully justifiable feeling that with him an epoch of financial policy was closing whose highest aim had been the greatest frugality, in order that the burden borne by the citizen might be reduced to the minimum.

His friends, of course, did their best to keep him entertained. A particular friend of these last years was Lord Rendel, once an influential Welsh Member of Parliament, whom Gladstone, on his resignation, had translated to the House of Lords. In the winter the well-known director of the Armstrong works lived at Cannes, where he had a château. Here Gladstone was almost yearly his honoured guest, and his host kept records of much of his conversation, which touched upon the personalities of the present and the past, his own experiences since his schooldays at Eton, and his anxieties for the future. He spoke of the Queen's dislike of him, and of the difficult situation of the Prince of Wales, who saw his best years slipping by in idleness, and he even hinted at the Queen's jealousy of her son. Of Bismarck he said: "Bismarck was a great man—a nation-maker. No other man like him in this respect but Cavour. He put Cavour rather above Bismarck as being somewhat more scrupulous and having effected as much with smaller means. . . . He thought Bismarck perfectly unscrupulous. He was full of 'devil.' " He was thankful for the destiny that had allowed him to work in "a period of emancipation and liberation," and he expressed his regretful belief "that in the next fifty years political labour would be in less fruitful soil and under more ambiguous conditions." Here his premonition was assuredly not mistaken. He often pondered, as he had done all his life, the reciprocal influence of religion and politics, and here again he had a feeling that the foundation on which the efficacy of religion was based was tottering. It seemed to him that the fear of God was dying out in the human heart.

Once more, at the age of eighty-six, Gladstone undertook one of those sea voyages which had refreshed him so in earlier years. At the opening of the Kiel Canal, which Wilhelm II celebrated with the greatest pomp, Sir Donald Currie fitted out his yacht *Tantallon Castle*, and invited Gladstone to join him, with his family and a few of his most intimate friends, such as Lord Rendel and Sir Algernon West. They visited Kiel and Hamburg, and rumour had it—though it was not true—that Gladstone intended to go to Friedrichsruh in order to visit Bismarck. However, he saw the Kaiser Wilhelm in all his glory at the opening ceremonies, and it is regrettable that we have no record of the impression which the Kaiser made upon him; but when he saw the great warships of the various navies forging past one another, and someone tried to persuade him that they were the guarantees of peace, he shook his head and said, laconically: "That means war!"

Copenhagen, too, he saw again, and the Danish King; but this time he had no need to fear a scolding from the Queen, as in 1883. This time he could without misgiving propose the health of King Christian, in words that so moved that sovereign that he could hardly reply to it. Of this visit we have a particularly vivid description from the pen of another guest, by no means a political follower of Gladstone, the manager of *The Times*, Moberly Bell:

"The most striking picture . . . was the little cabin in the very centre . . . where with his back to the door so as to get the light, sat Mr. Gladstone, reading a Danish pamphlet, laboriously looking out words in a dictionary and writing them in the margin with a pencil." The Queen of Denmark wanted to see his cabin, "so he rose, and in a pretty old formal manner, received her, showed her his books, etc., then, as she left, he quietly sat down and began again." Just outside his door there was laughter and music and the dancing of reels to the bagpipe, but he sat there reading "as completely absorbed and as utterly indifferent as if he were in his own study." Twice or thrice he was interrupted, once by the King, once by the Crown Princess; then he laid his book aside for a moment, with "no shade of annoyance on his face, but a genial movement of welcome," yet no sooner had they passed the threshold than he was deep in his book again. For that matter, on the whole of the cruise there was for him "not one single moment of quietly doing nothing."

Anyone was free to come on board, and some thousands of

Copenhageners did so. So that the people should not block the light from Gladstone's cabin, a rope had been stretched outside the door, but it was almost carried away by the pressure of the throng that was constantly standing there. Although only a few of them could just catch sight of the back of his head, there were 200 people standing there and craning their necks to see him. Gladstone came to the accommodation steps, and immediately there was a shout of "Gladstone!" and a cheer at least four times as loud as the others. Moberly Bell, who was standing beside him, said: "The people are cheering you." "Oh, nonsense!" he said, and he moved back a few steps. Then Sir Donald persuaded him to stand "at the top of the gangway. The cheer that came might be heard in London. I think it almost took him over. He took off his hat, bowed twice and disappeared." A minute later he was sitting in his cabin again, and "then had book, pencil and dictionary at work as if he had never stirred." This faculty of concentration—Bell continues—was what made the greatest impression on him; even more than his wonderful mental alertness.

When the *Tantallon Castle* returned to England, Gladstone learned that Rosebery had been overthrown by a snap division in the House of Commons, little more than a year after he had taken office. The feelings with which the old man received this news may be imagined. But he refrained from any expression of opinion. He had retired from public life, and he wished to have no more to do with Ministers and Parliaments.

And yet he was once more drawn into the conflict, by an event of the same nature as that which had ended his premature withdrawal in 1876. Once more the world was shocked by the news of Turkish atrocities. This time the Armenians were the victims. In the tragic history of this people the years 1894 to 1896 constitute an especially terrible chapter. Massacres in Asia Minor had moved Gladstone, in August 1895, to address a meeting at Chester, which is not far from Hawarden. No one took greater umbrage at this speech—excepting, of course, the Sultan—than Wilhelm II, who spoke of "a shabby trick of the Grand Old Man." When a year later the Sultan had thousands of Armenians slaughtered in the streets of Constantinople, he could contain himself no longer, and on the 24th of September, 1896, he addressed a public meeting for the last time. This last speech of his life he delivered in his native city of Liverpool. Thousands had crowded into the vast hall. Lord Derby, Disraeli's colleague 1878–1880, was in the chair. "The speech, an hour and twenty minutes," writes his enthusiastic daughter, "was very, very wonderful, not of the burning eloquence sort, but full of reserve, dignity and strength, careful beyond measure, and yet shadowing forth a policy as wise as it would be effective. The audience were quick to see and respond to the points . . . nothing could have been more impressive than the sight of him standing there, 86, full of wisdom and dignity, while the thunders of applause again and again echoed around."

Unfortunately not all the competent politicians joined in this applause. Lord Rosebery saw in Gladstone's recommendation of an active policy against the Turks an interference with his leadership of the Liberal policy, and he resigned his position as Party leader. In the correspondence which followed Gladstone wrote: "Our political relations have become tragic enough." And indeed, neither of them had had the joy of them that they had promised themselves in the days when the young Rosebery had introduced to his Scottish compatriots the great crusader against the Bulgarian atrocities. But who was there who could look back with unclouded satisfaction on his brotherhood in arms with Rosebery, in the last resort unproductive, despite his brilliant gifts?

In the Spring of 1897, as chance would have it, Queen Victoria was staying in the South of France while Gladstone also was sojourning there. This it was that led to their last meeting; the first at which she gave him her hand. A thing, said Gladstone, "which had never happened with me during all my life, though that life, be it remembered, had included some periods of rather decided favour." She had, however, allowed him to be seated in her presence during the last few years.

. . . . .

But now came the time when even his astonishing constitution began to yield before the assaults of age. His infirmities became more distressing, and when a friend encouragingly exclaimed that he might live another ten years, he replied: "I trust that God in His mercy will spare me that!"

His old friends and comrades in arms came to see him once more. John Morley, so closely bound to him by his last and hardest battle, visited him in the autumn of 1897, and was fascinated by the wealth of ideas and suggestions which the old man, now so visibly standing by the last frontier of life, still lavished in his conversation, grave and gay. There were, of course, few so fitted to follow him in all the domains of knowledge as the sometime journalist whose encyclopaedic learning and great intellectual powers had found expression in a whole library of volumes. But what drew Gladstone most strongly to Morley was his character. He had first met Morley —as he told Jusserand in 1891—at an age when one does not readily form new friendships. But he felt, at their very first meeting, that he had found a friend; "and I told myself that if my honour and that of my family were dependent on a secret, Morley would be the man to whom I could without a moment's hesitation entrust it." And all Morley's actions since then had confirmed his impression.

There was, of course, one great difference between them: the religious difference. For Morley was an outspoken freethinker. But never, as Morley himself averred, had this difference cast the faintest shadow on their relations. Firmly as Gladstone was rooted in his Christian faith, he was far from requiring of others that they should follow the same path in their quest of truth.

And then came the gradual and painful end. The organs that had so long remained intact put up a stubborn fight against the onset of senile decay, and the strength that had so long been his great good fortune was now the source of continual pain. He had need of all his piety to bear it without complaint. For months the struggle with death continued. Music at times assuaged his sufferings, and he would sometimes even attempt to sing a verse of a hymn to Mary's accompaniment. His old friends came yet again to his sickbed, to see him for the last time, and many to whom his life-work had given unforgettable moments wrote him words of sympathy and gratitude. Nothing touched him more deeply than the farewell greeting of his old University, and with

455

a last output of his failing energies he dictated his reply to his daughter:

"There is no expression of Christian sympathy that I value more than that of the ancient University of Oxford—the God-fearing and God-sustaining University of Oxford. I served her, perhaps mistakenly, but to the best of my ability. My most earnest prayers are hers, to the uttermost and to the end." So his last thoughts returned yet once again to the scene of the spiritual conflicts of his youth, and his earliest success.

On the 19th of May—it was Ascension Day—came at last the long-desired deliverer, Death.

.   .   .   .   .

Gladstone's death was felt by the whole British world as a national loss. The highest honour that England can accord to one of her sons was paid to his mortal remains: they were laid to rest in Westminster Abbey. Both Houses of Parliament unanimously moved "that Her Majesty be pleased to give directions" for a public funeral, and "that a monument be erected in the Collegiate Church of St. Peter, Westminster," after the leaders of the two parties, in solemn and moving words, had duly honoured his personality and his achievements. Lord Salisbury, the Conservative Prime Minister, "was thought," as Morley says, "to go nearest to the core of the solemnity."

"What was the cause of this unanimous feeling?" It was "that men recognized in him a man guided—whether under mistaken impressions or not, it matters not—but guided in all the steps he took, in all the efforts that he made, by a high moral ideal." In words that have not been forgotten, he celebrated in Gladstone "a great Christian statesman. . . . He will be long remembered not so much for the causes in which he was engaged or the political projects which he favoured, but as a great example, to which history hardly furnishes a parallel, of a great Christian man."

Rosebery also sounded a personal note, when he alluded to "the solitary and pathetic figure, who for sixty years shared all the sorrows and all the joys of Mr. Gladstone's life, who received his confidence and every aspiration, who shared his triumph with him and cheered him under his defeats; who by her tender vigilance, I firmly believe, sustained and prolonged his years."

"To be thus celebrated by friend and foe—that is the finest thing that can happen to a human being," wrote old Theodor Fontane, in Berlin, who had likewise come to the limit of his days; and the incarnate Prussian continued: "The outside world agrees. For the mere 'ruler' there is a lesson in all this."

The solemn funeral procession was the overwhelming expression of a national mourning in which all classes of society took part in numbers past estimation. Among the bearers of the coffin the future Kings of England, Edward VII and George V, walked beside the dead man's closest friends. And all bowed their heads in sorrow before Catherine Gladstone, who was taking her pathetic farewell of her life's partner. As the coffin was lowered into the vault it seemed as though she would have kissed the stone flags, and her lips whispered: "Only once more!" Two years later she was laid to rest beside him.

Solemn and pathetic, the funeral hymns of the Church echoed through the Abbey, and "when the high sentence rang out—'and their name liveth for evermore'—the effect was marvellous. One seemed to hear the voice of the future already pealing through the Abbey—as though the verdict were secured, the judgement given."

Returning from the funeral, George Trevelyan, who had left the House of Commons for his study, wrote: "It was by far the finest and noblest thing I ever saw. . . . One thing came home to me—the transitoriness of calumny. As long as he was in affairs, there was . . . in society continuous talk about his being bad, absurd, a Jesuit, a madman, moved only by his own interests, a hypocrite—what not? And the lighter, but almost more offensive weapons were largely directed against Mrs. Gladstone. And now, where is it all? The personal estimate is unanimous among those who are capable of making an estimate at all."

And across the ocean and across the continent not only the President of the United States and the Tsar of all the Russias greeted the great dead, but the peoples whom he had taken to his heart in the hour of their distress, because he had never learned to tolerate injustice in silence.

457

CHRONOLOGICAL TABLE

1809, Dec. 29	William Ewart Gladstone born at Liverpool.
1821, Sept.	Eton.
1828, Oct.	Christ Church, Oxford.
1830, July	Revolution in France. Overthrow of Charles X.
1831, May 17	Gladstone speaks on the "Reform Bill" in the Oxford Union Debating Club.
1832	Reform Act.
1832, Dec. 13	Gladstone M.P. for Newark.
1834, Dec. 26	Junior Lord of the Treasury in Peel's ministry.
1835, Jan.	Under-secretary for War and the Colonies.
1837, June 20	Accession of Queen Victoria.
1838	"The State in its relations with the Church."
1839, July 25	Gladstone marries Miss Catherine Glynne.
1840, Feb. 10	Queen Victoria marries Prince Albert.
1841, Sept.	Gladstone Vice-President of the Board of Trade in Peel's ministry.
1843, May	Gladstone enters the Cabinet as President of the Board of Trade.
1845, Jan.	Gladstone resigns office on Maynooth Bill.
1845, Oct.	Newman joins Roman Catholic Church.
1845, Dec.	Colonial Secretary.
1846, June	Repeal of the Corn Laws and Peel's fall.
1847	Gladstone M.P. for Oxford University.
1848, Feb.	Overthrow of King Louis Philippe by revolution in France.
1850, June	Don Pacifico Debate.
1850, July 2	Death of Sir Robert Peel.
1851, April	Manning received into the Roman Catholic Church.
1851, July	Gladstone's letters to Lord Aberdeen on Neapolitan misgovernment.
1851, Dec. 2	Louis Napoleon's *coup d'état*.
1852, Dec.	Gladstone on Disraeli's budget.
1852, Dec.	Gladstone Chancellor of the Exchequer in Lord Aberdeen's Government.
1853, April	First Budget.
1854–1856	Crimean War.
1855, Jan.	Aberdeen resigns. Palmerston Cabinet.
1855, Feb.	Gladstone resigns.

1857, March	Palmerston dissolves Parliament on Chinese war.
1857, July	Gladstone opposes Divorce Bill.
1858, Nov.	Gladstone High Commissioner for Ionian Islands.
1859, June 4	Battle of Magenta.
1859, June 20	Gladstone Chancellor of the Exchequer in Palmerston's Government.
1859, June 24	Battle of Solferino.
1859, July 11	Preliminaries at Villafranca.
1860, Feb.	The Great Budget. Commercial Treaty with France.
1861, May–June	Repeal of the Paper Duty.
1861–1865	American Civil War.
1861, Dec. 14	Death of the Prince Consort.
1862, Sept, 23	Bismarck Prussian Prime Minister.
1862, Oct. 7	Gladstone's speech at Newcastle on American Civil War.
1864, Jan.—July	War in Schleswig-Holstein.
1865, July	Gladstone defeated at Oxford University, elected for South Lancashire.
1865, Oct. 18	Death of Palmerston, Gladstone Leader of the House of Commons.
1866, March	Introduction of the Parliamentary Reform Bill.
1866, June–July	Austro-Prussian war.
1866, June	Resignation of Lord Russell's Government. Third Derby Cabinet.
1867	Disraeli carries Parliamentary Reform.
1868, Feb.	Disraeli Prime Minister.
1868, March	Gladstone's resolutions on Irish Church Disestablishment.
1868, Nov.	Gladstone elected M.P. for Greenwich.
1868, Dec.	Gladstone Prime Minister.
1869	Disestablishment of Irish Church.
1870	Irish Land Bill, Elementary Education Bill.
1870, July 15	French declaration of war against Prussia.
1870, Sept. 2	Battle of Sedan.
1870, Oct.	Russian Circular on Black Sea.
1871	Army Regulation Bill, University Tests, Ballot Bill, Opening of Civil Service.
1871, May	Washington Treaty on *Alabama* Claims.
1872, Sept.	*Alabama* award.
1873, March	Irish University Bill defeated, Gladstone resigns, resumes office.
1874, Jan. 26	Gladstone dissolves Parliament.
1874, Jan.–Feb.	General Election. Conservative majority of 50.
1874, Feb. 17	Gladstone resigns. Disraeli Prime Minister.

1874, Sept.	Gladstone visits Döllinger.
1874, Nov.	Pamphlet on "Vatican Decrees."
1875, Jan.	Gladstone retires from Leadership of the Liberal Party.
1876, Spring	Bulgarian rising against the Turks.
1876, May	Berlin memorandum.
1876, Aug.	Disraeli becomes Lord Beaconsfield.
1876, Sept.	Pamphlet on "Bulgarian Horrors."
1876, Dec.	St. James's Hall Conference on Eastern Question.
1877, April	Outbreak of Russo-Turkish war.
1877, May	Gladstone moves his first resolution on Eastern Question.
1878, March	Treaty of San Stefano.
1878, June 13– July 13	Berlin Congress.
1878, July 30	Gladstone criticizes Berlin Treaty in the House of Commons.
1879, Nov.	Midlothian Campaign begins.
1879, Dec. 5	Inaugural address at Glasgow University.
1880, April	General Election: 347 Liberals, 240 Conservatives, 65 Irish. Gladstone elected in Midlothian and Leeds.
1880, April 21	Lord Beaconsfield resigns.
1880, April 23	Gladstone Prime Minister for the second time.
1880, May	Bradlaugh case begins.
1880, July	Irish Compensation for Disturbance Bill rejected by the House of Lords.
1881, Jan.	Forster's Irish Protection of Person and Property Bill.
1881, Feb. 26	Majuba Hill.
1881, April–July	Irish Land Bill in the House of Commons.
1881, April 19	Death of Lord Beaconsfield.
1881, Oct. 2 & 8	Speeches in Leeds.
1881, Oct. 13	Parnell arrested.
1882, May	Parnell released. Forster resigns.
1882, May 6	Lord Frederick Cavendish murdered in Phoenix Park.
1882, July 11	Bombardment of Alexandria.
1882, July 12	Bright resigns.
1882, Sept. 13	Battle of Tel-el-Kebir.
1882, Dec. 31	Death of Gambetta.
1883, April 26	Speech on Oaths Bill.
1883, Sept.	Cruise to Copenhagen.
1884	Franchise Bill.
1884, Jan.	Gordon sent to the Sudan.
1884, August	Cabinet decides for expedition to Khartoum.
1885, Jan. 26	Fall of Khartoum. Death of Gordon.
1885, Feb. 28	Vote of Censure defeated by 14 votes.

1885, March 2	Bismarck attacks Granville in the German Reichstag.
1885, April 27	Gladstone moves vote of war supplies on account of Penjdeh incident.
1885, June 8	Defeat of Budget in House of Commons.
1885, June 9	Gladstone resigns.
1885, June 23	Lord Salisbury Prime Minister.
1885, Nov.–Dec.	General Election.
1885, Dec. 17	Herbert Gladstone's statement: "Hawarden Kite."
1886, Jan. 28	Salisbury resigns.
1886, Feb. 1	Gladstone Prime Minister for the third time.
1886, Feb. 2	Marriage of Mary Gladstone.
1886, March 26	Chamberlain resigns.
1886, April 8	Gladstone introduces Home Rule Bill.
1886 May 27	Liberal Party meeting.
1886, June 8	Defeat of Home Rule Bill. Parliament dissolved.
1886, July	General Election: 316 Conservatives, 196 Liberals, 74 Liberal Unionists, 84 Irish.
1886, July 30	Gladstone resigns. Second Salisbury Ministry.
1886, Dec. 23	Lord Randolph Churchill resigns.
1887, Jan.–Feb.	Round Table Conference.
1887, April 18	*Times* publishes "Parnell's letter on Phoenix Park murders."
1888, July	Government proposes Special Commission.
1888, Sept. 17– 1889, Nov. 22	Special Commission's sittings.
1889, Feb. 21–22	Pigott's examination.
1889, March 1	Pigott's suicide.
1889, July 25	Golden wedding.
1889, Dec.	Parnell at Hawarden.
1890, Feb. 13	Report of the Special Commission.
1890, March 20	Bismarck resigns.
1890, Nov. 15–17	Divorce trial O'Shea *v.* O'Shea and Parnell.
1890, Nov. 20–21	Sheffield meeting of the Liberal Party organization.
1890, Nov. 24	Gladstone's letter to Morley on Parnell.
1890, Dec.	Break-up of the Irish Party.
1891, Oct. 6	Death of Parnell.
1892, July	General Election: Liberals and Irish 355, Conservatives and Liberal Unionists 315.
1892, Aug. 11	Government defeated on address amendment. Lord Salisbury resigns.
1892, Aug. 15	Gladstone Prime Minister for the fourth time.
1893, Feb. 13	Gladstone introduces second Home Rule Bill.
1893, Sept. 1	House of Commons passes Home Rule Bill.
1893, Sept. 8	House of Lords rejects it.

1894, March 3	Gladstone resigns. Lord Rosebery Prime Minister.
1895, June	Lord Rosebery resigns. Salisbury's third Government.
1896, Sept. 24	Gladstone speaks at Liverpool on Armenian atrocities.
1898, May 19	Death of Gladstone.
1898, July 30	Death of Bismarck.
1900, June 14	Death of Catherine Gladstone.
1901, May 22	Death of Queen Victoria.

BIBLIOGRAPHY

A. General

W. E. GLADSTONE. Gleanings of Past Years, 8 vols. 1878 and 1897.
   The State in Relation with the Church. 1839.
   German translation with preface by Tholuck. Halle, 1843.
   Chapter of Autiobiography. 1868.
   Studies on Homer. 3 vols. Oxford, 1858.
   Special Aspects of Irish Question. 1892.
   Bulgarian Horrors, etc. Leipzig, Tauchnitz, 1876.
   Vatican Decrees. 1874.
   Studies about Butler. Oxford, 1896.
   Speeches. Edited by A. Tilney Bassett. 1916.
   Financial Statements. 1863.
   Political Speeches in Scotland. Edinburgh, 1879 and 1880.
   Letters to his wife. Edited by A. Tilney Bassett. London, 1936.
   Correspondence on Church and Religion. Edited by Lathbury.
      2 vols. London, 1910.

JOHN MORLEY. Life of Gladstone. London. 2 vols. 1905.

E. W. HAMILTON. Gladstone. London, 1898.

WEMYSS REID. Gladstone. London, 1898.

WILLIAMSON. Gladstone, Statesman and Scholar. London, 1898.

G. W. RUSSELL. Gladstone. Everyman Libr., 1923.

H. W. PAUL. Gladstone. Nelson.

OSBERT BURDETT. Gladstone. London, 1928.

FRANCIS BIRRELL. Gladstone. London, 1933.

RAMSEY MUIR. Gladstone in Hearnshaw, Political Principles of some
      Notable Prime Ministers. London, 1926.

BAGEHOT. Gladstone in "Biogr. Studies." London, 1881.

J. BRYCE. Gladstone in "Studies in Contemporary Biography."
      London, 1903.

GOLDWIN SMITH. My Memory of Gladstone. London, 1904.

GEORGE EDINGER AND E. F. C. NEEP. The Grand Old Man. London,
      1936.

D. C. SOMERVELL. Disraeli and Gladstone. London, 1926.

HERMANN ONCKEN. Gladstone und Disraeli in Rhoden, "Menschen die
      Geschichte Machten." 1933. Vol. ii.

FELIX SALOMON. Gladstone in "Deutsche Rundschau." October
      1898.

465

RUDOLF CRAEMER. Gladstone als Christlicher Staatsmann. Stuttgart. 1930.

HERBERT PAUL. A History of Modern England. 5 vols. 1904.

SIR SPENCER WALPOLE. The History of Twenty-five Years. 4 vols. 1904.

JUSTIN MCCARTHY. History of our own Time. Tauchnitz. 5 vols. From 1880 to the Diamond Jubilee. London, 1897.

J. A. SPENDER. Great Britain. Empire and Commonwealth, 1886–1935. London, 1936.

ALFRED STERN. Geschichte Europas in neunzehnten Jahrhundert. 10 vols. Stuttgart, 1894–1924.

CARL BRINKMANN. Englische Geschichte, 1815–1914. Berlin, 1924.

CHAPTER I. THE HOPE OF THE TORIES

1. *"A Man is Uprisen"*

BERNHARD GUTTMAN. England, im Zeitalter der bürgerlichen Reform. Stuttgart, 1923.

G. M. TREVELYAN. Lord Grey of the Reform Bill. London, 1920.

HERB. A. MORRAH. The Oxford Union, 1823–1923. London, 1923.

CHARLES E. MALLET. University of Oxford. Vol. iii. London, 1927.

LORD ACTON. Letters to Mary Gladstone. London, 1904. P. 43. Lett., 14th December, 1880.

ULRICH NOACK. Katholizität und Geistesfreiheit. Nach den Schriften von John Dalberg-Acton. Frankfurt, 1934.

LATHBURY. Gladstone's Correspondence. Vol. i, 3, 199, 225. Vol. ii, 49.

REID. Lord Houghton. London, 1890. Vol. i, 78.

2. *The Young Parliamentarian*

GLADSTONE. To his Wife. 241. 35. 163–4. *The Times*, 30th October, 1935. (Letter to Robertson. 13th December, 1882.)

LORD ROSEBERY. Sir Robert Peel, in "Miscellanies." Vol. i. London, 1921.

KITSON CLARK. Peel and the Conservative Party. 1832–1841. London, 1929.

LORD STANMORE. Lord Aberdeen. London, 1921.

LADY FRANCES BALFOUR. The Earl of Aberdeen. London, 1923. 2 vols.

DISRAELI. Coningsby. Book ii, Chap. 5.

GREVILLE. Diary. Edited by Reeve. III, 257.

PAUL KNAPLUND. Gladstone and Britain's Imperial Policy. London, 1927.

BERTRAM NEWMAN. Lord Melbourne. London, 1930.

LATHBURY. Correspondence. Vol, i, 23. Vol. ii, 428, 440.

JOHN MORLEY. Burke. London, 1909.

466

JOHN MACGUNN. The Political Philosophy of Burke. London, 1913.

RICHMOND LENNOX. E. Burkes politisches Arbeitsfeld. München, 1923.

FRIEDRICH MEINECKE. Weltbürgertum und Nationalstaat. München, 1915. P. 134.

MACAULAY. "Church and State"; in Constitutional Essays.

OTTO BAUMGARTEN. Religiöses und Kirchliches Leben in England. Leipzig, 1922.

About Manning

PURCELL. Life of Manning. London, 1896. (Gladstone's Letter 14th January, 1896. Lathbury. Vol. ii, 338.)

LYTTON STRACHEY. Manning in "Eminent Victorians." London, 1922.

BRYCE. H. E. Manning, Archbishop and Cardinal, in "Studies in Contemporary Biography." London, 1903.

4. *Marriage*

GLADSTONE. Correspondence with his wife. 120 (Jan. 2, 1858).

MARY GLADSTONE. Diaries and Letters. Edited by Lucy Masterman. London, 1930.

VISCOUNT GLADSTONE. After Thirty Years. London, 1928.

CHARLES MALLET. Herbert Gladstone. London, 1932.

IVOR THOMAS. Gladstone of Hawarden. London, 1936.

EDWIN A. PRATT. Catherine Gladstone. London, 1898.

LORD RENDEL. Personal Papers. London, 1931. P. 134.

CHAPTER II. PEEL'S CHANGE OF FRONT

1. *From Theory to Practice*

KITSON CLARK. Peel, 448, 457, 469, 473.

F. E. HYDE. Gladstone at the Board of Trade. London, 1934.

LUJO BRENTANO. Eine Geschichte der wirtschaftlichen Entwickelung Englands. Vol. iii, 1, p. 207.

ALGERNON WEST. Private Diaries. 192 (29th August, 1893).

Railways

DR. GUSTAV COHN. Die Entwicklung der Eisenbahngesetze in England. Leipzig, 1874. Pp. 112, 115, 138–140.

R. MUIR. P. 240.

2. *The Paladin of Principle.* 3. *Peel Victorious—and Defeated*

GLADSTONE. Chapter of Autobiography. 25, 26.

CHARLES STUART PARKER. Private Papers of Sir Robert Peel. London, 1891. Vol. iii, p. 163, ss.

MACAULAY. Speech on Maynooth. 14th April, 1845.

MONYPENNY AND BUCKLE. Life of Benjamin Disraeli. 2 vols. London, 1920. Vol. I, pp. 510, 723.

QUEEN VICTORIA. Letters. London, 1908. Vol. i, 2; 63.

B. DISRAELI. Life of Lord Bentinck.

JOHN MORLEY. Life of Cobden. Nelson.

G. O. TREVELYAN. Life of John Bright. London, 1913. Life and Letters of Lord Macaulay. Nelson.

CHAPTER III.   PACIFICO AND POERIO

1. *Oxford, Döllinger, Gorham and Manning*

GLADSTONE. Letters to his wife. 45.

LATHBURY. Correspondence. Vol. i, 65, 79.

CRAEMER. Gladstone. Pp. 180, 181.

DISRAELI. Lord Bentinck. Chapter 24.

BUCKLE. Disraeli. Vol. i, 883.

CH. E. MALLET. Oxford. Vol. iii, 277.

2. *Don Pacifico and Political Intervention*

GLADSTONE. Speeches, 100–154.

QUEEN VICTORIA. Letters Vol. i, 2; 252.

C. F. BELL. Palmerston. 2 vols. London, 1936.

PHILIPP GUEDALLA. Palmerston. London, 1928. Pp. 306–309. Palmerston and Gladstone, p. 35.

BUCKLE. Disraeli. Vol. i, 1076.

CH. H. PARKER. Life and Letters of Sir James Graham. London, 1907. Vol. ii, 105.

MORLEY. Cobden. 274.

KINGSLEY MARTIN. The Triumph of Lord Palmerston. London, 1924. Pp. 59–64.

G. W. E. RUSSELL. Collections and Recollections. (Tauchnitz.) Vol. i, 195.

R. MUIR. Gladstone. 246.

HEINRICH LAMMASCH. Das Völkerrecht nach dem Kriege. Kristiania, 1927. 128.

WOLFGANG WINDELBAND. Die auswärtige Politik der Grossmächte. Stuttgart, 1925. Chaps. v and vi.

3. *The Prisons of Naples and Moral Intervention*

QUEEN VICTORIA. Letters Vol. i, 2; 267. (8th October, 1850.)

GLADSTONE. Gleanings. Vol. iv, 1.

G. M. TREVELYAN. Garibaldi and the Thousand. London, 1920. Chap. iii.

Manin and the Venetian Revolution of 1848. London.

468

CHARLES LACAITA. An Italian Englishman. London, 1933.

GUEDALLA. Palmerston. 317.

T. WEMYSS REID. Life, Letters, and Friendships of Lord Houghton. 2 vols. London, 1890. Vol. i, 451.

SIR HENRY DRUMMOND WOLFF. Rambling Recollections. Vol. i, 145.

KARL HILLEBRAND. Antonio Panizzi. Deutsche Rundschau. Vol. viii, 235.

CHAPTER IV. THE FIRST ENCOUNTER WITH DISRAELI

1. *Criticism*

QUEEN VICTORIA. Letters Vol. i, 2; 385, 403–406, 411, 413.

GLADSTONE. Speeches. 155–181.

Correspondence with his wife. 95.

GUEDALLA. Palmerston and Gladstone. 86.

Palmerston. 335.

GEORGE SAINTSBURY. The Earl of Derby. London, 1892.

LORD MALMESBURY. Memoirs of an Ex-Minister. 3 vols. (Tauchnitz.) Vol. ii, 86–92.

2. *Construction*

QUEEN VICTORIA. Letters Vol. 1, 2; 415–418, 421, 427, 428, 446, 524.

GLADSTONE. Speeches. Pp. 182–252.

HIRST. Gladstone as Financier. Pp. 142 ff.

PARKER. Peel. Vol. iii, 560.

GUEDALLA. Palmerston. P. 346.

EDWIN R. SELIGMAN. The Income Tax. New York, 1921. Pp. 51, 55, 128, 172.

OTTO VOCKE. Geschichte der Steuern der Britischen Reichs. Leipzig, 1868.

CHAPTER V. ERA, PALMERSTON

1. *A Reluctant War*

QUEEN VICTORIA. Letters, 1st Series; Vol. ii, 451, 454–5, 460, 467, 471. Vol. iii, 72, 77–87, 102, 108.

GLADSTONE. History of 1852–1860 and Greville's Latest Journals. English Historical Review, 11, 281. April 1887.

The Cambridge History of British Foreign Policy. Edited by Sir Aug. Ward and George P. Gooch. Cambridge, 1923. Vol. ii.

H. A. L. FISHER. History of Europe. Book III, Chap. xvi.

KINGSLEY MARTIN. The Triumph of Palmerston. Pp. 185, 202.

P. GUEDALLA. The Second Empire. London, 1932.

Palmerston and Gladstone. P. 100.

HIRST. Gladstone as Financier. P. 156.

FRANCES BALFOUR. Aberdeen. Vol. i, 125. Vol. ii, 178, 281, 282.
STANMORE. Aberdeen. Pp. 31, 257, 271, 281, 288.
BUCKLE. Disraeli. Vol. i, 1342, 1387, 1383.
W. REID. Lord Houghton. Vol. i, 503–505.
PARKER. Graham. Vol. ii, 264, 267, 268, 283.
TREVELYAN. Bright. Pp. 216, 245, 247.
MORLEY. Cobden. P. 306.
SIR H. MAXWELL. Life of Clarendon. 2 vols. London, 1913. Vol. ii,
    31.
E. T. MALCOLM-SMITH. Life of Stratford-Canning. London, 1933.
GEORGE P. GOOCH. Later Correspondence of Lord John Russell.
    London, 1925. Introduction, p. xlvi.
SIR EDWARD COOK. Delane of the Times. London, 1915. P. 90.
ALGERNON WEST. Diaries, p. 325.
G. W. E. RUSSELL. Collections. Vol. i, 77.
KINGLAKE. Invasion of the Crimea. Vol. i.
CARL FREIHERR VON VITZTHUNM AND ECKSTÄDT. St. Petersburg and
    London, 1852–1864. 2 vols. Stuttgart, 1886. Vol. i, 145,
    227.
KARL MARX AND FRIEDRICH ENGELS. Gesammelte Schriften, 1852–1862.
    2 vols. Stuttgart, 1917. Vol. ii, 112, 160, 265.
FRANZ MEHRING. Karl Marx. Leipzig, 1918. Chapter 9.
EMIL DANIELS. Englische Staatsmänner, von Pitt bis Asquith. Berlin,
    1925. P. 127.
HEINRICH FRIEDJUNG. Der Krimkrieg und die österreichische Politik.
    Stuttgart, 1911. P. 149.
BRYCE. Studies. P. 466.
F. E. SANDYS. History of Classical Scholarship. Cambridge, 1908.
    Vol. iii, 423.

2. "Civis Romanus Sum" in China

QUEEN VICTORIA. Letters Vol. i, 3 ; 226, 228.
BELL. Palmerston. Vol. ii, 167.
GUEDALLA. Palmerston. P. 390.
MAXWELL. Clarendon. P. 139.
TREVELYAN. Bright. P. 258.
MORLEY. Cobden. P. 321.
COOK. Delane. P. 102.
PARKER. Graham. Vol. ii, 291, 293, 302, 347.
SPENCER WALPOLE. Life of Lord John Russell. 2 vols. London,
    1889. Vol. ii, 286.
LORD EDMUND FITZMAURICE. Life of Lord Granville. 2 vols. London,
    1905. Vol. i, 227.

A. G. GARDINER. Life of Sir William Harcourt. 2 vols. London, 1933. Vol. i, 83.
GLADSTONE. Correspondence with his wife, 114.
BELL. Palmerston. Vol. ii, 180.
VITZTHUM. Petersburg. Vol. ii, 257, 247.

Marriage Bill

CRAEMER. Gladstone. 284.
FITZMAURICE. Granville. Vol. i, 281.
T. A. NASH. Life of Lord Westbury. 2 vols. London, 1888.
T. B. ATLAY. The Victorian Chancellors. 2 vols. London, 1906–08.

Ionian Islands

DRUMMOND WOLFF. Recollections. Vol. i, 280, 281.
LACAITA. Italian Englishman, 78.
SIR A. HARDINGE. Life of Lord Carnarvon. 3 vols. London, 1925. Vol. i, 135.
G. MASSARI. Cavour. Leipzig, 1874. P. 246.

3. Italy, and the Great Budget

QUEEN VICTORIA. Letters. 1st Series, 3; 270, 292, 307, 322, 327, 341, 343, 349, 357–366, 377.
HANSARD. Debates. Vol. 155, pp. 1130–1156.
G. M. TREVELYAN. Garibaldi and the Making of Italy. London, 1905. P. 20, 105.
H. A. L. FISHER. Europe. Book III, Chap. 17.
WALPOLE. Russell. Vol. ii, 309, 327.
LACAITA. Italian Englishman, 105.
GOOCH. Correspondence of Russell. Introduction, viii, ix.
FITZMAURICE. Granville. Vol. i, 325, 355.
PARKER. Graham. Vol. ii, 389.
HARDINGE. Carnarvon. Vol. i, 144.
MALMESBURY. Memoirs. Vol. iii, 50.
MAXWELL. Clarendon. Vol. ii, 188.
MALLET. Oxford. Vol. iii, 374.
DASENT. Delane. 2 vols. London, 1908.
SCHULTHESS. Europäischer Geschichtskalender. Nördlingen. Vol. i, 327. Vol. ii, 22.
HENRICH VON TREITSCHKE. Cavour. (Historische und politische Aufsätze II.)
Preussische Jahrbücher. Vol. iii. 1859. P. 358.

About Cobden

GLADSTONE. Speeches, 253–311.

T. A. HOBSON. Cobden, the International Man. London, 1918.

W. E. WILLIAMS. Rise of Gladstone to the Leadership of the Liberal Party. 1859–68. Cambridge, 1934.

S. BUXTON. Gladstone as Chancellor of the Exchequer. London, 1901. P. 29.

HIRST. Gladstone as Financier. P. 176.

HYDE. Gladstone at the Board of Trade. P. 220.

MARTIN. Life of Prince Consort. Vol. v, 33, 35, 37.

MORLEY. Cobden. Chapter xxvii.

G. VON SCHULZE-GAVERNITZ. Britischer Imperialismus und Englischer Freihandel. Leipzig, 1906.

F. MEISEL. Britische und deutsche Einkommensteuer. Tübingen, 1925.

LUDWIG BAMBERGER. Errinerungen. Berlin, 1900. P. 426.

Differences with Palmerston

QUEEN VICTORIA. Letters Vol. i, 3; 401–3, 423.

GUEDALLA. Palmerston and Gladstone. Pp. 123, 124, 126, 138, 146, 161, 166–7, 181, 313.

MARTIN. Prince Consort. Vol. v, 99, 100.

GLADSTONE. Speeches. P. 300.
Financial statements. P. 404.

F. W. HIRST. The Six Panics. London, 1913.

WEST. Diaries. P. 324.

MALMESBURY. Memoirs. Vol. iii. Pp. 93, 94.

VITZTHUM. Vol. ii, 94, 133.

BRENTANO. Wirtschaftsgeschichte. Vol. iii. Pp. 1, 216, 222.

Paper Duties

GUEDALLA. Palmerston. Pp. 418, 419, 457.

HIRST. Gladstone as Financier. Pp. 192, 292–7.

BUXTON. Gladstone as Chancellor. Chapter ix.

LECKY. Democracy and Liberty. London, 1899. Vol. i, 407.

LEONARD COURTNEY. The Working Constitution of the United Kingdom. London, 1920. P. 26.

JULIUS HATSCHEK. Englisches Staatsrecht. Tübingen, 1905. Vol. i, 248.

H. SUSSMANN. Das Budgetprivileg des Hauses der Gemeinen. Mannheim, 1909. P. 193.

EDUARD LASKER. Zur Verfassungsgeschichte Preussens. Pp. 271, 277.

COOK. Delane. Pp. 139, 141.

"THE TIMES." Anniversary Number, 1st January, 1936.

4. *A Singular Error*

QUEEN VICTORIA. Letters Vol. i, 3; 469.

GUEDALLA. The Queen and Mr. Gladstone. Vol. i, 123, 124.
Palmerston and Gladstone. Pp. 232, 233.

E. W. ADAMS. Great Britain and the American Civil War. 2 vols.
London, 1925.

SIR WEMYSS REID. Memoirs. London, 1905. P. 55.

GARDINER. Harcourt. Vol. i, 132.

5. *Schleswig-Holstein*

HANSARD. Debates. Vol. 173, pp. 862, 869; vol. 176, pp. 777, 1219.

GUEDALLA. Palmerston and Gladstone. Pp. 289, 290.

Cambridge History of Foreign Policy. Vol. ii, Chap. xiii.

LORD SALISBURY. Essays on Foreign Policy. London, 1905. P. 229.

WALPOLE. Russell. Vol. ii, 368.

FITZMAURICE. Granville. Vol. i, 453.

MAXWELL. Clarendon. Vol. ii, 293.

BISMARCK. Gedanken und Erinnerungen. Vol. i, Chap. xv.
Gesammelte Werke. Vol. iv, 56 (Alvensleben-Convention, pp. 59, 91).

ERICH BRANDENBURG. Die Reichsgründung. Leipzig, 1922. Vol. ii, 67.

SCHULTHESS. Europäischer Geschichtskalender. 1863, 1864.

CHAPTER VI. THE SECOND ENCOUNTER WITH DISRAELI

1. *Leader of the House*

WILLIAMS. Rise of Gladstone. Chapter v, pp. 104, 108.

MALLET. Oxford. Vol. iii, 331.

A. B. ELLIOTT. Life of Lord Goschen. 2 vols. London, 1911.
Vol. i, 61–64.

GARDINER. Harcourt. Vol. i, 78.

W. REID. Houghton. Vol. ii, 142.

GLADSTONE. Chapter of Autobiography. P. 197.

GUEDALLA. Palmerston and Gladstone. P. 281.

HANSARD. Vol. 175, 324 (11th May, 1864).

A. P. MARTIN. Life and Letters of Robert Lowe. 2 vols. 1893.
Vol. ii, 253.

ERNST VON PLENER. Erinnerungen. Vol. i, 376.

2. *Gladstone's Franchise Reform Defeated.*

HANSARD. Debates. Vol. 182, pp. 43, 147, 164, 218, 219, 1134.

Annual Register, 1866. Pp. 107, 113, 116, 117.

GLADSTONE. Speeches. Pp. 342–379.
TREVELYAN. Bright. Pp. 355–56.
BARRY O'BRIEN. Bright. P. 340.
P. MARTIN. Lowe. Vol. ii, 263, 267.
REID. Houghton. Vol. ii, 151, 152.
GOOCH. Correspondence of Russell. XV. Vol. ii, 351, 352.
SIR JOHN ROBINSON. Fifty Years in Fleet Street. P. 60.
J. BRYCE. Studies (Robert Lowe). P. 293.

3. *Disraeli Reforms the Franchise*

BUCKLE. Disraeli. Vol. ii, 218–99.
LADY GWENDOL. CECIL. Lord Salisbury. London, 1921 ff. Vol. i,
    233, 291, 272.
LADY BURGHCLERC. A Great Lady's Friendship. London, 1932.
    P, 126.
REID. Houghton. Vol. ii, 175.
GOOCH. Correspondence of Russell. Vol. ii, 362.
Annual Register, 1867. Pp. 27, 41, 88, 109.

4. *Gladstone's Triumph*

QUEEN VICTORIA. Letters. Second Series. London, 1926. Vol. i,
    517, 518, 539, 562.
BUCKLE. Disraeli. Vol. ii, 341–89, 426–41.
GLADSTONE. Chapter of Autobiography. Pp. 30, 37, 41.
    To His Wife. P. 64.
SIR JAMES O'CONNOR. History of Ireland. 1798–1924. London, 1925.
    2 vols. Vol. i, 122. Vol. ii, 3.
MAXWELL. Clarendon. Vol. ii, 346.
Annual Register, 1868. Pp. 57, 60.

CHAPTER VII. THE GREAT MINISTRY

1. *Prime Minister*

QUEEN VICTORIA. Letters, Series II. 1; 562, 561, 564.
GUEDALLA. The Queen and Mr. Gladstone. Vol. i, 47, 141.
MAXWELL. Clarendon. Vol. ii, 121, 353.
TREVELYAN. Bright. Pp. 387, 400.
FITZMAURICE. Granville. Vol. i, 94.
P. MARTIN. Lowe. Vol. ii, 268, 361.
SIR ALGERNON WEST. Recollections, 1832–1886. 2 vols. London,
    1899.
LORD KILBRACKEN. Reminiscences. London, 1931.

SIR EDWARD W. HAMILTON. Mr. Gladstone, A Monograph. London, 1898.

GEORGE LEVESON-GOWER. Memories of Gladstone. Contemporary Review, October, 1934.

FURST BÜLOW. Denkwürdigkeiten. Berlin, 1930. Vol. iv, 552.

MARY GLADSTONE. Diaries. P. 4.

LORD ACTON. The History of Freedom and other Essays. London, 1907.

Historical Essays. London, 1907.

Letters to Mary Gladstone, with biographical introduction by Herbert Paul. London, 1904.

W. E. BLENNERHASSETT. Political Career of Lord Acton. Dublin Review, April 1934, No. 389.

Selections from the correspondence of Lord Acton. London, 1917.

ULRICH NOACK. Geschichtwissenschaft und Wahrheit. Frankfurt a.M., 1935.

Annual Register, 1869. P. 276.

F. W. HIRST. Early Life and Letters of John Morley. 2 vols. London, 1927. Vol. i, 146.

2. *Ireland*

Annual Register, 1869. Pp. 23–119, 158.

QUEEN VICTORIA. Letters. Vol. ii, 1; 55, 277 (note), 577, 578, 604, 616,

GUEDALLA. The Queen and Mr. Gladstone. Vol. i, 181, 183, 187.

GLADSTONE. Chapter of Autobiography.

F. MCCARTHY. Outline of Irish History. P. 95.

FITZMAURICE. Granville. Vol. ii, 1.

TREVELYAN. Bright. P. 402.

BUCKLE. Disraeli. Vol. ii, 444.

JAMES BRYCE. Lord Chancellor Cairns (Studies, 184).

Irish Land Act

Annual Register, 1870. Pp. 20, 36, 40.

JAMES O'CONNOR. Ireland. Vol. ii, 21.

BUCKLE. Disraeli. Vol. ii, 458.

MAXWELL. Clarendon. Vol. ii, 361, 364.

M. J. BONN. Ireland. München, 1918.

Englische Kolonisation in Ireland. 2 vols. Stuttgart, 1906.

3. *Reforms*

Education Bill

T. WEMYSS REID. Life of William G. Forster. 2 vols. London, 1888.

Memoirs and Correspondence of Lyon Playfair. London, 1899. P. 271.

GARDINER. Harcourt. Vol. i, 215.

COOK. Delane. P. 225.
TREVELYAN. Bright. P. 406.
BUCKLE. Disraeli. Vol. ii, 461.
HATSCHEK. Englisches Staatsrecht. Vol. ii, 558, 563.

Universities

MALLET. Oxford. Vol. iii, 323, 332.
ELLIOTT. Goschen. Vol. i, 61.
E. ABBOTT AND L. CAMPBELL. Life and Letters of Benjamin Jowett.
2 vols. London, 1897. Vol. i, 184; ii, 25.
LORD COLERIDGE. Life and Correspondence. 2 vols. London, 1904.
Vol. ii, 49–67.
LORD SNOWDEN. Autobiography. 2 vols. London, 1934. Vol. i, 35.
Annual Register, 1871.

Army Reform

Annual Register, 1871. P. 69.
GARDINER. Harcourt. Vol. i, 227.
HATSCHEK. Staatsrecht. Vol. ii, 276.
CARDWELL. Dict. National Biography. Vol. ix, 93.
GUEDALLA. The Queen and Mr. Gladstone. Vol. i, 111, 283, 285.

Trade Unions

FREDERIC HARRISON. Autobiographical Memoirs. 2 vols. London,
1911. Vol. i, 317.
E. VON PLENER. Erinnerungen. Vol. i, 302.
BRENTANO. Wirtschaftsgeschichte. Vol. iii, 1, 454.
G. M. TREVELYAN. History of England. London, 1934. P. 639.

4. The Franco-German War

Annual Register, 1870. Pp. 107, 110.
FITZMAURICE. Granville. Pp. 2, 32 ff.
ALG. WEST. Contemporary Portraits. London, 1920. P. 46.
LORD REDESDALE. Memories. London, 1916. P. 110.
LACAITA. Italian Englishman. P. 128.
LORD NEWTON. Lord Lyons. 2 vols. London, 1913. Vol. ii,
208, 334.
MRS. ROSSLYN WEMYSS. Memoirs and Letters of Sir Robert Morier.
2 vols. 1911. Vol. ii, 210.
COOK. Delane. Pp. 226, 230.
HARRISON. Memoirs. Vol. ii, 4, 15.
HIRST. Morley. Vol. ii, 176.
GUEDALLA. The Queen and Mr. Gladstone. Vol. i, 169, 238–9, 242,
244, 249, 251, 261.

476

QUEEN VICTORIA. Letters. Vol. ii, 2; 10, 27, 28, 46, 52, 54, 74.
EMPRESS FREDERICK. Letters, edited by Ponsonby. London, 1928.
  P. 71.
GLADSTONE. Gleanings. Vol iv, 197.
KNAPLUND. Gladstone's Foreign Policy. New York, 1935. Pp. 47,
  50, 55, 62.
Cambridge History of Foreign Policy. Vol. ii, 31, 33, 70.
R. H. LORD. The Origin of the War of 1870. Cambridge, 1924.
DORA NEILL RAYMOND. British Policy and Public Opinion during the
  Franco-Prussian War. New York, 1921.
DELBRÜCK. Weltgeschichte. Berlin, 1928. Vol. v.
K. RHEINDORF. England und der deutsch-französ: Krieg. Bonn, 1923.
H. V. TREITSCHKE. Deutsche Kämpfe. P. 280.
DANIELS. Englische Staatsmanner. Pp. 285, 288.
W. E. LINGELBACH. Belgian Neutrality. American Historical Review.
  Vol. 39, 48.

Black Sea

Cambridge History of Foreign Policy. Vol. iii, 43 ff.
K. RHEINDORF. Die Schwarze-Meer-Frage, 1856–1871. Berlin, 1925.
KNAPLUND. Foreign Policy. Pp. 61, 63 (note 32).
QUEEN VICTORIA. Letters. Vol. ii, 2; 83, 85, 123, 187.
BISMARCK. Gesammelte Werke. Vol. vii, 407.
Die Grosse Politik der Europäischen Kabinette. Vol. ii, 13.
M. BUSCH. Tagebuchblätter. Vol. i, 409.

5. *Fighting for Peace*

QUEEN VICTORIA. Letters. Vol. ii, 1; 594; ii, *pass.*
SCHULTHESS. Europäischer Geschichtskalender. 1869, p. 481; 1872,
  336, 339, 346.
Nouveau Recueil Général des Traités. Vol. ii, s.I., 37.
STRUPP. Urkunden zur Geschichte des Volkerrechts. Vol. i, 405.
Convention concernant les Droits et les Devoirs des Puissances neutres
  en cas de Guerre Maritime. 18 Octobre, 1907.
TH. W. BALCH. The Alabama Arbitration. Philadelphia, 1900.
E. D. ADAMS. Biography of his Father (American Statesmen). Boston.
  1900.
FITZMAURICE. Granville. Vol. ii, 81–108.
GARDINER. Harcourt. Vol. i, 144, 172, 196, 202, 257.
L. WOLF. Ripon. Vol. i, 237 ff.
ANDREW LANG. Sir Stafford Northcote. 2 vols. Edinburgh, 1890.
ATLAY. The Victorian Chancellors. Vol. ii, 396. (Lord Selborne.)
REID. Forster. Vol. ii, 23, 27, 31.

WALPOLE. Russell. Vol. ii, 365.
GOOCH. Correspondence of Russell. P. 411.
BARRY O'BRIEN. Bright. P. 274.
KARL SCHURZ. Erinnerungen. Vol. ii, 187.

6. *Decline*

GUEDALLA. The Queen and Mr. Gladstone. Vol. i, 66 ff., 299, 316–338, 374.
GLADSTONE. Correspondence with his wife. P. 188.
  Speeches. Pp. 401–425, 426–469.
VISCOUNT GLADSTONE. After Thirty Years. Pp. 101, 331–334.
HENRY NEV. GLADSTONE, in Hirst, "Gladstone as Financier." P. 304.
BUCKLE. Disraeli. Vol. i, 1201; ii, 210, 534, 570, 649.
FITZMAURICE. Granville. Vol. ii, 21.
LADY BURGHCLERK. Friendship. P. 292.
KNAPLUND. Gladstone and Imperial Policy. P. 127.
MUIR. Gladstone. P. 242.
BRENTANO. Wirtschaftsgeschichte. Vol. iii, 2, 77.
ERNST VON PLENER. Erinnerungen. Vol. i, 367.
J. BRYCE. Sir George Jessel in "Studies in Cont. Biogr." P. 170.

CHAPTER VIII.   THE LAST ENCOUNTER WITH DISRAELI

1. *Resignation from the Leadership*

QUEEN VICTORIA. Letters. 2 ser. ii, 371, 377.
GUEDALLA. The Queen and Mr. Gladstone. Vol. i, 394, 453, 454.
GLADSTONE. Correspondence with his wife. Pp. 207–209.
GARDINER. Harcourt. Vol. i, 273, 285, 286.
WEMYSS. Morier, Vol. ii, 248, 301.
LUISE VON KOBELL. Ignaz von Döllinger. München, 1891. Pp. 47–54.
LYTTON STRACHEY. Manning. Pp. 93, 95.
WOLF. Ripon. Vol. i, 207.
FITZMAURICE. Granville. Vol. ii, 140.
LORD REDESDALE. Memoirs. P. 549.
LORD ESHER. Journals. Vol. i, 46, 125 (about Hartington).
B. HOLLAND. Life of Duke of Devonshire. 2 vols. London, 1911.

2. *The Bulgarian Atrocities*

QUEEN VICTORIA. Letters. 2 ser. ii, 453, 499, 504, 538.
GLADSTONE. Speeches. Pp. 470–552.
MARY GLADSTONE. Diaries. Pp. 109, 132.

VISCOUNT GLADSTONE. After Thirty Years. P. 125.

MARY GLADSTONE. Hawarden Letters. P. 20.

BUCKLE. Disraeli. Vol. ii, 896, 898, 915, 917, 938, 1196, 1170–73, 1213.

LORD BEACONSFIELD. Letters to Lady Bradford. London, 1929. Pp. 154, 196, 251, 256, 273.

REID. Forster. Vol. ii, 175.

Houghton. Vol. ii, 344.

ELLIOTT. Goschen. Vol. i, 219.

LORD REDESDALE. Memoirs. P. 650.

LORD BALFOUR. Chapters of Autobiography. London, 1930. P. 106.

GARDINER. Harcourt. Vol. i, 312.

W. T. STEAD. The M.P. for Russia. London, 1909.

G. W. E. RUSSELL. Sir Wilfrid Lawson. P. 241.

R. W. SETON WATSON. Disraeli, Gladstone, and the Eastern Question. A Study in Diplomacy and Party Politics. London, 1935.

The Southern Slav Question. London, 1911. Gladstone's Correspondence with Bishop Strossmaier.

W. L. LANGER. European Alliances and Alignments, 1871–1890. New York, 1931. Pp. 87, 155, 165.

ALFRED SPENDER. Fifty Years of Europe. P. 60.

HAROLD TEMPERLEY. Disraeli and Cyprus. Engl. Histor. Review. Vol. 46, p. 274 (April 1931).

J. A. R. MARRIOTT. The Eastern Question. Oxford, 1924. Pp. 341–345.

H. A. L. FISHER. Europe. P. 1043.

BISMARCK. Gedanken und Erinnerungen. Chapter xxviii.

Die Grosse Politik der Europ. Kabinette. Band ii.

J. M. VON RADOWITZ. Aufzeichnungen und Erinnerungen. Stuttgart, 1925. Vol. ii, 165.

3. *The Decision*

GLADSTONE. Speeches. Pp. 553–579.

Political Speeches in Scotland. 2 vols. Edinburgh, 1879 and 1880.

Selected Speeches on British Foreign Policy, 1738–1914 (World Classics, 201). P. 371. (West Calder Speech, 27th November, 1879.)

MARY GLADSTONE. Diaries. P. 177–188.

Hawarden Letters. P. 175.

MRS. HUMPHRY WARD. A Writer's Recollections. London, 1918. P. 198.

BALFOUR. Autobiography. P. 129.

KILBRACKEN. Reminiscences. London, 1931.

ELISABETH PAULI, REINHOLD PAULI. Lebenserinnerungen. P. 331.

REID. Memoirs. Pp. 276–285.

1. *Prime Minister Once More*

QUEEN VICTORIA.   Letters.   Vol. ii, 3; 82, 87, 87–88, 91, 95.

GUEDALLA.   The Queen and Mr. Gladstone.   Vol. ii, 23, 113.

BUCKLE.   Disraeli.   Vol. ii, 1398, 1400.

FITZMAURICE.   Granville.   Vol. ii, 193, 194, 199, 206, 208, 219, 225–228.

GARDINER.   Harcourt.   Vol. i, 359.

ELLIOTT.   Goschen.   Vol. i, 208–214.

KILBRACKEN.   Reminiscences.   P. 132.

ESHER.   Journals.   Vol. i, 37, 211.

LORD ACTON.   Correspondence.   P. 170.

WEST.   Recollections.   Vol. ii, 57.

J. L. GARVIN.   The Life of Joseph Chamberlain.   London, 1932 ff. Vol. i.

GWYNN AND TUCKWELL.   Life of Sir Charles Dilke.   2 vols.   London, 1917.   Vol. i, 323, 337.

WINSTON CHURCHILL.   Life of Lord Randolph Churchill.   2 vols. London, 1906.

H. E. GORST.   The Fourth Party.   London, 1906.

MARY PONSONBY.   A Memoir by her Daughter.   London, 1927.

BISMARCK.   Gesammelte Werke.   Vol. viii, 370, 387.

Grosse Politik.   Vol. iv, 16, 22.

BUSCH.   Tagebuchblätter.   Vol. iii, 7, 13.

FURST HOHENLOHE,   Denkwürdigkeiten.   2 vols.   Stuttgart, 1907. Vol. ii, 306.

Parnell

R. BARRY O'BRIEN.   Life of C. S. Parnell (Nelson).

KATHERINE O'SHEA (MRS. PARNELL).   Parnell, His Love Story and Political Life.   2 vols.   London, 1914.

ST. JOHN ERVINE.   Parnell.   London, 1925.

W. O'BRIEN.   The Parnell of Real Life.   London, 1926.

JAMES BRYCE in Studies in Contemporary Biography.

Bradlaugh Case

GLADSTONE.   Speeches.   Pp. 580–600.

BRYCE.   Studies.   P. 438.

W. H. LUCY.   A Diary of Two Parliaments.   London, 1884.

HATSCHEK.   Staatsrecht.   Vol. i, 265.

COURTNEY.   Constitution.   P. 98.

2. *Ireland Again*

QUEEN VICTORIA.   Letters II.   Vol. iii, 130, 143, 148, 152, 163–165, 186–192, 208, 210, 220–234, 241, 275, 285–290, 319.

GUEDALLA. The Queen and Mr. Gladstone. Vol. ii, 121, 124, 127, 130, 138, 153, 155.

GLADSTONE. Letters to his Wife. Pp. 145–6.

Mr. Forster and Ireland. (Special Aspects of Irish Question.)

VISCOUNT GLADSTONE. Thirty Years. Pp. 46–7, 55, 185, 193.

MARY GLADSTONE. Diaries. Pp. 204, 213, 225, 249–50.

Hawarden Letters. Pp. 288–89.

LORD ACTON. Letters. Pp. 45, 48, 99, 114 note.

BUCKLE. Disraeli. Vol. ii, 1387, 1457–8.

B. O'BRIEN. Parnell. Chapters 11–14.

K. O'SHEA. Parnell. Vol. i, 207. Chapters 23–6.

REID. Forster. Vol. ii, 244, 246, 258, 286, 287, 300, 339.

Playfair. P. 292.

Memories. Pp. 292, 328.

GARDINER. Harcourt. Vol. i, 420 ff.

MALLET. Herbert Gladstone. P. 302.

ABBOTT. Jowett. vol. ii, 202.

BALFOUR. Autobiography. P. 155.

CECIL. Salisbury. Vol. iii, 41, 42.

LORD NEWTON. Lord Lansdowne. London, 1929. P. 22.

GWYNNE-TUCKWELL. Dilke. Vol. i, 440.

LORD ESHER. Journals. Vol. i, 319.

MRS. WARD. Recollections. P. 178.

WEST. Private Diaries. P. 5.

J. O'CONNOR. Ireland. Vol. ii, 100.

BONN. Ireland. P. 93.

MARTENS. Agrarreformen in Ireland. München, 1915. Pp. 108, 224–238.

3. Africa

Majuba

GUEDALLA. The Queen and Mr. Gladstone. Vol. ii, 108, 128, 133.

QUEEN VICTORIA. Letters II. Vol. iii, 124, 148, 166, 167, 179, 180.

VISCOUNT GLADSTONE. After Thirty Years. P. 213.

ESHER. Journals. Vol. i, 78.

FITZMAURICE. Granville. Vol. ii, 229.

MARY GLADSTONE. Hawarden Letters. P. 85.

ALFRED E. PEASE. Elections and Recollections. London, 1932. P. 60.

Egypt

QUEEN VICTORIA. Letters II. Vol. iii, 305, 315, 332, 402, 439, 460, 470.

GUEDALLA. The Queen and Mr. Gladstone. Vol. ii, 203–5, 215, 224.

R. RECOULY. De Bismarck à Poincaré. 60 ans de diplomatie républicaine. Paris, 1932. Pp. 134 ff.

FITZMAURICE. Granville. Vol. ii, 252, 253, 255, 256, 265.
TREVELYAN. Bright. P. 433.
LORD CROMER. Modern Egypt. Vol. i.
LORD ZETLAND. Lord Cromer. London, 1930.
LORD NEWTON. Lyons. Vol. ii, 277.
GARDINER. Harcourt. Vol. i, 459.
LANGER. European Alliances. P. 268.
Grosse Politik. Vol. iv, 26, 38, 418, 434.
BUSCH. Tagebuchblätter. Vol. iii, 85.
HUGO GRAF LERCHENFELD-KÖVERING. Erinnerungen-Denkwürdigkeiten.
Berlin, 1935. Pp. 142, 338.

Gordon

D. C. BOULGER. Life of General Gordon. Nelson.
BERNARD M. ALLEN. Gordon. London, 1935.
PIERRE CRABITÈS. Gordon, The Sudan, and Slavery. London, 1933.
P. 203.
LYTTON STRACHEY. End of General Gordon, in "Eminent Victorians."
VALENTINE CHIROL. Fifty Years of a Changing World. London.
P. 43.
RENDEL. Papers. Pp. 39 ss.
VISCOUNT GLADSTONE. After Thirty Years. Pp. 246, 252, 369, 434.
FITZMAURICE. Granville. Vol. ii, 325, 381–403.
CECIL. Salisbury. Vol. ii, 98, 104.
REID. Forster. Vol. ii, 500.
LORD CREWE. Lord Rosebery. 2 vols. London, 1931. Vol. i, 216.
QUEEN VICTORIA. Letters. Pp. 480–484, 487, 491, 495, 507, 528, 532,
597, 603, 605, 619, 633, 643.
LORD RIBBLESDALE. Impressions. London, 1927. P. 122.

Penjdeh

GARVIN. Chamberlain. Vol. i, 573.
LUCY. Parliament. P. 462.
Grosse Politik. Vol. iv, 120, 122.
RADOWITZ. Denkwürdigkeiten. Vol. ii, 246.

4. Bismarck

QUEEN VICTORIA. Letters. Vol. iii, 2; 624.
HANSARD. Debates. Vol. 205, 435, 436, 977.
British Documents on the Origin of the War. Edited by G. P. Gooch
and H. Temperley. Vol. iii, 404. (Memor. by Sir Eyre
Crowe, 1st January, 1907.)
Grosse Politik. Vol. iv, 50, 51, 56, 76, 104, 113, 124; vol. iii, 135, 176.
(Drei-Kaiser-Abkommen.)

Das Staatsarchiv. Vol. 44, 252, 270 (with the articles of the
   Norddeutsche Allgemeine Zeitung of 2nd and 4th March, 1885).
FITZMAURICE. Granville. Vol. ii, 422, 426, 427, 430.
CECIL. Salisbury. Vol. iii, 92.
GWYNNE-TUCKWELL. Dilke. Pp. 2, 81.
RENNELL RODD. Diplomatic Memories. Vol. i, 77, 119.
LORD ACTON. Letters to Mary Gladstone. Pp. 201, 205, 212; Intro-
   duction, xiii.
EMPRESS FREDERICK. Letters. P. 195.
VISCOUNT GLADSTONE. After Thirty Years. P. 102.
BISMARCK. Gesammelte Werke. Vol. xiii, 4–8, 22.
BUSCH. Tagebuchblätter. Vol. iii, 186.
BÜLOW. Denkwürdigkeiten. Vol. iv, 580.
RADOWITZ. Aufzeichnungen. Vol ii, 245.
GRAF WALDERSEE. Denkwürdigkeiten. Stuttgart, 1922. Vol. i, 256,
   275.
HOHENLOHE. Denkwürdigkeiten. Vol. ii, 358.
HERMANN ONCKEN. Rudolf von Bennigsen. 2 vols. Stuttgart, 1910.
   Vol. ii, 15.
SCHWEINITZ. Denkwürdigkeiten. Vol. ii, 299.
POSCHINGER. Ein Achtundvierziger (L. Bucher). Berlin, 1894.
   Vol. iii, 367.
A. K. MÜLLER. Zur ausseren Politik Bismarck in den achtziger Jahren
   in Brauer-Marcks, Erinnerungen an Bismarck.
Die Nation: Wochenschrift, edited by Th. Barth. Vol. ii, 328; vol. iii,
   345 (A. Milner), 387, 737.
THIMME, in Berliner Monatshefte, August and September 1929.
ALFRED RAMBEAU. Jules Ferry. Paris, 1903.
JOSEPH REINACH. Leon Gambetta. Paris, 1918.

6. *Franchise Reform and Defeat*

QUEEN VICTORIA. Letters. Vol. ii, 3. 513, 520, 522, 523, 531, 547,
   564, 581, 662.
GUEDALLA. The Queen and Mr. Gladstone. Vol. ii, 165, 289, 297,
   309, 317, 364, 368.
VISCOUNT GLADSTONE. After Thirty Years. P. 362.
GARVIN. Chamberlain. Vol. i, 463–487, 549, 557.
GARDINER. Harcourt. Vol. i, 504, 509, 521, 524.

CHAPTER X.   IN ALLIANCE WITH PARNELL

1. *Interval*

QUEEN VICTORIA. Letters. Vol. iii, 3; 441, 439, 687; iii, 1; 147.
GUEDALLA. The Queen and Mr. Gladstone. Vol. ii, 50, 166, 243.

MARY GLADSTONE. Diaries. Pp. 355, 362–365, 369.

LORD ACTON. Correspondence. P. 265.

Letters to Mary Gladstone. Pp. 157–159, 214.

VISCOUNT GLADSTONE. Thirty Years. Pp. 296, 303, 339, 366, 367, 391.

FITZMAURICE. Granville. Vol. ii, 463, 466.

BALFOUR. Autobiography. P. 207.

CREWE. Rosebery. Vol. i, 165.

GARVIN. Chamberlain. Vol. i, 548–573, 575 ff.; ii, 25, 86–119.

GARDINER. Harcourt. Vol. i, 286, 467, 527, 540, 542, 544, 574.

H. A. L. FISHER. Life of Lord Bryce. 2 vols. London, 1927. Vol. i, 209, 211, 212.

LORD EVERSLEY. Gladstone and Ireland. London, 1912. Pp. 264, 276, 277, 282.

VICT. HICKS-BEACH. Life of Sir Michael Hicks-Beach. 2 vols. 1932. Vol. i, 230, 245.

HARDINGE. Carnarvon. Vol. iii, 146, 155, 158, 178.

PEASE. Elections. P. 94.

A. L. THOROLD. Life of Henry Labouchere. London, 1913. Pp. 230–263.

GWYNNE-TUCKWELL. Dilke. Vol. ii, 190.

MALLET. Herbert Gladstone. P. 114.

BUSCH. Tagebuchblätter. Vol. ii, 430.

C. VON TIEDEMANN. Sechs Jahre Chef der Reichskanzlei unter Bismarck. Leipzig, 1910. Pp. 132–133.

2. *Home Rule*

QUEEN VICTORIA. Letters. Vol. ii, 707, 713, 718; iii, 25, 48, 102, 105, 108, 113, 119, 122.

GUEDALLA. The Queen and Mr. Gladstone. Vol. ii, 65, 405, 407.

GLADSTONE. Speeches. Pp. 601–644.

MARY GLADSTONE. Diaries. P. 385.

VISCOUNT GLADSTONE. After Thirty Years. Pp. 308, 312, 396. (Correspondence with Balfour, December 25th.)

GARDINER. Harcourt. Vol. i, 552, 554–560, 577.

THOROLD. Labouchere. Pp. 245, 246, 248, 251, 263.

GARVIN. Chamberlain. Vol. ii, 171–172, 192 ff., 210, 238, 242, 245.

HARDINGE. Carnarvon. Vol. iii, 249.

MALLET. Herbert Gladstone. P. 129.

TREVELYAN. Bright. P. 454.

LORD MORLEY. Recollections. 2 vols. London, 1919. Vol. i, 214.

RENDEL. Private Papers. P. 33.

W. O'BRIEN. The Parnell of Real Life. P. 116.

PEASE. Elections. P. 135.

BARRY O'BRIEN. Parnell. P. 403.

HICKS-BEACH. Life of Sir Michael Hicks-Beach. Vol. i, 216.

HARDINGE. Carnarvon. Vol. iii, 223.

FISHER. Bryce. Vol. i, 216.

T. M. HEALY. Letters and Leaders. 2 vols. London, 1928.

T. P. O'CONNOR. Memoirs. 2 vols. London, 1929.

R. C. K. ENSOR. England, 1870–1914. Oxford, 1936. P. 558, App.
A and P. 183 note.

ALFRED MILNER in Die Nation. Vol. iii, 334–402, 426, 441, 618.

3. *The Great Forgery*

QUEEN VICTORIA. Letters. Vol. iii, 1; 233, 279, 517.

W. CHURCHILL. Lord Randolph Churchill. Vol. ii, 416, 514.

GARVIN. Chamberlain. Vol. ii, 257, 286.

GARDINER. Harcourt. Vol. ii, 16, 27.

FISHER. Bryce. P. 216.

CECIL. Salisbury. Vol. iii, 333.

PEASE. Elections. Pp. 153, 226, 231.

SIR RICHARD TEMPLE. Life in Parliament. London, 1893. Pp. 143,
264.

Parnellism and Crime. Reprinted from The Times. London, 1887.

SIR ALFRED ROBBINS. Parnell, the Last Five Years. London, 1926.
Pp. 44, 47, 52, 56, 61, 76, 103.

BARRY O'BRIEN. Parnell. Chapter xxi.

Lord Russell of Killowen (Nelson). Chapter xii.

F. H. O'DONNELL. History of the Irish Parliamentary Party. 2 vols.
London, 1910.

THOROLD. Labouchere.

LORD ASKWITH. Life of Lord James of Hereford. London, 1930.

GARDINER. Pillars of Society. P. 126. (Mrs. Humphry Ward.)

MRS. WARD. Recollections. P. 238.

JAMES O'CONNOR. Ireland. Vol. ii, 128.

J. ALFRED SPENDER. Great Britain, 1886–1935. Chapter iii.

CHAPTER XI.   THE BREACH WITH PARNELL AND THE LAST
MINISTRY

1. *O'Shea v. O'Shea and Parnell*

QUEEN VICTORIA. Letters. Vol. iii, 1, 665.

HENRY HARRISON. Parnell Vindicated. London, 1930.

K. O'SHEA. Parnell. Vol. ii, chapters xii and xiii.

BARRY O'BRIEN. Parnell. Chapters xxii–xxvi.

ROBBINS. Parnell. Pp. 147, 153.

SIR JAMES O'CONNOR. Ireland. Vol. ii, 142.

GARDINER. Harcourt. Vol. ii, 81, 83, 87, 90.
GARVIN. Chamberlain. Vol. ii, chapter xxxviii.
MORLEY. Recollections. Vol. i, 253, 256, 259, 263, 268.
A. SPENDER. Life, Journalism, and Politics. 2 vols. 1927. Vol. i, 44.
RENDEL. Papers. Pp. 26, 126.
LUCY. A Diary of the Salisbury Parliament. London, 1872. P. 314.
AUGUSTE SCHLÜTER. A Lady's Maid in Downing Street. London, 1922.

2. *The Last Ministry*

QUEEN VICTORIA. Letters. Vol. iii, 2; 144, 145, 172–175, 181, 182, 189, 328.
GUEDALLA. The Queen and Mr. Gladstone. Vol. ii, 71, 75, 437, 446, 454, 455, 458, 462, 474.
SIR ALGERNON WEST. Private Diaries. Pp. 18, 52, 57, 83, 80, 145, 154, 213.
MORLEY. Recollections. Vol. ii, 5.
GARDINER. Harcourt. Vol. ii, 170, 194, 246, 254.
L. WOLF. Ripon. Vol. ii, 203.
A. SPENDER. Sir Henry Campbell-Bannerman. London, 1924. Vol. ii, 194.
    Great Britain, 1886–1935. Chapter 5.
HAROLD SPENDER. Fire of Life. P. 109.
THOROLD. Labouchere. P. xii.
CREWE. Rosebery. Vol. ii, 402, 403.
AUSTEN CHAMBERLAIN. Down the Years. London, 1936. P. 78.
GARVIN. Chamberlain. Pp. 2, 563.
MALLET. Herbert Gladstone. Pp. 148, 150.
VISCOUNT GLADSTONE. After Thirty Years. P. 348.
JUSSERAND. What Me Befell. London, 1933. P. 146.
VON ECKARDSTEIN. Lebenserinnerungen. Leipzig, 1919. Vol. i, 196.
LORD ESHER. Journals. Vol. i, 161, 217.
LORD KILBRACKEN. Reminiscences. P. 114.
AUG. BIRRELL. Sir Frank Lockwood.
Die Nation, Jahrgang. x, pp. 313 and 348.
LORD OXFORD. Fifty Years of Parliament. London, 1926.
    Memoirs and Reflections. London, 1928.
    Speeches. London, 1927.
MARGOT ASQUITH. Autobiography (Penguin Books). Vol. i, chapter ix.

3. *Epilogue*

MORLEY. Recollections. Vol. ii, 68–73.
ALGERNON WEST. Diaries. Pp. 323, 350, 427, 432.
MARY GLADSTONE. Diaries. P. 432.
LATHBURY. Correspondence. Vol. ii, No. 457.

GARVIN. Chamberlain. Vol. ii, 594.

BALFOUR. Autobiography. Pp. 76–82.

MRS. WARD. Recollections. Pp. 238, 304–306.

ROBINSON. Fleet Street.

RENDEL. Papers. Pp. 92, 95, 116, 138.

CREWE. Rosebery. Vol. i, 347, 552.

MOBERLY BELL. Life and Letters. London, 1927. P. 206.

Hawarden Letters. P. 278.

Grosse Politik. Vol. x, 257.

THEODOR FONTANE. Briefe an Freunde. Berlin, 1909. Vol. ii, 466.

G. M. TREVELYAN. G. O. Trevelyan. A Memoir.

INDEX

ABERDEEN, EARL OF, 1784–1860; Foreign Secretary 1828–1830, 1841–1846; Colonial Secretary 1834–1835, p. 22; Gladstone's letters on prisons of Naples, p. 65; Prime Minister 1852–1855, pp. 77–91; persuades Gladstone to enter Palmerston's Cabinet, p. 93; death, p. 149.

ACTON, JOHN EMERICH DALBERG-ACTON (1869 Lord A.); historian and politician. A Liberal and a Roman Catholic; friend of Gladstone, p. 192; M.P., 1859–1869; Professor of Modern History in Cambridge, 1895–1902; on Gladstone's correspondence with his father, p. 14; informs Gladstone about proceedings of Vatican Congress, p. 249; on House of Lords, p. 300; on Gladstone's position in English history, p. 307; against Gladstone's eulogy of Beaconsfield, p. 316; wishes Gladstone to continue, p. 366; thinks "Parnell king," p. 372; on Gladstone's authority, p. 376; Gladstone's visit, 1886, p. 405; court appointment, p. 437.

ADAMS, CHARLES FRANCIS, 1807–1886; United States ambassador in London 1861–1868, pp. 142, 223; American member of court of arbitration, p. 229.

ALBERT, PRINCE CONSORT, 1819–1861; married to Queen Victoria 10.2.1840, p. 35; against Palmerston, p. 59; congratulates Gladstone on budget of 1853, p. 84; admires Great Budget, p. 122; intervention in *Trent*-affair, p. 139; death, p. 140.

ALTHORP, LORD (1834 Lord Spencer); 1782–1845; Chancellor of the Exchequer 1830–1834, p. 18; succeeds his father in the peerage, p. 21.

ANDRASSY, COUNT GYULA; 1823–1890; Hungarian statesman, insurgent against Austria 1849; Austrian-Hungarian minister for foreign affairs 1871–1879, p. 254.

ARABI, AHMED, leader of Egyptian nationalist movement, pp. 333–338.

ARGYLL, DUKE OF, 1823–1900; India Secretary 1868–1874; supports Gladstone's Eastern agitation, p. 262; Lord Privy Seal 1880—April 1881; resigns on introduction of Irish Land Bill, p. 312.

ARNOLD, DR. THOMAS, 1795–1842; headmaster of Rugby 1828–1842, p. 449.

ASQUITH, HERBERT HENRY (1925 Earl of Oxford), 1852–1928; called to the bar 1876; entered parliament 1886; before Parnell Commission, pp. 415, 416; Home Secretary 1892–1895, pp. 437, 441; Chancellor of the Exchequer 1905–1908; Prime Minister 1908–1916.

BALFOUR, ARTHUR (1922 Lord B.), 1848–1930; nephew of Lord Salisbury; on General election of 1880, p. 277; Gladstone offers non-party solution of Home Rule question, p. 390; Irish Secretary 1887–1892, pp. 409–410; leads opposition against Home Rule Bill 1893, pp. 440,

441; last visit to Gladstone, p. 449; Prime Minister 1902–1905; Foreign Secretary 1916–1919.

BAMBERGER, LUDWIG, 1823–1899; leading German Liberal; member of German Reichstag 1871–1893, p. 115.

BARING, SIR EVELYN, *vide* Cromer.

BATTENBERG, PRINCE ALEXANDER, 1857–1893; prince of Bulgaria 1879–1885, p. 386.

BELL, CHARLES MOBERLY, 1847–1911; manager of *The Times* 1890–1911, p. 452.

BENEDETTI, COUNT VINCENT, 1817–1900; French diplomatist, ambassador in Berlin 1864–1870, pp. 215, 217, 360.

BENNIGSEN, RUDOLF VON, 1824–1904; leader of German National Liberal party, member of German Reichstag and Prussian Chamber 1866–1898, p. 357.

BENTINCK, LORD GEORGE, 1802–1848; leader of protectionist Tories, p. 50.

BISMARCK, PRINCE OTTO, 1815–1898, Prussian Prime Minister 1862, p. 142; conflict with chamber of deputies, p. 126; Danish war, p. 143; informs British ambassador of occupation of Hanover 1866, p. 165; universal suffrage, p. 166; on Clarendon's death, p. 211; Franco-German war, pp. 212–222; Berlin Memorandum, p. 254; Berlin Congress, p. 266; on Beaconsfield and Salisbury, p. 266; offers Beaconsfield alliance, p. 289; "Professor Gladstone," p. 288; on Dulcigno, p. 290; conference with Goschen, p. 291; on Transvaal, p. 332; on Suez Canal, p. 33; on lack of foresight in English Foreign policy, p. 339; attacks Granville in German Reichstag, 2.3.1885, p. 358; sends Herbert Bismarck to London, p. 360; farewell to Empress Frederick, p. 440; Gladstone on Bismark and Cavour, pp. 117, 451.

BISMARCK, HERBERT, 1849–1904; eldest son of Prince Bismarck; on Gladstone's foreign policy, p. 270; proposes annexation of Egypt to Granville, p. 338; conference with Jules Ferry (October 1884), p. 340; wishes Anglo-Russian conflict, p. 356; mission to London 1885, p. 360; friend of Rosebery, p. 360; German Foreign Secretary 1886–1890.

BLOWITZ, M. DE, pseudonym of Fritz Oppert 1825–1903; chief correspondent of *The Times* in Paris since 1873, p. 360.

BRADLAUGH, CHARLES, 1833–1891; free-thought advocate and politician; elected M.P. for Northampton 1880, p. 292; re-elected 1881 and ejected by force; expelled 1882 and re-elected, excluded 1883; re-elected 1884; excluded 1885; again elected 1885 and allowed to take his seat 1886; death, p. 296.

BRAND, HENRY, later Viscount Hampden, 1814–1892; Speaker of the House of Commons 1872–1884, pp. 165, 309.

BRENTANO, LUJO, 1844–1931; German economist; professor, pp. 40, 120.

BRIGHT, JOHN, 1811–1889; leader of Anti-Corn-Law League, p. 40; entered parliament 1843; against Palmerston, p. 59; against Crimean War, p. 86; "Angel of Death" speech, p. 95; warns Gladstone not to enter Derby's cabinet, p. 184; attempts reform movement, p. 128; letter to Gladstone 1861, p. 130; on American civil war, p. 138;

answers Lowe, p. 160; reform meetings, pp. 166, 173; difference with Disraeli, p. 183; enters Gladstone's cabinet 1868, p. 187; illness and resignation, p. 201; advocates ballot, p. 210; *Alabama* affair, p. 224; against Gladstone's abusers, p. 264; Chancellor of Duchy, p. 283; opposes coercion in Ireland, p. 303; quarrel with Irish members, p. 308; resigns on bombardment of Alexandria, pp. 336–337; declines to join cabinet 1886, p. 391; against Home Rule, p. 401; death, p. 403.

BROUGHAM, LORD, 1778–1868; Lord Chancellor 1830–1834, pp. 21, 155.

BRYCE, JAMES (1914 Viscount B.), 1838–1922; historian and parliamentarian, Professor; entered parliament 1880; "American Commonwealth" 1888, p. 439; Chancellor of Duchy 1892–1894, p. 439; President of the Board of Trade 1895; on Gladstone's speech on Oath Bill, p. 295.

BUCHER, LOTHAR, 1817–1892; democratic member of Prussian National Assembly 1848; exile in England 1849–1860; friend of the socialist leader, Ferdinand Lassalle; enters Prussian Foreign Office 1864, to become Bismarck's collaborator; secret mission to Spain 1870; calls Gladstone "Freudenstein," p. 356.

BURKE, EDMUND, 1729–1797; leading Whig in House of Commons and political writer; *Reflections on the French Revolution"* 1790. His doctrine of the State, p. 26; influence on Gladstone, pp. 163, 207, 235.

BURNE-JONES, SIR EDWARD, 1833–1898; painter, friend of Mary Gladstone, p. 260; welcomes peace with Boers, p. 332.

BUSCH, MORITZ, 1821–1899; journalistic mouthpiece of Bismarck, p. 356.

CAIRNS, LORD, 1819–1885; Lord Chancellor 1868, 1874–1880; Leader of Conservative peers, p. 198.

CAMBRIDGE, GEORGE WILLIAM DUKE OF, 1819–1904; Commander-in-Chief of the Army 1856-1895, p. 209.

CAMPBELL-BANNERMANN, SIR HENRY, 1836–1908; entered parliament 1868; Irish Secretary 1885, p. 368; War Secretary 1886 and 1892–1895, pp. 437, 439; Prime Minister 1905–1908, p. 434; on Parnell, p. 426.

CANNING, GEORGE, 1770–1827; Foreign Secretary 1822–1827; Prime Minister 1827; friend of Gladstone's father, p. 12; views on intervention, p. 62; influence on Gladstone, p. 163.

CANNING, STRATFORD, later Viscount Stratford de Redcliffe, 1786–1880; ambassador in Constantinople 1842–1856, p. 88.

CARDWELL, EDWARD, later Viscount Cardwell, 1813–1886; entered parliament 1842; becomes Secretary for War 1868, p. 189; army reforms, p. 208.

CARNARVON, EARL OF, 1836–1890; Colonial Secretary 1874–1878, p. 259; annexation of Transvaal 1877, p. 271; resigns 1878 on Eastern question, p. 265; Lord Lieutenant of Ireland 1885–1886, p. 378; secret interview with Parnell, p. 379; resigns, p. 387.

CARLYLE, THOMAS, 1795–1881; historian and essayist; "Shooting Niagara," p. 176; against Turks, p. 260.

CAVENDISH, LORD FREDERICK, 1836–1882; brother of Lord Hartington; entered parliament 1865; Chief Secretary for Ireland 1882, p. 324;

murdered in Phoenix Park 6.5.1882, pp. 325, 326; Gladstone's speech in his honour, p. 328.

CAVENDISH, LUCY, niece of Mrs. Gladstone, pp. 328, 398.

CAVOUR, COUNT CAMILLO, 1810–1861; Italian statesman; conversation with Gladstone, p. 109; alliance with Napoleon, pp. 110, 114; death, p. 117.

CHAMBERLAIN, SIR AUSTEN, 1863–1937; eldest son of Joseph Chamberlain; enters parliament 1892; maiden speech, p. 441; Chancellor of the Exchequer 1903–1905, 1919–1922; Irish Treaty, p. 385; Foreign Secretary 1924–1929.

CHAMBERLAIN, JOSEPH, 1836–1914; leader of the "Birmingham League," p. 203; enters parliament 1876; becomes in 1880 President of the Board of Trade, pp. 283, 284; opposes coercion in Ireland, p. 303; supports negotiation with the Boers, p. 331; on Egyptian policy, p. 336; radical agitation, p. 367; negotiations with Parnell, pp. 322, 368; advocates Irish Central Board, p. 368; "unauthorized programme," p. 377; affronted by Parnell, p. 381; visit to Hawarden, p. 382; joins Cabinet of 1886, p. 392; resigns, p. 395; attacks Home Rule Bill, pp. 398–401; "Round Table" conference, p. 407; parliamentary fight against second Home Rule Bill, pp. 440, 441; last visit to Gladstone, p. 449; Colonial Secretary 1895–1903.

CHILDERS, HUGH C. E., 1827–1896; Secretary for War 1880–1882; Chancellor of the Exchequer 1882–1885, p. 369.

CHRISTIAN IX, KING OF DENMARK, 1818–1906; becomes king 1863, p. 143; father of King George I of Greece, Queen Alexandra of England, Dagmar, Russian Tsarina, and Thyra, Duchess of Cumberland; visits of Gladstone 1883, p. 372, and 1895, p. 452.

CHURCHILL, LORD RANDOLPH, 1849–1895; entered parliament 1874; "Fourth Party," pp. 286, 292; attacks evicted tenants bill, p. 300; against reform of standing orders, p. 309; aspires to leadership of Conservative Party, p. 316; votes for extension of Irish franchise p. 365; joy about Gladstone's defeat 8.6.1885, p. 369; seeks understanding with Parnell, p. 378; becomes Indian Secretary, p. 369; on Maamtrasna assassinations, p. 380; Chancellor of the Exchequer 1886, p. 405; resigns, p. 406; speech about Pigott, p. 421; admires Gladstone, p. 441.

CHURCHILL, WINSTON, born 1875; son of Lord Randolph Churchill; M.P. since 1902; Colonial Secretary 1921–1922; Irish Treaty, p. 385.

CLARENDON, LORD, 1800–1870; Foreign Secretary 1853–1858, p. 94; 1865–1866, 1868–1870; opposed by the Queen, p. 187; on open competition, p. 208; death, p. 212; treaty on *Alabama*, p. 224.

CLARKE, SIR EDWARD, 1841–1931; barrister and parliamentarian; Solicitor-General 1886–1892; on Parnell, pp. 418, 422, 425.

CLEMENCEAU, GEORGES, 1841–1929; French statesman; enters parliament 1876; leader of Radicals, overthrows Freycinet 29.7.1882, p. 337; and Ferry 30.3.1885, p. 361; Prime Minister 1906–1909, 1917–1920.

COBDEN, RICHARD, 1804–1865; leader of Anti-Corn-Law League, p. 40; enters parliament 1841, p. 41; praised by Peel, p. 51; opposes Palmerston in Pacifico case, p. 59; on Chinese war, p. 100; declines Palmerston's offer, p. 112; Anglo-French Commercial Treaty, pp. 117–119; death, p. 150.

COHEN, DR., family physician of Bismarck, p. 290.

COLERIDGE, SIR JOHN DUKE (1873 Baron C.), 1820–1894; Liberal M.P. 1865–1873; Solicitor-General 1871; Chief Justice 1873–1894, p. 205; Bradlaugh case, p. 293.

COLLIER, SIR ROBERT (1885 Lord Monkswell), 1817–1886; entered parliament 1852; Solicitor-General 1863; Attorney-General 1868; appointed judge in Court of Common Pleas, November 1871; shortly afterwards in Judicial Committee of Privy Council, p. 233.

COURTNEY, LEONARD (1905 Baron C.), 1832–1918; leader-writer of *The Times* 1865–1881; professor of political economy in London 1872–1875; enters parliament 1875; Under-Secretary for Home Office 1880, p. 305.

COWPER, LORD, 1834–1905; Lord Lieutenant of Ireland 1880–1882, p. 303.

CROMER, LORD (formerly Sir Evelyn Baring), 1841–1917; British Commissioner of Egyptian debt 1876–1880; British Agent and Consul-General in Egypt 1883–1907, pp. 342–351.

CURRIE, SIR DONALD, 1825–1909; founder of Castle Steamship Co.; entered parliament 1880; Liberal Unionist 1886–1900, p. 374.

DARWIN, CHARLES, 1809–1882, p. 263.

DAVIS, JEFFERSON, 1808–1889; president of Southern States in American Civil War 1861–1864, p. 141.

DAVITT, MICHAEL, 1846–1916; founder of Irish Land League 1879; sentenced 1870 to 15 years penal servitude for treason felony, released 1877, p. 298; imprisoned 1881–1882, p. 310; relation to Parnell, p. 328.

DELANE, JOHN THADDEUS, 1817–1879; editor of *The Times* 1841–1877, p. 125.

DERBY, 14TH EARL OF (formerly Lord Stanley), 1799–1869; Irish Secretary 1830; "Rupert of Debate," p. 19; for extinction of slavery, p. 19; declines Peel's offer 1834, p. 21; joins Peel's cabinet 1841, p. 36; resigns 1846, p. 49; Pacifico case, p. 59; Conservative Prime Minister 1852, p. 70; declines, in 1855, to form government, p. 91; advances to Gladstone, p. 99; Prime Minister 1858–1859, p. 103; invites Gladstone, p. 104; against abolition of paper duty, p. 126; Prime Minister 1866–1868, p. 168; "leap in the dark," p. 175; resigns, p. 176; opposes Irish Land Bill, p. 197; death, p. 198.

DERBY, 15TH EARL, formerly Lord Stanley, 1826–1893; joins his father's cabinet, p. 168; Foreign Secretary in Disraeli's cabinet 1874–1878, pp. 259–265; Colonial Secretary 1882–1885; chairman of Gladstone's last meeting, p. 454.

DERBY, 16TH EARL, 1841–1908; second son of fourteenth Earl, Secretary for War 1878, p. 454.

DICKENS, CHARLES, 1812–1870; "Eatanswill Election," p. 16; on House of Commons, p. 17; *Hard Times*, p. 102; *David Copperfield*, p. 207.

493

DILKE, SIR CHARLES, 1843–1911; enters parliament 1868; becomes in 1880 Under-Secretary for Foreign Affairs, p. 283; on Odo Russell and Bismarck, p. 289; responsibility for Gordon's appointment, p. 345; on Herbert Bismarck's mission 1885, p. 360; pilots franchise reform, p. 365; divorce case, p. 382.

DISRAELI, BENJAMIN (1876 Earl of Beaconsfield), 1804–1881; enters parliament 1837, p. 46; author of *Coningsby* and *Sybil*, pp. 47, 156; derides Gladstone, p. 46; attacks Peel, p. 50; becomes Chancellor of the Exchequer 1852, p. 70; budget, p. 72; urges Derby 1855 to form government, p. 91; correspondence with Gladstone 1858, p. 105; against removal of paper duty, p. 132; attacks Palmerston's Danish policy, p. 146; on Gladstone's reform speech of 1831, p. 162; Chancellor of the Exchequer 1866, p. 168; Reform Bill, pp. 169–176; becomes Prime Minister 1868, p. 177; on Irish Church, p. 181; evades dissolution, p. 182; differences with Bright, p. 183; resigns after general election 1868, p. 184; opposes Irish Land Bill, p. 200; on Army reforms, pp. 209, 210; increasing popularity, p. 231; attacks government, pp. 233, 242; on colonies, pp. 234–236; death of Lady Beaconsfield, p. 239; Prime Minister 1874, p. 245; against Gladstone's critics, p. 246; "coffee-house babble," p. 255; becomes Earl, p. 256; Turkish policy, pp. 259–266; Berlin Congress, p. 266; annexation of Cyprus, pp. 268–270; on Midlothian campaign, p. 272; resigns, p. 280; as leader of cabinet, p. 285; manifesto on Irish unrest, p. 296; opposes evicted tenants Bill, p. 300; death 19.4.1881, p. 313; Gladstone's appreciation, pp. 313–316.

DÖLLINGER, IGNATIUS, 1799–1890; German theologian and historian, friend of Gladstone and Lord Acton; on account of opposition against dogma of infallibility excommunicated, p. 249; Gladstone's visits 1845, p. 55; 1874, p. 249; 1886, p. 405.

DUFFY, SIR CHARLES GAVAN, 1816–1903; Irish revolutionist; arrested in 1848; Minister and Speaker in Australia 1857–1880, p. 379.

EDWARD VII, 1841–1910; King of Great Britain 1901–1910; marries 10.3.1863, Alexandra, daughter of Danish King, p. 143; on Franco-German War, p. 216; illness 1871, p. 237; lack of employment, p. 239; negotiates with Hartington, p. 329; veneration for Gladstone, p. 435; urges Rosebery to take over Foreign Office, p. 437; among bearers of Gladstone's coffin, p. 457.

EYTH, MAX VON, 1836–1906; German engineer and writer, p. 319.

FERDINAND II, 1810–1859; King of Naples 1830–1859, pp. 65–67, 116.

FERRY, JULES, 1832–1893; French statesman, Minister of Education 1879; Prime Minister 1880–1881, p. 334, and 1883–1885, pp. 340, 361.

FONTANE, THEODOR, 1819–1898; German poet and novelist; lived in London 1850–1856, p. 457.

FORSTER, w. e., 1818–1886; Liberal M.P. 1861–1886; Vice-President, p. 202; Education Bill, pp. 203–204; for settlement of *Alabama* question, p. 228; becomes in 1880 Irish Secretary, pp. 283, 296; against coercion, p. 299; thinks coercion inevitable, p. 305; "Protection of Persons and Property Bill," p. 308; Parnell's arrest, pp. 318–320; opposes his release and resigns, pp. 322–324; against Zobeir, p. 347; attacks Gladstone, p. 348.

FOX, charles james, 1749–1807; parliamentary leader of Whigs; prohibition of slave trade 1807, p. 19; rivalry with Pitt, pp. 76, 107.

FREEMAN, edward a., 1823–1892; historian, professor at Oxford 1884–1892; against Turkish cruelties, p. 260.

FREYCINET, charles, 1828–1923; French statesman; Prime Minister, 1879–1880, 1882, 1886, 1890–1892, pp. 335–337.

FROUDE, james a., 1818–1894; historian and man of letters; chief disciple and biographer of Carlyle, p. 260.

GAMBETTA, leon, 1838–1882; French statesman; opposes Napoleon III; organizes national defence 1870–1871; President of the Chamber 1879; foreign policy, p. 334; Prime Minister 14th November, 1881–26th January, 1882, pp. 334–335; last speech, p. 337; death, p. 335.

GARIBALDI, giuseppe, 1807–1882; the hero of Italian *risorgimento*; landing in Sicily, p. 67; visit to London, p. 156.

GEORGE V, king, 1910–1936; among the bearers of Gladstone's coffin, p. 457.

GIBBON, edward, 1737–1794; historian, pp. 28, 207.

GLADSTONE, catherine, 1813–1900; marries Gladstone, p. 31; letter to Graham, p. 132; on reception in Newcastle, p. 141; against resignation 1874, pp. 248, 251; accompanies Gladstone to meeting, p. 278; in Leeds October 1881, p. 319; welcomes Granville, p. 394; learns of final resignation, p. 444; last farewell and death, p. 457.

GLADSTONE, john, 1764–1851; Gladstone's father; friend of Canning, p. 12; M.P. 1818–1827; correspondence with son, p. 12; proprietor of slave plantations, p. 19.

GLADSTONE, herbert (1910 Viscount Gladstone), 1854–1930: youngest son of Gladstone; enters parliament 1880, p. 279; on Katherine O'Shea, p. 383; "Hawarden kite," p. 388.

GLADSTONE, mary, later Mrs. Drew, 1847–1927; correspondence with Ruskin, p. 263; on Gladstone's Inaugural Address, p. 273; correspondence with Lord Acton, pp. 306, 307; "crisis of Liberal party," p. 373; wedding, p. 394; on Parnell's visit in Hawarden, p. 419; on Gladstone's last speech in Liverpool, p. 454.

GODLEY, arthur, later Lord Kilbracken; Gladstone's private secretary, pp. 189, 444.

GOERRES, josef, 1776–1848; German political writer against Napoleon I, and for Roman Catholic Church, p. 55.

GORDON, CHARLES, general, 1833–1885; suppresses Taiping rising in China 1863; Egyptian Governor-General of Equatorial provinces 1874–1876; of the Sudan 1877–1879; Private Secretary to Lord Ripon, Viceroy of India, 1880; character, p. 343; appointed British Commissioner for Sudan, p. 344; in Khartoum, pp. 348–351; death, p. 351.

GORHAM, clergyman; his case, p. 56.

GORTSCHAKOFF, PRINCE, 1798–1883; Russian Foreign Minister 1856–1880; denounces Black Sea Treaty, pp. 220–222; Berlin Memorandum, p. 254.

GOSCHEN, GEORGE JOACHIM (1900 Lord G.), 1837–1907; grandson of G. J. Göschen, Leipzig publisher; author of *Theory of the Foreign Exchanges* (1861); enters parliament 1863; talk with Palmerston about reforms, p. 148; advocates University Reform, p. 205; President of the Poor Law Board 1868–1871; First Lord of the Admiralty 1871–1874; special embassy to Constantinople 1880–1881, pp. 289–290; 1885 appealed to by the Queen for help against Gladstone, p. 386; Chancellor of the Exchequer 1887, p. 406.

GRAHAM, SIR JAMES, 1792–1861; entered parliament 1818; First Lord of the Admiralty 1830–1834; declines Peel's offer 1834, p. 21; Home Secretary in Peel's government 1841–1846, pp. 36, 39; in Aberdeen's government 1852–1855, pp. 77, 91; resigns, p. 94; last speech, p. 133.

GRAMONT, DUKE OF, 1819–1880; French Foreign Minister 1870, p. 214 ff.

GRANT, ULYSSES, 1822–1885; victorious general of Northern States in American civil war; President of United States 1869–1877, p. 228.

GRANVILLE, EARL OF, 1815–1891; Foreign Secretary 1851–1852; fails in 1859 to form government, p. 111; opposes Gladstone's Italian policy, p. 114; Colonial Secretary 1868–1870, p. 188; Leader of the House of Lords, p. 194; negotiates with Cairns, p. 197; becomes Foreign Secretary July 1870, p. 212; negotiations on Franco-German, pp. 214–220; Black Sea controversy, p. 221; *Alabama* question, pp. 225–231; on "Bulgarian Horrors," pp. 258, 261; during crisis of 1880, p. 282; becomes Foreign Secretary, p. 283; intimacy with Gladstone, p. 286; on Salisbury's leadership of Lords, p. 330; visit of Herbert Bismarck, p. 338; recommends Gordon to Baring, p. 344; appoints him, p. 245; conflict with Bismarck, pp. 356–360; for Irish Central Board, p. 369; Colonial Secretary 1886, p. 393; death, p. 437.

GREVILLE, CHARLES C. F., 1794–1865; political annalist; *Journal of the Reigns of George IV, William, and Queen Victoria*, p. 87; Secretary for Jamaica, p. 207.

GREY, EARL, 1764–1845; Prime Minister 1830–1834, p. 11.

GREY, GENERAL CHARLES, 1804–1870; son of Earl Grey; Private Secretary to Queen Victoria 1861–1870, pp. 180, 186, 195, 196, 213; death, p. 237.

HAMILTON, SIR EDWARD, 1847–1908; Gladstone's Private Secretary 1880–1885, p. 189; correspondence with Ponsonby, p. 351; Permanent Secretary to the Treasury 1902–07.

496

HAMMOND, EDMUND, later Lord Hammond, 1802–1890; Permanent Under-Secretary at the Foreign Office 1854–1873, p. 212.

HARCOURT, SIR WILLIAM, 1827–1904; entered parliament 1868; Solicitor-General 1873, p. 244; criticizes Gladstone, p. 248; becomes Home Secretary in 1880, p. 283; Gladstone "the only universal amalgam," p. 377; Chancellor of the Exchequer 1886, p. 393; on Parnell, pp. 426, 430; Chancellor of the Exchequer 1892, p. 437; farewell in Gladstone's last cabinet, p. 445; conflict with Rosebery, p. 447.

HARCOURT, LEWIS (1917 Viscount H.), 1863–1922; son of Sir William Harcourt; private secretary to his father 1881–1904; M.P. 1904–1917; Colonial Secretary 1910–1915, p. 428.

HARRISON, FREDERIC, 1831–1923; historical and miscellaneous writer; positivist; member of the Trade Union commission, p. 211; on Franco-German war, p. 218.

HARTINGTON, LORD, later Duke of Devonshire, 1833–1908; enters parliament 1857; Secretary for War 1866; Irish Secretary 1871, p. 188; Leader of the Liberal Party in the House of Commons 1875, pp. 252, 257, 261; sent for by the Queen 1880, p. 281; Indian Secretary, p. 283; supports evicted tenants Bill, p. 299; responsibility for Gordon's appointment, p. 345; defends Gladstone against Forster, p. 348; forces decision about Khartoum expedition, p. 350; opposes Irish Central Board, p. 369; contrast to Chamberlain, p. 377; declines to join Gladstone's cabinet, p. 391; speech against Home Rule, p. 398.

HAYNAU, BARON, 1786–1853; Austrian general, p. 64.

HEALY, TIMOTHY, 1855–1931; Irish Nationalist; M.P. 1880–1918; Governor-General of the Irish Free State 1922–1928, pp. 308, 380, 389, 415.

HEGEL, G. WILHELM, 1770–1831; German philosopher; pp. 54, 61.

HERBERT, SIDNEY, 1810–1861; enters parliament 1832; First Lord of the Admiralty 1841; Secretary for War 1845 and 1852–1855, p. 72; joins Palmerston's cabinet, p. 91; resigns, p. 94; Secretary for War 1859, p. 112; death, p. 149.

HERSCHEL, FARRER, later Lord Herschel, 1837–1899; enters parliament 1874; Lord Chancellor 1886, p. 393, and 1892–1895, p. 437.

HICKS-BEACH, SIR MICHAEL (1906 Viscount St. Aldwyn), 1837–1916; Chancellor of the Exchequer 1885, 1895–1905; Irish Secretary 1886, pp. 369, 380, 402, 409.

HOHENLOHE, PRINCE CHLODWIG, 1819–1901; German Ambassador in Paris 1874–1885; Imperial Governor of Alsace-Lorraine 1885–1894; Imperial Chancellor 1894–1900, p. 291.

HOUGHTON, LORD, formerly Monckton Milnes, 1809–1885; writer and parliamentarian, pp. 152, 160, 176.

JAMES, SIR HENRY (1895 Lord James of Hereford), 1828–1911; enters parliament 1869; Solicitor-General 1873; Attorney-General 1880–1885; declines to join Gladstone's cabinet 1886, p. 391; Parnell commission, p. 414.

JESSEL, SIR GEORGE, 1824–1883; called to the bar as first Jewish barrister 1847; enters parliament 1868; Solicitor-General 1871; Master of the Rolls 1873, p. 244.

JOWETT, BENJAMIN, 1817–1893; Master of Balliol 1870–1893; on Gladstone's *Homer*, p. 97; on University Reform, p. 206; meets Gladstone, p. 311.

JUSSERAND, J. J., 1855–1932; French diplomatist and writer; attached to London embassy 1887–1890; ambassador in Washington 1902–1925, pp. 432, 455.

KIMBERLEY, LORD, 1832–1902; Colonial Secretary 1870–1874, 1880–1882; Indian Secretary 1882–1886, 1892–1894, p. 445.

KRÜGER, PAUL, 1825–1904; leads Boer insurrection 1880–1881, p. 331; President of the Boer Republic 1883–1900.

LABOUCHERE, HENRY, 1831–1912; parliamentarian and journalist; in the diplomatic service 1854–1864; enters parliament in 1865; founds in 1876 weekly journal *Truth*; on Irish obstruction, p. 309; arachnoid talents, pp. 380, 389; on Mitchelstown affair, p. 410; excluded from cabinet 1892, p. 435.

LACAITA, GIACOMO (Sir James), 1813–1895; advocate in Naples, assisted Gladstone to collect information about Bourbon misrule; comes in 1852 to London; naturalized in England 1855; secretary to Gladstone's mission to Ionian islands, p. 108; deputy to first Italian parliament 1861–1865, p. 116.

LANSDOWNE, MARQUIS OF, 1845–1927; Governor-General of Canada 1883–1888; Viceroy of India 1888–1893; Secretary for War 1895–1900; for Foreign Affairs 1900–1905, pp. 299, 310.

LASSALLE, FERDINAND, 1825–1864; German socialist agitator and political and philosophical writer, p. 115.

LERCHENFELD, COUNT HUGO, 1843–1928; Bavarian member of German Bundesrat 1880–1918; on Bismarck and Egypt, p. 339.

LEVY, JOSEPH MOSES, 1812–1888; chief proprietor of *Daily Telegraph* from 1855, p. 124.

LEWIS, SIR GEORGE, 1833–1911; solicitor, p. 422.

LINCOLN, ABRAHAM, 1809–1865; President of United States 1860–1865, pp. 138, 140, 156.

LINCOLN, LORD, afterwards Duke of Newcastle, 1811–1864; friend of Gladstone in Oxford, p. 12; recommends Gladstone to his father, p. 13; unseated by his father, p. 49; enters Aberdeen's cabinet, p. 77; Palmerston's cabinet 1859, p. 112; death, p. 149.

LOWE, ROBERT (1880 Lord Sherbrooke), 1811–1892; Vice-President of the Council 1859, p. 159; attacks reform, pp. 159–175; refuses to join Derby's cabinet, p. 168; Chancellor of the Exchequer 1868, p. 188; difficulties on Irish Land Bill, p. 199; for reform of civil service, p. 208; duty on matches, p. 233; resigns, p. 244.

LLOYD GEORGE, DAVID, born 1859; Chancellor of the Exchequer 1908–1915; Prime Minister 1916—1922; concludes Irish Treaty, p. 385.

LUBBOCK, SIR JOHN (1900 Lord Avebury), 1834–1913; banker; parliamentarian; scientist; M.P. 1870–1900; Liberal Unionist, p. 263.

LYNDHURST, LORD, 1772–1863; Lord Chancellor 1827–1830, 1834–1835, 1841–1846, pp. 36, 127.

LYONS, LORD, 1817–1887; British diplomatist; ambassador in Paris 1867–1887, p. 215.

LYTTELTON, LORD, 1817–1876; Gladstone's brother-in-law, pp. 31, 33.

LYTTELTON, ALFRED, 1857–1913; nephew of Mrs. Gladstone; marries in 1885 Laura Tennant, p. 274; joins Liberal Unionists, p. 408; enters parliament 1895; Colonial Secretary 1903–1905.

MACAULAY, THOMAS BABINGTON (1857 Lord M.), 1800–1859; historian, essayist and statesman; enters parliament 1830, p. 18; criticizes Gladstone's *State and Church*, p. 29; on Disraeli's budget, p. 72; on Palmerston's Chinese policy, p. 101; on reform of civil service, p. 702.

M'CARTHY, JUSTIN, 1830–1912; Irish politician, historian, and novelist; enters parliament 1879, pp. 427, 430.

MAHDI—MOHAMED ACHMED OF DONGOLA, 1840–1885, pp. 341–351.

MALET, SIR EDWARD, 1837–1908; British ambassador in Berlin 1884–1895, p. 359.

MALMESBURY, LORD, 1807–1889; Conservative Foreign Secretary 1852, 1858–1859, pp. 111, 128.

MANIN, DANIELE, 1807–1857; Italian patriot; leader of revolution in Venice 1848–1849, p. 68.

MANNING, HENRY EDWARD, 1808–1892; cardinal; Gladstone's friend in Oxford, p. 27; joins Roman Catholic Church 1851, p. 56; for Irish University reform, p. 241; for infallibility dogma, pp. 249, 250; supports Irish Central Board, p. 368; his biography, p. 450.

MARX, KARL, 1818–1883; German socialist; lived in London 1849–1883, pp. 98, 153.

MASON, JAMES M., 1798–1871; commissary of Southern American states; *Trent* affair, p. 139.

MELBOURNE, VISCOUNT, 1779–1848; enters parliament 1806; Irish Secretary 1827–1830; Home Secretary 1830–1834; Prime Minister 1834–1841, pp. 21, 25, 35.

MIALL, EDWARD, 1809–1881; leading Nonconformist, p. 204.

MILL, JOHN STUART, 1806–1873; philosopher and politician; M.P. for Westminster, p. 152; speeches for reform, p. 160; defeated, p. 192.

MILNER, ALFRED (1902 Viscount Milner), 1854–1925; High Commissioner for South Africa 1897–1905, p. 408.

MOLESWORTH, SIR WILLIAM, 1810–1855; radical politician; enters parliament 1832; Colonial Secretary in Palmerston's cabinet, p. 77.

MORIER, SIR ROBERT, 1826–1893; diplomatist; appointed to German courts 1853–1876; on Franco-German war, p. 216; on Gladstone's personal charm, p. 249; Berlin appointment declined by Bismarck, p. 359; ambassador at St. Petersburg 1884–1893.

MORLEY, JOHN (1910 Viscount M.), 1838–1923; journalist, essayist, parliamentarian, and biographer (Burke, Voltaire, Rousseau, Diderot, Walpole, Cromwell, Cobden, Gladstone); editor of the *Fortnightly Review* 1870–1882; *Pall Mall Gazette* 1880–1883; entered parliament 1883; on Gladstone and Disraeli, p. 106; on Gladstone's family, p. 191; on "The Chamber of Mediocrities," p. 193; visit to Darwin, p. 263; demands evacuation of Sudan, p. 353; thinks 1884 Gladstone aged, p. 336; Irish Secretary 1886, pp. 392–395; Parnell's divorce case, pp. 422–431; on physical decline of Gladstone, p. 432; Irish Secretary 1892, pp. 437–439; informs Mrs. Gladstone of impending resignation, p. 444; last visit, p. 455.

MÜLLER, MAX, 1823–1903; philologist; of German origin; professor in Oxford, p. 220.

MÜNSTER, COUNT (1899 Prince), 1820–1902; German diplomatist; Ambassador in London 1873–1885; in Paris 1885–1900; approaches Beaconsfield 1879 with suggestion of alliance, p. 289; on German colonial policy, p. 357; Bismarck's Note of 5.5.1884, p. 359.

NAPOLEON III, 1808–1873; *coup d'état* 2.12.1852, p. 69; Orsini's attempt, p. 103; Italian policy, pp. 110, 117; commercial treaty with England, p. 119.

NAPOLEON, PRINCE LOUIS, 1856–1879, only son of Napoleon III, p. 271.

NEWCASTLE, 4th Duke of, 1785–1851, pp. 12, 15, 49.

NEWMAN, JOHN HENRY, 1801–1890; theologian; initiates the Tractarian movement; 1845 received in the Roman Catholic Church, p. 27; 1879 Cardinal.

NICHOLAS I, 1796–1855; Tsar 1825–1855, pp. 85, 97.

NORTHBROOK, EARL, 1826–1904; Governor-General of India 1872–1876; First Lord of Admiralty 1880–1884; High Commissioner in Egypt July 1884; responsibility for appointment of Gordon, p. 345.

NORTHCOTE, SIR STAFFORD (1885 Earl of Iddesleigh), 1818–1887; Gladstone's private secretary, p. 207; commission on *Alabama* question, p. 225; Chancellor of the Exchequer 1874; Leader of the House of Commons 1876; Leader of the Opposition 1880, pp. 286, 309; death, p. 406.

O'BRIEN, RICHARD BARRY, 1847–1918; barrister and author; biographer of Parnell, Charles Russell, John Bright, p. 431.

O'BRIEN, WILLIAM, 1852–1928; Irish journalist and parliamentarian; M.P. 1883–1918; nine times prosecuted for political offences; on Gladstone's Home Rule speech 1886, p. 397; "Plan of Campaign," p. 408.

OLLIVIER, EMILE, 1825–1913; French Premier in 1870, pp. 217, 221.

ORSINI, 1819–1858; Italian patriot; attempt against Napoleon III, p. 103.

O'SHEA, KATHERINE, wife of William O'Shea, mistress of Parnell, p. 321; correspondence with Gladstone, p. 383.

O'SHEA, WILLIAM, 1840–1905; Irish politician; captain retired 1862; marries Katherine Wood 1867; enters parliament 1880 for County Clare; negotiates between Parnell and the Government, pp. 322–323; between Parnell and Chamberlain, p. 368; stands 1885 in Liverpool as a Liberal, p. 383; with Parnell's help elected for Galway, p. 422; witness before Parnell Commission, p. 415; petition for divorce 1889, p. 423.

PALMER, SIR ROUNDELL (1872 Lord Selborne), 1812–1895; called to the bar 1837; enters parliament 1847 (Peelite); Solicitor-General 1861; Attorney-General 1862; *Alabama* affair, p. 223; declines to join cabinet 1886, p. 391.

PALMERSTON, VISCOUNT, 1784–1865; enters parliament 1807; enters cabinet 1827; Foreign Secretary 1830–1834, 1835–1841, 1846–1851; Don Pacifico affair 1850, pp. 58–63; on General Haynau, p. 64; on Bourbon misrule in Naples, p. 67; dismissed 1851, p. 69; Home Secretary 1852–1855; forms government 1855, p. 91; Chinese war, p. 100; falls on Conspiracy Bill 1858, p. 103; Prime Minister again 1859, p. 110; differences with Gladstone, pp. 123–132, 136–137; Note on *Trent* affair, p. 139; declaration on Danish policy, p. 144; death, p. 148; on Gladstone's reform speech 1864, p. 154.

PANIZZI, ANTONIO, 797–1879; born in Modena; compelled to fly as conspirator 1822; sentenced to death in his absence, comes to England, Chief Librarian at the British Museum 1856–1866, p. 68.

PARNELL, CHARLES STEWART, 1846–1891; enters parliament 1875, p. 287; chairman of Home-Rule Party in the House of Commons 1880, p. 288; controls Irish Land League, p. 298; invents "boycott," p. 301; obstructs Forsters coercion Bill, p. 308; on Land Bill, pp. 313, 317; arrest, p. 320; liaison with Katherine O'Shea, pp. 321, 383; on Phoenix Park murder, p. 326; vote on Gordon question, p. 353; helps to overthrow Gladstone's Government, p. 370; secret interview with Carnarvon 1.8.1885, p. 379; electoral manifesto of 21.11.1885, p. 380; affronts Chamberlain, p. 381; preparation of Home Rule Bill, p. 395; speech for Home Rule Bill, p. 395; *The Times* letter, pp. 411–418; invited to Hawarden, p. 419; divorce case, pp. 422–425, split of Irish Party, pp. 426–430; death 430.

PEEL, SIR ROBERT, 1788–1850; enters parliament 1809; defied by Oxford on introducing Catholic emancipation, pp. 12, 17; takes interest in Gladstone, p. 20; Prime Minister 1834, p. 21; appoints Gladstone p. 22; Tamworth manifesto, p. 23; resigns, p. 24; on Gladstone's book about State and Church, p. 30; again Prime Minister 1841, p. 35; appoints Gladstone Vice-President of the Board of Trade, p. 36; letter to Gladstone's father, p. 38; Maynooth, p. 44; difference with Disraeli, p. 47; defeated, p. 51; death, p. 63.

PIGOTT, RICHARD, 1828–1889; Irish journalist; forger of Parnell letter, pp. 416–417.

PITT, WILLIAM, 1759–1806; Prime Minister 1783–1801, 1804–1806; rivalry with Fox, pp. 76, 107; income tax, p. 81; Act of Union of 1800, p. 178.

PIUS IX, POPE, 1846–1878, pp. 113, 167.

PLENER, ERNST VON, 1841–1923; Austrian diplomatist and parliamentarian, Leader of German Liberals in Austrian Reichsrat 1873–1895; Minister of Finance 1893–1895, p. 243.

POERIO, CARLO, 1803–1867; Italian patriot; Neapolitan minister; prosecuted by King Ferdinand, pp. 65–67; in Italian parliament, p. 116.

PONSONBY, SIR HENRY, 1825–1895; Major-General; Private Secretary to Queen Victoria 1870–1895, pp. 285, 364, 434.

PUSEY, EDWARD B., 1800–1882; scholar and divine, leader of Oxford Movement; Professor at Oxford since 1828, pp. 55, 206.

REID, SIR WEMYSS, 1842–1905; journalist and biographer; editor of *Leeds Mercury* 1870–1887, p. 318.

RENDEL, STUART (1894 Lord Rendel), 1834–1912; industrialist and parliamentarian; M.P. 1880–1894; friend of Gladstone, p. 451; his daughter, Maud Ernestine, marries 1890 Henry N. Gladstone, later Lord Gladstone of Hawarden.

RHODES, CECIL, 1853–1902; Prime Minister of Cape Colony, 1890–1896, p. 429.

RIPON, 1ST EARL OF, 1782–1859; as Mr. Robinson, Chancellor of the Exchequer 1823–1827; as Viscount Goderich, Prime Minister 1827; in Peel's Government, President of the Board of Trade; resigns finally 1843, pp. 36, 41.

RIPON, 2ND EARL (1871 Marquess, formerly Lord de Grey), 1827–1909; leads Washington Commission on *Alabama* question, pp. 225, 228; controversy with Gladstone about his conversion, p. 251; Viceroy of India 1880–1885; Colonial Secretary 1892, p. 437.

ROEBUCK, JOHN ARTHUR, 1802–1879; enters parliament 1849; motion in Pacifico case, p. 59; on Crimean War, p. 89.

ROSEBERY, EARL OF, 1847–1929; introduces Gladstone in Midlothian, p. 272; Under-Secretary at Home Office 1881–1883; enters cabinet after Gordon's death as Lord Privy Seal, p. 352; on Gladstone's lack of personal interest, p. 376; Foreign Secretary 1886, p. 394; 1892–1894, pp. 436, 438; Prime Minister 1894–1895, pp. 447, 453; resigned Party Leadership, p. 454; eulogizes Gladstone in House of Lords, p. 456.

ROTHSCHILD, LIONEL NATHAN, 1808–1879; elected for the City of London 1847, p. 54; allowed to take seat 1858.

RUSKIN, JOHN, 1819–1900; writer on arts, economics, and sociology, pp. 260, 263.

RUSSELL, LORD JOHN, 1792–1878; member of Grey's ministry, pp. 11, 18; on corn laws, p. 41; Prime Minister 1846–1852, p. 52; Ecclesiastical Titles Bill, p. 57; dismisses Palmerston, p. 69; enters Aberdeen's cabinet, p. 77; resigns, p. 89; joins Palmerston's cabinet 1859, p. 111; Note on Italian policy, p. 116; introduces Reform Bill 1860, p. 125; becomes Prime Minister after Palmerston's death, p. 148; for reform 1866, p. 153; on Irish Church, p. 179; *Alabama* affair, pp. 223, 228.

RUSSELL, ODO (1881 Lord Ampthill), 1829–1884; nephew of John Russell; British minister at Vatican, p. 113; mission to Versailles 1870, p. 221; ambassador at Berlin 1871–1884; wishes to dispel English prejudices against Bismarck, p. 289; on Bismarck's jealousy, p. 291; death, p. 359.

SALISBURY, MARQUIS OF, 1830–1903 (formerly Lord Robert Cecil, then Lord Cranborne); on Church and Party, p. 151; against Gladstone's Reform Bill, p. 158; joins Derby's cabinet 1866, p. 168; difference with Disraeli, pp. 170–172; "Conservative Surrender," p. 175; opposes army reforms, p. 209; Secretary for India 1874–1878, p. 259; mission to Constantinople, p. 259; becomes Foreign Secretary 1878, p. 265; at Berlin Congress, p. 266; Leader of Conservative Lords, p. 316; on appointment of Gordon, p. 345; Reform of 1884, pp. 363–365; Prime Minister 1885–1886, p. 370; relation to Carnarvon, pp. 380, 387; resigns January 1886, p. 391; Hottentot speech, p. 403; Prime Minister 1886–1892, pp. 404, 433; praises Gladstone as "Christian statesman," p. 456.

SCHWARZENBERG, PRINCE FELIX, 1800–1852; Austrian Prime Minister 1850–1852, p. 66.

SEMON, SIR FELIX, 1849–1921; laryngologist, born in Germany; 1901 naturalized as a British subject and appointed extraordinary physician to King Edward, p. 372.

SHAFTESBURY, EARL OF (formerly Lord Ashley), 1803–1885; enters parliament 1826; devotes his life to the amelioration of the lower classes; advocates factory legislation; stepson-in-law of Palmerston, p. 135.

SHUVALOV, COUNT PETER, 1827–1889; Russian diplomatist; ambassador in London 1873–1879; concludes secret convention with Salisbury 24.5.1878, p. 266; represents Russia at Berlin Congress in common with Gortschakov.

SLIDELL, JOHN, 1793–1871; American politician; with Mason appointed agent of Confederate States to England 1861, p. 139.

SPENCER, EARL, 1835–1910; Lord-Lieutenant of Ireland 1868–1874 (without a seat in the cabinet), 1882–1885 (with seat in the cabinet), pp. 323, 326, 329, 268; opposes Irish Central Board, p. 369; converted to Home Rule, p. 388; praised by Gladstone, p. 397; First Lord of the Admiralty 1892, pp. 437, 443; Gladstone's wish to recommend him as his successor, p. 447.

STANLEY, *vide* DERBY.

STEAD, W. T., 1849–1912; journalist; editor of *Pall Mall Gazette* 1883–1889; interviews Gordon January 1884, pp. 341–342; against Parnell, p. 425.

STROSSMAYER, JOSEPH, 1815–1905; bishop of Bosnia 1850; leader of the Croatian opposition to Hungarian predominance; opposes dogma of infallibility; correspondence with Gladstone, p. 256.

SUMNER, CHARLES, 1811–1874; American statesman; chairman of Senates committee for foreign relations 1861–1871, p. 224.

TENNANT, LAURA, 1862–1886; daughter of Charles Tennant; marries 1885 Alfred Lyttelton, pp. 274, 353.

TENNANT, SIR CHALRES, 1823–1906; M.P. 1879–1886, p. 403.

TENNANT, MARGOT, married 1894 H. H. Asquith, now Lady Oxford, pp. 274, 277.

TENNYSON, ALFRED, 1809–1892; Poet-laureate 1850; Lord Tennyson 1884; peerage offered by Gladstone, pp. 311, 374.

TREITSCHKE, HEINRICH VON, 1834–1896; German historian and politician; on Cavour, p. 117; on English politics 1870, p. 216.

TREVELYAN, SIR CHARLES, 1807–1886; Permanent Secretary of the Treasury; Governor of Madras; appointed to inquire into the organization of civil service, p. 207.

TREVELYAN, SIR GEORGE OTTO, 1838–1928; son of Charles Trevelyan, statesman and historian; enters parliament 1865; opposed by Queen, p. 306; Irish Secretary 1882, p. 329; advocates franchise reform, p. 362; against Home Rule Bill 1886, p. 401; rejoins Liberal Party, p. 407; Scottish Secretary 1892, p. 437; last words on Gladstone, p. 457.

TREVELYAN, PROFESSOR GEORGE MACAULAY, born 1876; son of Sir George Trevelyan; historian; on Gladstone's reforms, p. 211.

VICTORIA, QUEEN, 1819–1901; succeeds to the throne 20.6.1837, p. 35; marries Prince Albert 10.2.1840, p. 35; first meeting with Gladstone, p. 37; against Palmerston, pp. 59, 64; on Peel's death, p. 63; on Aberdeen's cabinet, p. 77; rebukes Russell, p. 90; on non-intervention in Italy, p. 115; widow, p. 140; against Palmerston's Danish policy, p. 144; praise of Disraeli, pp. 177, 183; problems of Gladstone's cabinet 1868, p. 187; against "radical" ideas, p. 194; retirement from public life, p. 195; negotiations about Irish Church, p. 197; correspondence with Prussian Crown-Princess about Hohenzollern candidature in Spain, p. 213; on principles of English foreign policy, p. 213; on conduct of French Government 1870, p. 214; on *Alabama* question, p. 227; estrangement from Gladstone on personal questions, pp. 237–239; offers a peerage to Gladstone 1874, p. 245; on Gladstone's resignation from leadership, p. 251; on Berlin Memorandum, p. 255; blames Gladstone's agitation, p. 262; unhappy about his victory, p. 280; sends for Hartington, p. 281; receives Gladstone 23.4.1880, p. 282; against Dilke, p. 284; against Irish Land League, p. 302; wishes information about cabinet discussions, p. 304; against Courtney and Trevelyan, p. 305; intervenes on Land Bill, p. 317; warns Gladstone before speeches in Leeds, p. 320; Chamberlain "evil genius,"

p. 329; for bombardment of Alexandria, p. 336; on annexation of Egypt, p. 341; open telegram on Gordon's death, p. 351; correspondence with Lady and General Wolseley, pp. 353, 355; on franchise reform 1884, pp. 363–365; offers 1885 an earldom to Gladstone, p. 371; difficulties for Gladstone, p. 373; on Gladstone's trip to Copenhagen, p. 375; desires formation of Centre Party, p. 386; on Home Rule Bill 1886, p. 399; on Parnell's divorce case, p. 425; against Home Rule Bill 1893, p. 440; for increase of Navy, p. 443; Gladstone's farewell audience, p. 446; last meeting, p. 454.